The View From The Back Of The Band

The Life and Music of Mel Lewis

By Chris Smith

Foreword by John Mosca

Afterword by John Riley

D0770804

Number 10 in the North Texas Lives of Musicians Series

University of North Texas Press
Denton, Texas

10 9 8 7 6 5 4 3 2

Permissions:
University of North Texas Press
1155 Union Circle #311336
Denton, TX 76203-5017

The paper used in this book meets the minimum requirements of the American National Standard for Permanence of Paper for Printed Library Materials, z39.48.1984. Binding materials have been chosen for durability.

Library of Congress Cataloging-in-Publication Data

Smith, Chris, 1981- author.
The view from the back of the band : the life and music of Mel Lewis /
by Chris Smith.
     pages cm. -- (Number 10 in the North Texas lives of musicians series)
Based on: Thesis (D.A.)--University of Northern Colorado, 2012.
Includes bibliographical references and index.
ISBN 978-1-57441-574-2 (cloth : alk. paper)
ISBN 978-1-57441-587-2 (ebook)
ISBN 978-1-57441-653-4 (paper : alk. paper)
1. Lewis, Mel, 1929-1990. 2. Drummers (Musicians)--United
States--Biography. 3. Jazz musicians--United States--Biography. I.
Title. II. Series: North Texas lives of musicians series ; no. 10.
ML419.L46S65 2014
786.9'165092--dc23
[B]
                    2014024513

The View from the Back of the Band: The Life and Music of Mel Lewis
is Number 10 in the North Texas Lives of Musicians Series

The electronic edition of this book was made possible
by the support of the Vick Family Foundation.

For my wife Nina

Special Thank You—
John Riley, John Mosca, Jim White, Dick Oatts, Ed Soph, Norm Peercy, Matthias Kuert, Steve and Linda Smith, Paul Wells, UMKC LaBudde Special Collections, Donna Sokoloff Bauman, Lori Sokoloff Lowell, Doris Sokoloff

CONTENTS

Foreword

Uncle Mel

Uncle Mel. It was a perfectly apt moniker that came into general use in the band for a while after a Carnegie Hall concert around 1976. The reviewer after heaping praise on the band and Thad's arrangements, turned lukewarm when describing the drummer as "the avuncular Mel Lewis sitting back there hooking rugs." One of us looked it up. Mel laughed when we showed it to him as he generally got a kick out of a critic exposing his ignorance so plainly, which happened quite often when the band was reviewed. For a musician's reaction let's go to master arranger Don Sebesky at age 17, hearing Mel for the first time with Stan Kenton:

> Since I heard him the first time in Carnegie Hall to the present, he's always been my favorite drummer and I think he's the most musical drummer I ever heard.
>
> I was a kid in high school, 16 or 17, something like that, and we were big Kenton fans, my group and I. So we decided to go to Carnegie Hall, and I was a little hesitant about it since Stan Levey had just left Stan's band and I was used to the way he played, which was pretty loud and he didn't catch everything, which looking back on it, was a little strange. But we decided to go, even though I wanted to hear Stan Levey. So the band comes on stage and the last one to come out is Mel, and he looks like a tailor with the glasses, and I said, 'this is going to be something, he's probably a pick up guy.' So anyway, the band starts to play and it was a Bill Holman arrangement and Mel was playing his usual musical self and I was slumped down in my seat, my head resting on the back. I heard 8 bars and sat up straight, the next 8 bars went by and I was leaning forward, the next 8 bars went by and I'm touching the guy in front of me,

and I don't know what happened on the last 8 since he may have gotten the wrong idea. But anyway, Mel showed me at that time, what a drummer is capable of doing as far as being integrated as an inescapable component of the arrangement as a whole. Not just something stuck in there at the last minute. You don't replace Mel Lewis, you just hope to get somebody who's like him—maybe.

But anyway the concert was over and I'm on fire. I went home and I couldn't sleep, so I got up and wrote a tune called Humbug, which I recorded a few years later with Maynard Ferguson's band. So thanks to Mel and the whole band, Stan included.

What makes the critics' under-appreciation of Mel so incorrect is what most every musician and many listeners know: that while a band can play poorly with a great drummer, no band can be great without one. The Thad Jones-Mel Lewis Orchestra was a great band. As a teenager paying, I think $3.50 to get in, I was so struck by the perfection of what he chose not to play. That and the sound of the cymbals, and the way the bass drum seemed to lift the whole club. It was the only big band I really wanted to be a part of, so when Mel called (on a dial phone) I never asked about money or anything. I couldn't say yes fast enough. Playing Thad's great music every night with Mel and Al Porcino was really a finishing school for ensemble playing. They had all this history together by then, so all you had to do was listen and this very deep, complex and groundbreaking music became self-explanatory. Of course, my involvement with Mel was confined to the last 15 years of his life, so I'm thrilled to have this beautifully written and researched treatise as a reference. I've learned so much about his earlier career, only snippets of which he ever mentioned, usually when one of us found a record and quizzed him about it. Although, since my roommate was Al Porcino (subject for another book), and his tape machine was *always* on, I had a pretty good indoctrination to the things Mel and Al did together.

There are countless moments of beauty in the work listed here and nearly all of them are about the band or the music. Almost never is attention concentrated on the drummer. It's inevitable though, that sometimes the drums alone are important as a device, one of my favorites from a Hi-Lo's recording of "Of Thee I Sing," which if you don't know it, is usually done in double time like "Cherokee." Well, they're sailing along and Mel has to interrupt the whole flow with a four bar fill in an entirely new, unrelated slower tempo. He has the new tempo in his head and you'd better be holding onto something when it comes up. Another was the first time I heard him hit the Chinese cymbal on the out chorus of Thad's "Sixty-First and Richard." It was one perfect stroke, not real loud. I thought my scalp would come off. Many other instances involved drum solos which he was not known for, but if you listen closely, or better yet see him on film, he keeps the hi-hat going on two and four through the whole solo, which puts it into a new level of complexity. On one extended solo, he did the history of the drums, playing seamlessly through the styles of Baby Dodds, Papa Jo Jones, Kenny Clarke, Max Roach, Philly Joe Jones, and Elvin Jones. I wonder if there's a tape out there somewhere. Sometimes on the great vehicle Thad wrote for him, "Tip Toe," he'd throw us a curve ball on one of his fills, just to keep us sharp, and if somebody fell in the hole, he'd laugh and give us the business later.

There were almost as many great and revealing moments off the bandstand as well. The phrase "honest to a fault" is not an idle cliché when applied to Mel. He was far from bashful when voicing an opinion, even if it wasn't the best public relations to do so. One instance that stands out revolves around the fact that he detested rock. Space doesn't permit that case to be made here, but for a master of rhythm like Mel it must have been like Rembrandt regarding the canvas with one dot. It was a common opinion among jazz musicians, especially his generation, who saw their place in the popular culture usurped. Two ironies here: one—the great eclectic genius of Thad Jones saw a way of incorporating this music into his ideas with big works like, "Central Park North," "Suite for Pops," and "Forever Lasting"; the other is that Mel played it great. He played this wide-open beat that just let Thad work all sorts of magic. He didn't even like doing too much of Thad's straight eighth stuff. This is a long way of setting up our arrival one day in either Sweden or Denmark, by one of those big ocean going ferries, and I have no idea how it happened since we weren't even on shore yet. We were still on the gang plank when one of the crowd waiting to greet us held up a newspaper, which headline said so plainly it wasn't necessary to know the language, "MEL LEWIS SAYS ROCK IS SHIT." He loved it. I don't remember the program that night, but Thad probably programmed every rock chart in the book.

There's some mention here of the arduous bus trips. They were common, more the rule than the exception. One stands out. We were doing what was known as a hit and run to Chicago. That is, we played a concert (hit) and instead of going back to the hotel and riding the next day, we got right on the bus to drive all night (run) and part of the next day. Not our favorite way to travel, though sometimes it was preferable to make such a trip to have the day in a town like Chicago as opposed to any number of other places. This trip was just many hours that had to be done as we were starting a week at the Jazz Showcase on Rush Street at that time. When you're nearing the end of such a trip all you want is a hot shower, a toothbrush, and some time in the prone position. We were about 90 minutes out after about 16 hours driving when Mel announced (bad news was always delivered by Mel) that instead of checking in, we were going right to the club, set up, and do a matinee. There was a general hue and cry of course, but Mel said, "Look it will work out great. We'll blow a set, then check in, clean up and eat and play tonight." At that moment it became clear that here was a completely happy fulfilled guy who couldn't be beaten by anything in this life, since he was doing exactly what he wanted and was here on earth to do.

As it's turned out, with this work, the many studies of the Thad Jones-Mel Lewis Orchestra, and the reappraisals of his work, Mel has achieved the impact he hoped for beyond his time. While this is a book about Mel, he and Thad are inextricably linked in greatness. Mel needed something to grow into, to fully exercise that talent which had been so thoroughly developed by his work up till then. Thad needed to be free of concerns about whether this or that could be played and so could give full rein to that singular conception. What would have happened if the band had never come to fruition? Mel would still be celebrated and studied for what he did with Kenton, Gibbs, Goodman, and Mulligan. And Thad would have written great music and might have gotten the recognition he deserved as one of the greatest pure improvisers in jazz history. Happily this is academic. Mel was immensely proud of the trust Thad placed in him. One measure of his greatness is how many of the best arrangers shared that trust. When Bob Brookmeyer came back to New York and the band after Thad departed for Denmark, he came to work. We rehearsed at the Vanguard every Monday afternoon before work. The rehearsals were pretty intense as the music was new and Bob wanted it right, period. He was also very specific about the way things were to be played. Most times when a conductor stops a rehearsal to make a correction, it's done in 30 seconds. This one time he talked to us for what must have been 10 minutes about pitch, attack, attitude, duration, vibrato, dynamics, and every conceivable variable in this next section. We're leaning in, concentrating, making notes on the parts, conferring with each other on how we were going to give him what he wants. In other words it was plainly serious business. Now he was going to count it off, and just as he's about to start, he interrupts himself and without looking up from the score, said, "Mel, do something there."

— *John Mosca*

Preface

Mel Lewis's extensive recorded career of over 630 recordings serves as evidence that he is among the most important jazz drummers of all-time.[1] His unique style of jazz drumming has been highly regarded by fans and critics for almost sixty years, but more importantly, Mel was highly respected by his contemporaries in the jazz community. Trombonist and composer Bob Brookmeyer was one of Mel's closest friends and spoke of him in the highest esteem:

> When Mel died, it was one of the biggest losses the music ever had. People all over the world suffered. And they'll never recover. We were sitting in Cologne, a key producer and I. We said, "Mel," and were silent for five minutes because there's no replacement. All of the bands, big and small, amateur and professional, that he made sound good have to feel a terrible, terrible loss. There will never be another like him. Mel was one of the greatest drummers of all. I'd stake my life on that.[2]

As the generations of musicians who worked with Mel grow older with each passing year, fewer first-hand accounts of his career are available. It was important to research and preserve Mel's history before information was lost forever. Thus, a major aspect of my research relied on interviewing musicians and friends who had a professional and/or personal relationship with Mel. The stories they offered are the true highlight of this book. Their memories reflect the sincere love and respect they have not only for Mel's drumming, but also for him as a person.

The Mel Lewis Collection, part of the LaBudde Special Collections at the University of Missouri-Kansas City, was an invaluable resource for this project. Donated to the university in 1996, thanks to Mel's family and the urging of Danny Gottlieb, the collection contains many of the articles, interviews, personal datebooks, pictures, and correspondence needed to codify Mel's sixty-year career. If you are in Kansas City go spend time at UMKC's LaBudde Special Collections and thank them for the amazing service they provide the jazz community.

Several informative interviews with Mel have previously been published in *Modern Drummer, Crescendo,* and *DownBeat* magazines. He also did a series of three lengthy interviews with Bob Rusch for *Cadence* magazine in 1989. These interviews are now out of print and difficult to purchase, but are available through the New York Public Library in New York City.

Several important audio interviews were conducted with Mel during the 1970s and 1980s, the best known being his WKCR radio interviews with Loren Schoenberg. The multiple installment radio show consisted of Mel talking about the history of jazz drumming and innovative jazz drummers. While these interviews are informative and entertaining, most do not consist of Mel speaking about his own career and life. Luckily one installment of the radio show, recorded in 1989, focused on the beginning of his career from 1936 to 1955. That interview was an important part of my research because Mel provided dates, names, and locations for many of the important events during his pre-1956 career.

Another important interview with Mel was recorded in 1978 in Rochester, New York. Radio personality Will Moyle hosted a weekly jazz show titled the *Essence of Jazz*. During his hour segment with Moyle, Mel spoke at length about his career from 1956 through 1970. This very rare interview is the only known recording of him speaking about his first meeting with Bob Brookmeyer, his introduction to Thad Jones in Detroit, and the formation of the Thad Jones/Mel Lewis Orchestra. The interview has never been commercially available, and its only known location is in the Mel Lewis Collection at the University of Missouri-Kansas City. With permission, the interview was digitally copied and transcribed.

One of the most useful and important resources to my research was the Online Jazz Discography by Tom Lord. Currently, the Lord Online Discography lists Mel as being on over 626 recordings sessions and radio transcriptions. Of these, an amazing three hundred of them took place during the ten-year span of 1956 and 1966. One of the most important tools to my research was Mel's vast recorded history, and the Tom Lord Discography was the most valuable resource for finding record titles, dates, and locations. Additionally, liner notes to many of these albums provided information about Mel that cannot be found in any other source. Bill Kirchner's extensive research for Mosaic's *The Complete Solid State Recordings of the Thad Jones/Mel Lewis Orchestra* was also a tremendous resource.

When an album title initially appears in the text, I chose to include its original record label in parentheses. The original record label is an important part of the history of that recording; it also helps to show the history of the labels that Mel recorded for and will aid audiophiles in search of original pressings. In addition, a selected discography is included that lists every recording mentioned throughout the book. The recordings listed in the discography are the most current releases of the album, aiding in the process of finding and purchasing Mel's music. One purpose of this book is not only to preserve memories of a great drummer, but also to pique contemporary interest in some terrific sounds. So go purchase this music!

Chapter 1
Born a Drummer

Mel Lewis loved to sit in his living room at 325 West End Avenue #2C and listen to music. He sat in that room and listened for hundreds of hours, usually in the company of a young musician who intently absorbed his entertaining stories of the music business, life on the road, and the wide range of musicians he had worked with. When relaxing in his favorite lounge chair it was typically the music that encouraged Mel's stories of the past, and more importantly, sparked his excitement for the future. At only fifty-eight-years old Mel was a living jazz legend, one who still played drums every Monday night with his band at the Village Vanguard. He loved to talk about future musical projects, his band's next album, politics, or the New York Giants' upcoming season. However, by 1989 his four-year battle with cancer often forced him to silently reflect on the decades of music that defined his career. Mel cared about his legacy and hoped that his musical accomplishments would not be forgotten. "I'd like to leave a mark. I'd like fifty years from now for people to say that Mel Lewis was a pioneer in a way. I'd like to have had my share of doing something important for music," he said.[1] The desire to preserve his story led him to begin writing a memoir, which he aptly titled "The View from the Back of the Band." Mel was only able to complete several pages before passing away in February of 1990; however, the pages that he did complete offer remarkable insight into his thoughts and memories. There could be no more fitting way to begin this book than printing Mel's unfinished personal memoir for the very first time:

> "The View from the Back of the Band"
> Chapter 1—The Best Little Drummer in Buffalo
>
> I don't remember a time when it wasn't clear to me that I was to be a drummer in a band. My father was a drummer and it never occurred to me that I would do anything else. The final, irreversible decision was probably made when I was about two, when my cousins presented me with my own pair of drumsticks—I remember clearly that they were painted gold.
> My first musical triumph was as a cymbal player in the

kindergarten rhythm band, followed by my joining the first grade orchestra playing bass drum. First chair as I recall. I soon progressed to snare drum.

I sat in for my father at a Jewish wedding, and from that moment, considered myself a professional musician ready for anything. After that it was just job after job, band after band, record session after record session, until I found myself celebrating 20 years at the Village Vanguard. It all seems to have happened so fast—but I've never for a minute regretted that decision I made when I saw those gold drumsticks.

During the decades between 1890 and 1910 a remarkable wave of immigrants arrived in the United States from Eastern Europe, mostly Czarist Russia. Among the mostly penniless travelers, usually speaking little or no English, were Irving Berlin, Sam Goldwyn, and all four of my grandparents.

[Begins a new untitled chapter]

A jazz drummer generally sits at the rear of the bandstand or stage on a high stool called a throne. It provides a higher-than-normal seat, putting its occupant in a sort of half sitting, half standing position. From this stance, the drummer can operate both a bass drum pedal and a pedal-actuated cymbal. He can also reach and play on a 180-degree array of drums and tom-toms, perhaps six or eight cymbals, triangles, wood blocks or other tools of his unique trade.

Although he is often required to read music as carefully as other members of the band, he is sometimes called on to just play "time," counting measures almost subconsciously while he observes his surroundings.

He sees, first, the other musicians. From the dance floor, the audience sees smiles and shiny horns, freshly painted music stands, perhaps a pretty girl singer in a thousand dollar dress. The view from the drummer's throne is a little different, and surely closer to reality. The musicians, in fact, are often sweating and their tuxes don't often match. The floor around the players is cluttered with mic chords and spider boxes, empty cases and discarded reeds. And, if the lights are right, he can glimpse the singer's naked legs silhouetted through the thin fabric of the expensive gown.

Beyond the musicians, in the front of the bandstand, he sees the audience; the dancers, the drinkers, the listeners. Most of the time, the audience is a pretty accurate sample of society. From the throne the drummer sees class and beauty, priceless jewelry, attentive followers of the music, flirts and grumps, plus the usual variety of jerks, drunks, and hustlers. He sees Americans of all sorts in settings from Presidential inaugurations to Elk dances, from high school proms to basement jazz clubs.

Beyond the musicians and singers, the dancers, the drunks, the barroom fighters, this drummer has been privileged to see almost fifty years of music parade before the throne. In those fifty years jazz has grown from a private and almost secret art, passed on from player to player, to a skill taught in most American high schools. The record business, which began as an effort to preserve the very best of all kinds of music, has in those fifty years become little more than a very sophisticated way to market carloads of vinyl plastic. Radio, fifty years ago a vigorous and imaginative youngster, has gown virtually before my eyes, into a powerful and cynical handmaiden of the record business. Television, the great hope of all of us, has lost almost all contact with real American music.

My drums have played along or led—I hope, inspired—some of the greatest geniuses this nation has produced over the past century. Some are among the most famous names in music, honored by Presidential medals or Kennedy Center honors, or glorified by a six-foot shelf of biographies in every library. Some have gone from a saloon piano player to successful arranger to fabulously wealthy composer. Others have gone from saloon piano player to shoe salesman to nowhere close to the music business.

Some met and were captured by dope, or booze, or gambling, or their own personal demons before their talents could fully develop. No matter what their fate, many were authentic geniuses and I was privileged to be part of their world.

3

The view from the drummer's throne in the back of the band is a unique one. It'll be mostly fun, sometimes sad, sometimes inspiring; I think always useful to recall some of the sights and surely the sounds.[2]

—Mel Lewis

Great musicians can discover their love of music at different stages in life. Some musicians are in their thirties before it is clear to them that music is their true passion, yet to others, music seems to choose them before they ever have the chance to decide. Music chose Mel Lewis at a young age. He gladly accepted and devoted his next sixty years to a life through music.

I don't remember ever not playing drums. I can't remember any time in my life when I didn't play them, let alone want to be one. I don't even recall wanting, all I recall is doing, even as a very little baby![3]

Mel Lewis was born on May 10, 1929, as Melvin Sokoloff and was raised in Buffalo, New York. His mother Mildred and father Samuel Sokoloff were of Russian Jewish descent and many of the family's beliefs and customs were deeply rooted in their Jewish ancestry. Music, being one of these customs, was an important part of life in the Sokoloff household. Sam Sokoloff was a professional drummer who played regularly at Buffalo's famous Palace Burlesque Theater. As a result, many of Mel's earliest childhood memories involved watching his father play the drums. During a 1982 interview Mel spoke of what a great drummer his father had been:

He was a pit drummer and a show drummer. He was an excellent snare drummer, you know, he played Baby Dodds' style press rolls and was very good at it. He had impeccable time and impeccable taste, and was very much liked by an awful lot of dancers that came through the town. Most outstandingly, Bill Robinson, the famous Bojangles once told me, "I always look forward to getting to Buffalo because I know I am going to play with Sam."[4]

As two-year-old Mel discovered the drums, his father guided him through the snare drum rudiments and taught him the art of playing a press roll.[5] While other children his age were playing sports or attending summer camp, Mel was dreaming of playing drums in his own band:

> I always wanted to be me. I used to draw pictures on cardboard, you know those shirt cardboards? I used to draw my band, *my band Socky Brown,* because Socky was my father's nickname. All the guys called him Socky, S-O-C-K-Y, rather than Sucky, because he wouldn't have appreciated that. All right, so Socky they called him, and I was little socky ... Every musician in town knew me, I mean, since I was a baby.[6]

Thanks to his father, Mel's first experience on a bandstand occurred in 1935 during a cousin's wedding celebration. His father was playing drums during the party and decided to get up and dance so he called over to six-year-old Mel to take over the drumming duties. Having to stand, because he was too short to sit and play the bass drum, Mel's drumming propelled the dancers during the entire thirty-five-minute Jewish Hora (a traditional Jewish celebration dance). When his time on the bandstand was over, Mel recalled his father saying, "That's it, he's going to be a drummer."[7] After that moment Mel eagerly sought other performance opportunities in Buffalo, and did so by sitting in whenever and wherever possible.

> I used to sit in at all these wedding jobs, I sat in from six on, I mean talk about sitting in! I used to walk into any temple or church in the area, or I'd go on my bike, and no matter what union band was playing there, the drummer always let me sit in because he knew me. I sat in with everybody. Only regular dance music, on these little three-piece drum sets. Because there was no bass on these jobs, they were generally three men: drums, piano, and a horn, sometimes two horns. So, I didn't even know what it was like to play with a bass violin until I was grown up, you know, 'till I was a full-blown teenager.[8]

In addition to sitting in with bands, Mel also performed throughout town in amateur shows presented by Bob Smith, a local bandleader and entertainer. Bob Smith became a lifelong friend to Mel; children across the country would later know Smith as Buffalo Bob from *The Howdy Doody Show* television show.

Buffalo, New York, in the 1930s was a major road stop for touring musicians going to and coming from New York City. The interaction that Mel had with these touring musicians was an important aspect of his early musical development. In 1935, when he was only six years old, he went with his father to see a performance by the Benny Goodman Trio. The performance featured Gene Krupa on drums and left a deep impression on the young drummer. Mel remembered the evening clearly stating, "I did not meet him that night, but I saw him and that became very big with me. Two years later I met Gene and we remained great friends the rest of his life."[9] Throughout his childhood, Mel had the unique opportunity to witness and meet some of the greatest jazz musicians of the time as they traveled through town. Few had as much influence on Mel's career and drumming as Krupa.

Mel not only experienced music in Buffalo's clubs, but also at PS 74 elementary school in Buffalo. The same month he played drums at his cousin's wedding, he joined the elementary school orchestra. First grade students were usually not members of the school orchestra, but Sam Sokoloff pleaded for a special exception and his son was allowed to join his first band. During his first years playing with the eighty-four-piece orchestra Mel moved from playing the bass drum and cymbals to playing the snare drum. Finally, in the seventh grade, Mel showed so much musical potential that Mrs. Bert, his music teacher, put him on a drumset and let him be the one-man percussion section for the entire group. Years later Mel jokingly said, "Thanks to Mrs. Bert, the eighty-four piece . . . school orchestra was my first big band gig."[10]

Mel began high school in 1943 and attended East High, notorious for having the best music department in town. Even though he had been playing drums for over ten years, initially he was not allowed to the join the high school orchestra because he could not read music. Mr. Reshay, the East High music teacher, offered to teach Mel how to read music by playing the baritone horn. Mel's first weeks of school were diligently spent practicing the baritone; after just two months, he reached a satisfactory level of reading competency. Mel joined the high school orchestra percussion section, forever putting aside the baritone horn.[11]

During this period in Mel's life, he began to work professionally as a drummer throughout Buffalo. The start of World War II in 1939 had caused many local musicians to leave town as they either joined or were drafted into the military. This resulted in much of the musical work to be picked up by older musicians or, as was the case with Mel, younger musicians. By 1942, World War II was at its height and thirteen-year-old Mel played any gig that came his way. "I played a Polish wedding and was paid $3, which was pretty good. A big band gig was 75 cents, and a great gig paid $10. That's when a quart of milk cost 10 cents," he recalled.[12]

In the early 1940s, dancing and big bands were popular forms of entertainment, and most of Mel's early professional gigs involved playing music for people to dance to. He described his early work as "Mostly just dance jobs, trio, quartets, whatever. And I was involved in little big bands, rehearsal bands, and things like that. I played a Polish dance here or there, and Italian dance, a Jewish dance, that's mostly where your work came out of, the churches and temples. Non-union naturally."[13] Through steady work in these local dance and society bands, he began crafting his personal style of jazz drumming.

In the fall of 1943, at the age of fourteen, Mel found himself with the opportunity to play with the Bob Seib Band. The Bob Seib Band was a local Buffalo big band that played dances in the Northern New York region. As Mel stated, "The band wasn't one of the best dance bands in town," but they did work often and the experience proved to be an important opportunity for him.[14] One Friday night, Bob Seib's usual drummer broke his leg in a high school football game. When Mel's friend Tom Breach, who was the band's bassist, found out that the band needed a replacement drummer for the job that evening he recommended Mel. Rushing to St. Vincent's, the hall where the Bob Seib Band regularly played, Mel arrived with his worn and unimpressive looking drums, a contrast to the usual drummer's white marine pearl drums. As he unloaded his equipment he was met with skeptical looks from many of the band members.[15] Mel recalled the situation saying,

> So they called me frantically to come to St. Vinnie's. And they were all disappointed at my set of drums cause it was so beat-up and old, and their usual guy had a white pearl set you know. He couldn't play it, but he had it. But I had pieces of junk that I could play. They brought me in there and I was supposed to join the band temporarily and I ended up staying with the band.[16]

7

He did not have a nice set of drums in 1943, but Mel, the lifelong cymbal connoisseur, always had an ear for cymbals. It was only months after his first gig with Bob Seib that he acquired his famous 20-inch Zildjian ride cymbal that eventually had two sections cut out of it. That particular cymbal was so impressive that Buddy Rich proclaimed it to be the best cymbal ever made.[17]

Mel's initial appearance worried the older musicians, but on stage his musical feel and energetic drumming won over the members of the band before the night was over. Due in part to a high school football player's broken leg, fourteen-year-old Mel Lewis proved his musicianship and became a steady working musician in Buffalo.

Through his work with Seib, Mel's drumming was heard by an increasing number of local musicians. Many of Buffalo's Italian bandleaders such as Joe Gaglioni, Lou Powers, and Buddy Mack began to hire Mel in their bands. As a result of several higher profile gigs with Buddy Mack, Mel became a member of the local musician's union at the age of fifteen.[18] As a member of the musician's union, he had access to the better paying union jobs. Beginning in 1945, his professional work in Buffalo rapidly increased.

Late in the summer of 1946, Mel was asked to go on a four-month tour of the Midwest with a band led by Bernie Burns. Though it meant he would miss the first several weeks of school, Mel's parents approved of the tour and he headed out on the road. This was a pivotal point in his life, not only because it was his first chance to tour with a band, but also because he would never return to finish his high school education.[19] Mel Lewis was living his dream; he was a jazz musician making music out on the road. After his tour with Burns, Mel returned to Buffalo to pursue a fulltime career as a drummer.

By the fall of 1946, many local musicians who had been in the service during World War II returned to Buffalo in search of musical work. Even with more drummers competing for work, Mel steadily gained higher profile gigs. Local bandleader Harold Austin hired Mel when his former drummer, Sandy Graff, abruptly left the band. As a seventeen-year-old, Mel beat out every drummer in town, and joined one of the best big bands in Buffalo, the Harold Austin Band.[20]

Austin owned the Main Utica Ballroom, one of the premiere dance halls in Buffalo, and his band played there every Friday, Saturday, and Sunday night. In 1946, the Harold Austin Band's Sunday night performances were often broadcast live by local AM radio station WEBR. At the time, Bobby

Nicholson was the main arranger for the band, and one of his arrangements was of the popular song "Jealousy." Nicholson went on to work with Buffalo Bob Smith as Clarabell the Clown and J. Cornelius Cobb on the *Howdy Doody Show*.[21] During Mel's first Sunday evening broadcast with the Austin Band, his third night with the group, an acetate recording was made from the band's radio performance. This rare recording of "Jealousy" was the first ever recording of Mel playing the drums, and featured the seventeen-year-old maturely leading the band with swinging energy.[22] The recording can still be heard on the original acetate currently housed in the Dr. Kenneth J. LaBudde Department of Special Collections at the University of Kansas City-Missouri. The recording also exists via the independently taped radio interviews that Mel did on WKCR NYC with Loren Schoenberg.

In addition to owning the Main Utica Ballroom in Buffalo, Harold Austin also managed one of the largest open dance halls in North America called the Crystal Beach Ballroom. The Crystal Beach Ballroom was located in Ontario, Canada, directly across the Niagara River from Buffalo. As Mel worked steadily with Harold Austin, he performed frequently at Crystal Beach and met a very important figure in his career, trumpeter Maynard Ferguson:

> I have known Maynard since we were teenagers. I was in Buffalo and he was from Canada and he had a band. In the summertime we used to hang out together and we were both working for the same man who owned the ballroom. He was also a bandleader in Buffalo. His name was Harold Austin and he owned Crystal Beach Ballroom in Canada at Crystal Beach. Maynard's band was the house band there and I was in the Harold Austin Band ... So we got to know each other then. We were friends then 16, 17 years old, you know.[23]

As Mel's career progressed through the 1940s, so did the modernization of jazz music. The end of Union leader James Petrillo's recording ban in 1944, allowed Charlie Parker and Dizzy Gillespie to record their new style of music called bebop in May of 1945. By 1946, bebop had become a huge influence on musicians throughout New York City, even on young Mel Lewis who was living hundreds of miles away in Buffalo. Much like his meeting with Gene Krupa ten years earlier, he began to become acquainted with the bebop jazz

9

musicians who traveled through Buffalo. Mel remembered meeting many of his musical heroes, saying, "I fell into the bebop scene from the day it started through recordings. They were always coming through Buffalo—Bird, Diz, guys like that."[24] As a teenager Mel gained valuable experience by sitting in and playing at a local club called McVan's with musicians such as Art Tatum, Oscar Pettiford, Dorothy Donegan, Nat King Cole, Howard McGhee, and Coleman Hawkins.[25] The influence of bebop and the opportunity to play at jam sessions with New York City musicians further shaped Mel's style of drumming.

Between 1944 and 1948 Mel cultivated a friendship with another young drummer from Buffalo named Frank Dunlop. Mel remembered Frank Dunlop as the best bebop drummer in town and the two young drummers spent hours listening to records together and sharing drumming ideas.[26] Dunlop became a legendary jazz drummer in his own right, touring and recording with the likes of Sonny Rollins, Lionel Hampton, and Thelonious Monk.

Bebop was also a huge influence on one of Buffalo's best big bands, a band led by Lenny Lewis. In January of 1946, while still a regular with Harold Austin, Mel also began performing with the Lenny Lewis Band. The Lewis Band was one of the rare local mixed-race bands of the 1940s and contained many great African-American musicians from Buffalo, such as the saxophonists George Clarke and Elvin Shepherd, and bassist Lawrence "Skinny" Bergen.[27] The group was a true jazz band, which played music in the style of the Count Basie Orchestra but often featured more extended solos than Basie's group. Lenny Lewis himself would go on to be the road manager for Basie as well as Artie Shaw.[28] Lenny Lewis eventually expanded from the Count Basie model and used bebop influenced harmony and rhythm in his band's modern arrangements. Through much of 1946 and 1947, as Mel continued to play a variety of musical jobs in Buffalo, his steady work with Lenny Lewis improved his musicianship and his personal style began to solidify. Unfortunately, because of the second recording ban by union leader James Petrillo in 1948, no commercially available recordings of Mel with the Lewis Band exist. However, in a 1982 WKCR interview with Loren Schoenberg, Mel provided a rare acetate recording of the band performing a composition titled "One for Mel."[29] This song featured the seventeen-year-old drummer soloing and leading the band like a seasoned veteran. While his drumming on "One for Mel" exposes an undeniable Krupa influence, Mel was always quick to point out that Papa Jo Jones, Sid Catlett, Sonny Greer, and Davey Tough were the drummers who meant the most to his musical development during the era. In his interview with Schoenberg, Mel described his drumming on "One for Mel" and how the Lewis Band was pivotal in his career:

> In my playing you can hear the influences of the day. There's Jo Jones in my playing, there's Gene Krupa in my playing, there's not quite yet much of Max yet because I was playing bebop small group but I was still thinking big band then. You can hear touches of Shadow Wilson in there too, but I hadn't heard that much of him yet. Big Sid is there, you know. This is 1946 you know, nobody really got into anything yet. I am living in Buffalo, so we're still getting everything off of records and the groups coming through. And I was doing a lot of small group playing at that time too.
>
> Charlie White wrote an arrangement for me called "One for Mel," which was a drum number. Of course it actually had a beginning and an ending with a drum solo in the middle, the drum solo could be extended. But in those days on acetate you couldn't get more than about two and a half minutes at the most on a side, so we cut it down to 16 bars and we made this. So I still had that, it's another nice scratchy acetate. But this will give you an idea of the kind of music this band was playing. And you'll get the idea that it was a true jazz band. This is the band that I came to New York with and actually started my jazz career.[30]

As Mel continued working in Buffalo, Lenny Lewis continually mentioned a possible move to New York City with the band. For Mel, a move to New York City would be a childhood dream come true and the beginning of an exciting new chapter of his life. ▌

Chapter 2
Mel Meets New York City

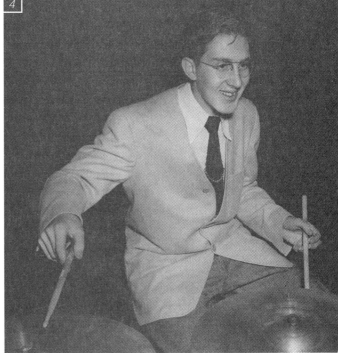

1 Young Melvin Sokoloff. *Used by permission of the Sokoloff family.*

2 Mel with his mother Mildred and father Samuel. *Used by permission of the University of Missouri-Kansas City Libraries, Dr. Kenneth J. LaBudde Department of Special Collections and the Sokoloff family.*

3 A teenager with his hero, Gene Krupa. *Used by permission of the University of Missouri-Kansas City Libraries, Dr. Kenneth J. LaBudde Department of Special Collections and the Sokoloff family.*

4 Mel drumming in Buffalo in 1946. *Used by permission of the University of Missouri-Kansas City Libra Dr. Kenneth J. LaBudde Department of Special Colle and the Sokoloff family.*

5 Mel with Bernie Burns in 1946 (notice the on the drumhead). *Used by permission of the Uni of Missouri-Kansas City Libraries, Dr. Kenneth J. LaBt Department of Special Collections and the Sokoloff fa*

Chapter 2
Mel Meets New York City

In January of 1948, after years of talking about relocating, Lenny Lewis finally moved his band and young drummer to New York City. When the Lewis Band arrived, the height of the big band era had passed and even after successful engagements at the Savoy Ballroom and Apollo Theater, Lewis found it much more difficult to find gigs than he had expected.[1] He broke up the band after only several months in the city. During a 1957 *DownBeat* interview, Mel reflected:

> If Lenny's band had stayed together, it would have been one of the *greatest* swing bands. We had guys like Al Killian, Harold (Shorty) Baker, and Fats Ford on trumpet; and Frankie Socolow, Eddie Bert, Sonny Russo, and Al Cohn. Basie loved that band. He still remembers it, too.[2]

Saxophonist Gene Cipriano had recently joined the Lewis Band and recalled the music and personnel of the band, saying, "That Lenny Lewis band was a true bebop big band and was stocked with great musicians. Unfortunately it was a really bad time for big bands, but for me it was great because I got to meet and play with Al Cohn and Mel."[3] Even though the Lewis Band did not last long in New York City, Mel had enough time in the city to meet several musicians who changed the course of his career.

In July of 1948, the Lewis Band rehearsed at Heartnet Studios in the basement of the Strand Theater building in Manhattan. During this same time, the Count Basie Orchestra featuring Billie Holiday played a weeklong engagement upstairs in the Strand Theater. Throughout the week, Count Basie came down to the basement studio to hear the Lewis Band rehearse. Mel recalled the situation:

> Basie kept coming down between shows to hear the band. And at that time he was looking to modernize his band because he felt like they were hurting. They were in very bad trouble by that time; they were not doing well at all. And he kept hearing our

band, which was like a modern Basie band. We were what Basie wanted to have. We had a good strong bebop tinged, but basically swinging book.[4]

The Monday after Basie finished his engagement at the Strand Theater, he fired many of his band members and began to hire younger musicians, hoping to achieve a more modern sound. In one of his more surprising moves Basie fired drumming legend Gus Johnson and asked Mel to join the Basie Orchestra. Of course, the eighteen-year-old boy from Buffalo accepted the offer and began to tell his family, friends, and anyone that would listen, that he was the new drummer in the famous Count Basie Orchestra.[5] Thanks in part to his playing in the Lenny Lewis Band, Mel had landed the gig of a lifetime.

On Thursday of that same week, Mel and the newly formed Basie Orchestra were scheduled to rehearse for their upcoming engagement at the Royal Roost; however, on Wednesday, Basie's manager Milt Ebbins called Mel to his office for an urgent meeting. Basie and Ebbins shocked Mel by telling him that management thought it would be best if he did not join the Basie Orchestra. Big bands in 1948 were facing many financial problems and even the famous Count Basie Orchestra was struggling to make ends meet. Consequently, Basie's management had booked a tour of dance halls in the South that was scheduled to begin directly after the Royal Roost engagement. Because of racial tension in the South at that time, Mel was told that it would not be safe for him to travel with the band.[6] Years later, Mel reflected positively on one of the greatest disappointments of his life:

> Because prejudice was running rampant in those days, a white guy, a white kid especially can't come down there with a black band. And, oh boy what a hurt! That's when it really struck me what was really going on. I never knew anything about that, you know, because I hadn't been there yet. And it hurt; it hurt. But they had been through more hurts. But now I realized why there had been black bands and white bands more than ever, and what the problems were. See a white band could take a Roy Eldridge, like Gene Krupa's band, and get away with it because Roy was a star. There were problems; you used to read about them. But with me, a little unknown, it wasn't even worth the attempt. And it

wasn't on Basie's mind, he was thinking strictly of hiring a young drummer he liked. He's not the kind of person who would have thought that way. But the office, they said you can't do it Bill. And he realized he couldn't, you know there was no sense in trying to be a hero, of any kind. And I certainly wouldn't have lasted long, no doubt. With my little temper and everything I would have been in all kinds of trouble. And there had already been stories about Red Rodney where they called him "Albino Red" and things like that with Charlie Parker. So, these things happen and I got wiped out.[7]

In the end Basie hired another young drummer from New York named Shadow Wilson, who played the Royal Roost engagement before traveling South, leaving Mel in New York City searching for his next steady gig.

Upon his arrival in New York City months earlier, Mel began spending every free moment out on the town watching the jazz drummers he grew up admiring. "When I first came to New York City, my evenings were all spent at the Royal Roost listening to Max, Kenny Clarke, and Shelly Manne. I made sure that I heard Sid Catlett, Cozy Cole, George Wettling, and Morey Feld. I listened to them all," recalled Mel.[8] At that time, he also loved to watch and listen to Norman "Tiny" Kahn, a young drummer from Brooklyn whose playing he greatly admired.[9] The two began a close friendship that lasted until Kahn's premature death at age thirty on August 9, 1953. Tiny was six years older than Mel, and having grown up in Brooklyn, was much more established in the New York City jazz scene. Characteristics of Tiny's drumming included modern bebop vocabulary, a buoyant ride cymbal beat that often broke from the repetitive ride cymbal pattern, and a quieter dynamic of playing than many drummers of that era. Listening to Tiny on recordings with Herbie Fields, Wardell Gray, and Stan Getz it is fascinating to hear him use many of the same stylistic characteristics (such as the aforementioned items) that have become so strongly associated with Mel's drumming. Strangely, in print interviews Mel often downplayed the influence Tiny had on his drumming. However, in an interview with Will Moyle, Mel clearly stated, "Tiny played so musically, he was a big influence on my playing. That great sound out of his bass drum and his constant motion. He used what we call 'Rub-a-Dub' feel, which I use too. That is what really makes a band move ahead and play inspired, it's that 'Rub-a-Dub.'"[10]

Because Tiny died at such a young age Mel was often credited as carrying on Tiny's style. However, Mel was always of the opinion that he carried on the style of playing that *they* were into at the *same* time.

Throughout 1948 Tiny worked with several jazz groups in New York City, one of which was the Boyd Raeburn Band. When Tiny left the Raeburn Band that August to start working for bassist Chubby Jackson, he recommended Mel as his replacement.[11] Mel's friendship with Tiny landed him a new job and after the disappointment of the Basie gig earlier that year, Mel was excited to join what he considered to be a musically satisfying Raeburn Band.

In August of 1948, several other young musicians joined the Boyd Raeburn Band, including saxophonist Harvey Estrin, and Mel's trumpet playing friend from his Crystal Beach Ballroom days, Maynard Ferguson. Maynard and Mel had stayed in touch and their friendship only grew while road roommates during their fall tour with Raeburn. Mel's relationship with Maynard proved to be very important, as only several years later Maynard recommended Mel to the famous bandleader Stan Kenton.[12]

Playing with the Raeburn Band, Mel only earned eighteen dollars per job, but it provided him the opportunity to play music nightly while remaining based in New York City.[13] Mel enjoyed working for Raeburn because he was treated with kindness and given the musical freedom to play the drums how he saw fit:

> Boyd never let himself get too close to the guys in the band. I mean he was busy fighting with his wife in front of us at the time. Ginny Powell. And he played, he played actually not too well, alto, alto clarinet, which is the hardest thing to play. He also played bass saxophone. But I'll tell you, he treated us nice, he was a nice guy, he was a lot of fun, and he really believed in what he was doing.[14]

While with Raeburn for only a few months, no commercial recordings were made to serve as an example of Mel's playing with the group. Both Mel and Maynard stayed with Raeburn through the summer and early fall of 1948. In October Raeburn broke up the band to move in another musical direction, Ferguson then went on the road with Jimmy Dorsey, and Mel returned to an uncertain future in New York City.[15]

Upon his return to the city, Mel stopped by Charlie's Tavern, the famous musician's watering hole located on 51st Street, between Broadway and Seventh Avenue. Charlie's was not only a place to get a meal and drink, but also a message center for many jazz musicians. When Mel checked in at Charlie's, the bartender handed him a message from his mother stating that bandleader Alvino Rey was in Buffalo and had called the Sokoloff house looking for a drummer. The next morning, Mel took the first train upstate to Buffalo to meet Alvino Rey.[16]

Mel joined the Alvino Rey Orchestra for the remainder of 1948. The band was much less of a modern jazz band than the Lenny Lewis and Raeburn Bands, and much more of a dance band.[17] However, by this time bebop was such an influence on Mel's drumming style that it came out in his playing regardless of the situation. The bebop influence resulted in Mel's increased use of the bass drum as a melodic voice, a more interactive approach to comping, and a focus on a triplet-based ride cymbal beat (sometimes referred to as a "wide beat"). Mel recalled trying to play in a style that was appropriate for Rey while still maintaining his bebop approach:

> Now I am with a dance band again, but the funny bit is that bebop had completely taken me over by this time; I was really a bop drummer. And the small group thing was really coming into my head now, this way of playing. But I wasn't thinking about it that way, I didn't even realize what I was doing. I wasn't saying, "oh, I'm going play small group drums in a big band." I'm just going to play and what's going to be is going to be. Alvino Rey never told me what to do. He had some bebop charts in the book, all the bands did. He had some modern stuff for the time and he also had some corny stuff.[18]

Even though his short tenure with Rey was not filled solely with the type of music he would have preferred to play, Mel enjoyed working for Rey and his time with the band. Rey was a forward-thinking musician, and that was something that Mel particularly respected. Rey was also fascinated with bebop music, especially guitarist Charlie Christian, and even though Rey did not normally play in a bebop style, Mel recalled that many times before gigs Rey would join the other members of the band for an impromptu bebop jam session.[19]

At the end of December, as the tour ended, it was apparent that Rey would not reorganize his band after the holidays. Famous leaders such as Benny Goodman and Woody Herman were breaking up their big bands because life on the road was not profitable, and for bands such as Rey's the times were extremely tough. Mel moved back in with his parents in Buffalo and held a slight glimmer of hope that Rey's manager Billy Young would get him a job with the Skitch Henderson Orchestra. Unfortunately, that gig never came through, and he ended up staying in Buffalo and taking whatever musical work came his way.[20]

After spending January and February of 1949 living and working in Buffalo, Mel told his parents that he had enough of small town Buffalo life and needed to be back in New York City. He packed a bag and his drums and took the nighttime Empire State train to New York City for the second time in as many years.[21]

Mel arrived at Grand Central Station in Manhattan the next morning and immediately called his friend Harvey Estrin, whom he met while playing with Boyd Raeburn. Estrin told him to leave his drum cases at the train station and meet him at Nola rehearsal studios in Midtown.[22] When he arrived at Nola's, Mel saw a gathering of young drummers in the lobby. Of the assembled drummers he recognized Buddy Lowell, a friend he had made while living in New York City the year before. Lowell proceeded to tell Mel that the twenty-five drummers had been invited to audition for a new band led by Ray Anthony, a trumpet player and bandleader recently signed to Capitol Records.

Young and brazen, Mel proceeded to walk up to the door where the auditions were taking place and knocked until someone answered. After being initially denied the chance to be added to the audition list, he literally stuck his foot in the door, and again asked for the chance to audition. This time Anthony looked up at Mel, who was dressed in a zoot suit, maroon jacket, peg pants, and Flagg Brothers shoes, and snidely shook his head no. However, it was during the exchange that Anthony's manager Fred Benson recognized Mel from his tenure with Alvino Rey. Years later Benson told Mel that he whispered, "I think you better listen to him. I heard him, he's good," in Anthony's ear.[23] Mel gained his audition, and after waiting all day, he was the last of twenty-six drummers to audition for Anthony. After a brief audition, he was offered the spot with the band. During a 1989 interview in *Cadence* magazine, Mel described his interaction with Anthony during the audition:

Anthony said, "Sokoloff what kind of name is that?" Lewis responded, "That's Russian, that's Jewish. So what?" Anthony responded by saying, "Well, I never had a Jew in my band before." And to that the young Lewis shot back, "*So*, you don't have one yet."[24]

Even after the hostile interview, Mel accepted the job and began his employment with Anthony.

In March of 1949, Mel hit the road with the newly formed Ray Anthony Orchestra. During the first several weeks, he quickly noticed that Anthony never announced him by his full name on stage, only by his first name. To Mel, it was obvious that Anthony was opposed to announcing a Jewish name, such as Sokoloff, on stage. After a show one night, Ray Anthony, whose own real name was Raymond Antonini, was introduced to Mel's younger brother Lewis Sokoloff. The very following night Anthony finally introduced Mel using a first and last name. The name used was not Mel Sokoloff, but the fictitious stage name Mel Lewis.[25]

After that night, Mel Sokoloff would forever be known as Mel Lewis. Of course the name change did not come lightly. To begin with, Mel's personal relationship with Anthony was far from pleasant, and he was initially very upset and offended. When he spoke to his parents about it, they assured him that they understood the circumstances and realized that it was a chance to further his career.[26] While his parents' understanding and the use of his brother's name made the name change easier to accept, unbeknownst to Mel the final decision had already been made. Anthony's management told the Gretsch Drum Company, Mel's first endorsement, that Mel Sokoloff wanted his name changed to Mel Lewis.[27] Shortly after the first on-stage introduction of Mel Lewis, *DownBeat* magazine published a Gretsch advertisement featuring a drumhead that read "Mel Lewis." There was no going back.

The Ray Anthony Orchestra of 1949 and 1950 was a stiff-sounding ensemble that performed popular dance music and often traveled with as many as five vocalists. There were, however, rare occasions in the music for Mel to inject his personality. Though most of the time when he played something he considered hip and tasteful, Anthony would later scold him for it. The relationship between Anthony and Mel was always strained. Both men seemed only to need each other for practical purposes. Mel's wife Doris explained the men's relationship by saying, "Mel had his way of doing things, and Ray had his way of doing things. The two never got along because they never wanted to do anything the same way!"[28] In a 1989 interview Mel recalled his relationship with Anthony and what he learned from the situation:

> I joined Ray Anthony and he was a total pain in the ass to work for, but I learned a lot. I learned I got that discipline going. My cocky attitude was cut down a little bit. He changed my name. When I finally left, *I* quit. But he did fire me, he fired me a lot of times. He just kept hiring me back before I could leave because he couldn't find anybody to play better than me. He knew it. He just didn't know it until he tried. And I knew it too because I could hear what was going on around. I found out all these so-called New York drummers were not great at all. They were ordinary, and there was a few good ones and no real competition for me, or for anybody for that matter. Good drummers were a rarity and that's all there was to it. There's no ego problem involved, it's just there weren't many good drummers. There still aren't.[29]

Mel also explained that his biggest source of musical tension with Anthony involved the spacing of his ride cymbal beat. "He always wanted me to play tight; I never knew what he meant ... I played tighter. I played clean that's all, but it was still too loose for him," said Mel.[30] The men co-existed, but Mel always played his cymbal beat based on the triplet subdivision he loved and Anthony always asked for, yet never received, the tight-sounding eighth/dotted-sixteenth ride cymbal beat he preferred.

Even with its negatives, the Anthony Orchestra did feature other talented young musicians. Al Simi, a bass player, and Bill Usselton, a tenor player, both played in Anthony's group with Mel. The friendship between Bill Usselton and Mel led them to later record their first small group album together titled *Bill Usselton Sextet: Modern Jazz Gallery* (Kapp) on October 17, 1956.[31]

During May of 1950, the Anthony Orchestra played an engagement at Café Rouge, the main ballroom at the Hotel Pennsylvania in New York City. For much of the 1950s, '60s, and '70s, the hotel was renamed the Statler Hotel. After their engagement at Café Rouge, they began a run at Frank Dailey's Meadowbrook in nearby Cedar Grove, New Jersey.[32] On a rare night off, Mel

21

ran into a friend and former Ray Anthony drummer at his hotel. The young man informed Mel that he was going to audition for the Tex Beneke Orchestra that night in New York City at Café Rouge, and he suggested that Mel tag along for the evening. Having just performed at Café Rouge with Anthony, Mel thought it would be fun to see the Beneke Orchestra play the same room and went along to his friend's audition.[33]

When the two drummers entered Café Rouge they were met by Tex Beneke's manager Vince Carboni and taken to a table at the side of the stage. As he watched the first set, Mel was in awe of the slow tempos and swinging feel of the Beneke Orchestra. Saxophonist Gene Cipriano, who was also a former member of the Lenny Lewis and Raeburn bands, recognized Mel and gave him a hello nod from stage.[34] Mel then observed Cipriano lean over to Beneke and whisper something in his ear. Mel later learned that Cipriano whispered, "There's the guy we should get on drums."[35]

After the first set ended, Mel's friend was scheduled to play the second set with the band as his audition. However, when Beneke approached their table during the set break, the course of events changed drastically. After a quick introduction from Carboni, Beneke immediately asked Mel if he would like to play the next set. Not wanting to be rude, he tried to politely tell Beneke that he was only there to watch and support his friend. After more pushing from Beneke, and the approval of his friend, Mel agreed to play the second set. Mel recalled auditioning that night, saying,

> It was a great saxophone section and it wasn't even like what you would think the Glenn Miller type band would be like. Nick Travis was up there, Joe Ferrante, Bobby Nichols, Dick Nash, Paul Tanner of course. Four trombones, four trumpets, but they were very laid back, you know. Moe Purtill was playing drums in the interim; he was helping them out while they were looking for a drummer.
>
> So I went up the next set and I sat in. And boy what a difference in the feeling of the band! Beneke pulled some good charts and I read them and everything felt good. Nick Travis turned around to me and said, "yeah!" Nick was just joining the band then and I realized that this was going to be an experience that might be a little nicer. I found out the money was much better! You know not even a little better, but much better. And while Johnny somebody was playing the last set, I was hired.[36]

For Mel, playing with the Beneke Orchestra after spending a year with the Anthony Orchestra felt like going from a bicycle to a sports car. Similarly, the entire band was knocked out with his drumming and Mel ecstatically accepted the job.[37] Mel had planned to give his two-week notice the next morning, but as he explained, things did not go according to plan:

> When Johnny and I came back to the hotel after the audition we walked into the lobby and noticed Greg Lawrence the singer in the Beneke Band, who didn't really know me from Adam. Lawrence was sitting at a table with Ray, his manager Benson, and his wife Dee. Johnny and I walked by their table, quickly said hello and kept moving. Apparently after we passed Benson, the manager who had been instrumental in me getting on Ray's band, turned to Greg Lawrence and said, "I know Beneke was looking for a drummer, did you guys get a new drummer yet?" And Lawrence replied, "Yeah that guy there, the red head that just walked by." So they *knew*! When I called the next morning Ray gave me a hard time. But I quit; I put my two weeks in and joined the Beneke band.[38]

Mel began his three-year association with Beneke in June of 1950. His first weekend with the Beneke Orchestra was at the Edgewater Beach Hotel on the north side of Chicago. Mel recalled the pressure of joining a new band in those days:

> My first gig, my first scene man, was at six o'clock in the evening on the air. There's no rehearsal you know. I sat down in the band and we went on the air, nothing man, there it was. The set was pulled out, I set up the music and we went, "Moonlight Serenade" and right into it, we're on the radio coast to coast. And I did another broadcast later that night. And this included the "St. Louis Blues March," all of these things. I had to play all of these on sight, and I did it.[39]

Saxophonist Gene Cipriano had played with Mel in both the Lenny Lewis and Boyd Raeburn Bands and was instrumental in getting him hired with Beneke. The two men became roommates and close friends while on the road with Beneke. Cipriano remembered the impact that Mel's drumming had on the band and their friendship at the time:

> The Beneke Band was a swinging band and Tex was really wonderful to work for. I had played with Mel on the Lenny Lewis Band and then I helped him get the gig with Tex Beneke. I am sure glad that I did because he was a great friend and a great drummer. He played so great night in and night out, hell he made "Little Brown Jug" and "String of Pearls" sound fresh and exciting!
>
> We roomed together on the road and man did we have some fun. Mel loved to talk, mostly about himself, but he loved to talk. We'd get back to the hotel room after a gig at one o'clock in the morning and I would lie down on the bed to relax. Well Mel would start talking and while I fell in and out of sleep, Mel kept talking. He could talk until four in the morning if I let him!
>
> Another thing I remember about Mel was that every time the Beneke Band stayed in a town, you know where we'd stay for a couple days, he would try to find the best Jewish deli. Eventually he'd find it and drag me with him every morning for a bagel. He would always say, "Cip it's good, but not as good as in New York." And I would say, "Mel nothing is as good as it is in New York, even the Italian food!" Even then, Mel's heart and stomach were still in New York.[40]

While working with Beneke in Chicago for much of the summer, Mel spent almost every night out on the town meeting musicians and playing at jam sessions. During one of these sessions he had the opportunity to play with a local bass player named Buddy Clark. Mel and Clark were the same age, enjoyed the same music, and from the very first time they played together had a great musical connection. In a 1957 *DownBeat* article, Mel spoke of Clark by saying, "I really dig him because he's always in tune and his time is great."[41] As luck would have it for Clark, Beneke's bassist Cliff Hill had just given his notice and was leaving the band. Mel recommended Clark for the position, and shortly after playing together for the first time, he joined Mel in the evolving Beneke Orchestra rhythm section. It marked the beginning of the Mel Lewis and Buddy Clark musical connection that can be heard on over fifty-eight recordings between 1951 and 1962.[42]

Later in the summer of 1950, several months into Mel's tenure with Beneke, his former boss Lenny Lewis contacted him out of the blue. No longer a bandleader, Lewis and had gone into the management side of the music business. In 1950 he was the manager for Count Basie, as Basie looked to form a new septet. Basie was still interested in hiring Mel, something he had been denied two years earlier. Twenty-one-year-old Mel Lewis was offered the drum chair with the new Count Basie Septet, a group that featured jazz musicians such as Wardell Grey, Clark Terry, and Buddy DeFranco. However, when Mel was offered only ninety dollars a week to play in the group, he decided to turn down the offer. At that point in his career Mel was sending money home to help support his parents and if he took the Basie gig he would not be able to continue taking care of his parents.[43] His pay cut would have been almost ninety dollars per week, as he was making 175 dollars a week with Beneke. Mel recalled the tough decision:

> Normally I would have taken the job for fifty dollars a week, for myself, who cares. But I couldn't do it. So there was my second opportunity to go with Basie. I could have gone from that into the famous big band, which could have meant possibly no Sonny Payne, if I would have stayed. It could've changed everybody's history.[44]

Incredibly, Mel later learned that ninety dollars a week was not the offer that Basie had intended for him. The offer was supposed to be $135 a week, but Lenny Lewis tried to get Mel to join for less money while pocketing the extra.[45] In a 1989 interview with Bob Rusch for *Cadence* magazine, Mel stated, "Basie didn't know I turned it down because of money, but if he'd [Lenny Lewis] offered me what he was supposed to have offered me, I'd have gone."[46] Having made a very mature decision for a twenty-one-year-old, Mel stayed on the road with Beneke.

With his decision, Mel unknowingly put himself in a position to meet the love of his life Doris Sutphin. Their unexpected meeting took place during the winter of 1951 while the Beneke Band performed in New York City. Beneke's pianist at the time had a girlfriend living in Washington D.C. who traveled to

New York City to catch up with the band. As fate would have it, she brought her friend Doris Sutphin with her. It was on that weekend that Doris and Mel met, beginning the couple's lifelong relationship. Doris recalled the circumstances that led to the meeting and how the couple truly fell in love months later in San Francisco:

> I was living and working in Washington D.C. at the time and my girlfriend asked me to go to New York City with her for the weekend. I didn't really want to go but I said ok. Mel was working with Tex Beneke at this time, and my friend was seeing Beneke's piano player. We got into New York on a Friday night and it was a terrible weather day, and by that I mean it was a blizzard! After we got in town my friend went over to the hotel where the Beneke Band was staying. She asked me if I wanted to go and I said, "No I am too tired, and I really don't want to go back out in that weather." So I didn't go out with her that night, but she ended up telling Mel that I was in town with her and she showed him my picture. I think Mel was disappointed he didn't get to meet me that night, I say this because on Saturday he kept calling the hotel leaving messages asking me to get a cup of coffee with him. He must have called a million times, but I never bothered to answer his call because in my mind he was a traveling musician and what interest does he have in me. Now for some reason, and I don't know why, I changed my mind on Sunday. We were getting ready to go back to Washington but I decided to call him back because he had been so persistent and left me so many messages. When I called him he said, "I'll meet you at a restaurant near Grand Central Station and we can have dinner before you leave town." So I went with my girlfriend and that is when I met Mel for the first time. Of course I thought he was very nice, but I didn't take the matter seriously because he was out on the road and all over the place.
>
> I did give him my phone number during that meeting in New York and to my surprise he started to call me from the road. Those phone calls were really how we got acquainted. Several weeks later he played in Washington D.C. and we got to go out again and spend time together. After that visit we continued talking on the phone

while he was on the road. Several months passed and Mel ended up working in San Francisco for several weeks. He called me and said that he wanted me to come out and spend time with him. So I went out to San Francisco and that is really when and how we fell in love. Our time in San Francisco was wonderful. After that, the next time I saw him was in Washington D.C. and he asked me to marry him. Of course I said yes! It's kind of funny to think about, because we really hadn't spent that much time together, but that's how we got started and fell in love.[47]

The couple talked on the phone daily, as Mel stayed on the road and Doris worked in Washington D.C. and prepared for the couple's upcoming wedding in Buffalo. With his budding romance and steady gig with Beneke, twenty-two-year-old Mel Lewis was living the life he had always dreamed of.

Chapter 3
Brookmeyer and Kenton's Initial Offer

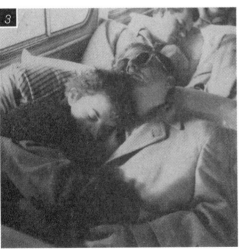

1 Mel and Doris riding a cable car in San Francisco. *Used by permission of the University of Missouri-Kansas City Libraries, Dr. Kenneth J. LaBudde Department of Special Collections and the Sokoloff family.*

2 Mel with Tex Beneke. *Used by permission of the University of Missouri-Kansas City Libraries, Dr. Kenneth J. LaBudde Department of Special Collections and the Sokoloff family.*

3 Mel and Doris sleeping on the band bus. *Used by permission of the University of Missouri-Kansas City Libraries, Dr. Kenneth J. LaBudde Department of Special Collections and the Sokoloff family.*

4 Mel and Buddy Clark with the Tex Beneke orchestra. *Used by permission of the University of Missouri-Kansas City Libraries, Dr. Kenneth J. LaBudde Department of Special Collections and the Sokoloff family.*

5 Mel with Ray Anthony in 1953. *Used by permission of the University of Missouri-Kansas City Libraries, Dr. Kenneth J. LaBudde Department of Special Collections and the Sokoloff family.*

5

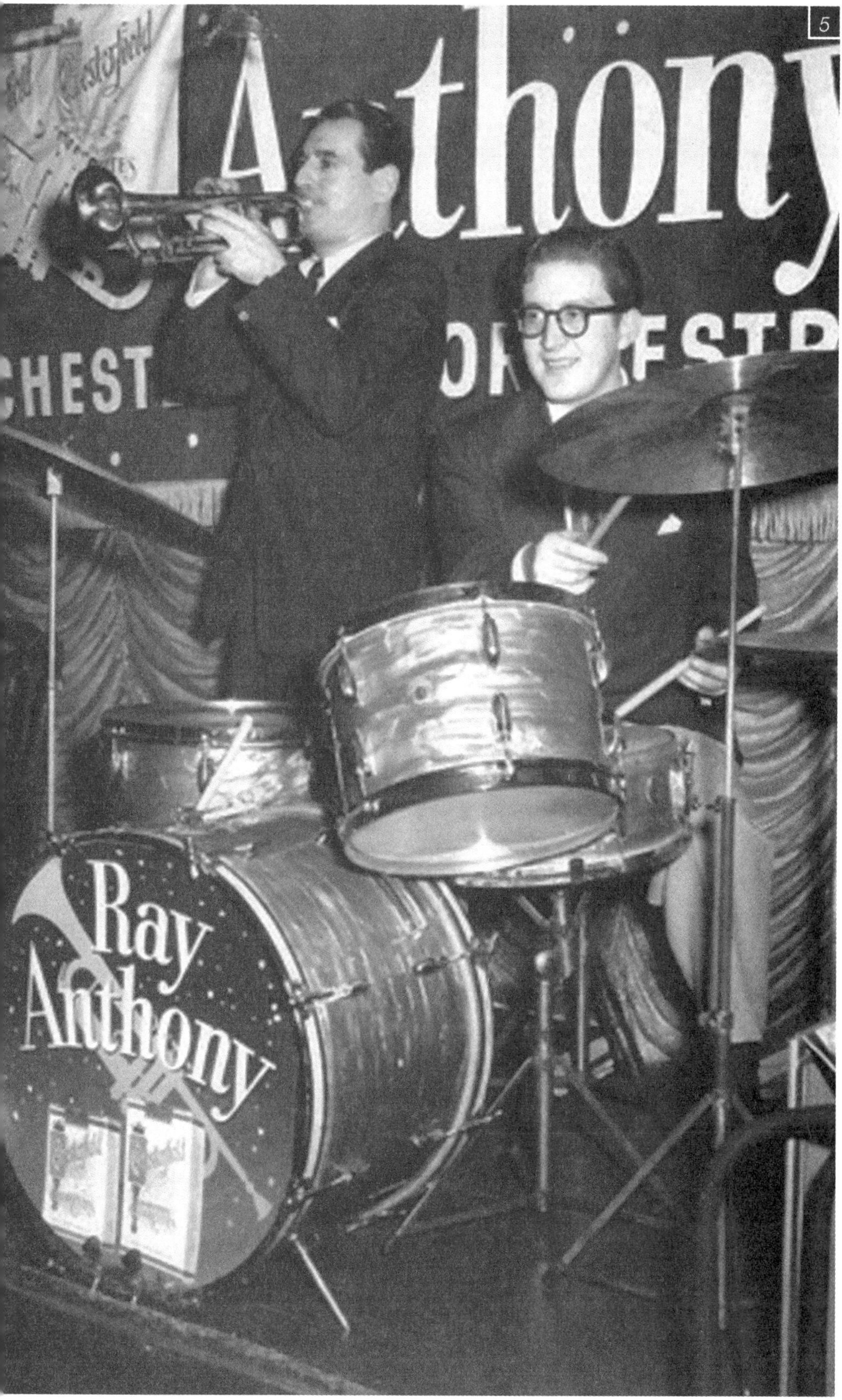

Chapter 3
Brookmeyer and Kenton's
Initial Offer

In 1951, Mel once again persuaded Beneke to hire another one of his friends, this time on piano. Bob Brookmeyer, a young pianist and valve trombonist from Kansas City, joined Mel and Buddy Clark in the rhythm section. Mel recalled his first meeting with Brookmeyer and how he eventually got him on the Beneke Band:

> Bobby and I met in 1949, in Chicago. I was playing drums with Ray Anthony; now this is before Anthony was really very well known, he was just starting to go out. The band was more or less a Les Brown type of band, not quite as good, but it was close. And Brookmeyer was playing piano with the Orrin Tucker Band, that's what he was doing.
>
> Bob and I met at a jam session at a little club called the High Note in Chicago. Also that night we met up with Al Cohn, Tiny Kahn, Frank Rosolino, they were all working in Chicago at the time. And we were with two commercial dance bands, Brookmeyer with the extreme commercial band, and he was down there with his valve trombone. We are the same age, in fact I am older than Bobby six or seven months. So we were both around nineteen years old then and met at that session. It was one of those things where we liked each other, liked the way each other played and we became fast friends.
>
> Bob went to the Army, we kept in touch, and as soon as he got out I got him on Beneke's band as the pianist. And then later he moved over to a trombone chair when it opened up. At that point Al Haig came into the band on piano. So we worked it all out, because we were waiting for a trombone chair to open up and when it did Bobby took it. Then we came to New York with the band and I started taking him around to Birdland and introduced him to different people and he started sitting in down there.[1]

The 1951 rhythm section of Mel Lewis, Buddy Clark, and Bob Brookmeyer transformed the Beneke Band from a Glenn Miller-inspired dance band to a more modern sounding jazz band. "We had a little thing going all our own in the corner. It was like the Beneke band plus a separate small combo within the band, and it was a ball all the way," recalled Mel.[2] The musical relationship that Brookmeyer and Mel formed during their time with Beneke continued developing over the next thirty-seven years. In 1952, Brookmeyer left the band to live permanently in New York City where he began working with Ray McKinley, Claude Thornhill, and Stan Getz.[3]

By 1952, Mel's second year with Beneke, the band's music had become more modern. Beneke began his career with Glenn Miller, and after Miller's death, he fronted his own band that was closely associated with the Miller estate. For years much of the music that the band played were famous Miller Orchestra arrangements such as "Moonlight Serenade," "In the Mood," and "Tuxedo Junction." However by the end of 1950, Beneke had officially cut ties with the Miller estate; the move allowed him to take more creative control of his band's music.[4] The music rapidly changed and by 1952 the band was playing a wide variety of more contemporary swinging arrangements. Mel recalled: "One of our chief arrangers in the band was Hank Mancini, now known as Henry Mancini. Brookmeyer did some writing for the band, as did Neal Hefti and Marian Evans."[5] Mel remained extremely happy to be with the band, playing music that complimented his triplet-based cymbal beat and light bebop touch. But just as he was hitting his stride with Beneke, Mel received yet another unexpected job offer, this time from jazz legend Stan Kenton.

In late June, Mel and the Beneke Band were performing in Walled Lake, Michigan. As he stepped off the stage for an intermission break, Mel heard a voice call him from the dark shadows behind the stage. A tall man said, "Mel, can I talk to you for a minute? My name is Leo Kern, and I work for Stan Kenton. Would you be interested in joining the Stan Kenton Orchestra?" Mel responded to the surreal moment by saying, "Are you kidding, of course!"[6] A meeting with Kenton was scheduled for the next day in nearby Detroit. Luckily, Mel had his car with him and could get into Detroit without anyone associated with Beneke knowing.

During the meeting, Mel learned that Kenton and his current drummer Stan Levey had had an argument, resulting in Levey's decision to quit the band. Levey was still on the road with Kenton, but the two men had decided that the relationship was over. As Kenton began to look for a new drummer, his star trumpet player Maynard Ferguson recommended Mel for the job.[7] Mel had been working for this opportunity his entire life, and at the end of the meeting when Kenton officially offered him the drum chair he gladly accepted. He gave Beneke his notice the very next day and unlike the attitude that he received from Ray Anthony upon giving his notice, Beneke was pleasant and assured him there were no hard feelings.[8]

Coincidentally, a week later, both the Beneke and Kenton Bands were working in Chicago. In less than a month, Mel was to begin rehearsals with Kenton and join the band on their first European tour. While in Chicago, Kenton visited Mel at his hotel and explained that Stan Levey had unexpectedly reconsidered and wanted to continue playing with the band. As far as Kenton was concerned, it was Mel's job if he wanted it and ultimately left the decision up to him.[9]

Musically Mel was more than ready for the gig, yet he didn't want to be known as the drummer who kicked Stan Levey out of the Kenton Orchestra. Again, showing maturity far beyond his years, Mel turned down the offer and allowed Levey to leave Kenton on his own terms. After telling Kenton of his decision, Mel was promised the drum chair whenever Levey officially left.[10] Luckily for Mel, Beneke had not hired a new drummer yet and he was welcomed back with open arms. He stayed on the road with Beneke during the fall of 1952 and anxiously awaited further word from Kenton. With all the uncertainty in his career, Mel found calm that fall in still having a gig with Beneke and often being joined on the road by his fiancée Doris. Mel and Doris ended the year on a high note, getting married at Temple Emanuel in Buffalo on Christmas Day, December 25, 1952. After the honeymoon Doris settled in Buffalo with the Sokoloffs and Mel headed back out on the road with Tex Beneke[11]

After spending January on the road, twenty-three-year-old Mel Lewis suddenly quit the Beneke Band and moved back to Buffalo. Mel wasn't unhappy with the Beneke situation, but was needed by Doris who was expecting the couple's first child. Ultimately Mel made the difficult decision to cut ties with Beneke and headed home. Spending the spring of 1953 in Buffalo he worked every musical job offered, but also had to take several day jobs to help make ends meet. Some of his day jobs included work as a factory inspector at Western Electric, a salesman at a men's clothing store, and a short stint selling women's shoes at a store called Beck's. For a man that had spent almost his entire life on a bandstand, these day jobs were incredibly tedious and awkward. Mel recalled his brief stint working day jobs in Buffalo:

I had to leave Tex because my wife needed me and I had to get back to Buffalo. So I went back and I started working day jobs and boy they weren't working out at all. I first went to work at Western Electric in the factory as an inspector. Once I was late to work three days in a row mainly because I was working some night gigs at the same time, you know I was getting home at four in the morning and had to be there at seven. I was only walking in two minutes after, three minutes after, but it's on the clock and I was late. A guy ended up telling me, "If you're late one more time you're fired." I said, "don't even bother" and I walked out. I quit. I didn't like it at all.

Then I got a job selling ladies shoes at Becks. [Mel laughs] That didn't last long! I quit that one by telling some lady the truth. She insisted she wore a size six, but I said, "Lady you wear an 8 and besides your feet stink!" After that I walked out and quit that job too. Turned in my shoehorn and split!

Then I went to work in a men's store. I was ok there, except all the guys in town were coming in stealing the store blind because I was in charge. You know they would just walk in and say, "Hey man I'm going to take a shirt." I said, "Aw come on man don't do that!" "Just say you didn't see it," they would tell me. I said, "yeah but that's not the idea." Truth was that all my broke Italian musician friends were coming in and stealing Mr. B shirts. I hate to say Italian, but they just so happen to be Italian. Finally I started telling them, "Just take some for me and I'll meet you later!" It was just funny you know. They were all my musician buddies. But nobody caught on to us, and as it turned out, everybody working at that store was also stealing. They're all stealing shirts and ties from my department and I had to look the other way even for the employees. It was ridiculous![12]

Mel knew eventually he would go on the road with Kenton; however, he had no idea when that call would come and had already been waiting over eleven months.[13] As fate would have it, early that spring the Ray Anthony Orchestra traveled through Buffalo. By this time, Anthony was a rising pop star, had better musicians in his band, a higher payroll, and a sponsorship from the Chesterfield Cigarette Company. The Anthony Orchestra was riding the success of their recent popular dance hits "The Bunny Hop," and "The Hokey Pokey." When word got to Anthony that Mel was living in Buffalo without a steady job, his manager immediately called Mel and offered him the opportunity to rejoin the Anthony Orchestra.[14]

Buffalo had run its course and Mel was more than ready to get back on the road, even if it meant working with Anthony. Mel recalled that the decision to rejoin Anthony was a fairly simple one:

> Man, I was itching to get back and the band was better. I thought to myself, "I'm going with Kenton next anyway." I mean I had the Kenton job; the next opening was mine. I figured it couldn't be too long. So I said to my wife, "Would you let me go?" She said, "Go ahead, I can't stand you the way you are now, you're miserable."[15]

In May of 1953, Mel hit the road with Anthony for the second time, but this was a much different Anthony outfit than the one he had toured with four years earlier. Band members were now paid between 250 and 300 dollars a week. Mel stated, "Man, that was great money for the time."[16] With higher pay came better musicians and an overall better band, resulting in a mostly happier Mel. While the money was welcome, he was growing more restless for the call from Kenton and his move to the jazz "big leagues."

After several weeks of touring, the Anthony Orchestra traveled to New York City. They were hired to be on television for eight weeks as the summer replacement for Perry Como on CBS. The promise of spending much of the summer in New York City while on salary with both Anthony and the CBS Network (two paychecks) was a major reason that Mel took the gig.[17] Spending the summer months in New York City also gave him the opportunity to play gigs and jam sessions whenever he wasn't required to work for Anthony. Mel remembered the summer of 1953, saying,

> It gave me a chance to stay around a little while again that summer, and I was doing a lot of outside stuff on my own. I was getting to know people, because I had Brookmeyer here and Sal Salvador, and different people. Joe Morello was working with Marian McPartland at the Hickory House every night, so I'd go

down there and blow and sit in with the trio, you know. And I'm with a big band three days a week and hanging around Birdland and sitting in on Monday nights and all that. I had a lot of nice things going.[18]

On June 20, 1953, the Anthony Orchestra headed into the studio to record several singles. Mel was featured on one of them, a Dick Reynolds arrangement of the theme from *Dragnet* (Capitol).[19] Thanks in apart to Mel's drumming, the single quickly became Anthony's greatest commercial success, selling over 500,000 copies during its first month of sales.[20] *Dragnet* went on to become Anthony's first million-selling record.[21]

After the summer, the Anthony Orchestra left New York and spent much of the next eight months on the road. When not with the band, Mel spent his breaks with Doris and their newborn baby girl in Buffalo. By January 1954, not much had changed for Mel; he and Anthony could not get along, and Stan Levey was still Kenton's drummer. In May 1954, he looked forward to spending another summer in New York City since the Anthony Orchestra was once again Perry Como's summer replacement on the television show *TV's Top Tunes*. Mel again spent the summer in the city playing jam sessions, the occasional gig, sitting in for drummer Joe Morello at the Hickory House with Marian McPartland's Trio, and seeing live music nightly. His summer was also spent hoping for that call asking him to join the Stan Kenton Orchestra. He had been waiting two and a half years and doubt that the call would ever come began to enter his mind.[22]

During an Anthony Orchestra rehearsal that August, Dean Kinkade brought in an arrangement of "South Rampart Street Parade." The drum part contained written drum fills in the style of drummer Ray Bauduc, and Mel was more than happy to play what was written as he felt it was similar to his own interpretation. After the band rehearsed the arrangement to Kinkade's satisfaction, Anthony joined the rehearsal. Immediately upon hearing Mel play the written drum part, Anthony stopped the orchestra and snidely gave him a hard time about his playing. As Mel later described, it was at that very moment that the two men had their final disagreement:

> Ray immediately stops the band and says to me, "Wait a minute what are you doing?" I said, "I'm playing the part." He said, "Don't play that, just play backbeats." I said, "Man, there is all this

35

interesting stuff that's written here, what do mean play backbeats?"
He responded by yelling, "Do what I say." He makes it a big issue
you know, he's going to show off how great he is. So he counts it off
again, and you know me, I start playing the same thing again! And
he stops again and says, "What did I just say?" And I said, "Listen to
it once, let us get through the chart first then make your decision."
He responded by saying, "I said don't do that, so you better not do
it." So we start again, and you *know* I did it again. I was *mad* now, I
was really angry. Ray was so frustrated that he finally stopped and
said, "Pick up that music, I don't want you to read it any more. I
don't want anything but time. Just pick up that book and throw it
away." I said, "Alright" and I picked up this huge book of music and
threw it right at him! With that I said, "Take that you little jerk."
Well, at that moment Ray completely fell apart. He started shaking,
turning red, and screaming. I used to call him all sorts of dirty
names, you know, but I never called him that. What I didn't know
was that Glenn Miller called him a "little jerk" when he had fired
him. I touched a nerve and I didn't have any idea. Well, that was
it. He's yelling, screaming for Benson, and everybody is running
around all over the set they don't know what happened. And I am
standing there ready to grab my hi-hat to hit him in case he comes
at me. I couldn't believe what I started, you know! It was a funny
scene. Anyway I was fired.

Naturally, of course I *had* to finish the show and the contractor
came over and told Ray, "Look you can't fire Mel, he's got to finish
out the series. Unless you want to pay him for the whole series,
but he's under contract under CBS and you can't do that." Well,
anyway this turned into a big scene. I finished the show; played
the arrangement the way I wanted to, he didn't talk to me any more
and he left me alone. Boy I really did it to him! In the meantime we
had a recording session that night that he canceled me off of. But
Ray was mad and made me come to that recording session even
though I wasn't playing. My wife was in town, so we went to the
session together and played cards in front of the band. The band
was laughing and eventually Ray threw us out. We get back to the
hotel; dig this, now this is the beginning of a whole new era. There

is a phone call, a message that said call operator six with a phone number in Los Angeles. And that was Stan Kenton. Oh man, talk about fate!

For six years, the opportunities for Mel to join a band led by a major jazz artist had not worked out. There was the first Basie offer in 1948, the second Basie offer in 1950, and the initial offer to join Stan Kenton in 1952. The message from Kenton gave him three weeks' notice to fly to California and join the Stan Kenton Orchestra. When he least expected it, Mel finally got his break. After many years of hard work and patience Mel Lewis was ready introduce his drumming to the mainstream jazz community. ‖

1 Mel and Doris on their wedding day December 25, 1952. *Used by permission of the Sokoloff Family.*

2 Mel Lewis publicity shot for the Stan Kenton Orchestra. *Used by permission of the University Missouri-Kansas City Libraries, Dr. Kenneth J. LaB... Department of Special Collections.*

Chapter 4
Kenton Presents Mel Lewis

In September of 1954, twenty-five-year-old Mel Lewis flew to Los Angeles and joined the reorganized Stan Kenton Orchestra. After four days of rehearsal the Kenton Orchestra set out on the second installment of their nationwide tour named The Festival of Modern American Jazz. The tour began in San Diego on September 16 and Mel quickly adapted his musical concepts into the Kenton Orchestra. He often told the story of his first night with the band, stating, "When I joined Kenton, that very first night, he came over and yelled, 'Hey Mel, can you play louder?' And I said, 'No.' He said, 'Okay, I just thought I'd ask.'"[1] For the remainder of his time with Kenton, Mel's softer dynamics and bebop-influenced style of big band drumming were a major influence on the band's sound.

The Festival of Modern American Jazz featured the Kenton Orchestra, along with the several other groups such as the Art Tatum Trio, Charlie Ventura's Quartet, and Shorty Rogers and His Giants.[2] The drummer touring with Shorty Rogers's group was former Kenton drummer Shelly Manne. By 1954, Manne was the top call jazz drummer on the West Coast, having gained national exposure and fame playing with Kenton from February 1946 to December 1951.[3] During his time with Kenton, Manne had provided the blueprint for how a drummer could add dynamics and color to the oftentimes loud Kenton Orchestra. The two-month tour gave Mel the opportunity to watch and learn from Manne every night. Mel later recalled the specific advice Manne gave him during the tour:

> He [Manne] was quite an influence, I learned about dynamics from him. On my first tour with Kenton, Shelly was there with Shorty's Giants. It was a great tour; it was with Shorty Rogers' Giants, Art Tatum Trio, Charlie Ventura Quartet with Mary Ann McCall singing and Sonny Igoe was the drummer. So we had Shelly, Sonny Igoe, and me with the Kenton Band.
>
> I had just joined the Kenton Band and Shelly used to stand in the wings and watch me play. And one day after we were out there, this is how we really got friendly, he came to me and said, "Can I

make a suggestion to you?" and I said, "Sure of course." He said, "Mel your cymbal beat is beautiful, but you're hitting too much two and four on the cymbal, because your hi-hat is there and you don't need that. I think you should give it a little more one and three." And he's the one that got me started on that. And I went right at it and it worked, and he gave me a high sign from the wings that it sounded great.

From then on I really developed the cymbal beat I have today. I mean it was the same spread, I didn't change my grace note, but I was hitting two and four a little more than was necessary. And I started giving it more one and three, which you can hear in his playing. So you have one, two, three, and four. That's it you know![4]

On September 21, 1954, the Kenton Orchestra played the Civic Auditorium in Portland, Oregon. The performance was privately recorded and later released in 2000 on a CD titled *Stan Kenton Festival* (Status). This performance was the first live recording of Mel drumming with the Kenton Orchestra. Having played with the orchestra for only a week, his playing was inspired and swinging. He was playing well, but still trying to figure out how to best support the orchestra and its soloists. Burt Korall heard the band perform that week and recalled Mel's drumming, stating, "I had the opportunity to see and hear Lewis on one of Kenton's first concert dates with the newly revised band, at a large Seattle auditorium in September of 1954. He didn't seem to be in full control of the band or comfortable in the job."[5] Mel was indeed learning on the job, but matured quickly over the next several months. He had the good sense to apply Manne's drumming advice and soon found himself more comfortably leading the band and beginning to impart more of his own style and drumming vocabulary.[6]

On stage, Mel was introducing his drumming to legions of Kenton fans. Meanwhile, in the confined quarters of the tour bus, he was introducing his personality to the other musicians. Composer and tenor saxophonist Bill Holman remembered getting to know him during the tour:

Mel joined the band for that tour, and he started playing really well right off. I remember after the first night we were on the bus traveling somewhere, and I noticed Mel was kneeling in his seat.

He was facing the rear, talking to the person behind him. I thought, "well it looks like Mel's a talker!" I woke up several times during the night, and he was still there talking to the guy. I don't know if the guy was a willing participant or a captive audience, but that was my introduction to Mel's personality.[7]

For two months the tour zigzagged across the country, playing one-nighters in cities both big and small. On November 6, the tour had a rare afternoon off in New York City; the day would produce another first for Mel's career. His association with Kenton not only gained him membership to a big band filled with great jazz players, but also the opportunity for small group recordings through Kenton's subsidiary label with Capitol Records called Stan Kenton Presents. Mel joined bassist Max Bennett, trumpeter Sam Noto, alto saxophonist Charlie Mariano, pianist Pete Jolly, and trombonist Frank Rosolino and recorded Bill Holman's arrangements of "I'm Gonna Sit Right Down and Write Myself a Letter," "Linda," "Embraceable You," "Ragamuffin," "Besame Mucho," and "Frank N' Ernest." The album was simply titled *Stan Kenton Presents: Frank Rosolino* (Capitol) becoming the first of hundreds of small group albums that Mel recorded in his career. Holman recalled the session, and Mel's introduction to small group recording:

It was one of my first flashes of being in a studio as well; I guess we were in New York. Mel had some trouble making the transition to the little band. I don't remember the exact issue, but some of the guys in the band had to talk to him about it. Anyway, after a few minutes he fit right in to that thing too, and sounded great.[8]

The Kenton Orchestra went back on the road for two weeks. Then on November 21, 1954, The Festival of Modern American Jazz came to an abrupt end because the attendance during the tour was not as high as the Festival tour the year before. The various groups went their separate ways and the Kenton bus headed back to Los Angeles.[9]

In December, Kenton disbanded his group for the holidays and promoted Bill Holman to chief arranger. He then sent Holman to New York City with the assignment to arrange Great American Songbook compositions for the orchestra. While in New York, Holman went out every night and listened for inspiration for his new arrangements. He was able to watch and hear some of the greatest big bands of the day, especially the Count Basie Orchestra, which featured arrangements by Ernie Wilkins and Neal Hefti. Holman recalled the experience in an interview with Marc Myers of JazzWax.com: "In 1954, when Stan Kenton sent me to New York for a couple of months to arrange 'What's New' and 'I've Got You Under My Skin,' I often caught Basie at Birdland. So the new Basie sound was a big influence as well."[10] Holman's new arrangements became an important factor in Mel's successful tenure with Kenton.

While Holman worked in New York City, Mel spent his five-month break from Kenton working in Los Angeles. Doris and the couple's young daughter Anita had also relocated from Buffalo to 13424 D Huston Street in Sherman Oaks and became year-round residents of California with Mel. Mel stated, "I've been on the road since I was seventeen, that's a straight ten years. Now it's good to sit down and stay home."[11] He played an increasing number of recording sessions and performed with various jazz groups, most led by current or former Kenton members. In December, he also worked and recorded with his friend from the Beneke Band, Bob Brookmeyer. Brookmeyer had moved to Los Angeles that September, and was playing valve trombone regularly with the Gerry Mulligan Quartet and the Stan Getz Quintet.[12] Brookmeyer lived on the West Coast for less than a year before moving back to New York City. During his time in Los Angeles, he and Mel performed together frequently including several residencies at The Haig jazz club located at 638 S. Kenmore Street.

On December 26, 1954, Brookmeyer began a weeklong residency at The Haig with his new quartet. The group included Brookmeyer on valve trombone, the quartet's usual bassist Buddy Clark, and the new additions of Jimmy Rowles on piano and Mel on drums. After their engagement at the Haig that evening, the group went into the studio and recorded with legendary producer Norman Granz.[13] The album was titled *The Modernity of Bob Brookmeyer* (Verve) and featured several jazz standards, as well as three original Brookmeyer compositions. The recording serves as a landmark in Mel's career, as it was his first recording with Brookmeyer and also his first small group date with Clark.[14]

Throughout the spring of 1955, Mel also recorded with some of the finest jazz musicians on the West Coast, including the Herb Geller Quartet, the Bud Shank-Bill Perkins Group, and the Pete Jolly Quintet.[15] Jolly's album, *Pete Jolly Quintet: The Five* (RCA Victor) is a fine example of Mel's small group playing during this period. On Shorty Rogers's composition "Perkin," Mel played his ride cymbal beat on slightly open hi-hat cymbals while perfectly placing melody counterpoint with his snare drum. The recording is also a good example of the cohesive time feel that Buddy Clark and Mel achieved together.

During his break from Kenton, Mel also played regularly in a trio with pianist Hampton Hawes and bassist Red Mitchell. The trio performed nightly throughout February, March, and April, and Mel greatly enjoyed playing in the format:

> We formed a trio with Red and I and Hampton, and we where tearing it up at the Haig. And I tell you, I wasn't that well known at the time, and I had already joined the Kenton band, and I had already committed myself to go back with Kenton. And I'm glad I did, because it turned out to be a very important move for me anyway, because that was a good Kenton band that I went back with. But I hated to leave that trio. I was just there a few months, working every night with Hamp. It was a delightful time; it really was wonderful. Hamp couldn't have been playing better. Red and I got to know each other inside out. It really worked out great.[16]

In May of 1955, Kenton reorganized his orchestra after the six-month layoff and headed back on the road. The group included many significant personnel changes, including new bassist Max Bennett, alto saxophonist Charlie Mariano, and tenor saxophonist Bill Perkins who rejoined the band. Perkins had spent time on the road in previous years with Kenton and the Woody Herman Orchestra. His smooth tone and legato time feel were heavily inspired by Lester Young, and his strong bebop soloing meshed perfectly with Mel's drumming style.

No personnel change to the 1955 Kenton Orchestra was more important than new lead trumpeter Al Porcino. Porcino had finished up a year with the Woody Herman Orchestra and was one of the most in-demand lead trumpet players in the world.[17] His bebop-inspired lead playing and brash personality brought an immediate change to the sound and personal dynamics of the band. In Michael Sparke's book *Stan Kenton: This Is an Orchestra!* Bill Holman recalled the Al Porcino and Mel Lewis team:

Porcino and Mel were kind of tight … so Stan sort of turned
the band over to Al and Mel as far as the direction was concerned.
They set about getting the band to swing, and had the guys playing
really close to a true jazz feeling. I think that was the most swinging
band Stan ever had.[18]

Mel's musical relationship with Porcino continued for over thirty years
and contributed to the sound of some of the greatest big bands of all-time,
including the Terry Gibbs Big Band, the Bill Holman Orchestra, and the
Thad Jones/Mel Lewis Jazz Orchestra. It cannot be overstated how much
the feel and sound of the 1955 Kenton Orchestra changed with their playing.
The two men were also not bashful as leaders and often told other band
members how to play, phrase, and interpret their parts.[19] Mel remembered
his role in the band:

I was the bad guy in the band. I used to get on everybody who
didn't pull their weight. People said the Kenton band never swung,
but it swung all the time I was there, and that had something to
do with all the players in the band. I didn't play any harder with
Kenton, and that band was as blasting as any band you ever heard.
I just didn't find it necessary to be loud—I don't push a band, I
cushion it. Woody Herman offered me a job when I was with
Kenton, but Stan's band offered more musical satisfaction. We
never really sounded like Woody, though we started to get a little
close. Really, we became a Bill Holman band.[20]

Under the close musical supervision of Mel and Al Porcino, the Kenton
Orchestra began performing Holman's new arrangements. The arrangements
perfectly suited their swing conception and featured standout soloists such
as Charlie Mariano on "Stella by Starlight" and Bill Perkins on "Yesterdays."
On May 13, 1955, the band played a concert at the Surf Club in Palo Alto,
California. The concert was privately recorded, released as *Stan Kenton and His
Orchestra: Live at Palo Alto* (Status), and featured a live version of Holman's
new arrangement "I've Got You Under My Skin." This live recording makes for
an interesting comparison to the same arrangement recorded two months later
on the famous commercial release *Contemporary Concepts*. Mel's drumming

on the live version of "I've Got You Under My Skin" is so thoughtful and interactive that it is hard to imagine that he had only played the arrangement a handful of times. Many of the phrases and melodic ideas that he played on the live recording were used in almost exactly the same fashion during the studio recording months later. Some of these musical ideas included: Mel's pick-up notes into the first measure, his melodic phrasing during the melody, his use of the low sounding floor tom to fill into a low brass figure, and the clever way that he slowed down and brought the arrangement to an end. After only a handful of times playing the complex arrangement, he was beyond reading the chart and had already interpreted the music in his own style. Even at the young age of twenty-six, Mel had the ability to quickly memorize music and play in a way that uniquely suited each arrangement. ‖

Chapter 5
Contemporary Concepts and Thad Jones

July of 1955 was one of the most important months in Mel's career. The Kenton Orchestra had hit their stride, and jazz critics began to notice Mel's drumming and the orchestra's lighter swinging style. Jazz journalist Nat Hentoff heard the band during their famous July engagement at Birdland in New York City and proclaimed:

> The new Stan Kenton band is still working itself into a more balanced, more relaxed shape, but as of its Birdland bow, it displays a crisp arsenal of power, exuberance, and several swinging soloists. In line with the last two years, this is a leaner, far less pretentious sounding band than some of the crews Stan used to front. In fact, in its better, unstiff moments, this band swings unusually hard to the extent that one late entrant on opening night shook a skeptical head and asked, "Are you sure this is a Kenton band?"[1]

Burt Korall also heard the band at Birdland and took note of Mel's control of the ensemble stating, "Mel Lewis plays with a surety that gives the band definition and much of the small group feel that is essential to moving it off the ground. He is technically proficient and very much at home in the band."[2] Korall's statement highlighted Mel's unique ability to play with the subtlety and interaction of a small group drummer in a big band setting. Though he never intended to, Mel truly invented a small group approach to big band drumming.

In July, after their successful run at Birdland, the Kenton Orchestra arrived in Chicago for a series of concerts. Drummer John Von Ohlen witnessed Mel with the Kenton Orchestra during that week in Chicago and recalled the immense impact it had on his life:

> I was fourteen years old and we had driven in from Indianapolis to see Kenton. At the time I was a trombone player and piano player. I had never even touched the drums, never even thought about it.

Well, we pulled up to the concert and I heard Mel's cymbal from out in the parking lot and boy it just went straight to my brain! He kept playing that cymbal when we got in there and I just couldn't get my mind off of it. The next day when I woke up, I was a drummer in my head. The reason I started playing drums was because I heard Mel playing that cymbal with Stan Kenton. He became my mentor after that; he was everything to me.[3]

While in Chicago, Kenton's new road manager Bob Martin felt that the band sounded phenomenal and persuaded Kenton to take it into the studio to record Holman's new arrangements.[4] Mel later recalled that Kenton did not initially want to record an album:

In 1955 the critics were saying the Kenton band was swinging for the first time in history. The band had a fresh, light feeling to it, and credit was being given to me—the new, young drummer on the scene—and to Bill Holman's writing. We had acquired an ex disc-jockey named Bob Martin as road manager, and when we got to the Blue Note in Chicago, Martin said to Stan, "You know, we really should record this music while it's fresh, and while the band is sounding so good." And Martin talked Stan into it, he even went and booked the studio time, so Stan gave in and we did it.[5]

On July 20 and 22, the band entered Universal Studios Chicago and recorded six Holman arrangements and one Gerry Mulligan arrangement for the album *Stan Kenton: Contemporary Concepts* (Capitol). Because of the impromptu nature of the session many of the soloists were reportedly unhappy with their playing on their features, but it was the band as a whole that had come into its own and was hitting on all cylinders.[6] *Contemporary Concepts* did not rely on solo features, a powerful brass sound, or even Kenton himself; the album was recorded to showcase the band's swinging interpretations of Holman's masterful writing. Mel explained his opinion of the album by saying,

If you notice, Stan doesn't play a drop of piano on it. He didn't really want to do this album, because it was not typical Kenton music. He wasn't sure. He had commissioned all this work for Bill

Holman, to write extended compositions based on standard tunes; really rewrite them, and this was what really made him somebody. The reviews of the album were spectacular, from all the important critics. It became the most swinging album Stan ever made, but it swings in a different way. It's not like Woody's band, with that hard forceful thing they had, and it didn't have the Basie 4/4 swing.[7]

With the release of the *Contemporary Concepts*, Mel Lewis was introduced to the legions of Kenton fans around the world. More importantly, the revitalized swinging sound of the Kenton Orchestra helped his drumming be heard by the larger jazz community. Mel's light touch, bebop comping, and ability to support the ensemble without overplaying, began setting a new standard of big band drumming.

During July the Kenton Orchestra also performed at a Monday night "Battle of the Bands" at the Greystone Ballroom on Woodward Avenue in Detroit. It was on that hot July evening that Mel met a thirty-two-year old trumpet player with the Count Basie Orchestra named Thad Jones.[8] Neither man could possibly know how intertwined their lives would become, or how many future Monday nights they would spend making music together. However, it was on that night that a lifelong friendship began. Mel recalled the evening he met Thad Jones:

> Thad and I always felt like it was meant to be. It really was, because I was with Stan's band at the time and he was with Basie's band at the time. And we played a dance together, a Battle of Bands, in Detroit on a ridiculously hot night. People have seen this in some of the biographies, but it's true, we met when it was 110 degrees at night in the Greystone Ballroom. There were 8,000 people there and both bands were sort of passing out, we were just drenched soaking up sweat. There was only one opportunity for anybody to possibly get near each other, as far as the two bands were concerned. It was during one particular break, when the two bands changed bandstands. We went outside, which made no difference between inside and outside as far as the heat was concerned, and Basie came inside. You couldn't get through the crowd at all, but somehow Thad and I were the only ones that met that night. The only ones

that met from the two bands, and we started talking and hanging out together during the break. And Basie saw it, he noticed it. He saw us talking, and he also remembers that night.

We sat around talking and Thad invited me out to play with him and his friends at a place called the West End Hotel. The West End was where all the guys used to jam after the job, and I went. After I got home to the hotel and got out of those soaking wet clothes I got in a cab and went out there. It was an area I hadn't even been in, you know. But I got there, and sure enough they were there, Billy Mitchell, Elvin was there, and all the Detroit guys were out there and I met them all. Thad introduced me to everybody and I played! Thad and I just stayed that way. Every time the bands ran into each other, we'd always get together.[9]

July of 1955 was a significant month for both men, as Mel recorded *Contemporary Concepts* and Thad headed into a New York City studio and recorded the song "April in Paris" with the Count Basie Orchestra.[10] "April in Paris" featured Thad playing a brilliant trumpet solo in which he quoted the melody of the children's song "Pop Goes the Weasel." The quote became such a hallmark that he was pressured into playing it on every solo he took on "April in Paris" for the reminder of his eight years with Basie.[11]

The Kenton Orchestra stayed on the road throughout the fall of 1955, while Kenton himself split time between touring and flying to New York every Tuesday to be the host of the short-lived CBS television series *Music '55*.[12] After more than seven months on the road, the band finally ended their grueling schedule with a two-week run at Birdland from November 24 to December 7. In only nine months' time, the band had gained new and exciting players such as Charlie Mariano, Bill Perkins, Al Porcino, and Carl Fontana. The writing of chief arranger Bill Holman allowed the group to play with the contemporary, swinging, and light feel that many of the members preferred. They did not sound like the Kenton Orchestra that its fans had grown accustomed to. However, Kenton was rapidly beginning to second-guess the direction of the band and his influence on its sound. As the group disbanded for its usual holiday break Kenton reshaped his band in major ways. In one decisive action, Kenton fired Al Porcino, road manager Bob Martin, and told Bill Holman that he would no longer be arranging for the group. To Holman, the firing was a shock. To this day he is not sure why Kenton changed his musical vision so hastily:

I don't know exactly what went on in Stan's mind, but he fired Al Porcino, the road manager, and called me and told me to stop writing, all at the same time. And I don't know what the reason was. Maybe he felt that the band was getting away from him, or maybe there was some tension between him and Al, and he lumped Al's playing and my writing in the same category. Either way he decided to make the clean sweep. I just don't know why.[13]

Kenton may have been disillusioned with the swing concept, or he may have simply felt the need to reclaim ownership of the ensemble, but no matter his reasons, the changes to the orchestra greatly affected Mel. Charlie Mariano also left the band that December, a move that prompted Kenton to hire two French horn players instead of a new alto saxophonist.[14] This move puzzled many and greatly irritated Mel. The French Horns altered the timbre of the ensemble and raised the overall volume, resulting in the four saxophonists and rhythm section competing against the powerful sound of twelve brass players.[15]

The Kenton Orchestra was searching for a new identity during the winter and spring of 1956. Their February recording *Kenton in Hi-Fi* (Capitol) could be viewed as a creative step backward, as the band recorded several previous Kenton hits including "Intermission Riff," and "The Peanut Vendor." While still finding itself musically, the band embarked on one of its most famous and highly publicized tours.

In March of 1956, the Kenton Orchestra began its second European tour; the first had taken place in 1953. This tour was different because the band had been granted special permission to perform in Great Britain. They were the first American group to officially perform in Britain since World War II, thanks to the British Musicians Union agreeing on an exchange visit with the Ted Heath Band, which toured the United States. On March 4, the band arrived on the west side of Manhattan and boarded the largest ocean liner in the world, the *Queen Elizabeth*. The transatlantic journey took a total of five days. For Mel and the other musicians, this was a chance to relax on the most luxurious ship in the world before a demanding tour schedule.[16]

On March 11, the Kenton Orchestra played the tour's debut concert to a capacity crowd of 7,000 people at London's Royal Albert Hall. They performed a mixture of Kenton's famous pieces, as well as the more recent arrangements by Gerry Mulligan and Bill Holman. The band and its featured soloists Carl Fontana, Bill Perkins, and Lennie Niehaus were under the close scrutiny of the media and thousands of British jazz musicians who were eager to size up the skill level of the American musicians. While many were enthusiastic about the sound of the band, there were some local musicians who were seemingly unimpressed by what they heard.[17] An article in the British publication *Melody Maker* expressed several of the local musicians' opinions. The following is an excerpt from an article titled "Kenton's Impact," published on April 7, 1956:

However one viewed the Kenton conception of jazz, by common consent, Stan had formed some great bands. Expectations were that he would awe and thrill us. Up at Luton, for example, Basil Kirchin stood on the pavement in unabashed hero-worship to watch the Kenton coach arrive. Then, with his band, he went inside to listen and learn. "I was brought up on that legend," says Basil. "British musicians hadn't a chance. These men were our gods. The curtains weren't even drawn when the Kenton men ambled on. Then Stan loped to the piano and started playing. Wonderful psychology, I thought, because we were all waiting for that fabulous Kenton brass. After I heard the trumpets, I felt sorry for Kenton. They had no range. I only heard a few F's and a couple of G's. And from one of the sections we saw a display of childish irritation over a fluff. Was this the legendary musicianship? It must have been a bad night. Thank goodness for that drummer. Great. But my band agrees with me that if Ted used those arrangements, he'd show up the Kenton band on that standard. Only a couple of numbers swung."

Possibly that is an anti-climactic judgment. Balance it with the words of Stan's staunchest protagonist, Vic Lewis. When I discussed the Kenton band with Vic, he'd already introduced and heard it eight times. "As a unit, it's as good as anything Stan's ever had, and it swings more than most. The program, I'd say, retrogresses from the music played by the innovations orchestra of 1950. Fontana at all concerts was the outstanding all-around soloist and improvisationally, Niehaus and Perkins were everything I expected. But I'd have to say that the Americans only lead us in two respects: their drummers are relaxed and they swing, and the arrangers know how to write and are free to write well. Our picked soloists are as good."

Neither of these opinions should be construed as unfriendly. Now that the idols are within reach, they are being lifted down from those pedestals and examined with almost brutal curiosity. Perspectives are being adjusted and here and there, we may guess, over-adjusted. What the American visits offer our musicians, is the chance to discover, first-hand, just where they stand. At least, they figure, let's away with the legend and find how much we really are behind.[18]

While the positive reviews greatly outnumbered the negative, it is significant to realize that this was the first time British jazz fans had seen live American jazz musicians since the end of the big band era and the development of bebop. Jazz music had changed greatly over the years, and not all of the music that Kenton programmed was modern or swinging. Because many people in the audience wanted to hear bebop, Mel's drumming was never criticized in the media and he became one of the brightest stars on the tour.[19]

During the grueling tour through England, the band performed an astounding sixty concerts in thirty-three days.[20] With the British leg of the tour completed, they set out on a month-long tour of Europe that included performances in West Germany, Denmark, Belgium, The Netherlands, Switzerland, Sweden, and France. Despite the exhausting schedule and several personnel issues along the way, the tour was a success and Mel gained his first taste of international recognition.[21] On May 10, the Kenton Orchestra boarded the *Queen Elizabeth* in Cherbourg, France, and headed back to New York City.[22]

Back in the United States, the popularity of rock and roll music was growing by the month. Elvis Presley and his number one hit "Heartbreak Hotel" had taken over the airwaves and ears of American teenagers. The golden era of big bands had long passed and Kenton's personnel changes in 1956 were likely a result of him realizing that the orchestra had to once again reinvent itself to remain relevant. Kenton wanted to move away from the swing feel that the band had established, so he took his love of Latin rhythms and the strengths of his new chief arranger Johnny Richards and created *Stan Kenton: Cuban Fire* (Capitol).[23]

Johnny Richards began writing for Kenton in 1950. Much like Holman before him, Richards was sent to New York City with a specific assignment. Kenton wanted Richards to immerse himself in the Latin music scene of New

York City, and use authentic Latin rhythms and instruments as the basis for new compositions for the Kenton Orchestra.

Richards's Latin-inspired arrangements were recorded in New York City on May 22, 23, and 24, only one week after the band had returned from its European tour. *Cuban Fire* brought back the dense orchestral writing and heavy brass sound for which the Kenton Orchestra was known. It was one of the first times an entire jazz album used Latin rhythms and Latin musicians, and it became a defining recording in the genre of Latin Jazz. While artists such as Juan Tizol, Dizzy Gillespie, and Mario Bauza had been playing and recording truly authentic Latin American rhythms since the 1940s, Kenton's commercial stature helped spread the sounds of Latin music to a large new audience.[24] In addition to Mel on drums, the recording featured Mario Alvarez on maracas, George Laguna on timbales, Willie Rodriquez on bongos, Tommy Lopez on congas, Roger Mozian on claves, and Saul Gubin and George Gaber on timpani.[25] The thick orchestration and added percussion, while effective, may have signaled the beginning of the end for Mel in the Kenton Orchestra. The music was moving in a decidedly less bebop direction, and by the fall of 1956, it was increasingly clear to Mel that it was about time for another musical change.[26]

Mel had been based out of Los Angeles for two years, and his work around town was steadily increasing. When not on the road with Kenton, he played in a variety of large and small band settings. During October of 1956, Mel record two albums with some of the best musicians on the West Coast. The first recording was led by tenor saxophonist Bill Perkins, titled *Bill Perkins: Just Friends* (Pacific Jazz), and included Red Mitchell on bass, Hampton Hawes on piano, and Richie Kamuca on tenor saxophone; it is one of Mel's finest recordings from 1956. The second recording that Mel made that month was the compilation album titled *Modern Jazz Gallery* (Kapp). The album featured Mel with tenor saxophonist Bill Usselton's Sextet as well as with pianist and arranger Marty Paich's big band. Mel's musical relationship with Paich had begun earlier that year when he recorded an album titled *Mel Torme with the Marty Paich Dek-tette* (Bethlehem). During the next five years, Marty Paich and Mel were one of the busiest and most musically successful teams on the West Coast jazz scene. The combination of Paich's arranging or piano playing, and Mel's drumming can be heard on forty-three albums recorded between 1956 and 1961.[27]

During the first two weeks of November 1956, Mel was back out with Kenton playing the Macumba Club in San Francisco. Lawyer and part-time recording engineer Wally Heider recorded the band almost every night at the club. Heider's recording resulted in an album titled *Kenton '56 in Concert* (Artistry) and serves as the last recorded performances of Mel with the Kenton Orchestra.[28] The album reveals the band playing many of the swinging arrangements from Gerry Mulligan and Bill Holman during the engagement. In addition to it being Mel's last recording with Kenton, it is also significant as being one of the earliest known recordings of baritone saxophonist Pepper Adams.[29] Adams only played with Kenton for a few months, but his playing at the Macumba Club was so strong that he immediately stood out among the group of gifted improvisers. One can only imagine Mel's excitement the first time he played with Adams in the Kenton Orchestra. The two men became great friends and were musically "cut from the same cloth." Before the Kenton engagement had ended in San Francisco, Mel was presented with the opportunity to record his first small group album as a leader, one that would feature his new friend Pepper Adams.[30]

When Pat Henry, the founder of San Francisco radio station K-Jazz, approached Mel with the idea of an album for San Francisco Jazz Records, he jumped at the chance and quickly began assembling musicians and arrangements for the date. He was excited to record his first album as leader, and through the process, learned how stressful being a leader could be:

> Pat Henry asked me to put together a record and I said sure. So I asked Pepper right away, Pepper was rooming with me at the time. And Lee Katzman was mad at me because I didn't ask him, but I asked Ed Leddy because I thought Ed Leddy was a classier trumpet player. Who has since disappeared totally, I don't really know what happened to him. He lives out in the Bay Area. Richie Kamuca was there, and Perk was supposed to be the other tenor player. Jerry Coker ended up doing it in place of Perkins because Coker was living in town and we'd already planned on the music being for two tenors.[31]

On Sunday afternoon, the day prior to the recording session, Mel learned that Bill Perkins had been injured the night before while defending a woman who was being molested. Perkins' injuries ended up being so severe that he was hospitalized for a week and was unable to play on the recording. At this point the project was almost called off entirely, but because the charts had been written and the group had rehearsed, Mel felt that the project should proceed.[32] Jerry Coker, a local tenor player, stepped into Perkins' vacated spot on the recording session, as well as with Kenton.[33]

The men gathered on the afternoon of Monday, November 19, and recorded "In a Mellow Tone," "Leave Your Worries Behind," and "One for Pat." The original location for the session had been canceled and the recording ended up taking place in the cavernous Sands Ballroom. The ballroom presented an entirely new set of challenges including a very out -of-tune piano. Mel recalled the session, stating,

> Oh, I was very excited to make my first record (as a leader), you know, and the only thing is everything went wrong. We had to go to this ballroom; it was freezing cold, so intonation problems and everything. But that was Pepper's first record too, I believe.[34]

Recording continued the next evening after the men had played their nightly engagement with Kenton. Starting well after midnight, the group battled cold temperatures and fatigue as they completed the recording. *Got'cha: Music of the Mel Lewis Septet* (San Francisco Jazz) was recorded amid many challenges, but the music shone through and provided a revealing snapshot of Mel Lewis and Pepper Adams's musical partnership in late 1956.

After his final tour with Kenton, Mel officially left the orchestra in December of 1956. He cited the orchestra's changing musical direction as his reason for leaving:

> At the end of 1956 we took our Christmas vacation, and I got a call from Stan saying he was going to Australia, but he's only taking a nucleus, and hiring guys down there. Now I knew that was going to be a catastrophe! And frankly, I also knew he was going to drop the Holman approach, and revert to the traditional style of Kenton Band again. It was going to get heavy, and I wanted to swing, so I decided I didn't want to be involved. When you're a jazz musician, you've gotta move on![35]

Mel considered his time with Kenton one of the best periods of his life.[36] Musically he respected Kenton and praised him saying, "In my opinion Stan Kenton has made such lasting contributions that he will go down in music history as one of the truly great innovators and bandleaders."[37] Kenton's personality as a bandleader also left a lasting impression on Mel. "Stan Kenton treated his musicians like gentlemen, and he knew how to draw the best out of you. He never told anybody how to play. And I thought that was very important," recalled Mel.[38] The lessons Mel learned from Kenton deeply influenced the way he treated fellow musicians when he became a bandleader. ‖

See Appendix Transcription and Listening Guide for this chapter: "Stompin' at the Savoy"

Chapter 6
Life in Los Angeles

Mel's career after Kenton provided him the opportunity to develop a wider network in Los Angeles and accept more studio work. In 1957, the Los Angeles jazz and studio scenes were very active, providing a wide variety of work for most musicians. During the winter and spring, he performed or recorded with Lennie Niehaus, Dave Pell, Bill Perkins, Jimmy Rowles, John Graas, Med Flory, and Quincy Jones, among others.[1] He was also being called for an increasing number of big band dates, many of them led by former members of the Kenton Orchestra.

Maynard Ferguson had recently led the Birdland All-Star Dream Band in New York City and was looking to establish his own thirteen-piece band on the West Coast. He asked several of the men who had just left Kenton's band to join his new outfit. In addition to his old friend Mel, Bob Fitzpatrick, Ed Leddy, and Richie Kamuca joined the first ever Maynard Ferguson Orchestra. "I've wanted to have a band like this for years, and now that it exists I darn well want to keep it going. If everything works out, I hope to keep at it for a long time," stated Ferguson.[2] Though Mel performed with Ferguson's band for only a very short time, it was one of the first examples of him being a first call big band drummer in Los Angeles.

In the spring of 1957, Mel joined another former Kenton musician who was also becoming a leader for the first time. Bill Holman had received a commission from producer Red Clyde to write new arrangements for what would be Holman's first big band album as a leader. Unfortunately, after the initial deal Clyde's budget became tight and the record was put off for months and eventually shelved for good.[3] Just when Holman thought his project was a lost cause, he received an unexpected phone call from drummer Shelly Manne. The Coral record label, a subsidiary of Decca Records, had recently hired Manne to be the producer of four jazz albums for the label. When he found out that Holman had an album of charts that were written and ready to be recorded, he approached him with the opportunity to record.[4]

The Fabulous Bill Holman (Coral) did not have the feel of a debut album for Holman, as he had more than proved his writing abilities with Kenton. Holman was ready and excited to make his own musical statement; his new compositions reflected the maturation of his arranging style and also marked the beginning of a new big band era in Los Angeles, one that featured the drumming of Mel Lewis.[5]

Holman was not leading a working band in April of 1957, so he quickly gathered many of the best jazz musicians in the city for the recording. As was usually the case with recording sessions, there was very little time for the musicians to familiarize themselves with the music. After one brief rehearsal the band headed into the studio on April 25 and recorded "Bright Eyes," "You and I," and "Evil Eyes." The remaining three compositions "Airegin," "Come Rain or Come Shine," and "The Big Street" were recorded on April 29.[6] While most of the musicians had previously played together in various settings (most within the Kenton Orchestra) they had never played or recorded together with that exact lineup. Holman later explained how quickly the musicians developed a cohesive sound during the recording:

> The band had one rehearsal, just to get out the wrong notes and everything. But at that time, there were so many guys that all had the same musical concept that the conception of the charts just fell in automatically. It was amazing that they came out as well as they did with that one rehearsal.[7]

The Fabulous Bill Holman was Mel's true big band follow-up recording to Kenton's *Contemporary Concepts*, which had been recorded two years prior. Mel's drumming on *The Fabulous Bill Holman* displayed the continued development of his style and sound. His ability to support every section of the ensemble was clearly evident during the melody statement of "You and I." Mel played fills that supported the rhythmic counterpoint in the saxophone section, while he simultaneously provided the brass with the subdivision and set-ups they needed to accurately play their parts.[8] Holman recalled Mel's drumming during the recording process:

> I realized during that recording how quickly Mel picked things up. He sounded like he had been playing the charts for years, finding the right concepts and always playing the right fills. And I

found out later, when we started going over to Germany to work
with the WDR Band, that he was like Buddy Rich, in that he could
play a chart the first time and have it almost down.[9]

Mel's wide cymbal beat, supportive fills, and ability to listen
throughout the entire ensemble continued to set his playing apart from
his contemporaries.

While *The Fabulous Bill Holman* showcased Mel's big band drumming,
the remainder of 1957 served as an opportunity for him to display his
playing in a small group setting. Prior to 1957, he had recorded in only a
handful of small group situations, but by the end of the year he added an
astounding twenty-five small group albums to his resume.[10]

Many of the small group dates that Mel recorded in 1957 were a result
of his new exclusive contract with producer Red Clyde and Mode Records.
During the spring and summer, he found himself in the studio several
times a month recording for the label.[11] In addition to Clyde, Marty Paich
was the musical director of Mode and also responsible for Mel's increased
studio work. Mel's 1957 small group output includes *Marty Paich 3*
(Mode), Marty Paich: *A Jazz Band Ball* (Mode), Bob Cooper: *Coop*
(Contemporary), Don Fagerquist Octet: *Eight by Eight* (Mode), Pepper
Adams: *Critics' Choice* (World Pacific), and the *Pepper Adams Quintet*
(Mode).

The musical partnership between Mel and Pepper Adams was
still strong as the men played gigs together in various configurations as
members of other bands. Earlier that November, Pepper and Mel had also
started their own small group. Unfortunately the group was short-lived
and did not perform frequently, but did produce two noteworthy studio
recordings. Journalist John Tynan observed the Pepper Adams/Mel Lewis
group at two rare live engagements in Los Angeles:

> The quintet played exactly two engagements, one night and one
> afternoon at Zucca's Cottage in Pasadena. At the close of the night
> engagement, for example the entire audience consisted of one
> waitress, Pasadena jazz columnist George Laine, and the writer!
> But Mel's quintet swung hard to the very end … Out of that brief,
> if swinging, alliance, however, came three record dates, the San

Francisco Jazz LP (*Got'cha*), and albums under Adams' name for Pacific Jazz and Mode.[12]

Pepper's first album as a leader, *Pepper Adams Quintet*, was recorded on July 10, 1957, at Radio Recorders studio in Hollywood, California. The album featured plenty of solo space for Adams, Stu Williamson on trumpet, and Carl Perkins on piano.[13] Bassist Leroy Vinegar created an incredibly solid foundation for the band, and Mel played with energy and a sense of urgency. His driving timekeeping and solo trading on "Baubles, Bangles and Beads" should forever debunk the notions that he "always played behind the beat" and "had no chops."

Pepper's next album as a leader, titled *Critics' Choice*, was recorded on August 23 and featured Pepper and Mel along with trumpeter Lee Katzman, pianist Jimmy Rowles, and bassist Doug Watkins.[14] The recording's straight ahead compositions included Tommy Flanagan's "Minor Mishap," Barry Harris's "High Step," and Pepper's "Blackout Blues." Trumpeter and composer Thad Jones, a close friend of Pepper from their hometown of Detroit, contributed two compositions, "Zec" and "5021," that rounded out the album. The album is an interesting piece of history because it was the first recording of Mel Lewis playing Thad Jones compositions.[15]

The Pepper Adams/Mel Lewis group may have received more popularity in Los Angeles following the favorable reviews of *Critics' Choice*, but several weeks after the recording was released, Pepper moved to New York City and left the West Coast for good.[16] Though their group was short-lived, their friendship was not. Pepper and Mel remained close and went on to perform music with each other in various groups throughout the 1960s and 1970s.

Mel's recent contract with Mode not only gave him steady studio work, but it also guaranteed him the opportunity to record an album as a leader.[17] In June of 1957, Mel gathered saxophonists Charlie Mariano and Bill Holman, trumpeter Jack Sheldon, pianist Marty Paich, and his old friend Buddy Clark on bass to record his second album as a leader, *The Mel Lewis Sextet* (Mode). The recording was finished in one day and Mel was very relaxed during the process. Holman recalled, "Mel was not a born leader so he would just play and say, 'well that felt good.' He kind of left it up to the producer (Red Clyde) to decide when we had a take."[18] Clyde and Mel deeply respected each other, and the friendly atmosphere made the recording a very enjoyable experience for Mel.[19] The excellent audio quality and Mel's tasteful drumming made The Mel Lewis Sextet a much more satisfying album for him than the previous year's *Got'cha*.[20]

Building on the momentum of The Mel Lewis Sextet, Mel and Bill Holman decided to co-lead their own small group and hired Lee Katzman on trumpet, Jimmy Rowles on piano, and Wilfred Middlebrook on bass.[21] For much of 1957 and 1958, the Bill Holman/Mel Lewis Quintet performed regularly at Terry Lester's Jazz Cellar on Las Palmas Avenue just south of Hollywood Boulevard.[22] Holman recalled the situation, saying, "We had the steady gig on Friday and Saturday nights. At 2:00 a.m., when all the other bars closed, we hosted a jam session. Musicians would come in after their gigs and play, guys like Ornette Coleman and Charlie Haden."[23]

The quintet's gig at the Jazz Cellar became a staple in the Los Angeles jazz scene and provided them the opportunity to develop a diverse book of music, including many originals and arrangements by Holman. The arrangements were often sparse, at least by West Coast standards at the time, because both leaders wanted the focus of the quintet to be on the soloists and the hard-swinging rhythm section, not the written music. Holman stated,

> Mel and I had decided that we had enough of West Coast jazz, and we were going to try to make a hard swinging group. West Coast jazz was getting awfully cute at that time. Musicians were so consumed with writing counterpoint, that they were bringing in fugues and passing them off as jazz charts. We were kind of fed up with that, so we tried to make a real jazz band. In some ways we succeeded, and in some ways we were still "West Coasters." We couldn't stop it entirely![24]

In a live performance review for *DownBeat* magazine, John Tynan fully comprehended the Holman/Lewis Quintet's musical direction:

> Clearly delineating the shift in taste of most west coast musicians to the hard (or semi-hard) school of playing is the newest addition to the combo league. Coincidentally, three of the five are Stan Kenton alumni but, unlike the Kentonites of seven or eight years ago who entrenched and pioneered "West Coast Jazz," they are less

concerned with innovation than with concentrating on relaxed and gusty playing.[25]

In regard to Mel's drumming, Tynan's description from the same review is so concise that it could be used to summarize nearly every Mel Lewis performance:

> The drummer-co-leader fulfills admirably his primary function of timekeeper justifying betimes his well-deserved reputation as one of the nation's top drummers. Mel's is a style devoid of useless technical showing off. He digs firmly, laying down the time with authority and when it comes time for fours (as in the very fast Liza) he makes his breaks count with intelligence and spirit.[26]

On May 29 and June 6, the quintet recorded *Bill Holman/Mel Lewis Quintet: Jive for Five* (Andex), an album of material that had been strengthened through their residency at the Jazz Cellar. Holman recalled the recording, stating, "That album may not have fully reached the 'East Coast energy' we aimed for, but the swinging rhythm section, simple compositions, and strong solos certainly made a statement on the West Coast."[27]

The Holman/Lewis Quintet continued to work through the summer of 1958 and, early that fall, was given the opportunity to perform at the first annual Monterey Jazz Festival. Inspired from his previous visits to the Newport Jazz Festival in Rhode Island, disc jockey Jimmy Lyons started a similar type of jazz festival in California. Lyons partnered with then San Francisco Chronicle jazz critic Ralph J. Gleason to develop the West Coast festival.[28] Saturday, October 4, and Sunday, October 5, 1958, marked the first annual Monterey Jazz Festival in Monterey, California.[29] The Holman/Lewis Quintet performed the 1:30 p.m. main stage show on Saturday afternoon, alongside other West Coast bands led by Med Flory and Shelly Manne. In addition to the exposure of his afternoon performance, Mel was able to spend time with the legendary musicians who performed during the evening concert. The evening concert featured the Gerry Mulligan Quartet, the Modern Jazz Quartet and the Dizzy Gillespie Quintet featuring Sonny Rollins.[30] Mel's 1958 performance at the Monterey Jazz Festival was just the beginning of his successful career at the festival.

The Holman/Lewis Quintet was an important group in Mel's career because it was the first time that he was the co-leader of a steadily working band. Much of his prior and future work was as a sideman; however he always seemed to have the desire to lead his own group.[31] Because of Mel's ambitious leadership of the quintet, his performances at the Jazz Cellar and at the Monterey Jazz Festival rapidly expanded his social and musical networks.

In 1958, Mel recorded a staggering number of vocal jazz albums. His swing feel, steady time keeping, and musical sensitivity were exactly what producers, studio contractors, and vocalists were looking for. Many of the recording sessions utilized a full big band or studio orchestra to accompany the vocalist or vocal group. The setting showcased Mel's ability to support a large ensemble and vocalist without overplaying or drawing attention to himself, yet still retaining his personal sound. The list of vocal artists with whom Mel recorded during 1958 includes: Jeri Southern (January), Anita O'Day (April), the Axidentals (May), June Christy (June-July), The Hi-Lo's (June-August), Sammy Davis Jr. (October), Carmen McRae (October), Bobby Troup (October), Ella Fitzgerald (November), and Mark Murphy (December).[32] Mel was hired for many of these recording sessions through Marty Paich, who was often the arranger and leader of the date. In what continued to be a running theme, Paich was the catalyst of much of Mel's studio jazz work, and steady income, throughout the late 1950s. Mel also continued performing regularly with Paich's instrumental jazz group the Marty Paich Dek-Tette. The group collaborated frequently with vocalists and many of their most successful albums, such as *Mel Torme Swings Shubert Alley* (Verve), featured singer Mel Torme.

It is unlikely that future generations of drummers will be able to match the diversity of studio work that Mel and other jazz drummers produced in the late 1950s. It was the last era when studios regularly hired jazz drummers and big bands to record popular records and television shows. This allowed drummers such as Mel Lewis, Shelly Manne, Irv Cottler, Alvin Stoller, and others to make studio income while utilizing their big band expertise.[33]

Of all of Mel's musical collaborations during 1958, none proved to be more important than his new associations with Shorty Rogers and Terry Gibbs. Trumpeter and composer Shorty Rogers represented the upper echelon of West Coast jazz musicians. Rogers received his first acclaim as a trumpeter in the bands of Woody Herman (1945–1951) and Stan Kenton (1950–1953), and went on to found his own small group, Shorty Rogers and His Giants. After the band's inception in 1950, fans, critics, and musicians on both coasts recognized the group as one of the finest in jazz.[34] Rogers always hired the best drummers on the West Coast, and his usual drummer of choice was Shelly Manne. Starting in 1958, when Manne was unavailable to make a performance, Rogers hired Mel. During 1958 alone, Mel was featured on Rogers's recordings *Gigi in Jazz* (RCA Victor), *Boots Brown and His Blockbusters* (RCA Victor), and *Chances Are It Swings* (RCA Victor). Additionally, the group made an appearance on KABC's television show, *Stars of Jazz*.[35] Mel's work with Rogers confirmed his spot as one of the top-call jazz drummers on the West Coast and helped to further his reputation around the globe. ‖

See Appendix Transcriptions and Listening Guides for this chapter:
"You Took Advantage of Me" and "Baubles, Bangles, and Beads"

1 Mel playing his famous "cut-out" cymbal with the Terry Gibbs Dream Band.
Used by permission of the Sokoloff family.

2 Coleman Hawkins, Ben Webster, Roy Eld
Mel Lewis, and Woody Herman at Monterey
© *Ray Avery/CTSIMAGES*

Chapter 7
Terry Gibbs and "The Tailor"

Mel first met vibraphonist Terry Gibbs in 1948 while both men were living in New York City. Gibbs remembered his initial encounters with Mel:

> Mel was with Tex Beneke, and he used to try to find me all the time because he loved Tiny Kahn's drumming. He knew that I grew up with Tiny, and had all of these things I could tell him about Tiny. So he would find me and we'd talk a little bit, but we never really got to know each other until I moved out to the West Coast.
>
> When I moved out to the West Coast and wanted to start a band, that's when we got really tight. Mel was looking for a band to play with, and even though he had Bill Holman's rehearsal band and Med Flory's band, all they did was rehearse and my band ended up as a working band almost immediately.[1]

The two men first recorded together in September of 1957 on an album titled *Jazz Band Ball—Second Set* (Mode).[2] It was during that session that Gibbs famously gave Mel his nickname, "The Tailor." Gibbs recalled the exact reason:

> I named him "The Tailor!" He was funny because he would tell people that I named him the tailor because I said he was tailor-made for the drums, but that wasn't the case at all. I named him "The Tailor" because there was a little Jewish tailor in my Brooklyn neighborhood, who had bunions on his feet, and never lifted his feet when he walked. Well, Mel shuffled his feet when he walked too. So I nicknamed him "The Tailor," and it stuck with him.[3]

Gibbs and Mel recorded together again in November of 1958, resulting in the album *Terry Gibbs: More Vibes on Velvet* (EmArcy). While their first album together featured a small group, More Vibes on Velvet featured Gibbs accompanied by a rhythm section and full saxophone section. The arrangements by Pete Rugolo allowed Mel to showcase his small group playing behind the soloing of Gibbs, and also his ability to support the saxophone section throughout the written arrangements.

It was also during that fall that Gibbs decided to form a big band on the West Coast.[4] Traditionally, Gibbs had recorded an annual big band album while living on the East Coast, and to continue the tradition he formed a new band in Los Angeles. In January of 1959 the Terry Gibbs Big Band rehearsed for the first time and prepared material for their upcoming recording in February. In addition to Mel on drums, Gibbs hired many of the best jazz players in Los Angeles including Conte Condoli, Frank Rosolino, Pete Jolly, and Joe Maini.[5] It was through his new band that Gibbs accidently fell into the most successful era of his career. In a 1962 *DownBeat* article, Gibbs recalled the making of his West Coast big band:

> A movie columnist friend of mine, named Eve Starr, called me one day in 1959. She told me about this club in Hollywood, a place called the Seville. She said the place was dying and the owner wanted to change the policy. He didn't really know whether he wanted jazz; he wanted anything that would bring customers into the joint. Eve suggested I go talk to him. His name was Harry Schiller.[6]

Initially Gibbs signed a contract with Schiller to play the Seville with his quartet. Gibbs's quartet had always been his most commercially successful group and was the main source of his income.[7] It was only because of his love of big band music that Gibbs recorded his yearly big band album. Journalist John Tynan explained the situation in a 1962 *DownBeat* article titled "Vamp Till Ready—Terry Gibbs' Big Band":

> It was a nice musical arrangement for Gibbs; he could record and work nightclubs with his quartet, commanding top money, and then, for kicks, he could cut loose and indulge his real love for big band jazz.[8]

Shortly after he signed his quartet contract with the Seville, Gibbs ran into a major hurdle with his upcoming big band recording. The Los Angeles Musicians Union rules prohibited any unpaid rehearsals for a recording, but permitted a band to rehearse unpaid for a nightclub job.[9] This meant that Gibbs couldn't rehearse for the recording, unless they were also rehearsing for an upcoming gig. Gibbs would have loved to pay the musicians for the rehearsals, but that was not financially possible. This left him with only one option; get the big band a gig:

> I made Schiller a proposition, I asked him if he'd let me take the big band into the club on Tuesday night only for the same amount of money as the quartet was getting. Schiller said it was okay with him if the quartet did business. If the quartet brought in some customers, he said, he didn't care if I brought in a band of apes on Tuesday. So we were set.[10]

With the Tuesday night confirmed, Gibbs began preparing for the big band's opening night. He made a guest appearance on the *Steve Allen Show* to promote his new big band and their upcoming Seville performance. In addition to the publicity from Steve Allen, word of mouth quickly spread that the band's show on Tuesday night was going to be one of the best jazz events of the year. By 1959, big bands, especially in Los Angeles, were not popular entertainment and did not even gain much attention from the music community. The Los Angeles big bands of Bill Holman and Med Flory were the most popular amongst musicians, but both were mainly rehearsal bands that released studio albums every year but did not perform live on a consistent basis. Mel played drums in both Holman's and Flory's bands during 1958 and 1959, but according to Gibbs, Mel really missed having the opportunity to play a steady live gig with a big band.[11]

While excitement for the band's debut was mounting, no one knew if the band would attract much of a crowd. But to Gibbs and the other members, it didn't really matter. They hoped to draw a crowd, but in reality they were still just rehearsing for their upcoming studio recording. They didn't have their sights set on being a steady working big band, but after opening night at the Seville their plans quickly changed.[12]

Opening night was a huge success and bigger than Gibbs or anyone could have ever imagined. In the packed club sat not only lovers of big band music, but also a remarkable mix of musicians and celebrities. By the end of the evening, Gibbs and Schiller decided that the group would perform again at the club the next Tuesday.[13] The turnout for the band's second week was just as successful as the first, and Gibbs found himself, and his band, the hottest event in Los Angeles:

The gigs were like a party. It was like a freak thing, and all of a sudden that band became the stars of Hollywood. You couldn't get in the club; there would be three hundred people packed inside, with a line full of movie stars waiting to get in. We were making fifteen dollars a night, the band was, and I was making nineteen dollars. Well, actually I made eleven dollars after I paid the band boy. See, we were making no money at all; we were just having fun. Everybody was so happy in that band because the music was so good. It didn't have anything to do with money, we just wanted to play that music together. We played twice a week most of the time, and sometimes we'd even play five days a week. The band was ecstatic because all the lead players in the band were the greatest lead players, but didn't have any place to play except in studios.[14]

As the band's popularity grew, composers and band members submitted their arrangements to Gibbs for use with the band. Bill Holman was playing tenor in the band and contributed several arrangements that he had previously recorded with his own group. As Holman noted, it was a great opportunity to have his arrangements played on a weekly basis to a large and enthusiastic audience:

> I didn't have a band; the records I made I had gotten a band together specifically for that. So I didn't have a band of my own that I was trying to promote, so having my music performed by a band that was working was beneficial for me. It was no sacrifice on my part.[15]

On February 17 and 18, several weeks after their first engagement at the Seville, the band went into the studio to record their first album.[16] *Terry Gibbs and His Orchestra: Launching a New Sound in Music* (Mercury) featured the arrangements of Bill Holman ("Stardust" and "Begin the Beguine"), Marty Paich ("Opus #1" and "I'm Getting Sentimental Over You"), Al Cohn ("Cotton Tail" and "Prelude to a Kiss"), Manny Albam ("Moten Swing" and "Jumpin' at the Woodside"), Bob Brookmeyer ("Let's Dance" and "Don't Be That Way"), and Med Flory ("Midnight Sun" and "Flying Home").[17] While the recording was well received by fans and critics, it was not a complete representation of the excitement that the band produced during their live performances.[18]

The packed crowds followed the Terry Gibbs Big Band for a total of nine weeks at the Seville and three weeks after that at the Cloister Club. The band then found a steady home at the Sundown Club on Sunset Boulevard. The band performed every Sunday, Monday, and Tuesday there for eighteen months. During that time the venue was sold to a new owner and renamed the Summit. The band's incredible live run from 1959 through 1961 was one of the most successful and longest-running steady gigs of any big band after the swing era.[19] More importantly, the gigs allowed Mel to play continually in a contemporary big band setting. When many other jazz drummers no longer played regularly with a big band, or performed the same material night after night, Mel had the opportunity to learn and perform new arrangements on a weekly basis, rapidly developing his concept of drumming within a big band.

It was the live performances of Terry Gibbs's Band in 1959, 1960, and 1961 that resulted in many of Mel's most well-known recordings. Gibbs knew that the band was at its peak during their live performances and that only a live recording would do his band justice. As a result, weeks after their debut at the Seville, Gibbs contacted Wally Heider about recording the band live.[20]

In 1959, Heider was a mildly successful lawyer in Eugene, Oregon, who was more interested in his hobby of recording music than his law profession.[21] (You may recall that Heider also recorded Mel with Kenton's Orchestra in November of 1956.) After speaking with Gibbs, Heider drove his customized U-Haul trailer of recording equipment to Los Angeles and began recording the band at the Seville for much of 1959. In 1960, the excitement of recording led Heider to quit his job as a lawyer and move to Los Angeles to pursue a career as a fulltime recording engineer.[22]

Heider became one of the most famous recording engineers of all time. In addition to his long career recording jazz music, he eventually relocated to San Francisco and recorded legendary pop and rock musicians such as Jimi Hendrix, The Grateful Dead, Jefferson Airplane, and Santana. He is responsible for what was known as the "San Francisco Sound."[23]

Throughout 1959, 1960 and 1961, Heider continued to record the Gibbs Big Band during their weekly gigs. At the Sundown/Summit Club, he improvised a control booth in a small backroom where he operated all of the recording equipment without being able to see the band.[24] His two-track, direct-to-tape masters had no EQ or post editing, but sounded absolutely incredible. *The Exciting Terry Gibbs Big Band* (Verve) and *Explosion: Terry Gibbs and His Exciting Big Band* (Mercury) were released in 1961 and evidence of Heider's ability to record the band hitting on all cylinders. Most importantly, the albums finally gave listeners throughout the country a chance to hear the band in a live setting.

In addition to the material on those albums, hours upon hours of Heider's recordings were not commercially released. Through the years these unreleased recordings became something of a legend in the jazz community. For twenty-six years, only the truly lucky heard them as they stayed in Gibbs's personal possession. It wasn't until 1986 that Gibbs finally began releasing the recordings on the Contemporary label.[25] Contemporary released all six volumes on digital compact disc under the name "Terry Gibbs Dream Band." This was the first time that Gibbs's band was called anything except the "Terry Gibbs Big Band" or "Terry Gibbs and His Orchestra."[26] *Terry Gibbs Dream Band: Volume 1*, *Terry Gibbs Dream Band: Volume 2—The Sundown Sessions*, *Terry Gibbs Dream Band: Volume 3—Flying Home*, and *Terry Gibbs Dream Band: Volume 6—One More Time* featured previously unreleased Heider recordings, many from the band's 1959 run at the Seville. By 1986 the LP versions of *The Exciting Terry Gibbs Big Band* and *Explosion: Terry Gibbs and His Exciting Big Band* had been out of print for nearly a quarter century and were reissued as *Terry Gibbs Dream Band: Volume 4—Main Stem* and *Terry Gibbs Dream Band: Volume 5—The Big Cat*.

The "Dream Band" recordings are a testament to the greatness of that band and feature some of Mel's finest drumming. In 1986, when asked about the release of *Terry Gibbs Dream Band: Volume 1* Mel responded,

> This recording brings back a memory of probably the best big band of its time. I was so proud to be a part of it. Everybody was a real jazz professional, and Terry evoked so much spirit. I think it was some of my best playing in my entire career also. I don't think there was ever a better band than this one, including my own. Different, but not better.[27]

Similar to Mel's recordings with Kenton, the "Dream Band" recordings display his ability to subtly take control of a band and make it his own. In a completely unselfish manner he was the greatest musical influence on Gibbs's band. Mel realized his influence:

> "I am a unique drummer. I have a style that nobody else has. I make music happen. I make bands do things that no other band can do. Any time I've played, any band I've played in, that band has become mine. Now, I didn't do it on purpose ... it just happened."[28] ‖

See Appendix Transcription and Listening Guide for this chapter: "Nose Cone"

Chapter 8
Webster and Mulligan

Mel's suddenly high profile work with Terry Gibbs introduced his playing to an increasing number of network contractors in Los Angeles. As a result, he joined the staff of ABC Studios Hollywood.[1] His 1959 studio work included playing on the *Eddie Fischer Show*, performing live dates with Frank Sinatra (subbing for Irv Cottler), and performing on numerous radio and television commercials.[2]

Mel was also involved with the motion picture *The Gene Krupa Story*. The movie was loosely based on the story of Gene Krupa's life, but while the movie was entertaining to audiences, it didn't succeed in portraying much reality. Krupa himself recorded most, but not all, of the drumming sequences for the movie. Mel was brought in to record the drumming audio for several scenes, including a montage from low periods in Krupa's career. The scenes depicted Krupa playing with bad groups, awkwardly forcing Mel to try and sound like Krupa on his bad nights. In the end, the opportunity for Mel to be a part of a movie about his lifelong drumming idol and friend was a nerve-racking, but enjoyable, experience.

While Mel spent much of 1959 trying to get accepted into the higher paying commercial studio scene, his jazz career continued to expand at a rapid pace. He began working with former Kenton members Art Pepper and Gerry Mulligan and also had the opportunity to work with jazz legends such as Ben Webster, Johnny Hodges, and Sonny Stitt. The year 1959 was one of Mel's most prosperous small group periods. As his career developed throughout the 1960s and 1970s, much of his recorded output was done in the big band setting; however, many of his most highly regarded small group recordings took place in Los Angeles during 1959.[3]

Over a three-month period (on March 14, 28, and May 12), he recorded Art Pepper's album *Art Pepper Plus Eleven: Modern Jazz Classics* (Contemporary).[4] Marty Paich's arrangements created the perfect backdrop for Mel to kick the "little" big band and at the same time show that he had the bebop fire to back a soloist the caliber of Pepper. The album represents one of the 1950s West Coast recordings that had the drive and intensity of its East Coast counterparts. Dizzy Gillespie and Charlie Parker's composition

"Shaw 'Nuff" and Bernie Miller's "Bernie's Tune" are fine examples of Mel's playing on *Modern Jazz Classics*, as his drumming propelled the soloists and also beautifully navigated the written arrangements.

It is worth noting that the sound of Mel's drums and cymbals on *Modern Jazz Classics* is an excellent representation of his "typical sound" at the time. Mel's "sound" was a combination of many aspects, two of which were his use of calfskin drumheads and tuning his drums medium-low in pitch, even when playing in a small group. His drum sound on *Modern Jazz Classics* is a prime example of the warm tone he pulled out of the calfskin heads and how the sound of his drums blended into the ensemble, yet were tuned high enough to cut through when needed. Another important aspect of Mel's "sound" heard on the album is his use of low-pitched cymbals and the master touch in which he played them. Fine audio quality, easy accessibility, and of course Mel's playing, make *Modern Jazz Classics* a great snapshot of his "sound" and a perfect starting point for the novice Mel Lewis listener. For others, a detailed examination of Mel's "sound," playing, and drum equipment are found in the transcription portion of this book.

In October of 1959, Mel once again performed at the Monterey Jazz Festival, this time as a member of the Monterey Festival Orchestra. The orchestra was assembled to perform with various artists during the three-day festival. Most importantly, it functioned as the "New Herd" for Woody Herman on Saturday, October 3. Many of its members, such as Zoot Sims and Al Porcino, had been members of previous Herman bands, but this was the first time Mel performed with Herman's famous band. After a brief rehearsal on Friday night, the "New Herd" took to the stage on Saturday afternoon and again that evening as the headlining act.[5] Mel's drumming during both sets proved why he was being considered one of the best big band drummers in the world. Leading the orchestra through compositions such as "Four Brothers," "Monterey Apple Tree," and "Skoobeedoobee," his control and support of the orchestra sounded as if he had been playing the music for years, not days. The orchestra's afternoon and evening performances were recorded, released as *Woody Herman's Big New Herd at the Monterey Jazz Festival* (Atlantic), and became one of Herman's most-loved recordings. Herman considered the briefly organized "New Herd" for the Monterey Jazz Festival one of the greatest bands that he ever stood in front of, yet he later commented that he did not prefer Mel's time feel and the two men never worked together again.[6]

On Friday, October 2, the evening prior to the Herman concert, Mel performed at the festival with legendary pianist Earl "Fatha" Hines. The Earl Hines Trio was joined by jazz legends Roy Eldridge on trumpet, Ben Webster on tenor saxophone, Coleman Hawkins on tenor saxophone, Woody Herman on clarinet, and Vernon Alley on bass. Finally, blues singer Jimmy Witherspoon took to the stage and performed an unrehearsed set with the all-star group. In the presence of some of the greatest blues improvisers in jazz, Mel provided the swinging beat for Witherspoon's singing, and masterful solos by Hawkins, Webster, Eldridge, and Hines. The emotion of the musicians swept through the audience, and the performance stands as the beginning of Witherspoon's most commercially successful period after spending years in obscurity working smaller clubs in the South.[7]

Witherspoon's initial performance at Monterey also helped promote the arrival of Ben Webster in Los Angeles. Webster had relocated to the area earlier that summer, but sadly was not getting called for much work yet. His performances that fall at Monterey and at the Los Angeles Jazz Festival helped West Coast jazz fans and critics rediscover his masterful tenor playing.[8]

Mel's drumming had caught the ear of Webster, and the two men began performing music together on a regular basis. On November 3, 1959, they began recording their first studio recording together with Gerry Mulligan titled *Gerry Mulligan Meets Ben Webster* (Verve). Webster and Mulligan had only been playing together for a short time, but their melodicism, tone, and impeccable time feel, greatly complimented each other. The rhythm section of Leroy Vinegar on bass, Jimmy Rowles on piano, and Mel provided an incredibly solid and swinging foundation. When the group went back into the studio on December 2, they recorded "Fajista," "Tell Me When," "Blues in B Flat," "Sunday," and "The Cat Walk" to finish the album. Mulligan regarded *Gerry Mulligan Meets Ben Webster* as his favorite in his "Mulligan Meets…" series.[9]

After their recording session on the afternoon of December 2, Webster, Mulligan, Vinegar, Rowles, and Lewis met at Ben Shapiro's Renaissance Club on the Sunset Strip. At 9:30 p.m., the Mulligan/Webster Quintet hit the stage backing none other than the star of the Monterey Jazz Festival, singer Jimmy Witherspoon. The performance was recorded and titled *Witherspoon, Mulligan, Webster at the Renaissance* (Hi-Fi).[10] In less than a twenty-four-hour period, Mel had recorded two classic albums with Webster and Mulligan. Little did he know at the time how important both men would be to his musical future and his eventual relocation back to New York City.

In the spring of 1960, Mel recorded small group albums with two jazz legends: Sonny Stitt and Benny Carter. *Sonny Stitt: Blows the Blues* (Verve) and *Benny Carter: Sax a la Carter* (United Artists) are further proof of Mel's expanding jazz career. All the while, he continued to play a variety of commercial studio work. It was during a commercial date that spring that Mel played drums on a song that became the number one pop song in the country. "I got called to do a date, I got there and found these pimple faced kids, and I found out their name was the Hollywood Argyles and I was the drummer on the famous 'Alley Oop,'" recalled Mel.[11] The Hollywood Argyles at the time was not a group at all; actually, it was just one college student named Gary Paxton who came up with a group name to avoid any legal hassles by using his own. Paxton was the singer on the hit song and hired the studio musicians on a very limited budget.[12] As Mel often told the story, he almost walked out of the session but ended up staying, teaching the "kids" a thing or two, and completed the track:

> I said to them, "Listen kids, you want a hit record? Did you ever hear of doing anything original?" I said, "I'll fill in those little holes with my bass drum. What you want is something that doesn't make any sense at all. All you're trying to do is copy somebody else's hit. That was a hit, that doesn't mean you're going to have a hit." I said, "Just let me do what I'm gonna do. If you don't like it, so you won't like it." I did the record, that son-of-a-bitch sold over 4 million records and they sent me a little note thanking me very much. I made $34 ... To me that was about the only compromise I ever made and from then on you couldn't get me on a rock and roll record date.[13]

On July 11, 1960, "Alley Oop" became the number one song in the country. It only stayed there for a week, and the "Hollywood Argyles" never had another hit.[14] For Mel, the whole experience left him with an amusing story to tell and a new level of dislike for the Los Angeles commercial music scene. Like so many other studio musicians through the years, Mel provided the musical expertise to make someone else a whole lot of money.

Throughout the spring of 1960, Mel continued playing his weekly big band gigs with Terry Gibbs. The band had been playing together for over a year at that point and headed into the studio on February 23 to record their second studio album. *Terry Gibbs and His Big Band: Swing Is Here!* (Verve) is a classic Gibbs recording and a better representation of the band's sound and energy than their first release, *Launching a New Band*. However successful the Terry Gibbs Big Band studio albums became, it was still their live performances that had jazz fans, journalists, and fellow musicians excited.

While the Terry Gibbs Big Band continued to gain attention on the West Coast, Gerry Mulligan had relocated to the East Coast and started his own thirteen-piece big band in New York City. In January of 1960, Mulligan and Bob Brookmeyer formed the Mulligan Concert Jazz Band.[15] While Mulligan was always the official leader of the band, Brookmeyer functioned as an unofficial co-leader and often helped by hiring, and sometimes firing, band personnel and writing arrangements for the group.[16] Verve founder Norman Granz was also an important figure in the band's formation because he financially backed the project and was involved in getting the band recorded and taking them on tour. "When I formed the Concert Jazz Band in 1960, Norman Granz's financial input was pretty extensive. He paid for a tour of the United States to prepare us for a European trip, but I paid for everything else," recalled Mulligan.[17] Drummer Dave Bailey had worked with Mulligan in the past several years and was the original drummer in the band.[18] Unfortunately for Bailey, the Concert Jazz Band's first tour to the West Coast in the spring of 1960 would also be one of his last with the band.

During the band's time in Los Angeles, Brookmeyer stayed with Mel and his family. The trip provided Mel and Brookmeyer the opportunity to record another small group album together. *Bob Brookmeyer Quartet: Blues, Hot and Cold* (Verve) was recorded on June 16 and included Jimmy Rowles on piano and Buddy Clark on bass.[19] While in Los Angeles, Brookmeyer also went with Mel to a Terry Gibbs rehearsal.[20] In an interview with Burt Korall, Brookmeyer recalled hearing the Terry Gibbs Big Band live for the first time, and immediately asking Mel to join Mulligan's Concert Jazz Band:

> I'd been writing some things for Terry and hadn't heard them performed. The band was just outrageous! Mel was fantastic, and all those guys were so strong. In comparison, Mulligan's band sounded

like a bunch of amateurs. So I said: "We've got to get this feeling!" I was staying with Mel and asked him to join the band. And he said yes. I hired Buddy Clark and Conte Candoli as well. They all came back east.[21]

There were two important decisions that Mel had to consider before officially accepting Brookmeyer's offer to join the Concert Jazz Band. First, his involvement with Mulligan's band would result in him splitting time between New York and Los Angeles. While it would be great for his career, it would also mean that he would be away from his family, who would still be living in Los Angeles. Second, in order to go with Mulligan, he would have to quit his staff job at ABC and give up what steady income that provided.[22] In the end, the choice was actually pretty simple for Mel; he quit his staff studio position and joined Mulligan. In a 1962 *DownBeat* article, he recalled his decision:

> The security of it (ABC staff position) didn't mean much on the job if I couldn't get to play. Then along came Brookmeyer who got me to come along with Gerry's band. The decision wasn't as difficult as you may think. I'd been working semi-regularly with Terry Gibb's big band, but that was only maybe one night a week.[23]

In a strange twist of events, just days after accepting the position with Mulligan, Mel received yet another offer, this one from legendary composer and bandleader Duke Ellington:

> Duke Ellington offered to hire me in 1960 to replace Sam Woodyard, when Woodyard was sick. It was on the behest of Johnny Hodges, and Juan Tizol recommended me. Ben Webster backed them on it, but it was only for two months. They wanted me to come out for two months while they put Woodyard in a hospital for rehabilitation; he was so screwed up. And I had just accepted the gig with Gerry Mulligan to join the Concert Jazz Orchestra to go on tour for a permanent situation, for much more money too.[24]

What notoriety and fame might have come from a limited two-month employment with Ellington were forgotten with the promise of steady work and higher pay with Mulligan. Mel thanked Ellington, but declined the offer, and prepared for his first gig with Mulligan on the East Coast.

In July of 1960, trumpeter Conte Candoli and bassist Buddy Clark joined Mel on a flight from Los Angeles to New York City to join the Gerry Mulligan Concert Jazz Band. On July 25 and 27, the band recorded their debut album *Gerry Mulligan and the Concert Jazz Band* (Verve).[25] Other members of the Concert Jazz Band included trumpet players Don Ferrara and Nick Travis, trombonists Bob Brookmeyer, Wayne Andre, and Alan Raph, and saxophonists Gene Quill, Dick Meldonian, Zoot Sims, Gene Allen, and Mulligan.[26] The piano-less rhythm section of Mel and Buddy Clark provided a nimble and interactive feel to the large ensemble while the solos of Brookmeyer, Candoli, Sims, and Mulligan beautifully combined contemporary ideas with time-honored lyrical playing.[27]

Mel's new association with Mulligan changed the entire course of his career. Though very successful in his four years in Los Angeles, Mel was quickly growing frustrated with the West Coast scene. Mulligan's band afforded him the opportunity to tour Europe and, most importantly, brought him to New York City on a frequent basis. It was through these trips to New York that he eventually realized that his playing and personality would be better suited to the East Coast.

After spending the first part of August in Los Angeles, Mel returned to New York City on August 24 to play with the Concert Jazz Band at the famous Village Vanguard jazz club. This was Mel's first performance at the club that became so closely associated with his career. Brookmeyer recalled Mel's Village Vanguard debut:

> Mel did just what I expected. I remember the first night at the Vanguard. We were playing Gerry's "Bweebida Bobbida," I looked over at him the first chance I had—and just grinned because it felt so good.[28]

In addition to his performances with Mulligan at the Vanguard that week, Mel recorded Al Cohn's *Son of Drum Suite* (RCA Victor) at New York City's Webster Hall. The recording featured a six-movement suite written and arranged by Cohn and showcased an orchestra that included Clark Terry on trumpet, Zoot Sims on tenor saxophone, Bob Brookmeyer on valve trombone, and Hank Jones on piano. The orchestra was then augmented with six jazz drummers who often played as a section, and traded solos during musical interludes. In addition to Mel, jazz drumming legends Don Lamond, Jimmy Cobb, Charli Persip, Louis Hayes, and Gus Johnson were featured.[29]

After his busy week in the city, Mel hit the road with the Mulligan Concert Jazz Band on an extensive tour of the United States and Europe. For much of September and October, the band traveled throughout the United States, performing at jazz festivals and clubs. In November, the band traveled to Europe for the first time. During a hectic three-week span, they performed all over the continent, including extended stops in Amsterdam, Berlin, Copenhagen, Milan, Paris, Stockholm, and Zurich.[30] The Concert Jazz Band was extremely popular with the European audiences and the tour ended as a huge success. The Paris and Zurich performances were recorded by national radio affiliates and later made into commercial albums: *Swiss Radio Days Jazz Series 12* (TCB) and *Live at the Olympia 1960* (Europe1).[31]After playing together nonstop for several months, the band was cohesive, musical, and swinging. However, when they arrived back in New York City during the last week of November, several personnel changes were made when Buddy Clark and Conte Candoli decided to leave the band and return to Los Angeles. Mel, not being as invested in the Los Angeles commercial studio scene, decided to stay on with Mulligan. Trumpet legend Clark Terry took the place of Conte Candoli and bassist Bill Crow replaced Buddy Clark.[32]

The Mulligan Concert Jazz Band was the first opportunity for Mel to perform with Bill Crow on a steady basis; however it was not their first experience playing together. Mel had briefly played with Crow back in the summer of 1954 when sitting in with the Marian McPartland Trio at the Hickory House. Mel and Crow went on to play together in several other groups between 1960 and 1966, but none were more important than the Concert Jazz Band. The men had a great musical connection, and the time feel they created was an important part of the band's sound. Each knew to mold his idea of time feel around the other's conception to create a pulse that simultaneously felt driven and relaxed.[33] Crow remembered his first experiences playing with Mel:

> The Concert Jazz Band was my first chance to really get to know Mel and get to play music with him on a steady basis. I thought

it was a hot rhythm section! I liked the sounds that he got out of his cymbals and I liked the general steam that he was able to turn on. You know it's funny, one time he told me, "I don't like to play what the brass section is playing, they got enough accent in their playing and they can do that on their own. If I play everything that they play, they get lazy. We need to get them more up on the time. I like to play what the saxophone players are playing." And I thought that was a very interesting insight into his conception of playing.[34]

Norman Granz's business plan for the Concert Jazz Band included a live recording at the Village Vanguard directly after the group returned from their European tour. On November 29, 1960, the new Mulligan lineup began its two-week engagement at the Village Vanguard. Several nights were recorded, but Mulligan selected only the takes from the band's final performance on Sunday, December 11, to be included on *Gerry Mulligan and the Concert Jazz Band at the Village Vanguard* (Verve).[35] In the album's liner notes, Mulligan said, "My conception of a band is that of a group which can communicate an emotion that comes from the interaction between its members as a unit."[36] An example of this interaction can be heard on Art Farmer's composition "Blueport." If the author could describe an emotion that was communicated by the band during this song, it would be sheer joy! Crow's bass lines settled perfectly with Mel's ride cymbal beat, creating a cushion for soloists Willie Dennis, Jim Reider, Clark Terry, and Mulligan. Crow described exactly how he and Mel created that swinging time feel:

> There's that long cut of "Blueport" where Gerry and Clark go on forever playing fours and eights. If you just listen to what Mel's doing in the back, it is really interesting the way he controlled the emotional quality.
>
> A lot of drummers will press the time a little bit when they want to get exciting, but Mel had a way of getting more exciting without ever pressing forward on the tempo. I found out that if I put my bass note on the front end of his cymbal beat that we really matched perfectly right down the line … with Mel it always felt like we had a good center together.[37]

In addition to the persistently swinging feel of the bass and drums, the solo trading between Mulligan and Terry made "Blueport" the prime example of the artistry of the band. Crow explained that the full live version of the song has unfortunately been lost forever:

> When they were preparing the LP Gerry said, "Geez I can't put a track on here that is this long." So they found a way to cut about three and a half minutes out of some of those exchanges. He found a couple of blank spaces where he could cut from. And unfortunately, Verve was not very aware of historical importance in those days, and if they cut a piece of tape out of the master they just threw it away. So that music is lost. But it's a hell of a take anyway![38]

The entire album featured great playing by the band, and especially Mel. If the jazz critics considered Mel having officially arrived on the jazz scene during his 1955 Birdland performance with Kenton, then his 1960 performance with Mulligan at the Village Vanguard gave them reason to proclaim him as one of the greatest drummers in jazz. ‖

See Appendix Transcriptions and Listening Guides for this chapter: "Bernie's Tune"

Chapter 9
Mel's New Cymbal
and Europe with Dizzy

Just as the Concert Jazz Band began to gain popularity, it received two major setbacks.[1] By the end of 1960, Mulligan began to devote more time to take care of his girlfriend Judy Holliday who had recently been diagnosed with cancer. Also in January of 1961, only a month after their successful second run at the Village Vanguard, Granz sold Verve Records to MGM for two and a half million dollars.[2] The move meant that Granz would no longer help promote, record, or financially back the band. While Mulligan financially kept the band performing and recording until 1964, the band was never able to take another European tour or record as often as Mulligan would have liked.[3] These two events destroyed the momentum that the band had built during their first year. The Concert Jazz Band performed sporadically throughout 1961, with most of their work consisted of jazz club dates in New York City.[4] For Mel, what had seemed like an opportunity for a busy steady job with Mulligan, turned out to be musically rewarding, but not nearly as steady as he had hoped.

In January of 1961, with the Concert Jazz Band on an extended break, Lewis returned to Los Angeles and picked up where he had left off with Terry Gibbs. The album *Terry Gibbs Dream Band Volume 4: Main Stem* was recorded during the band's performances at the Summit Club on January 20, 21, and 22.[5] Mel found himself back in Los Angeles while still keeping one foot in the New York City jazz scene. In an interview with John Tynan, he described the unique opportunity to perform with both the Gerry Mulligan Concert Jazz Band and Terry Gibbs's Big Band during 1961:

> This is a very good experience for me. The variety of music in both bands necessitated that I take a different approach with each one. And this has made me a better drummer. Actually, the past year has been one of the most rewarding I've ever spent.[6]

In addition to his recordings with Gibbs, Mel recorded several albums on the West Coast during the spring of 1961, including *Anita O'Day: Travelin'*

Light (Verve), *Shorty Rogers and His Orchestra: The Invisible Orchard* (RCA), *Johnny Hodges: The Complete 1960 Jazz Cellar Sessions* (Verve), *Bud Shank Quintet: New Groove* (Pacific Jazz), *Mavis Rivers: Mavis* (Reprise), and *Sammy Davis Jr. Accompanied by the Marty Paich Orchestra* (Reprise) to name a few. Thanks to the occasional work with Mulligan, he also traveled to New York City that spring to record *Judy Holliday: Holliday with Mulligan* (DRG), *Jimmy Hamilton: It's About Time* (Swingville), and *Gerry Mulligan's Concert Jazz Band: Gerry Mulligan Presents a Concert in Jazz* (Verve).[7]

On June 13 and 14, 1961, Mel was back in Los Angeles to record the album *Ray Charles and Betty Carter* (ABC Paramount).[8] Marty Paich was the arranger and conductor of the session and responsible for Mel's inclusion on the date. The recording featured Charles's regular rhythm section of Edgar Willis on bass and Bill Pittman on guitar, with the addition of Mel, who replaced Charles's usual drummer Bruno Carr.[9] Mel loved to tell the story of how he learned of Ray Charles's approval of his drumming during the session:

> Charles likes the drummer, he told Edgar, he says, "Boy, that cat can play good drums, I like that drummer, and all that." And Edgar says, "Ya, not bad for a White boy was he." "White, I didn't know. Was he White?" He (Ray Charles) says, "That's Mel Lewis." He said, "I didn't know Mel..." Then years later at the Vanguard Charles said, "I knew who you were, but I always thought you were Black." He says, "I didn't know you were White."[10]

Regardless of race, Mel's drumming was accepted by Charles and greatly contributed to the soulful music. The album is an important marker in Mel's career since it was the first recording in which he performed with the distinctive sound of a riveted Chinese cymbal, as heard on "You and I," "People Will Say We're in Love," "Side By Side," "Together," and "Just You, Just Me." He frequently played the cymbal during ensemble passages and behind the tenor saxophone solos by David "Fathead" Newman. Several months after the recording, in an interview for *Melody Maker*, Mel was asked if he owned a Chinese cymbal:

> Yes, in the past year I've started using one myself. I've used it on lots of vocal dates—with Ray Charles, Betty Carter and

some more—and on the Gerry Mulligan Concert in Jazz LP, the Brookmeyer big-band Verve album, and all my own dates. You can use it with any size group, but it's greatest for big-band work. Today it's a rare sight, but back in the old days, Sid Catlett and Cozy Cole and those guys, they used that kind of cymbal. When you shift gears, and get into high intensity with a big band, it's good then. My own cymbal is an A Zildjian, the only one I got. Normally I use K. Zildjian. But this one of mine has too many rivets in it. I must take some out.[11]

As fewer jazz drummers used Chinese cymbals, Mel's use of one became somewhat unique. The roaring low pitch and distinctive crash of the cymbal became a trademark of his sound for the remainder of his career.

In the fall of 1961, Mel continued splitting his time between Los Angeles and New York City. In Los Angeles, he played in a new big band led by trumpeter Gerald Wilson. The Gerald Wilson Orchestra was a hard swinging group that featured the arranging of Wilson, and superb solos by members such as Teddy Edwards, Harold Land, Richard "Groove" Holmes, and Wilson. On September 9, the band began recording their debut album titled *Gerald Wilson Orchestra: You Better Believe It* (Pacific Jazz). Only weeks after the Wilson recording, Mel was back in New York City recording the albums: *Bob Brookmeyer: Gloomy Sunday and Other Bright Moments* (Verve), *Anita O'Day: All the Sad Young Men* (Verve), and *Gary McFarland: How to Succeed in Business Without Really Trying* (Verve). It was during his time spent in New York City that fall that he landed one of the most important tours of his career.

In November Dizzy Gillespie asked Mel to join his group on a four-week tour of Europe. Dizzy's usual drummer Chuck Lampkin was suddenly recalled into the Army and not available. With the tour scheduled to begin in a matter of days, Dizzy was in a crunch to find a suitable replacement; thankfully for Mel, he received the call and accepted the offer.[12] Mel had never played a full gig with Dizzy Gillespie's small group, and only had the opportunity to briefly play two songs with them before the start of the tour:

> Dizzy and I were both working in New York, and on the closing night of Diz's quintet at Birdland, I went down to see what they were doing. Finally, I sat in and played two numbers, "Manteca,"

and "The Mooche." The final set was a jam session; everybody began to sit-in, so I climbed down. And that was my only rehearsal with Diz. Afterwards he said: "I got a feeling everything's going to be all right." He was pretty relaxed about it. So my first night with the group was quite an experience. Most of the music was new to me and I had to listen hard. Drummers should.[13]

The tour was part of Norman Granz's Jazz at the Philharmonic series and featured the John Coltrane Quintet along with Dizzy Gillespie's Quintet. It marked the first time that Coltrane led his own group on a European tour. Coltrane's group included Reggie Workman on bass, McCoy Tyner on piano, Elvin Jones on drums, and Eric Dolphy on flute and alto saxophone. Dizzy Gillespie's group consisted of Leo Wright on alto saxophone and flute, Lalo Schifrin on piano, Bob Cunningham on bass, and Mel on drums.[14]

For Mel, the tour was an eye-opening opportunity to observe Dizzy as a musician and bandleader. He later stated, "Those four weeks were worth a year in training. I learned so much from Diz."[15] Dizzy's kindness and encouragement towards Mel reinforced his belief that no matter how big the musical star, nurturing younger musicians was an important responsibility of jazz's elder statesman. In addition to observing Dizzy manage the group, the experience of playing with Dizzy was a highlight of Mel's career. An added perk of the tour was the opportunity to spend time with members of Coltrane's group and, in particular, drummer Elvin Jones. Mel and Elvin first met on that July evening in Detroit in 1955 when Thad Jones introduced his younger brother to Mel at the late-night jam session. During the tour, Mel and Elvin had the chance to hear each other play every night, were roommates, and quickly became close friends. Later in their careers, both drummers mentioned how much the other had influenced his playing. In his WKCR interviews with Loren Schoenberg, Mel talked about his experiences with Elvin Jones during the 1961 tour:

He gets his intensity from another way, you know. He is not loud; he is a dynamic drummer. It looks like he is playing loud, he is all sweaty you know, and he's making all that noise and all that, but he is not loud! Listen, I was on tour with him when I was with Dizzy and he was with 'Trane. And I would listen to him every night, and he and I played on the same set of drums, and you know

I don't play loud and he didn't play loud. And we talked about it all the time, about intensity, about getting it from not playing loud. But, you can get a strong feeling, and that is what he has. A very strong feeling.[16]

Prior to the tour, Coltrane's group had finished recording a live album at the Village Vanguard, and their music had received some very harsh criticism from jazz journalists and critics. Much of the criticism of the group revolved around the inclusion of alto saxophonist Eric Dolphy.[17] He was a talented improviser who came up through the bands of Gerald Wilson and Chico Hamilton, yet his sound, time feel, and intonation pushed the comfort boundary of many traditional jazz listeners.[18] Dolphy's extended solos were another source of frustration for Coltrane's fans, band members, and Norm Granz himself. Coltrane was the leader and the artist whom people were paying to hear, yet often Dolphy's solos lasted longer than Coltrane's.[19] Skepticism of Coltrane's new music and Dolphy continued throughout the European tour.

On the other hand, Dizzy's group performed straight-ahead jazz and was popular with the critics and fans alike. The group played several jazz standards that were easily recognized by the audience, and the duo of Bob Cunningham on bass and Mel on drums provided a joyous beat for Dizzy to play over. It is also important to note that many of the arrangements the group performed included Afro-Cuban influenced rhythms that had not been heard a great deal in Europe at the time and were enthusiastically received by audiences.

During the tour, Mel learned that Gillespie was as particular about the use of a Chinese cymbal as he was. Gillespie was famous for often requiring the drummer of his group to play a certain cymbal during his solos. Mel later recalled using Gillespie's personal Chinese cymbal during the tour:

And this guy knows his drums, believe me. He knows just what he wants from them. So I'm learning things from Dizzy; it's another lesson for me. In fact, it's unusual to work for a man who knows so much about what's coming out of the different instruments. Take this Chinese cymbal now. Dizzy's drummers always use this one; in fact they use the same one. This is Dizzy's cymbal; this is the sound he likes behind him. That low-pitched tone makes a nice frame around the trumpet. So he carries this cymbal with him. This is his, and when the drummer leaves, it stays with Diz.[20]

The tour produced two recordings: *Dizzy Gillespie Quintet: Live in Europe* (Unique Jazz) and *Eric Dolphy Quartet: Softly as in a Morning Sunrise* (Jazz Connoisseur). The Eric Dolphy album was the result of a bootleg recording of a jam session in Germany that included Mel with Eric Dolphy, McCoy Tyner, and Bob Cunningham.[21] Despite the poor audio quality it is fascinating to hear Mel's bebop drumming behind Dolphy's avant-garde approach to improvisation. *Dizzy Gillespie Quintet: Live in Europe* was recently remastered and released as *Legends Live: Dizzy Gillespie Quintet* on the Jazzhaus Musik label. This once hard-to-find recording of Mel and Dizzy, is now easily available and an important addition to any Mel Lewis collection.

After his December tour of Europe, Mel began 1962 with a new network staff position in Los Angeles, this time working for NBC Television Studios in Hollywood. "This gives me more time to put to good use all I've learned during the past few months," said Mel.[22] He spent much of the spring working in Los Angeles, playing drums on the *Bob Newhart Show* at NBC and recording albums with singer Peggy Lee and alto saxophonist Benny Carter.[23] ‖

alo Schifrin, Leo Wright, Mel Lewis and Dizzy Gillespie in 1961.
by Bill Wagg. Photo courtesy of Mitsuo Johfu.

Chapter 10
The Soviet Union
and a Move East

In April of 1962, Mel accepted an exciting offer from Benny Goodman's management to join an extensive tour of the Soviet Union for the U.S. State Department. At that time, the Cold War was growing increasingly tense; the previous ten months had seen both the construction of the Berlin Wall by the East German regime and the failed invasion of the Bay of Pigs. It would be only weeks after the conclusion of the tour that the two countries faced off in the Cuban Missile Crisis.[1] The State Department picked Goodman for the tour because he was quite possibly the best-known jazz musician in the world.[2] The goal of the tour was for Goodman and his musicians to present "an anthology of American jazz" to the Russian people.[3]

It took the first several weeks in April for the personnel of the group to be finalized, but when it was, the band was a dynamite cast of musicians. Joya Sherrill was the featured vocalist. Zoot Sims, Jerry Dodgion, and Phil Woods were part of the saxophone section. Joe Newman and Jimmy Maxwell were in the trumpet section. The rhythm section consisted of Bill Crow on bass and Turk Van Lake on guitar, and featured Victor Feldman on vibes and Teddy Wilson on piano.[4]

The band's first rehearsal took place in New York City on April 14. The musicians felt honored to be involved with the tour and were excited about how good the band sounded after only a short amount of rehearsal. On April 25 the band made its first national appearance on *The Bell Telephone Hour* television show. After completing tour preparations in New York City, the band hit the road for a short tour of the United States before heading to the Soviet Union. The band's first performance was a college dance in Chicago. They then played shows in St. Louis and San Francisco while making their way to Seattle to perform at the 1962 World's Fair. The Goodman Band performed several days as a featured act at the World's Fair before flying to the Soviet Union.[5]

The trip from Seattle to the Soviet Union took twenty-four exhausting hours; the party consisted of Goodman, his family, management, eighteen musicians, a television crew from NBC, reporters, photographers, and the State Department staff. After flying from Seattle to New York, New York to Copenhagen, and then from Copenhagen to Moscow, the entourage arrived safely on Russian soil on Monday, May 28.[6] On Wednesday, May 30, the Goodman Band performed their first concert in Moscow to a sold-out crowd of 5,000. The audience included Premier Nikita Kruschev and his family, who seemed to enjoy the show.[7] It was only the first of thirty concerts during the six-week tour. After five days and three concerts in Moscow, the band performed in Sochi from June 3 to 7, Tbilisi from June 9 to 14, Tashkent from June 15 to 17, Leningrad from June 18 to 24, Kiev from June 27 to 30, and then returned to Moscow on Monday July 2 for their final week of the tour.[8]

This was the first time that Mel had worked for Benny Goodman, and the tour provided him an introduction to Goodman's famously quirky personality. "All I know is that Benny ended up being one of the worst guys I was ever proud to work for," recalled Mel.[9] Goodman was notorious for being nervous, socially awkward, and hard to work with. This tour was no exception. Bill Crow explained the somewhat bizarre actions of Goodman during the trip:

> The whole tour was a strain because we never felt like we had Benny's approval as a band. We were proud of that band and we knew that we were good. But for some reason, Benny got competitive with everybody. For example, he would do underhanded things like if he thought you were a good soloist he'd take your solo away from you. If you were a good lead player, he would have somebody else take the lead spot. We kept saying to each other, "Look this is a good band and Benny is playing well, all he has to do is turn the band loose and go out there and take his bows and it'll be a piece of cake." But throughout the tour he seemed to want to make everyone as uncomfortable as possible.[10]

By all accounts, Mel never lost his cool when dealing with Goodman, even when the two didn't see eye to eye. "I wasn't afraid of him, I just did what I wanted ... I said, 'Screw you, I'm going to be me and do what I want. I'll play my best for you, you know, for what suits you. I'm going to play the best damn Benny Goodman drums I can play,'" remembered Mel.[11] That being said, one of the notorious musical moments of the tour happened the first time the band played Goodman's classic "Sing, Sing, Sing." When it was time for the famous "Gene Krupa style" floor tom solo Mel played some very modern-sounding musical phrases instead of the classic phrases that Goodman was used to. "I got very modern on him, I went out … I figured it was my solo, I may as well have fun with it, you know," he recalled.[12] Mel did have fun with the solo and so did the entire band; the only person on the stage who was not laughing was Goodman. During the solo, Mel kept his hi-hat playing on beats two and four and played free-sounding, arrhythmic phrases with his hands. While he and the rest of the band knew where beat "one" was, Goodman was completely lost and grew more flustered by the minute. Goodman had to count the band back in at the end of the drum solo, but because he could not feel where the downbeat was, he was frozen stiff with fear. After finally finding the downbeat, with help from Zoot Sims and the saxophone section, Goodman counted the band back in and brought Mel's drum solo to a close.[13]

The very next night Goodman called "Sing, Sing, Sing" again, but this time said, "No drum solo." Of course Mel couldn't resist messing with Goodman yet again:

So I went out on his solo, and he really didn't know where he was. And I purposely did it to screw him up. And when it came time where he wanted to bring the band in, I went into half time, half note triplets. And he didn't know where the hell "one" was. Well, man, every third bar it's one … It ended perfectly together, and I knew it would. But he didn't, and he almost, he lost his glasses, they fell off his face. He almost dropped his clarinet, and we never played "Sing, Sing, Sing" again on the whole tour in Russia. He didn't say a word. He just never called it again.[14]

Many musicians who played with Mel often mention his complete dedication to making music feel good. Taking that into account, his drumming during "Sing, Sing, Sing" was most likely tasteful, but much too modern for Goodman. Mel's actions were more than likely the way that he responded to some odd statement or action that Goodman took against him or another band member. Without disserving the music, or losing his temper with Goodman, his drumming let Goodman know that he wasn't to be disrespected.

As much as the musicians enjoyed the opportunity to spread jazz music through the Soviet Union, by the end of June, everyone involved was ready to go back to their families and lives in the United States. The bland Russian food, constant military presence, and Goodman's antics had taken their toll.[15] During the more difficult days of the tour, Mel realized that he was coming to another important fork in the road of his musical journey. He had many questions to answer in regard to his career, such as: should he continue with the commercial studio work, even though he didn't enjoy much of the music that he was being paid to play? The New York City jazz scene seemed like a more lucrative environment for a drummer of his caliber; should he stay in Los Angeles or move back to the East Coast?

On Wednesday, June 20, while in Leningrad, Mel wrote to his wife Doris and proclaimed that he was going to make a change:

> I've decided not to stay with the band because he's [Goodman] trying to hang us up for the whole summer with options and I can't make it any longer like this. I'm lonesome for you and I love you. This is no life for me, or you, or the kids, and I'm going to try real hard to make it at home.[16]

Of course Mel had been "making it" by most people's standards. He was a successful musician who made his living playing music and provided for his family. However, when his commercial studio work in Los Angeles began to diminish, he realized that he could gain more jazz work if he lived on the East Coast. By the end of the Goodman tour in July of 1962, the thought of relocating to New York City was already in the forefront of Mel's mind.

After the Goodman tour, Mel returned to Los Angeles and began playing once again with the Gerald Wilson Orchestra. Unlike many other big bands of that era, Wilson's band was a mixed-race band that included an almost-even split of white and black musicians. The diversity of the group was evident in the saxophone section, which often consisted of Joe Maini, Bud Shank, Don Raffell, Harold Land, and Teddy Edwards. These men came from many different social and ethnic backgrounds, but their common ground was playing music that was deeply rooted in the blues and swing. In August and September, the band recorded *Gerald Wilson Big Band: Moment of Truth* (Pacific Jazz).[17] The album became one of Wilson's most successful releases.[18]

Later that fall, the Gerald Wilson Orchestra performed on Frank Evans's live television series *Frankly Jazz*. Mel's drumming guided the band through

Wilson's arrangements of "Milestones" and "Latino" from their *Moment of Truth album*.[19] Mel was also featured on the band's up-tempo version of "Perdido." Because very little video footage exists of him playing with big bands in the early 1960s (Mulligan Concert Jazz Band, Terry Gibbs Big Band, and Benny Goodman), this television performance is an important visual example of Mel's drumming at the time. His two-cymbal set-up, with his Chinese cymbal as the only one on his right side, was the same cymbal set-up used by his drumming idols Cozy Cole and Dave Tough. Mel's drumming on *Frankly Jazz* is also a wonderful visual example of just how physically relaxed Mel was when he played, creating so much intensity while making the whole process look effortless.

September of 1962 once again found Mel drumming at the Monterey Jazz Festival. He and bassist Buddy Clark were again members of the Monterey Festival Orchestra. Over the course of five days, Mel and Clark rehearsed and performed almost constantly in a wide variety of groups, including performances with the Benny Carter Ensemble, Stan Getz, the Al Porcino Big Band, the Quincy Jones Orchestra, and the Gerry Mulligan/Paul Desmond Quartet.[20] The festival also gave Mel the opportunity to once again work with Dizzy Gillespie. The directors of the Monterey Jazz Festival commissioned Dizzy's pianist Lalo Schifrin to compose an extended piece for Dizzy to debut during the festival. Schifrin's composition *The New Continent* was a six-movement tone poem featuring shifting styles, rhythms, and textures for Dizzy to solo over. The composition was debuted by the Monterey Festival Orchestra during opening night on September 21.[21] In addition to Dizzy, saxophonist and flutist James Moody, who had recently joined Dizzy Gillespie's Quartet, played an important musical role during the performance. The concert was the first documented performance of Mel playing with Moody, a musical relationship that was important for Mel throughout the 1960s.

Mel's performance on *The New Continent* led to another opportunity for him to perform with Moody and Dizzy later that fall at the University of California, Los Angeles. On Saturday, November 3, he joined the Dizzy Gillespie Quartet to perform another Lalo Schifrin extended composition, *Gillespiana*, featuring a jazz quintet and brass choir.[22] The UCLA concert was the last major performance of the year for Mel. He had traveled the world for much of 1962, and as he expressed to Doris he was tired of traveling and wanted to "make it" at home.[23] The real question he had to answer was, should home be in California or New York?

From November 1962 through April 1963, Mel's career was in a period of great transition. His work with Terry Gibbs had completely stopped by November of 1962. After the band's eighteen-month engagement at the Sundown Club, Gibbs focused his energy on booking and playing with his small group. The financial burden of running a big band had taken its toll on Gibbs, and even though the band was still popular (although not like that first year) he decided not to book a weekly gig for the band. By January of 1963, Gibbs had left Los Angeles and relocated to New York City, marking the end of his famous big band and musical relationship with Mel.[24]

Gerry Mulligan had begun performing more with his New York City based small group and by 1963 only booked the Concert Jazz Band a few times a year. The band still played their usual spring engagement at Birdland, but extensive touring and recording for the band was over. Because Mel was still based in Los Angeles, he did not perform with Mulligan's small group; Mulligan used Gus Johnson frequently during 1962 and early 1963.[25]

In addition to Mel's high-profile jazz jobs ending or slowing down, he was not recording in the Los Angeles studios as often as he had the previous five years. One reason for his lack of work could be attributed to the increase of rock and roll music and its musicians in studios. Younger drummers such as Hal Blaine, Earl Palmer, and Jim Gordon began getting much of the studio work as part of a group of musicians known as the "Wrecking Crew." While many of these drummers were raised as jazz players, they made their living by playing rock and roll studio dates. The era of big bands being the main source of L.A. studio accompaniment was gone, and the sound of guitars, electric instruments, and rock drumming had taken over. Jazz musicians such as Mel, who didn't want to play rock and roll music, began to see their studio work drastically decline.

Another reason that Mel's studio work was diminishing was his personality.[26] Mel was well known as being very opinionated, outspoken, and often quite blunt.[27] Bill Holman recalled Mel's tendency to speak his mind:

> You know some people thought he was a terrible person because he was so outspoken, so dogmatic, and so positive about his beliefs. If you were on the other side of his opinion you were bound to think he was a bad guy. But many times, his opinions on situations were correct. It just might have been better judgment to

not express them. But he always stuck to his guns, and there is a lot to be said for that![28]

A prime example of Mel's outspoken personality was a musical blindfold test that he did for *DownBeat* magazine in September of 1962. During the test, he listened to several musical examples and was then asked what he thought of each example and whom he thought performed it. Of course the *DownBeat* reader gets to see all the album information, yet unless Mel had previously heard the album, he was simply giving his musical opinion and taking an educated guess at the performers. Mel ended up giving some unfavorable opinions about some very famous jazz musicians, yet in no way was he trying to be malicious. Mel's blindfold test is reprinted below and serves as a prime example of his candid personality. (*DownBeat* still prints a blindfold test in each issue. Possibly due to a lack of opinion, or more likely political posturing, current participants rarely say anything negative or highly opinionated about the musical examples.)

BLINDFOLD TEST—Mel Lewis by Leonard Feather (*DownBeat* September 27, 1962)

Mel Lewis' victory this year as a new star in the *DownBeat* International Critics Poll was a belated but welcome recognition of a fact recognized by musicians for some years. Lewis is among the most consistently exciting drummers in jazz.

Son of a professional drummer, Lewis was born in Buffalo, N.Y., in 1929 and made his professional debut at 15. Between 1946 and 1954 he worked with a number of name bands, including those of Boyd Raeburn, Alvino Rey, Ray Antony, and Tex Beneke. It wasn't until his 1954–6 tenure with the Stan Kenton Orchestra that he attained any jazz prominence.

Since then, Lewis has been consistently in demand in the Hollywood area, working with Terry Gibbs' big band whenever it is operative. He visited Europe some months ago with Dizzy Gillespie's quintet and most recently was a member of the Benny Goodman band during its tour of the Soviet Union.

This was Lewis' first Blindfold Test. He was given no information, before or after the test, about the records played.

THE RECORDS

1. Buddy Rich-Max Roach, *Big Foot* (from Rich vs. Roach, Mercury). Buddy Rich (left), Max Roach (right), drums; Willie Dennis, trombone; Julian Priester, trombone; Phil Woods, alto saxophone; Stanley Turrentine, tenor saxophone; Tommy Turrentine, trumpet; John Bunch, piano; Phil Leshin, Bass.

ML: There were at least two drummers ... actually, they were a little too busy for the size of the band; there was too much going on. I don't recognize too many of the soloists, except Willie Dennis.

The recording balance on this is fairly bad; I couldn't hear all the parts, what was going on. I don't know who the two drummers are, either ... One of them has some pretty good chops.

The one on the left seemed to lean toward the Louis Bellson sound; I don't think it was Louis, though. And the one on the right sounded like Charlie Persip, but I'm not sure. I would give this about 2 ½ stars for effort.

2. Miles Davis, *Salt Peanuts* (from Steamin', Prestige). Davis, trumpet; John Coltrane, tenor saxophone; Philly Joe Jones, drums; Paul Chambers, bass; Red Garland, piano.

ML: The ensemble—the guys played the heck out of it, considering what was going on. It wasn't swinging at all, and as far as the drummer is concerned, he's got a lotta chops, but he played way too long; I don't like drum solos that well. This was quite unmusical. I hope it wasn't my buddy, Elvin Jones—it didn't sound like Elvin, because he plays much more musically, and actually, after Buddy Rich, I don't see why anybody bothers playing drum solos, because he puts them all away. Hearing fast technical things of this sort doesn't please me too much.

The horns, whoever they were, were struggling to keep up. In the early part the bass player was dying; it was way too fast for him ... In fact it sounded to me like the tempo lifted some more. For this I can only give two stars.

3. Sam Jones, *The Chant* (from The Chant, Riverside). Victor Feldman, composer, arranger, piano; Sam Jones, bass; Les

Spann, guitar; Nat Adderley, cornet; Cannonball Adderley, alto saxophone; Jimmy Heath, tenor saxophone.

ML: That was a nice record; a lot of spirit, I don't know the tune. The bass player was very good. I thought there was a little too much guitar, though, coming through too strong, sort of blotting them out. The bass player was very good though—was that Sam Jones?

The trumpet player was good too—sounded like one of the Adderleys. The tenor seemed to have some intonation problems, some idea problems. The alto was good ... They got a nice bouncy feeling. I liked the arrangement too. I'll give that 3 ½ stars.

4. Shelly Manne, *Poinciana* (from Sounds Unheard Of, Contemporary). Shelly Manne, percussion; Jack Marshall, guitar.

ML: Well, I'd like to have heard that one with just the guitarist alone. What was all that racket behind there? I got panicked in the beginning; I thought it was going to be a rock-and-roll record there for a second. But, as time went on, I could see ... the guitarist, he played very well, his inclination is toward the classical; his intonation was fine; he knew his instrument very well. But all the racket in the background, it was just plain racket—just for the sake of stereo, I'm afraid.

I don't know who they were. Sounds like it might be some of my friends out here on the coast, trying to cash in on the percussion album sales. I really can't rate that at all.

5. Dukes of Dixieland, *Honeysuckle Rose* (from Now Hear This, Columbia). Frank Assunto, trumpet; Herb Ellis, guitar; Gene Schroeder, piano; Jim Atlas, bass; Charles Lodice, drums.

ML: Well, that proved its point. I like this kind of music. It's always refreshing to come back and hear something like this.

The opening trumpet sounded like Ruby Braff or somebody like that, and the rhythm section sounded nice. It was the old swing school, of course; guitar player had nice time; drummer was good and loose, bass player had a tendency ... I didn't like him in his high register ... but still, you could tell he had spirit. And the piano player was definitely out of the Teddy Wilson school, and Teddy, of course, is one of my favorites, so anybody who wants to play like him can, as far as I'm concerned—as long as they do a good job of it.

The second trumpet—the muted trumpet—I don't know if that was the same guy or not ... sounded like there was more than one, almost Joe Newman-y sounding. I like this record; this is worth at least 3 ½ stars.

6. Quincy Jones, *Straight No Chaser* (from Quintessence, Impulse). Joe Newman, trumpet; Curtis Fuller, trombone; arranger not credited.

ML: Yeah, that was a good arrangement of Straight, No Chaser. Good sounding little band, too ... or big band, I should say.

The trombone player sounded a lot like J. J. The trumpet was good, too, coming on with that pecking—Joe Newman always did a lot of things like that.

I don't know whose record this is, or whose arrangement, but it sure had a lot of fire to it, sort of reminiscent of Dizzy's old band. I like this very much. Four stars.

7. John Coltrane, *Softly as in a Morning Sunrise* (from Coltrane Live at the Village Vanguard, Impulse). Coltrane, soprano saxophone; McCoy Tyner, piano; Reggie Workman, bass; Elvin Jones, drums.

ML: I thought I recognized Elvin Jones early in the beginning ... behind the piano. You know, Elvin is the only drummer, to me, of what you would call the busy school; while he's got this constant thing going—movement at all times—he played lightly. He was still light behind the piano. You were able to hear everything the piano did. And even through the whole record, he kept this thing going, which, if you notice, has a lot to do with what Trane is doing up front. He's listening all the time. Plus the interplay between him and the piano, it's musical, it's strong, but still I could hear everything the piano played, I could also hear everything Trane doing. I could also hear the bass player. He wasn't drowning them out.

I like McCoy; I enjoy his playing very much. He's a guy that should be heard from a lot more.

And just to get to Trane for a second, the soprano is not the kind of instrument I enjoy listening to too much; after a while it gets a little grating, but still of this new school Trane knows what he's doing. There are so many guys that just don't know what they are doing. I can listen to him any time and enjoy it. Four stars.

8. Tribute to Benny Goodman, *Let's Dance* (from Tribute to Benny Goodman, Crown). Mahlon Clark, clarinet.

ML: Well, to be polite, that was pretty bad. I don't know who that could have been; it was a very poor imitation—no swinging. There was nothing there. I just can't even say anything about it. No Stars.

I've heard that tune sound good, even in the Goodman band that I was with. All these old things sounded good, even though they were no fun to play.

For Mel, the political atmosphere of the Los Angeles studios did not lend itself to his thoughts and opinions. By January 1963, he was no longer on staff at NBC Studios or being called by many of the top studio contractors. "I was a very bad politician. I'd say I was really abrasive to people who I just couldn't kiss their ass. Because I didn't believe in it … I couldn't do that. I just couldn't do that, I wasn't raised that way," stated Mel.[29] The contractors determined who got hired for the well-paying studio jobs in Los Angeles, and when Mel fell out of favor with the major contractors he lost his opportunity for the best paying studio work such as television shows and motion pictures:

Politics, that was one of the reasons I left the town. It was a political town, terrible. And you really had to do things that I won't do! Same things I wouldn't do in grammar school, you know. And I had to get out of there eventually. But between '52 and '62 that town was romping, I mean there was a lot of music, a lot of wonderful musicians, and although they were talking about east coast versus west coast, I think we did just as much back there in L.A. as they were doing here.[30]

Mel still worked frequently in the Los Angeles jazz scene, but he had burned too many bridges to get called for the high paying commercial work that would have made living in Los Angeles worthwhile. In the end, because he was making his living as a jazz drummer, he knew that his career would be better served by living in the jazz capital of the world, New York City.[31] Mel himself said,

> I did some studio work in Los Angeles, but actually it was pretty polite. Out there, (Los Angeles) I was pretty typed and in California you have to be a big name or you need to be a star to really work. I wasn't a star and I didn't get a star on my dressing room, as far as a lot of the contractors were concerned. Actually, I was a big band drummer and I was doing all the good big band dates, and I did some of the good small group dates. I did quite a few things for Pacific Jazz, Contemporary, and some of the Atlantic things when it was strictly a jazz company. But I didn't get the cream work, I got very little of the television or the movie work. Those were the things you needed to keep your family going; you know to live! Because you could take all these jazz dates, add them all up, all the albums and everything I did out there over the period of nine years, and it would all add up to maybe one year's worth of good studio work, as far as finances were concerned. Actually I was traveling to New York so often anyway that eventually I was getting more work in New York than L.A., even though I my family was still out west. Every time I came into New York I got record dates, jingles, and things like that because the jazz musicians knew I was coming.[32]

The same personal traits that cost Mel studio work in Los Angeles also shaped his career in positive ways. His absolute refusal to change the style of his drumming or the sound of his drums for a recording session made a lot of recording engineers and contractors upset, yet made his playing very recognizable and familiar to listeners. Mel's opinions on drumming, and what he considered good music, never changed. The beliefs that he held during his years in Los Angeles were bluntly restated during the next two and a half decades; case in point is the following quote from a 1987 interview with Ben Sidran. Mel's statements about music and drumming may have seemed old-fashioned to some, but to read his words again today, one smiles knowing that his thoughts are more than valid, they are correct:

It is shame because electronics have taken over and it has hurt musicians terribly. I mean it's probably one of the worst things that happened in the business and people don't realize this you know. In fact, I am glad that I get a chance to even talk about it ... It's not the coming in of electronics, because many good things have happened because of electronics, but the fact is that instead of using these electronic instruments as instruments to enhance they have been used to replace. And I think that is the rottenest thing man! This is just like big business, you know, like computers taking the place of people and I think it is completely wrong!

Not only is it wrong, it doesn't even sound good. I wonder how many people realize they are listening to machines. The drums are the worst! They are absolutely terrible! They do not sound anything like a drum and I don't know why they keep thinking it does. Except that in today's popular music these particular drummers that do this type of work and who play pop music don't even know what a drum is supposed to sound like anyway. I mean, I don't mean to put you down kids but you don't know! You don't know anything about drums. You can't play them, you don't know what they sound like, and you can't play! And I am on record as saying it. Now I am not talking to the fusion drummers because there are some great ones out there. But you'll sit there and watch a television show like Saturday Night Live or something like that, and they'll have some rock group on there. On the stage I'll see a huge set of drums and there's a guy sitting up there behind this huge set and all he's doing is playing on his closed hi-hat, and his bass drum which you can see through the plastic head with a big hole in the front, and he's got cymbals ten feet up in the air which he can't reach anyway. And he's playing (Mel vocalizes a rock beat and fill) Boom Boom Pop, Boom Boom Pop, Do-Ka-Da-Ka-Ding. He plays a fill and then hits a cymbal real loud and he never even touches all these drums. It's just a big show. He can't even play them and he's only got two hands anyway. He's got to play really loud and of course it's probably triggered into some stupid electronic drum that makes the backbeat sound like a gunshot instead of a drum, and they say that's a drum! That is because these kids don't know what a drum is sounds like.

Now I have gone into recording studios where when I get through with them they have had a lesson in what a drum is supposed to sound like, as I remove all the tape on the drumheads! You can say I am an old man, the kids can say "Oh what does he know he is from the old school." Man, I am not from the old school! I am a musician and I play drums and cymbals. I use cymbals that are real cymbals. It's like driving a good car as opposed to a piece of junk, you know ... But man, once you really know how to play a drum, meaning you can play it, you know what it sounds like, and you can sit and create music on that drum, then you've achieved something. I don't mean play songs where you sit there playing backbeats and play a fill here and you do this there. I mean where you can actually make music on an instrument, then you'll know exactly what I am talking about. The late Buddy Rich, who was one of my dearest friends, man he was really one of a kind! He and I played drums with completely different approaches, but you can't beat the way he played. We used to sit and talk about young drummers and he used to say to me, "What is happening to the art form?" The funny bit is that all of these rock drummers admired him; there isn't a drummer in the world that didn't admire him. Yet, none of them even thought about playing like him. If they did, they'd never be doing what they are doing because he hated that stuff...

See what happened was, these drummers were fools! They allowed a sound to take over that could be duplicated by a machine and now all the machines are doing the work and the drummers are out of jobs. But no machine can replace me, no way![33]

Mel never stopped speaking up for what he believed in and he always stayed true to his belief that jazz music should be swinging *and* innovative. Due in part to his unapologetic honesty, his career wasn't filled with the fame and fortune that other drummers achieved. Yet Mel stayed true to himself and developed artistically throughout his entire life, in turn leaving the world with a recorded legacy that is priceless. ‖

Chapter 11
Back in the Big Apple

In April of 1963, Mel finally made the decision to move himself and his family back to New York City. This ended up being one of the best decisions he ever made, beginning the most artistically satisfying period of his career.

Arriving in New York City in May of 1963, Mel gigged on the jazz circuit almost immediately:

> I started working and playing with everybody, and playing jazz gigs within two weeks after I arrived. In two weeks I started making a living, not just a job here or a job there, I mean it started and it went bam! It's hard to believe, but that's the way it was.[1]

His first month in the city was better than he could have imagined, and June proved to be a successful and important month as well. Earlier that spring while still living in Los Angeles, Mel had told Ben Webster of his plans to move to New York City. According to Mel, Webster responded by saying, "Well, if you are leaving I am leaving too, you got room?"[2] Mel was playing with Webster on a regular basis in L.A., and as he told it, his decision was the tipping point of Webster's decision to also move back to the East Coast. Just a week before the two men planned to drive to New York City together, however, Webster told Mel that he was not going to travel with him because he wanted to stop in Kansas City on his way east. He told Mel that he would eventually meet up with him at the famous musician establishment Jim and Andy's on West 48th Street in Manhattan. In early June, Webster did find Mel at Jim and Andy's and their musical association quickly resumed.[3] Mel recalled seeing Webster in New York City for the first time:

> He said, "I'll meet you in Jim and Andy's in a few weeks." And that's exactly what we did. And when I ran into him he said, "Boy I am glad you are here. We got a gig. Get me a bass player!" So I got Richard Davis, because I had worked a gig with Richard already with Don Friedman on piano, and Zoot (Sims) and Al (Cohn) at the New School. I loved playing with Richard, I liked him personally

and I liked the way he played. I called him and he took the gig, he said that I got him his first gig in Harlem. And we (Richard Davis and Ben Webster) went to work at a place called the Shalimar.[4]

Along with Mel and Richard Davis, Webster's Quartet of 1963 included pianist Dave Frishberg.[5] With Webster's newfound popularity among New York City jazz fans and critics, the group turned what was supposed to be a one-week stay at the Shalimar Club in Harlem into a six-week engagement.[6] Their stay at the Shalimar ended up being as important for Mel as it was for Webster. In addition to the exposure he received with Webster, he had the opportunity to build a strong musical rapport with Richard Davis. The men had the ability to make any style or tempo of music feel good, allowing the other musicians on the bandstand to play their best. As a result of their musicality and sight-reading abilities, the combination of Mel and Richard Davis became the first-call rhythm section for much of the jazz and studio work in New York City for the remainder of the 1960s.[7] After the Webster Quartet's initial run at the Shalimar, they continued to perform for much of the summer, including a concert at Philharmonic Hall, seven weeks headlining the Half Note, several nights at the Village Vanguard, and two weeks at Birdland.[8]

In addition to his work with Webster, another great opportunity presented itself to Mel during his first few weeks in New York City. On June 17 and 18, he played a recording date with Dizzy Gillespie's former saxophonist James Moody. The resulting album, *James Moody: Great Day* (Argo) is an important piece of history as Mel's first recording with Thad Jones. The album also included Richard Davis on bass, Johnny Coles on trumpet, Hubert Laws on flute, Hank Jones on piano, Bernie Leighton on piano, Jim Hall on guitar, and the arrangements of Tom McIntosh.[9] Mel had stayed in touch with Thad after their initial meeting in Detroit in 1955, and in what seemed like fate, both men unknowingly moved to New York at about the same time. Mel recalled, "Without ever talking about it, in 1963 I quit L.A. and moved to New York, Thad quit Basie and moved to New York. There we were!"[10] Only weeks after both men arrived in the city, they found themselves in the studio recording music together. Rarely can the beginning of an era be pinpointed to an exact date but the *Great Day* recording session on June 17, 1963, marked the official beginning of Thad and Mel's musical collaboration, an association and friendship that defined both of their careers for the next seventeen years.

Mel's first summer back in New York City was a busy one. In addition to his steady gigs with Webster and his recording with Moody, he also started to get called for studio work. Most importantly for Mel, his work that summer consisted of once again playing straight-ahead jazz in small groups. Through his live small group work, he began to record with some of the best jazz musicians in the city. In July he recorded the album *Jimmy Smith/Kenny Burrell: Blue Bash* (Verve), and in August he recorded *Clark Terry and Friends: What Makes Sammy Swing* (20th Century Fox).[11] After spending his last years in Los Angeles being typecast as "only a big band drummer," as Mel put it, he happily found a resurgence of small-group work on the East Coast.[12]

Soon after Mel relocated, Doris and the couple's three daughters, Anita, Lori, and Donna lived briefly in Tarrytown, New York, before eventually settling into a new house in Irvington, New York.[13] In addition to his new home just north of the city, Mel found stability with a new staff job for ABC Studios. For jazz musicians who were good sight-readers, improvisers, and had their personal life fairly organized, a studio job was still the best way to make a steady income.[14] Even with Mel's general dislike for the commercial studio scene, he accepted the ABC job and the consistent paycheck it provided. The steady income made supporting his family easier, and also afforded him the financial stability and time to further his jazz career.[15] His work in New York City studios was a more positive experience than in Los Angeles. In a *DownBeat* interview with Dan Morgenstern, Mel explained:

> On more and more of the dates, jingles and records that I've been doing in the past year or two, I'm being allowed to play fairly free, and restricted only where absolutely necessary. The rhythm section can get pretty loose; we even get into some free things … In this kind of environment, it takes real ability and a halfway decent personality to make good. I don't mean you have to be a phony and charm everybody, but you've got to be the kind of person that people enjoy being around. I had to learn that myself—it comes with growing up. Anybody who has the ability, and really wants to, can make it. But you've got to have the ability.[16]

New York City jazz musicians such as Clark Terry, Frank Wess, and Hank Jones had already proven that daytime studio work did not hinder their progress or development as jazz musicians. Mel joined this elite crowd and took advantage of the last great era for the studio jazz musician in New York City. Throughout the fall of 1963, he played drums for various commercials, jingles, and television shows including the *Jimmy Dean Show*.[17]

The weekly hour-long *Jimmy Dean Show* aired on ABC from September 1963 to April 1966, and Mel was the drummer for almost the entire run.[18] The variety show featured, among other things, live musical acts. Mel and the ABC staff orchestra, under the leadership of Peter Matz, accompanied many of the guest musical acts. While he was never seen on screen, Mel's drumming accompanied artists such as Johnny Cash, Eydie Gorme, Red Buttons, The Four Seasons, Patty Duke, and puppeteer Jim Henson's first national television creation, Rowlf, the piano-playing dog.[19] Mel's association with Peter Matz continued throughout the 1960s in an extremely wide variety of musical situations, including the first five albums by rising star vocalist Barbra Streisand, various jazz and pop record dates, and two major television series conducted by Matz, the *Kraft Music Hall* and *Hullabaloo*.[20] Mel greatly respected Matz and considered him one of the best studio musicians and conductors in New York City.[21]

For Mel, one of the most exciting aspects of relocating to New York City was the opportunity to play and record music with a larger scene of jazz musicians.[22] Some of his new musical associations became steady work, while others ended up being a one-time gig or recording session. A short list of his recordings from the fall of 1963 includes *Gary McFarland Sextet: Point of Departure* (Impulse!), *Stan Getz: Reflections* (Verve), and *Brother Jack McDuff Big Band: Prelude* (Prestige). After his short time working in the city, word had spread that Mel was one of the best drummers in town, and someone who was completely dedicated to making every ensemble he played with sound great.[23]

In November of 1963, with his jazz and studio career in New York City on the rise, Mel received an unexpected offer to join another State Department Tour. Duke Ellington was once again looking to replace ailing drummer Sam Woodyard and asked Mel to join his band. The main difference between this offer and Ellington's proposal three years earlier was that the new offer was for a fulltime steady position in the band. Even considering his ABC staff job and the fact that he had just relocated, Mel couldn't turn down the chance to be in Ellington's orchestra. He gratefully accepted Ellington's offer and prepared to hit the road as Woodyard's replacement:

I got another call from Ellington to join the band on its worldwide tour, state department tour. I was to meet the band in Athens, Greece. On Thursday I was supposed to leave … I accepted the gig; that would have been permanent, or as long as I wanted to stay. And for the same reason though, Woodyard was sick again, only this time it wasn't to replace him temporarily, it was to replace him.[24]

On Friday, November 22, 1963, less than a week before Mel was to fly to Europe and join Ellington, President John F. Kennedy was assassinated in Dallas, Texas. The Kennedy assassination paralyzed the nation and put an immediate end to Ellington's State Department Tour. Ellington and his orchestra flew back to New York after the cancelation of their tour, with no future tour plans.[25] By the time Ellington reorganized and toured South America three months later, Sam Woodyard was healthier and stayed on with the band. Mel never received another call to join Ellington's orchestra.[26]

As with his two offers to join Basie in 1948 and 1950, his two offers to join Ellington in 1960 and 1963 never came to fruition. By 1963, Mel had established a successful career and did not necessarily need the exposure of working with Ellington. Also, a positive result of never working for Basie or Ellington was that he never got typecast as a "Basie-type of drummer" or "Ellington-type of drummer"; letting their iconic music drastically shape his drumming. Mel was able to freely develop his style with Kenton, and as soon as he felt his drumming style was being compromised by Kenton's conception, he left the band. The steady creative opportunities that he had with Holman, Gibbs, and Mulligan from 1957 through 1963 allowed him to continually develop his unique style of big band drumming. Unlike so many other drummers, Mel's career was spent in bands where the leaders, composers, and arrangers actually based their musical conception around his drumming.

In 1964 Mel continued his work at ABC, worked throughout New York City in various jazz groups including a newly formed small group with Thad Jones and Pepper Adams, and played drums on several recordings featuring jazz vocalists. When East Coast musicians experienced how great Mel played with vocalists, he began to get called frequently for that type of work. Mel's drumming can be heard on a wide variety of vocal albums released in 1964, including: *Morgana King: With a Taste of Honey* (Mainstream), *Sylvia Syms:*

The Fabulous Sylvia Syms (20th Century Fox), *Carmen McRae: Haven't We Met?* (Mainstream), *Carmen McRae: Alfie* (Mainstream), and *Joe Williams: The Song Is You* (RCA Victor).[27]

Truth be told, Mel enjoyed recording with vocalists because he realized the format showcased his ability to musically support the group and the vocalist simultaneously. "I like working with singers because it gives me a chance to play another little way," stated Mel.[28] Throughout his career he continually performed with the world's greatest vocalists, many with quirky and distinct personalities. Mel recalled his experiences with several:

> Peggy Lee was difficult. She was like Benny Goodman because she learned from him how to treat musicians, which is bad you know. And then she's got that woman stuff, a woman treating men like "ah ha, I got you by your balls"... I worked with Jimmy Rushing a lot at the Half Note with Al Cohn and Zoot Sims and I also worked there with him and Ben Webster. He was great ... I think Mel Torme is a great singer, I really like him, you know. I mean as a singer you can't fault him; he's this great artist. But to work with he's a pain in the ass. He made comments about my band I didn't like. And I've had the tendency to let him know how to keep his mouth shut ... Jo Stafford she's wonderful and a sweetheart too ... I enjoyed working with Joe Williams ... Jimmy Witherspoon was easy to work with too. Witherspoon was just a plain, down home guy, just like he sang. I mean, the way he sings, that's the way he is.[29]

That spring Mel accepted a new musical opportunity that took him back to Europe. In May he flew to Austria to participate in a newly formed jazz orchestra led by world-renowned classical pianist Friedrich Gulda. A famed concert pianist with a deep love and respect for jazz, Gulda began playing jazz in the late 1950s and also composed works that mixed elements of jazz and classical music. The Euro-Jazz Orchestra marked one of Gulda's first opportunities to perform his original music with his own jazz orchestra.[30] After the initial concert on May 30, 1964, Mel was invited back to Austria in 1965 and 1966 to perform again with Gulda and his orchestra.[31] During those three years the Euro-Jazz Orchestra featured a rotating cast of some of the greatest jazz musicians in the world including

J. J. Johnson on trombone; Freddie Hubbard, Kenny Wheeler, and Art Farmer on trumpet; Ron Carter on bass, Joe Zawinul on piano, and Julian "Cannonball" Adderley on alto saxophone.

Despite the previously mentioned vocal recordings, Mel's overall recorded output from 1964 was fairly small. He wasn't in the studio recording jazz albums nearly as often as he had been in Los Angeles. In all fairness, he had set an incredibly high standard between 1957 and 1963, usually recording several albums a week. On the positive side, in New York he was performing live more frequently than he had during his final L.A. years. In 1964 many of his gigs in New York City were with small groups led by Al Cohn, Zoot Sims and, most importantly, Thad Jones.

Chapter 12
Thad and Mel
Get Their Opening

Throughout 1964, Thad and Mel performed together on a regular basis in their small group with Pepper Adams. However, the most high profile work that Thad and Mel shared was with the Mulligan Concert Jazz Band. Earlier in the year trumpeter Clark Terry had left the Concert Jazz Band, accepting a contract to work for NBC Studios in Los Angeles. Famously, Terry's contract was the first ever offered to an African-American musician by NBC and resulted in his decade of high profile work on *The Tonight Show*. Amazingly, ABC and CBS had already hired African-Americans in their studio orchestras, but it wasn't until Terry in 1964 that NBC finally followed suit. On Mel and Brookmeyer's recommendation, Mulligan hired Thad Jones to take over Terry's trumpet chair in the Concert Jazz Band.[1] The band was not touring or recording at the time, but still played several long residencies at clubs in New York City. Thad soon found himself sitting next to Mel during the Concert Jazz Band's three-week residency at Birdland during March and April of 1964. Even though there are no commercially available recordings of Thad with the band, Bill Crow remembered Thad's performances by saying, "Those gigs were testament to his musical interaction and connection with Mel."[2]

The bond that Thad and Mel formed during their time in Mulligan's Concert Jazz Band became a life-changing event. Many of the musical experiences they shared made them realize how exciting and innovative a big band could be. Unfortunately, all of the experiences with Mulligan were not positive ones. As Thad explained, Mulligan often would not let the best soloists in the band stretch out, leaving him and Mel to imagine the possibilities of such a group without musical limits:

> Mel and I were working with Gerry Mulligan, who had a very good band at the time. He didn't use a piano, incidentally. And Bobby Brookmeyer, one of the original members of our band, was also in that band. Phil Woods was in there—and can you imagine Phil Woods sitting up in a band and not playing a solo all night long?

But this is what used to happen, because Phil's got so much fire, and when he started playing it would just take things away, you know. Gerry started cutting him off, then leaving him out: how can you do this to a musician?

This isn't putting the knock on Gerry, but the band always seemed to reach a certain level of intensity—and it never went beyond that. Mel and I always felt that there was an area beyond this.[3]

Late in the summer of 1964 Mulligan informed the members of his Concert Jazz Band that he was breaking up the band to focus more on his small group. The news was disappointing to all of the members, but especially to Thad and Mel who greatly enjoyed playing in the large group setting. However, as Mel explained, the end of the Concert Jazz Band led directly to the creation of the Thad Jones/Mel Lewis Jazz Orchestra. Mel recalled the moment he and Thad realized that if they wanted to play in a big band, they were going to have to form their own:

I was back with the Mulligan Band, and Clark Terry had left and Thad joined the band. Now we're sitting next to each other, and there we are! Then we started getting each other on gigs, hanging out, and starting to make all kinds of scenes. We'd always talk and say, "Well we need to do something ourselves." And then one day Mulligan just gave us the opening, he said "Fellas, I am breaking up the band," and we said, "There goes the last of the big bands," and we thought that was it for us. We were through, unless we wanted to go back on the road with Count Basie or Stan Kenton, which we couldn't do at this point in our lives. No way could we do that anymore, we'd have to be something new or forget it completely. So we looked at each other and somebody said "Zing! You two guys are going to do it," and we did it![4]

By the end of 1964, the two men had a verbal agreement to start their own big band, yet it would be another year before they actually formed the group. Mel spent much of 1965 pushing Thad to start the band, but until Thad composed new music the group couldn't get off the ground.[5]

In 1965, as Mel waited, he worked in a huge variety of musical situations. For much of the year he continued playing with Zoot Sims and Al Cohn's co-led small group at the Half Note, located at 289 Hudson Street, subbed frequently in Lucky Thompson's new quartet, and played clubs throughout the city with the Thad Jones/Pepper Adams Quintet.[6] He also recorded albums including: *Oscar Peterson Trio: With Respect to Nat* (Limelight), *Shirley Scott: Latin Shadows* (Impulse!), *Stan Getz: Plays Music from the Soundtrack of Mickey One* (MGM), *Jimmy Ricks: Vibrations* (Mainstream), *Gary McFarland and Clark Terry: Tijuana Jazz* (Impulse!), and *Jimmy Witherspoon: Blues for Easy Livers* (Prestige).[7] Mel also continued his musical collaboration with Peter Matz and recorded two Barbra Streisand albums: *My Name Is Barbra* and *My Name Is Barbra Two* (Columbia).[8] Both albums reached number two on the Billboard Top 200 and have since become platinum, selling over one million copies each worldwide.

On most of the Peter Matz's projects, including the Streisand albums, Matz also hired bassist Richard Davis. Together, Mel and Davis continued to work several times a week as a rhythm section on jazz and commercial recording dates. During 1965 the duo could be heard on everything from Schaefer beer commercials, to a pop record, to a singing puppet sketch on a network television show.[9] Mel recalled his studio work with Davis during the mid-1960s:

> Richard and I have spent days together, where we start with a Dixieland jingle on Tiger Rag, go on to a Jimmy Dean country-and-western date, and wind up playing something really far out—from one extreme to the other. In a week we might come up with every kind of music imaginable. And it's all well-written and played with the best musicians.[10]

In addition to their employment with Matz, the men started doing a large amount of recording for composer and arranger Manny Albam who hired the duo to play on jazz recordings, radio jingles, and television commercials.[11] Albam was a jazz baritone saxophonist who had begun composing and arranging in the bands of Georgie Auld and Charlie Barnet. During the 1950s, Mel and Albam got to know each other through the Terry Gibbs Big Band; Mel played several of Albam's arrangements with Gibbs including "Moten Swing" and "Jumpin' at the Woodside." During the 1960s, Albam continued his career on the East Coast and arranged for Buddy Rich, Coleman Hawkins, Gerry Mulligan, Stan Getz, and Dizzy Gillespie.[12] In 1965, Albam became the musical director for a new record label called Solid State, which was the jazz subsidiary of United Artists Records. The label was co-founded by producer Sonny Lester and recording engineer Phil Ramone. In the next several years, Mel, Richard Davis, Manny Albam, Sonny Lester, and Phil Ramone teamed up to create some of the greatest big band music ever recorded.

Similar to Mel's work at ABC Studios, Thad Jones was on staff at CBS Studios. Because of his busy staff position and regular playing engagements throughout the city, Thad still had yet to write music for his big band with Mel. But as Mel later discovered, Thad rarely composed or arranged music unless he had a paid commission to do so.[13] As fate would have it, that spring, Count Basie commissioned Thad to compose and arrange an entire album of new music for the Count Basie Orchestra. From 1954 through 1963, Thad had contributed several of his original compositions and arrangements to Basie's book, including "The Deacon" and "To You." In addition, he was the arranger of most of the material on Basie's 1959 recording *Dance Along with Basie* (Roulette).[14] Now, three years removed from his employment with Basie, Thad had the opportunity for his full-scale arranging debut. With his new arrangements complete, Thad delivered the music to Basie and patiently waited for a response to his work. In the end, Basie rejected every single arrangement that Thad had written. Mel recalled the situation and the positive effect it had on the development of his band:

> He [Jones] had the staff job over there at CBS, so man I was on his butt for about a year and a half [to start a band]. And then finally the truth of the matter is that Thad got an assignment to write an album for the Basie Band. And he wrote ten or eleven arrangements for Basie's band that had nothing to do with Basie's band at all. That's number one through twelve in our book![15]

The arrangements that Thad wrote for Basie included, "The Second Race," "Lowdown," "Backbone," "All My Yesterdays," "Big Dipper," and an arrangement of his brother Hank's composition "A-That's Freedom." In addition, Thad finished his composition "Little Pixie," which he had originally started writing for the Mulligan Concert Jazz Band.[16] It was not that these arrangements were poor; as a matter of fact, they are among the most highly regarded big band music ever written. However, the style and difficulty of Thad's music did not mesh well with the members of Basie's band or its existing repertoire. When all was said and done, Basie allowed Thad to keep the scores and individual parts, and never used any of the arrangements with his band.[17] It must have been a true disappointment for Thad, but ironically now that he had new music, he contacted Mel and told him they were finally ready to start their band. ‖

1 The Thad Jones/Mel Lewis Jazz Orchestra at the Village Vanguard in February 1966.
© *Raymond Ross Archives/CTSIMAGES*

2 Mel's 1966 datebook, "Village Vanguard ● Band 9:30" February 7. *Used by permission of t*
University of Missouri-Kansas City Libraries, Dr. Kenn
LaBudde Department of Special Collections.

Chapter 13
Opening Night at the
Village Vanguard

In November of 1965, Thad and Mel quickly put together a list of the musicians they wanted for their band. While Thad had certain friends at CBS whom he wanted to hire, and Mel had musicians he wanted, they easily agreed on the personnel. Thad remembered the process of forming the group, saying, "We agreed on *everything*. And that's ridiculous. Musically it bordered on fantastic. And then, when we finally started calling, nobody turned us down. Not a soul."[1] Eugene "Snooky" Young, Bob Brookmeyer, Pepper Adams, and Richard Davis were the first musicians hired, as Thad and Mel loved all four men as both musicians and friends. Next came Jimmy Nottingham, Jack Rains, Cliff Heather, and Hank Jones, all of whom were on staff with Thad at CBS. Jimmy Maxwell, Bill Berry, Danny Stiles, Jerome Richardson, and Jerry Dodgion were all accomplished jazz musicians active in the New York City studio scene, and were soon invited into the band.[2] It is important to note that while Thad and Mel were previously friends with many of the musicians they hired, this wasn't true in every case. Thad himself stated, "We weren't all friends in the beginning. We were acquaintances who respected each other as individuals and musicians. The friendship came through our association together with our band."[3] The two men were determined to fill their band with great musicians, regardless of age or race. When promising young players such as Joe Farrell (who was recommended by Wayne Shorter), Garnett Brown, Jimmy Owens, and Eddie Daniels were asked to join the band, often Thad and Mel were going on musical ability alone.[4] Eddie Daniels recalled the chance meeting that got him hired into the band:

> Tony Scott had hired me to play with him at the Half Note, and it was one of my first jazz gigs ever. One night Thad and Mel came in and heard me. I was only playing saxophone because Tony Scott wouldn't let me play clarinet. But, they came in and heard me and I got a call several weeks later to join their band. I was shocked. You never know![5]

Jerry Dodgion was a much more established musician than Daniels at the time. He had previously worked with Mel in several musical settings, including a recording session with singer Peggy Lee and as a member of the Benny Goodman tour in 1962. Even though he was a contemporary of both Thad and Mel, he recalled a similar joy and surprise when asked to join the all-star band:

> Mel is the one who called me, he said, "Thad Jones and I are starting a band together and we wanted to know if you wanted to be a part of it?" I said, "Of course!" So I knew these two individuals separately, but not as a team. And I thought to myself, "I wouldn't miss this for the world," because in a way they are sort of the "odd couple." They are totally different individuals, and I'm thinking, even if this lasts for one rehearsal, or twenty, I need to be there and I wouldn't miss it for anything. So I was in the place I wanted to be, and they were in the place that they wanted to be.[6]

After the all musicians confirmed their availability, Thad and Mel had assembled an incredible group of musicians. They had also unintentionally created a very racially diverse band. As saxophonist Dick Oatts explained, the diversity of the band was very significant to the jazz community at the time:

> When Thad and Mel started the band in 1965 it was so unique. During that turbulent time in the mid-1960s, they were able to form a truly mixed-race band. Everyone in the band had a distinct personality and direction in life and music. It broke through a lot of barriers and it was a good time for that to happen. It was really revolutionary. Not just what was going on musically, but it was also a sign of racial harmony. And I think the band represents that harmony, as much as it does the music. Thad's writing brought differences in life and music together, as did Mel's passion for putting the music "first above all" and the way he tailored the rhythmic direction. The glue for success was the respect of the differences of each member.[7]

The group's first rehearsal took place sometime on November 26, 27, or 28, Thanksgiving weekend of 1965.[8] The all-star band gathered at A&R Studios in Manhattan, located at West 48th Street near Sixth Avenue, just above the famous musician hangout Jim and Andy's.[9] As Thad later recalled, even a major delay didn't dampen the musicians' excitement for their first rehearsal:

> Our first rehearsal was at A&R Studios, and was scheduled for eleven o'clock. Everybody got there at ten-thirty. The latest cat was there by that time; I got there around ten o'clock, bringing with me a bottle apiece of brandy, Scotch and vodka. Hank, who doesn't drink, brought three bottles of whisky; he came in five minutes after I did.
>
> And you know what happened? The studio we were to rehearse in was occupied; they were recording a jingle. They were supposed to be out by eleven, but the jingle went on until around twelve-thirty. We sat there and we waited. *Nobody left.* When the studio was finally open we went in, had our first rehearsal, and everybody fell in love. We had a ball![10]

Even though they did not have gigs scheduled when they began rehearsing, the band was formed to be a performing and touring ensemble. Thad and Mel did not create the group as a rehearsal band, and even though critics and journalists often stated otherwise, the men were adamant about their reasons for forming the band.[11] In an interview with Les Tomkins, Mel emphatically stated, "We are not a rehearsal band. We're an organized, living, working band." Thad echoed Mel's comment stating, "We have never been a rehearsal band. The band wasn't formed just to rehearse. This is a point we've discussed many times."[12]

During the mid-1960s there were several rehearsal big bands in New York City, including bands led by pianist Duke Pearson, tenor saxophonist Clifford Jordan, as well as tenor saxophonist Joe Henderson and trumpeter Kenny Dorham. These bands usually met once a week late at night, and served two purposes. First, the bands were an opportunity for composers to have their new music and arrangements played. Second, they served as a chance for jazz musicians who worked in the daytime studio scene to stretch out and play jazz during the evening. Even though Duke Pearson's band would frequently gig in New York City during the mid-1960s, none of the previously listed bands performed or recorded anywhere to the extent of the Thad Jones/Mel Lewis Orchestra.[13] "I think because so many of the members of the band were the most respected and busy studio musicians in the city, the term 'rehearsal band' was incorrectly applied for years," stated Jerry Dodgion.[14]

To further contradict the rehearsal band label, the group rehearsed only six times before playing their first show.[15] For these rehearsals Thad and Mel had worked out a deal with Phil Ramone, who promised his studio as free rehearsal space if they allowed his recording engineer students to practice their recording skills during the rehearsals. Unfortunately, surviving recordings of these first rehearsals seemingly do not exist. The rehearsals usually began at midnight and went until the early morning hours. Mel commented on the dedication of the band members by saying, "Everybody'd be there. They'd be putting in their whole day at work; they finished rehearsing at four or five in the morning, got home at six and had to be back in their studio jobs by nine or ten a.m. And it wouldn't matter to them at all."[16] These late night rehearsals were usually held at A&R Studios on 48th Street, but also took place at A&R Studios on Seventh Avenue between 51st and 52nd Streets and at Soundmixers Studio at Broadway and 49th Street.[17]

Thad and Mel invited several important guests to witness their new band in action during the December and January rehearsals. WABC disc jockey Alan Grant and *DownBeat* magazine's New York editor Dan Morgenstern visited an early rehearsal and were so amazed by the group that they took it upon themselves to help the band find a gig. Grant and Morgenstern urged Max Gordon, the owner of the Village Vanguard, to book the group on a Monday night in February, as Monday was the slowest night of the week for business. Monday nights at the club were usually jam sessions prior to 1966 and rarely, if ever, did a group of this caliber perform then. Gordon was successfully persuaded to hire the band, and gave them the first three Monday nights in February. To make the booking financially possible for Gordon, each band member agreed to play for only seventeen dollars a night.[18] In addition to his help with the booking, Grant also promoted the band on his weekly radio broadcasts leading up to opening night.[19] Word spread quickly throughout the city that Thad and Mel would be debuting their all-star big band at the Village Vanguard in February.

Another important visitor to the band's first rehearsals was Manny Albam. In addition to previously working with many of the band members on various jazz and studio projects, he was working closely with A&R studio engineer Phil Ramone on the new Solid State record label. In February, as Thad and Mel began looking for a record label for the band, their close friendship with Albam made Solid State a clear favorite.

On Monday night February 7, 1966, the Thad Jones/Mel Lewis Jazz Orchestra made their debut at the Village Vanguard. The group was originally billed as The Jazz Band, but the title quickly changed to the Thad Jones/Mel Lewis Jazz Orchestra because fans and critics usually used Thad and Mel's names when mentioning the group.[20] On opening night, Thad and Mel arrived at the club early in the evening to set up for the performance. Because the Village Vanguard wasn't equipped to handle a big band, they had to bring their own music stands and create makeshift music stand lights so that all eighteen musicians could read their music in the dimly lit club. The two men also had to figure out how to fit a full big band set-up on the small stage of the Vanguard. Eventually, the saxophone chairs and stands were pushed as far as possible to the front of the stage area allowing drums to fit in the far back corner by the trumpet section. After setting up the bandstand, a task that may have been more suited for two engineers, Thad and Mel joined club owner Max Gordon in the back office. Thad recalled the multitude of emotions that he experienced while waiting for the band's first downbeat:

> Mel and I bought music stands, which we hoped were strong enough to hold the music and set them up on the stage. Then around 9 p.m. we sat in the back of the club with Max who was getting more nervous every minute. I told him: "There's no sweat. The people will come." But I was whistling in the dark.
>
> We went on talking for a while, then around 9:30 I heard a buzz from outside. I looked out, and to my amazement, the place was packed. They were four deep on the stairs and when we hit at 10 o'clock it was almost impossible to get through to the bandstand.[20]

Thad and Mel knew from the very first rehearsal that they had assembled an amazing group, yet it wasn't until minutes before their first public performance that they realized New York City would embrace their band. Jazz fans, musicians, and record company executives paid the $2.50 cover charge and crammed into the basement jazz club to witness history.[21] At ten o'clock the orchestra began their first set. In addition to its leaders, Thad conducting and playing cornet and Mel setting the musical pace on drums, the opening-night orchestra consisted of Jimmy Nottingham, Jimmy Owens, Snooky Young, and Bill Berry in the trumpet section; Bob Brookmeyer, Jack Rains, Garnett Brown, and Cliff Heather (bass trombone) in the trombone section; Joe Farrell (tenor), Jerry Dodgion (alto), Eddie Daniels (tenor), Jerome Richardson (alto/soprano), and Marv Holliday (baritone) and possibly Pepper Adams (baritone) in the saxophone section; and joining Lewis in the rhythm section were Hank Jones (piano), Sam Herman (guitar), and Richard Davis (bass).[22]

Jerry Dodgion recalled there being only ten arrangements in the band's book on opening night, yet they still managed to play three sixty-minute sets. Thanks to the level of musicianship in the band, and Thad's ability to conduct and reshape his arrangements during performances, the band could perform the same arrangement twice in a night and not get a complaint from the audience. By replaying certain sections of the arrangement, opening new solo sections, and improvising new backgrounds on the spot, the band almost never played an arrangement the same way twice.[23] Even during that very first night, the music was changing and growing. As Thad stated, "We want to establish a style, a musical pattern. But it should have a lot of elasticity. Once you begin over-listening for something, what you're striving for is gone. And there has to be both freedom and discipline."[24]

With a nearly full audience at all three sets, the Thad Jones/Mel Lewis Orchestra's opening night was a huge success. Jerry Dodgion recalled the excitement at the Vanguard that night,

> I remember the place was packed, I mean *really* packed! After we played that first set, it took us forever to get back to the kitchen because so many people were stopping us to express their delight at the sound of the band. The spirit of the occasion was very memorable and just to be there was a great feeling. Everyone who was at the Vanguard that night knew something very special was happening.[25]

Critics and fans who were lucky enough to witness the band that first night quickly spread word that the new group led by Thad and Mel was the hottest jazz show in town. John S. Wilson was in the audience on opening night and wrote a review for the *New York Times*:

> The all-star band—it includes Bob Brookmeyer, Hank Jones, Richard Davis, Snooky Young, and Jerome Richardson among others—ripped through Thad Jones's provocative, down-to-earth

arrangements with surging joy that one remembers in the early Basie band or Woody Herman's First Herd. Those were young bands whose skills sometimes could not keep up with their desires. But these are old pros, having a wonderful time and rising to each other's challenges.[26]

More than thirty years after that historic night, Alan Grant released a recording titled *Opening Night: Thad Jones/Mel Lewis Big Band February 7, 1966* (Alan Grant Presents). While the recording has been marketed as the only existing one of that evening, saxophonist Jerry Dodgion is not positive that all of the material on the album was from opening night:

> I remember playing "Big Dipper," "All My Yesterdays," "Morning Reverend," "Low Down," "Little Pixie," "Mean What You Say," "Don't Ever Leave Me," and "Willow Weep for Me," which was Brookmeyer's chart. But on the *Opening Night* album that came out several years ago, it contained "Lover Man." That was Joe Farrell's arrangement, and I don't recall playing it until we'd been at the Vanguard for a while. They may have had access to other tapes to put this together, but a lot of people don't have the highest scruples when it comes to releasing something that could make them money.[27]

Additionally, baritone saxophonist Marv Holliday subbed for Pepper Adams at several January rehearsals and is believed to have played in the saxophone section on opening night. Holliday continued to regularly substitute for Pepper, who had previously scheduled tours, until later that summer. The track "Once Around" on *Opening Night* features a baritone solo that is undeniably Pepper Adams, meaning that if indeed Adams did not play on opening night, then "Once Around" was not recorded on February 7.[28] It is possible that Pepper came to the club later that evening and played on the final set; however, those who where in attendance cannot confirm Pepper's involvement. While all the songs on the album may or may not have been from February 7, 1966, Grant did record the band during its first several months at the Village Vanguard. His recordings presented on *Opening Night* are a testament to the band's early greatness and the audience's enthusiasm for the new music.

The band's second Monday night at the Vanguard produced an even larger audience than the first. Lines to get into the first two sets stretched out the door and down Seventh Avenue, causing Gordon to promptly offer the band the Monday night gig on a permanent basis. Thad and Mel gladly accepted.[29]

As a teenager growing up in the New York City area, trombonist John Mosca went to see the band on Monday nights during 1966 and 1967. He remembered the excitement of hearing the band, and in particular Mel's drumming during that time:

> I remember pretty distinctly because it was such a big deal in town. There wasn't all that much happening in 1966 or '67 on the big band front, so it was quite a newsworthy event. There were really long lines to get in, and it was just exciting to be down there. I remember distinctly the first time I heard Mel, how impressed I was with how little he had to play and what he would leave out. It made him different than everybody else you were hearing at that time … and of course the sound of his bass drum in the club. I found out later that he had it tuned below the lowest note on the piano, so it would give that low lift to the band. And the sound of his cymbals too, which those unfortunately were stolen. Those cymbals from the early band were a little bit lighter than the cymbals he played later.[30]

Thanks to the Thad Jones/Mel Lewis Orchestra, Monday quickly became one of the busiest nights of the week at the Vanguard.[31] The band was so successful in February that Gordon gave them a full week at the club, which the band played from Monday, March 7 to Saturday, March 12. The band also made its formal concert debut that month at Hunter College in Manhattan on Friday, March 18.[32]

In April, as the Thad Jones/Mel Lewis Orchestra quickly became the focus of Mel's career he maintained a busy schedule as a studio musician and sideman. Much of his studio work at the time was for Grant and Murtaugh Productions, recording one to four commercial sessions for the company during a normal week.[33] The company was run by two former jazz musicians, John Murtaugh and Hal Grant, and specialized in producing music for commercials. Grant often claimed he hired more jazz musicians than anyone else in the commercials business. In addition to Mel, Grant hired musicians such as Clark Terry, Herbie Hancock, Thad Jones, and Richard Davis.[34] Grant stated, "Your first obligation is to the commercial itself—to pick out the one type of music to give it a new climate. But next, your obligation is to elevate the taste of the listeners."[35] The company's unique philosophy of trying to elevate listeners' taste resulted in a steady source of income for the jazz musicians they hired. Mel worked for Grant and Murtaugh between 1966 and 1970. During that period, the company recorded commercials for brands such as Coca-Cola, Hanes Stockings, Lee's Carpets, Monsanto, Hertz, and Country Club Liquor.[36] Mel's work with the company is yet another example of his incredible versatility as a musician.

Sadly, there is no official documentation of which Grant and Murtaugh commercials Mel recorded during the late 1960s. Most of the time, musicians had no idea what product or brand their recording would be used for. Trumpeter Marvin Stamm worked with Mel on numerous commercial recording sessions, and recalled that studio work in the late 1960s was so frequent that musicians rarely remembered the specifics of a project:

> Most of the studio work I remember doing with Mel was radio or television commercials. Around the time I got there [New York City], we did a number of studio dates, but as far as what they were for I am not sure. Things were so busy at that time that you might have two or three dates a day. If you had a day where you were doing a lot of commercials, you might even have four or five recording sessions a day, starting in the morning and ending in the evening. A lot of the time, with two or three things happening each day, you couldn't even remember what you had done the day before. Everything was flying by so quickly.[37]

Mel played on hundreds, if not thousands, of radio and television commercials during his career, but which exact ones will never be known. As Stamm's comment illustrates, Mel himself most likely did not know the final products of his many hours of studio work.

Mel finished April of 1966 by recording two classic jazz albums in one day, *Thad Jones/Pepper Adams Quintet: Mean What You Say* (Milestone), and *Manny Albam: Brass on Fire* (Solid State). On April 26 he headed into the studios and recorded both albums. From 3:00 p.m. to 6:00 p.m. he was at Plaza Sound Studios recording with Thad and Pepper Adams, and later that evening from 9 p.m. to midnight he recorded his first album with Manny Albam at A&R Studios. Around midnight, after his session with Albam, Mel headed down to Greenwich Village to attend a benefit and jam session at the Village Gate.[38] The day would have seemed like a "career" day for many other drummers, but for Mel, recording two classic albums with two different groups was just a typical day in his life. ‖

1 Bob Brookmeyer soloing with the Thad Jones/Mel Lewis Orchestra in 1966.

Photo by Lee Tanner ©

Used by permission of Lee Tanner.

Chapter 14
The Thad Jones/Mel Lewis Orchestra and Solid State

After the initial success of the Thad Jones/Mel Lewis Orchestra, several record companies quickly approached Thad and Mel about recording the band. Creed Taylor, who was working for Verve at the time, had set up a meeting with Thad and Mel in February of 1966. Both men had previously had their personal and professional disagreements with Taylor, and neither of them was thrilled about attending the meeting. Mel remembered the earlier incident that caused the rift in his relationship with Taylor:

> Creed and I weren't even talking at the time, because we had had scenes at Verve. That's how I ended up not being on Verve anymore. Because when I moved back to New York Creed said, "You'll be my drummer here." But I had a big scene with Stan Getz, he was drunk one night. In fact, I drove him to the date and he was drinking all the way to the date [*Stan Getz: Reflections*]. When we got there he ended up getting in some kind of scenes and started picking on me, because I was the only guy he knew there. And I let him have it, and Creed says, "You can't talk to my star like that." I said, "who the hell are you, you're going to sit here and take shit from him? I ain't going to take any shit from you either." I told them both off ... and I never worked for Creed again.[1]

In the end, Thad did not attend the meeting, leaving Mel to negotiate the possibility of the Thad Jones/Mel Lewis Orchestra recording for Verve. During negotiations, Taylor argued with Mel about the musical direction of the group, and more specifically how much the label should be involved in that musical direction. Not willing to compromise the music, Mel quickly ended the possibility of a recording contract with Verve:

> Thad didn't want to go so I went ... And he (Creed Taylor) said, "The band is fantastic, if we can find a saleable idea." I said, "You

just said so. You said the band was fantastic, what do you need, what's more saleable than that? You're sold on it." He said, "We've got to ... that's not the kind of music we can sell though." I said, "Well that's the type of music we're going to sell Creed. If we can't leave it the way it is then we're not interested. I can't come with you ... Our idea is to play music. We're not looking for anything commercial. Either take it the way it is, or forget it." And it was forget it, and I walked out.[2]

Days after Mel's frustrating meeting with Taylor, he met with Sonny Lester, the head of Solid State Records. During the meeting, Lester promised Mel that if he and Thad signed with Solid State they would be able to maintain the musical direction of the band and that Solid State was only there to record and promote their music, not to tell them how it should sound.[3] Equally important to Thad and Mel was the fact that with Solid State they would be working closely with musical allies Manny Albam and Phil Ramone.

Thad and Mel initially signed a ten-album contract with Sonny Lester and Solid State.[4] Their relationship with the label eventually produced seven albums in four years: three studio albums, two live albums, and two albums featuring vocalists Joe Williams and Ruth Brown. The 1969 sale of Solid State voided their contract before all ten albums were recorded. The musicianship of Albam, combined with recording knowledge of Ramone, allowed the Solid State recordings of the Thad Jones/Mel Lewis Orchestra to properly reflect the precision, creativity, and joyous spirit of the band.

On May 4, 5, and 6, Thad and Mel took the band into A&R Studios to record their debut album *Presenting Thad Jones/Mel Lewis and The Jazz Orchestra* (Solid State). There had been several personnel changes in the band since their live debut in February. Lead trumpet player Danny Stiles temporarily replaced Snooky Young, trumpet player Richard Williams replaced Jimmy Owens, and trombonist Tom McIntosh replaced Garnett Brown. Because studio time was cheaper later at night, the band began recording at 9:00 p.m. and ended around 1:00 a.m. each evening.[5] Eddie Daniels remembered the attitude of the band during their first night of recording:

We never overdid anything, you know, one or two full takes of each song. It was not an overly edited type of band. It was such a gutbucket type of band, and everybody was happy to be there with each other. There was a lot of laughter. It was a band that laughed a lot.[6]

During that first night in the studio, the band recorded Thad's lyrical and hard-swinging original "Kids Are Pretty People" as well as Bob Brookmeyer's masterpiece "ABC Blues," which combined a tone-row melody with variations on blues harmony and form. The next night of recording, May 5, resulted with the recording of two of Thad's original compositions "Don't Ever Leave Me" and "Once Around." "Three and One," "Mean What You Say," "Balanced Scales = Justice," and "Willow Weep for Me" were recorded on May 6, the final night in the studio.[7]

While Thad composed the majority of the music on the album, two other band members made important contributions. Recently added trombonist Tom McIntosh provided his original composition titled "Balanced Scales = Justice."[8] The arrangement's rubato interludes and waltz feel provided a modern framework for solos by Thad, Bob Brookmeyer, and Pepper Adams.

In addition to his composition "ABC Blues," Brookmeyer contributed a ballad arrangement of Ann Ronell's composition "Willow Weep for Me." His use of orchestral inspired textures created an eerie-sounding backdrop for outstanding solos by Thad and Brookmeyer himself. As with Thad's composition "Little Pixie," Brookmeyer had originally arranged "Willow Weep for Me" for the Gerry Mulligan Concert Jazz Band; however, Mulligan hated the arrangement and it was never performed. Brookmeyer rescored the arrangement for full big band, brought it to the Thad Jones/Mel Lewis Orchestra's first rehearsals, and it quickly became a staple in the band's repertoire.[9] It cannot be stressed enough how important Brookmeyer's compositions were to the evolving style of the Thad Jones/Mel Lewis Orchestra. His concepts of harmony, form, and texture both contrasted and complimented Thad's compositional style.[10]

During the summer of 1966 the band performed every Monday night at the Village Vanguard. They performed three sets: the first set started around 10:00 p.m., the second set around 11:30 p.m., and the third set began around 1:00 a.m. attracting local musicians coming from their earlier gigs.[11] The cover charge had risen to three dollars, putting eighteen dollars in the pocket of each band member at the end of the night.[12] The band's music was evolving on a weekly basis, and every performance became a musical adventure for the musicians and the audience. Thanks to the summer influx of tourists visiting the club, articles about the band in *DownBeat* magazine, and their debut studio album, the Thad Jones/Mel Lewis Orchestra began gaining recognition throughout the United States.

The summer also gave the band the opportunity to perform for the first time at the Newport Jazz Festival in Newport, Rhode Island. On Saturday, July 2, the band performed an afternoon set that began with a few instrumental numbers before vocalist Joe Williams joined them and sang several arrangements that Thad had written for the occasion. Williams was always a crowd favorite at Newport, and his vocal performance, coupled with the swing and energy of the band, sent the crowd to their feet in elation.[13] Coming off of their success at Newport, the band made their New York City debut with Williams during an evening concert in Central Park on August 8.[14]

On September 30, 1966, the band returned to A&R Studios to record their second album *Presenting Joe Williams and Thad Jones/Mel Lewis Orchestra* (Solid State). The album featured Thad's arrangements of classic jazz and R&B songs, many which were clearly inspired by his time with Basie, meticulously built to showcase Williams at the height of his powers. On the album's first song "Get Out of My Life Woman," Mel supported Williams and the band with some of his funkiest drumming to date. Even though Mel rarely played in funk or rock styles he was not uncomfortable or unconfident in those realms, once stating in an interview, "I can play the hell out of funk."[15] In addition to his soulful funk playing on the recording, Mel masterfully swung the band through some very mature tempos on "Gee Baby, Ain't I Good to You" and "Come Sunday."

The album also featured the newest member of the band, pianist Sir Roland Hanna. Hanna replaced Hank Jones and brought his blues and gospel-inspired style of piano playing to the Joe Williams record date. Like Jones, Hanna was a masterful pianist as comfortable playing modern jazz as he was playing in the classic stride-piano style. The recording also marked the return of Snooky Young, whose trumpet playing was a hallmark of the band's sound.

Away from the band, Mel continued his work as a sideman and recorded two highly respected albums during the fall of 1966. The first was a small group recording with Eddie Daniels, the young saxophonist in the Thad Jones/Mel Lewis Orchestra. *First Prize* (Prestige) was recorded on September 8 and 12, and was Daniels's first album as a leader. In addition to Mel, the recording included the rest of the Thad Jones/Mel Lewis rhythm section, Roland Hanna on piano and Richard Davis on bass.[16]

Mel's second major recording occurred during October and November with saxophonist James Moody at Plaza Sound Studios in Manhattan. *James Moody: Moody and the Brass Figures* (Milestone) featured Moody and Mel along with the all-star duo of Bob Cranshaw on bass and Kenny Barron on piano. The quartet recorded "Cherokee," "The Moon Was Yellow," "Ruby, My Dear," and Moody's original "Never Again," before being joined by the "Brass Figures." Trombonist and fellow Thad Jones/Mel Lewis Orchestra member Tom McIntosh wrote five arrangements that featured the quartet plus the Brass Figures: Snooky Young, Joe Newman, and Jimmy Owens on trumpet, Jimmy Cleveland on trombone, and Don Butterfield on tuba.[17]

McIntosh's original composition "Smack-A-Mac" opened the album on a very swinging note with Mel playing a beat reminiscent of Sam Woodyard, utilizing his open hi-hat and cross stick. A famous highlight of Mel's playing on the album was his solo introduction to Charlie Parker's bebop classic "Au Privave." With the melodic phrasing of an instrumentalist, Mel played the twelve-measure melody on his cymbals before the ensemble entered with the melody. Mel was not known for being a soloist, yet when he did play a solo, he had the ability to turn the single pitched drums and cymbals into a melodic instrument. Drummer Jeff Hamilton described Mel's introduction on "Au Privave" saying, "His phrasing on the cymbals was like a horn player, he was ghosting and swallowing the notes that were not as important in the phrase."[18] Mel's introduction also stands out because his cymbals were in the key of the song, allowing him to play the pitches of the melody on his cymbals. In a 1969 interview he was asked about his playing on "Au Privave" and specifically how he was able to play the melody on his cymbals. Mel replied, "Those cymbals are sort of freak. They were purchased. I picked them up at the factory. I acquired the two cymbals two years apart. I had no idea that they were relative at all."[19] The interviewer then asked him why there was fabric tape underneath one of the cymbals, Mel responded:

> The cymbal without the tape wasn't right. I put on too much at first, so the cymbal actually became dead. Then I started tearing it off a piece at a time. I play on it a little bit then I tear off another piece. I keep doing that until I reach the sound I want and stop there. In fact, it gets the cymbal down to the pitch I want it to be. On the other hand, with the Chinese cymbal that I have, I experimented

with the number of rivets in that cymbal. I have 27 rivets in that cymbal. I did that the same way—kept adding rivets because they, too, alter the sound of the cymbal. That cymbal I had with Stan? I still have it, only there are two large chunks cut out of it now. That's the one with just two rivets in it. It's a very famous cymbal. I use it a lot on sessions.[20]

His recording with James Moody capped a very busy year. Even with his wide variety of work, it was the development and early success of his band with Thad Jones that defined 1966. The Thad Jones/Mel Lewis Orchestra was the focus of his energy and continued to be for the next thirteen years.

The beginning of 1967 brought a major change to Mel's career when his staff position at ABC Studios was terminated.[21] Even though the job was not always musically satisfying, it had provided steady income that helped him support his family.[22] Mel was not the only staff musician let go by ABC; in fact, in 1967 all of the major studios in New York City (CBS, NBC, ABC) drastically reduced the size of their musical staffs. Much like the Los Angeles studios, the use of electronic instruments and the influence of rock and roll radically changed how many jazz musicians worked in the studios. Marvin Stamm recalled the changing New York City studio scene of the late 1960s:

> Things were starting to change from the big band and orchestra type of style, towards more of the rock field. Around that time the music of the Beatles, and other groups, began to change the landscape of the studio recording business. There were still jazz record projects going on, but it was not necessarily the same group of people that had been busy during the late 50s and early 60s.[23]

Mel continued to play freelance studio work for Peter Matz, Don Elliot, Manny Albam, and Hal Grant for the next several years, but he never held another salaried network job.[24]

In 1967, the business of running the Thad Jones/Mel Lewis Orchestra was the focal point of Mel's life. On February 3, 1967, he and Thad took the next major step as bandleaders and signed papers to incorporate; legally they now operated Thad Jones/Mel Lewis Orchestra Inc.[25] The two men were extremely focused and hoped to begin extensive touring with the band during the year.

In addition to Monday nights at the Village Vanguard, the Thad Jones/ Mel Lewis Orchestra began playing hit and run gigs throughout the Northeast. In the spring of 1967, the most notable of these were a trip to Philadelphia to perform on the *Mike Douglas Show* on January 26, a concert at the Stratford Motor Inn in Bridgeport, Connecticut, on February 14, a dance job at the United Nations on March 3, a concert at Stony Brook College on April 8, and a dance job at the Governor Morris Hotel in Morristown, New Jersey on April 21.[26] In regard to the band playing occasional dance jobs, Mel stated,

> I'd like to see people start dancing to jazz again. Jazz has always been danceable. We're not going to change anything, we have a few concert-type pieces that can't be danced to, and we'll present them that way. Other than that, I'm sure people will be able to dance to our music.[27]

On April 28, the Thad Jones/Mel Lewis Orchestra recorded their third album for Solid State. This time they did not go into the studio; rather they recorded live at the Village Vanguard. The band always performed at its peak on Monday nights at the club, and even though every studio recording the band made was phenomenal, the band's music and spirit were at their best in the live setting. Thad himself once said that the enthusiasm generated by a live audience was more important than the aural control of the studio and that even the band's mistakes were more exciting during a live recording.[28]

Flawlessly recorded by Phil Ramone, *Thad Jones and Mel Lewis: Live at the Village Vanguard* (Solid State) debuted many of the band's most popular songs, such as "A-That's Freedom," "Don't Git Sassy," and "The Little Pixie." Since Alan Grant's album *Opening Night* wasn't released until 2000, *Live at the Village Vanguard* was the first opportunity for many people outside of the New York City area to hear the band in a live setting. The live recording displayed many of the traits that made the band so special: the vocal hollers of joy from the band during Roland Hanna's solo on "Bachafillen," the cohesive playing of the saxophone section during "The Little Pixie," Bob Brookmeyer's beautiful orchestration on his arrangement of "Willow Tree," Mel's swinging shuffle on "Don't Git Sassy," and Thad's intricate and rhythmic writing on "The Little Pixie." Thad's arrangements always contained a tremendous sense of spontaneity, and as Mel explained, Thad's music challenged every member of the band:

He writes the unexpected, interesting under parts, interesting jumps for the guys who are not playing lead. His placing of the notes as opposed to the rests is never obvious. You can't anticipate his charts. He stays away from the eighth rest-dotted quarter note routine. His whole rhythmic conception—the way everything falls—his use of space—it's so beautiful to play from a drummer's standpoint.[29]

It wasn't only Thad's written music that made the recording special, but also his method of reshaping his arrangements during the performance. The unreleased version of "The Second Race" from the *Live at the Village Vanguard* recording, compared to the live version of the same song released a year later on the album *Monday Night*, reveals different tempos, solo orders, and completely different backgrounds behind the trumpet solo. Thad's ability to reshape his arrangements during live performances was a result of his unique conducting style. Using hand signals, he had the ability to select soloists, signal members of the rhythm section to drop out, control dynamics, skip or repeat certain sections of an arrangement, cue the band to play a written insert, or select an individual to improvise a background on the spot.[30] Thad explained his conducting style by saying,

My technique of reshaping things on the stand, by hand signals and such—this represents the way I've always felt that music should be played. I don't think it should ever be confined to any one particular area, one straight and narrow road. No road is ever engineered that perfectly.[31]

Many people knew Thad as a great musician, great writer, and a great cornet player, but they never realized what a great conductor he was.[32] Even though he stood in front of the band as a leader, Thad approached his conducting as if he were a member of the rhythm section, always shaping and developing the music in the moment.[33] Many of the musical aspects that make *Live at the Village Vanguard* so interesting to listen to were a result of Thad's impetuous conducting during the performance.[34]

Thad's spontaneity had an effect on everyone in the band. While all members played their written part with the utmost precision, soloists were given complete creative freedom. In a story that defines the spontaneous atmosphere in the band, Eddie Daniels described the unexpected clarinet solo that changed his career:

> When we did "Little Pixie" on the *Live at the Vanguard* recording, I picked up the clarinet on a whim and played my solo. I had always played a tenor solo, but that night I don't know what got in me! The funny thing was that I won the *DownBeat* new star award for clarinet that year, for those thirty-two bars of "I Got Rhythm." Years later, when I was a guest artist at the Vanguard, Mel told a story that I had never heard. He said that as soon as my clarinet solo on "Little Pixie" was over, Thad leaned over to him and said, "What in the hell did he do that for?" But Thad never complained to me about it, and my clarinet career really took off after that.[35]

While Thad expanded the role of a big band leader with his conducting, Mel further developed the art of big band drumming. Instead of only thinking of himself as the drummer, Mel approached his playing as a member of the trumpet, trombone, and saxophone sections. Marvin Stamm recalled Mel's big band drumming approach:

> The thing that was so amazing about Mel was that he heard everything that was going on in the band. Mel would give it up for the band. In other words, he felt that he was not only a part of the rhythm section, but that he was a part of each section of the band. And depending on which section had the lead, whether it was a sax soli, a trombone soli, or the trumpets were leading the ensemble through the out chorus, Mel knew every part. Inside of what he did, as far as the overall sound of the drums, he would also accentuate things that other drummers would never hear. He would do it so subtly that you felt it more than you heard it. He was just so unique in his ability to be a total part of the orchestration … He never got in the way, and Mel never made the drums a prominent instrument in the band. His sound was always something that the band sat on top of, and he was the most supportive drummer that I have ever heard. For me, I have never heard anyone be so giving musically, as part of a big band. I don't think he ever thought of

himself as a drummer, I think he probably thought of himself as just a band member. But as it ended up, he *was* the band![36]

Mel carefully orchestrated to fully support the band while he simultaneously followed Thad's interactive conducting. Mel respected Thad as much as any musician he ever worked with, and trusted him musically one hundred percent. The two had a constant nonverbal dialog during performances; the connection between them was so strong that a simple look or small gesture could take the music in an entirely new direction.[37] When asked to describe Mel's respect for Thad, Jerry Dodgion emphatically stated, "Mel was in Thad's corner all the way. As far as tempo goes, Mel wouldn't change a tempo for God, but if Thad said, 'Let's pick it up a little right here,' he'd do it!"[38] The two men unselfishly worked together to develop an environment of creativity and freedom within the big band, and the music on *Live at the Village Vanguard* is evidence of their success.

Throughout 1967, Mel's career continued with the usual wide variety of musical work. He played every Monday night at the Vanguard with the Thad Jones/Mel Lewis Orchestra, played a week-long engagement at the Riverboat Room in Manhattan, made an appearance at the first annual Spring Jazz Festival at the State University of New York in Albany, worked with Richard Davis and Peter Matz on the *Kraft Music Hall* television program, and recorded several jazz albums for Solid State.[39]

The most notable albums he recorded for the label in 1967 were *Jimmy McGriff: A Bag Full of Blues* (Solid State) and *Dizzy Gillespie: Jazz for a Sunday Afternoon* (Solid State) also titled *Dizzy Gillespie: Live at the Village Vanguard* (Blue Note). The latter was an afternoon jam session recorded live at the Village Vanguard that featured the rare combination of Mel on drums, Richard Davis on bass, Chick Corea on piano, Garnett Brown on trombone, Ray Nance on violin, Pepper Adams on baritone saxophone, and Dizzy Gillespie on trumpet. "Sweet Georgia Brown" "and "Tour De Force" displayed swinging drumming by Mel as he accompanied exciting solos from Dizzy, Pepper, and twenty-six-year-old prodigy Chick Corea.

Jazz for a Sunday Afternoon is well known amongst jazz drummers because it featured the playing of both Mel Lewis and Elvin Jones. Mel was the drummer hired for the date, but during the lengthy jam session Elvin came down to listen and Mel invited him to sit in. On "Birk's Works" and "Lullaby of the Leaves" Elvin is heard playing on Mel's bebop-size Gretsch kit (14 X 18" bass drum, 8 X 12" mounted tom, 14 X 14" floor tom, and 5 ½ X 14" snare drum), several of Mel's cymbals (left side ride and hi-hats), and Dizzy Gillespie's famous Chinese cymbal set-up as the main ride cymbal on his right. Even with the tone of Mel's drums and distinct sound of Dizzy's Chinese cymbal (which Elvin played nearly the entire time) the touch, phrasing, and vocabulary were pure Elvin. The recording reveals many interesting similarities between Mel and Elvin's playing, including: the broadness of their cymbal beats and the nearly constant underlying feel of 12/8, the wide range of dynamics they used while maintaining a personal sound out of the drums and cymbals, their soft use of the bass drum while keeping time, the ability to play a non-repetitive cymbal beat that still provided a strong quarter note pulse and forward momentum, and their use of the Chinese cymbal behind Dizzy. Mel and Elvin sounded remarkably similar, no one would mistake them for each other, but the recording revealed two drummers with a parallel musical concept. ‖

*See Appendix Transcriptions and Listening Guides for this chapter: "Three and One"

1 The Thad Jones/Mel Lewis Jazz Orchestra performing in Europe 1969.

Used by permission of the University of Missouri-Kansas City Libraries,
Dr. Kenneth J. LaBudde Department of Special Collections.

Chapter 15
Thad and Mel Hit the Road, and the Road Hits Back

1968 marked the first time that the Thad Jones/Mel Lewis Orchestra took extended tours of the United States and Japan. The tour of the United States began on April 20 with a performance at the second annual Bay Area Jazz Festival in Berkeley, California. Joe Williams was the guest vocalist with the band, which included several new members, including Danny Moore and Randy Brecker on trumpet, and Seldon Powell taking the place of Joe Farrell in the saxophone section. From Berkeley the band traveled to San Francisco to perform on Ralph J. Gleason's television show *Jazz Casual*.[1] The group performed "Just Blues," "St. Louis Blues," "Kids Are Pretty People," and "Don't Git Sassy." The entire performance, plus on-air interviews with Thad, Mel, and Brookmeyer, has been reissued on DVD and is the earliest commercially available footage of the band.[2] After the band taped their afternoon performance, they traveled to Los Angeles for an evening performance at the club Marty's on the Hill. The band performed at the club from Monday, April 22, through Saturday, April 27, before heading back home to New York City.[3]

On June 18 and July 2, the band recorded their second album featuring a vocalist, this time with the versatile singer Ruth Brown. Ruth Brown had recorded nearly one hundred jazz and R&B sides for Atlantic records between 1949 and 1961 and was one of the top-selling female recording artists of the early 1950s. *The Big Band Sound of Thad Jones/Mel Lewis featuring Miss Ruth Brown* (Solid State) was an opportunity for Brown to reestablish her career after a brief retirement. Thad wrote all of the arrangements for the album, and similar to the Joe Williams recording the year before, his writing showcased Brown's earthy voice and soulful phrasing. Her voice was a perfect match for the band and Mel always considered the album an artistic success, even though it wasn't the crossover hit that he, Thad, or Sonny Lester hoped it would be.[4]

The same week they finished recording with Ruth Brown, the band was scheduled to depart on their first extensive tour of Japan. Lacking proper management, Thad and Mel had decided to book the tour themselves with the help of Elvin Jones's wife Keiko, Thad's sister-in-law. Keiko was from Japan, so it made perfect sense that she set up the tour. Throughout May and June, Thad and Mel made plans for the two-week tour and looked forward to spreading their music to a new part of the world.

The band originally planned to leave New York City on July 4, but that date was pushed back one week, and July 11 became the new departure date.[5] As the band members arrived at LaGuardia airport there was a very jovial mood among them. Jerry Dodgion recalled the atmosphere by saying, "The first day we went to the airport, we didn't have banners, but it was very exciting and we had lots of relatives, kids, and dogs to see us off."[6] But as Dodgion and the rest of the band soon learned, there were no airline tickets reserved for them. As the musicians waited around to see if they would make their flight, they took shifts calling their families and friends on the airport pay phone. It was directly after a call to his wife that Dodgion learned that something more serious was wrong with the trip:

> I had just finished talking to my wife on the payphone when Thad walked over. He went to the phone right next to me and said, "I'm going to call Elvin." So I hear him dial the number, and say, "Hello Elvin, Thad. Do you know any good spirituals?" And he said it in a very serious voice! So they talked for a while and I didn't listen to their conversation, but I remember the stern tone of his voice and his words so well.[7]

After a call to Keiko in Japan, Thad and Mel were told that there was a problem with the money for the airfare, but the band's tickets would be ready and waiting for them the next day. In what had to be a very defeating turn of events, they were forced to tell the band members that they would not be flying out until the next morning. The enthusiasm of the musicians had been drained, and everyone left the airport trying to stay positive, but a bit discouraged.[8]

The next morning, the band once again assembled at LaGuardia to fly to Japan. As Dodgion recalled, "The second day we show up, there were fewer people seeing us off, fewer relatives and kids, and no dogs!"[9] Unbelievably, Thad and Mel found out that they still did not have tickets to Japan. They had to quickly figure out what to do, as the tour was beginning to look like a disaster to their band members. Thad was confident that once the band got to Japan everything would be fine and the tour would be a success. Dodgion later explained that even

147

though the flights were a mess, the band did not have many concerns about the rest of the tour. "It was common knowledge that Keiko had a wealthy father in Japan who was a big shoe manufacturer in Yokahama, so the band wasn't too worried," said Dodgion.[10] After much deliberation between Thad and Mel, Red Keller, the band's road manager, stepped in with an idea that the men hadn't thought of. Keller suggested that if they were truly confident that there was money to be made in Japan, they purchase the band's airfare with their personal credit cards. In a move that could be described as either extremely dedicated or incredibly foolish, Thad and Mel split the band's airfare on their credit cards and booked one-way tickets to Japan. With each ticket costing hundreds of dollars, both men were thousands of dollars in debt before even leaving New York City.[11]

On the evening of July 13, the band finally arrived in Japan and stayed at a hotel near the airport. Many band members including Thad, Mel, Richard Davis, Snooky Young, Garnett Brown, Eddie Daniels, and Seldon Powell had brought their wives on the trip, and that first night at the hotel was a much-needed opportunity for everyone to relax and enjoy a nice dinner.[12] The next day, the band traveled into Tokyo to begin their two-week, thirteen-concert tour of Japan.

When meeting with Keiko in Tokyo, Thad and Mel abruptly learned that nearly all of their scheduled performances had been canceled, or were possibly never booked in the first place. If the lack of airline tickets in New York was viewed as a minor hitch in plans, then the news of canceled concerts was cause for major concern. By this time it was obvious that even though Keiko had the best intentions, the money for the tour did not exist, and she was simply too embarrassed or scared to tell anyone that the tour was never properly scheduled. The truth was, as Dodgion recalled, "Keiko always maintained that her father was a rich shoe manufacturer, which is true, but she never told anybody that he disowned her when she started going with Elvin Jones!"[13] With only one or two scheduled performances, it was evident to Thad and Mel that there would be no money coming in during their time in Japan. They contacted the U.S. State Department to see what could be done about the canceled concert dates; however, because there were no signed contracts for any of their "scheduled" concerts there was nothing the State Department could do to help.[14]

While all of these issues were piling up on Thad and Mel, the rest of the band was making the best of the bad situation. Even with canceled performances and money issues, Eddie Daniels recalled that everyone had a great time on the trip.[15] Thad and Mel surely had less of a great time as they were forced to pay for the hotel rooms out of pocket and tried to set up as many gigs in Tokyo as they could on short notice. When all was said and done, the band only performed two or three times in Tokyo and never had the opportunity to travel to the other cities on the itinerary.[16]

After about a week in Japan Thad and Mel finally decided to cut the trip short, but because they couldn't afford to purchase airfare again, they were forced to find another option to pay for the group's tickets back home. It was not an option to ask the band members to pay their own way; the two men had to save face and luckily they found an option. During their time in Tokyo, they had met and spent time with the famous jazz photographer K. Abe. Abe was an ally and friend to Thad and Mel during their time in Tokyo. He translated Japanese for them and also helped by trying to book them gigs in the city. When Abe learned that the men did not have enough money to pay for the band to return to the United States, he offered to pay for all of the airfare using his life savings. Thad and Mel accepted his gracious offer and agreed to pay him back in full once they returned to New York.

K. Abe purchased the band's tickets, and after a Japanese vacation that happened to include a couple of gigs and no income, the band returned to New York City. While they didn't leave their mark on Japan as they had hoped, the band certainly made history on their trip home. Dodgion summed up the trip with a story he learned weeks after returning home:

> Eddie Daniels stayed in Japan an extra week, because he was making an album there. Eddie said that when he came back it was also on Northwest Orient Airlines out of Seattle. When he landed back in Seattle and went through customs, a man working in customs said to him, "Say, weren't you with that band that went over to Japan and they came back last week?" And Eddie responded, "Yeah I was with the band." The man replied, "Did you know you made history in the airlines?" Eddie said, "What do you mean?" The man then told him, "There was more alcohol consumed on the band's return flight from Japan to Seattle than in the history of the whole airline!"[17]

In the end, the tour was a disappointment for Thad and Mel, but everyone in the band remained positive despite the circumstances. Mel summed up the trip saying,

Thad and I, it ended up costing us $30,000, we had to pay Northwest Airlines. These guys [band members] didn't get paid, but they got their expenses paid, we covered their hotel bills, we covered their wives' tickets, you know. They had a few days in Japan; they had a good time. There was no work, they knew we got burned terrible. It was poor judgment on our part, but we were all so eager at the time.[18]

Thad and Mel had used very little business sense and lost a lot of money as a result. In order to pay off his credit card debt and reimburse K. Abe, Mel took out a second mortgage on his home in Irvington.[19] The trip was a learning experience for the new leaders, and made it apparent that if they were to tour successfully in the future, they'd need the assistance of a booking agency to take care of the details.

After returning from Japan, Mel recorded several albums in New York City during the late summer and fall of 1968, the first being *Jimmy McGriff: The Worm* (Solid State). It has become one of Mel's most well-known small group recordings from the 1960s. Recorded in August for Sonny Lester and Solid State, *The Worm* exhibited a soulful mix of funk, jazz, and gospel music. From the hard swing of the song "Keep Loose," to the gritty funk of "The Worm," Mel played with intensity on six of the album's eight songs. In addition to the previously listed songs, his drumming can also be heard on "Think," "Girl Talk," "Heavyweight," and "Lock It Up." Mel was always proud of his playing on the album and stated, "I am on the record called *The Worm*, but they got my name down and Grady Tate, a lot of people don't realize that I'm on three quarters of the album. The only two tracks he's on are the ones that sound like the white drummer. It's true."[20] The fact remains that no matter if Mel was white, brown, or purple, his drumming on *The Worm* was swinging and very funky.

Mel recorded Stanley Turrentine's album *Always Something There* (Blue Note) in October 1968, at Rudy Van Gelder's studio in New Jersey. The album contained Thad Jones's arrangements of popular rock songs such as the Beatles "Hey Jude" and the Doors' "Light My Fire." The arrangements were scored for an eleven-piece jazz group and string section, and while the players were fantastic and the concept a good one, overall the album was not a hit. Even so, Mel's musical interaction with pianists Hank Jones and Herbie Hancock on the date is well worth a listen.

On Monday, October 21, Mel recorded his second live album at the Village Vanguard with the Thad Jones/Mel Lewis Orchestra. Simply titled *Monday Night* (Solid State) the album was the band's third instrumental album for Solid State, and included Thad's compositions "Say It Softly," "Mornin' Reverend," "Kids Are Pretty People," "The Second Race," and "The Waltz You Swang for Me." "St. Louis Blues," Bob Brookmeyer's final written contribution to the band before he left for the West Coast was also featured. The recording showcased the band's new tenor player Seldon Powell on "The Second Race," contained what many consider the definitive version of "Kids Are Pretty People," and included "Mornin' Reverend," Thad's first recorded arrangement that mixed jazz and funk styles.[21] With the exception of its inclusion in Mosaic's *The Complete Solid State Recordings of the Thad Jones/Mel Lewis Orchestra*, the album *Monday Night* has never been reissued, making it quite possibly the band's least known Solid State album.

Monday Night reflected several major changes in the band's personnel. A month prior to the recording, founding member Bob Brookmeyer moved to Los Angeles and accepted a steady television studio job with the *Merv Griffin Show*.[22] Brookmeyer was replaced by Jimmy Knepper, a trombone legend in his own right. The loss of Brookmeyer's trombone playing was felt, but his absence as an arranger was even more noticeable. Thad and Mel did not necessarily need Brookmeyer in the band as a soloist because the group was stocked with great soloists. However, the fact remained that Brookmeyer's brilliant arrangements were a defining and important part of the band's early sound. Guitarist, auxiliary percussionist, and music copyist Sam Herman was also no longer in the band, marking the first time that the rhythm section consisted of only piano, bass, and drums. The change gave the rhythm section freedom musically, and created the space for Mel and Roland Hanna to accompany in a more modern and interactive fashion.

Throughout Mel's career, the months of January, February, and March were consistently the slowest months for performing opportunities, and 1969 proved to be no exception. Aside from the studio work that came his way, Mel's sideman work was fairly slow and he remained focused on his band. The Thad Jones/Mel Lewis Orchestra continued to perform every Monday night at the Village Vanguard and, thanks to their three years of success at the club, found themselves to be the leaders of an unexpected big band resurgence in New York City.

The spring of 1969 was a changing time in the New York City jazz scene. The avant-garde music forged by John Coltrane was a heavy influence on many musicians, as were the growing popularity of jazz/fusion music and the use of electronic instruments. Despite the new influences vying to take over the jazz scene, big bands slowly started to gain popularity again. The Thad Jones/Mel Lewis Orchestra was making the Village Vanguard profitable on Monday nights, and their success helped to generate other weekly big band gigs throughout the city.[23] Additionally, many of the best jazz musicians in the city started writing big band arrangements, hoping to have them performed or recorded by these bands. One example of this was tenor saxophonist Wayne Shorter, who wrote an arrangement of his composition "Dolores" for the Thad Jones/Mel Lewis Orchestra. Ultimately, the arrangement was never recorded, but Thad recalled Shorter's writing:

> Wayne Shorter is a coming star in the writing business. We are rehearsing a piece of his called Dolores. He doesn't write easy, rhythmically or harmonically. You have to work it out with the band and with the section you play in, in order to really comprehend what he's doing. Once it hits you, it really knocks you out.[24]

During this period of 1969, Thad and Mel did not lead the only big band in New York City performing new music, just what most considered the best. Thad's writing and conducting and Mel's drumming were on the forefront of what many hoped would be the next great era of big bands. Other bands that held weekly gigs in 1969 included the Clark Terry Big B-A-D Band, which performed Monday nights at Club Baron on Lenox Avenue in Harlem. In February 1967, the Duke Pearson Big Band began performing regularly at the Half Note, and by April of 1969, the band performed every Sunday night at the Village Vanguard.[25] In 1969, Pearson commented on the changing jazz scene and resurgence of New York big bands:

> I've noticed from some of the smaller groups I've heard over the past couple of years, that it is time for the big band once again, and I think that in the near future the public will accept big bands more than they will smaller groups, mainly because of the music the small bands are playing. It seems that no one knows exactly

what to play these days as far as a small group conception is concerned; you don't know if it's avant-garde, or a holdover from the bebop days, or the post-bop era.[26]

While Pearson's prediction did not come true, his statement reflected the somewhat uncertain direction of jazz music in the late 1960s and early 1970s. In the end, big bands gained more exposure in the jazz community, but did not create much renewed interest from the general public. Pearson continued to lead his big band, which also contained many members of the Jones/Lewis Orchestra, until 1972, and Clark Terry led his Big B-A-D Band through most of the 1970s. But it was Thad and Mel who were able to create a band and music that ultimately stood the test of time.[27]

Thad Jones/Mel Lewis Jazz Orchestra: Central Park North (Solid State) was recorded on June 17–18 and is an album that reflected the changing New York City jazz scene of 1969. The funkier rock influenced tracks such as "Central Park North," "Jive Samba," and "Tow Away Zone" featured the sound of electric rhythm guitar played by Barry Galbraith and Sam Brown, the use of electric bass by Richard Davis, and Mel's rare use of a metal shell snare drum and a muffled bass drum.[28] Thad's compositions seemed to be an experiment of mixing the traditional timbre of a big band with the modern sound of electric instruments and funk music. While certain aspects of the instrumentation sound dated, the creativity and ingenuity of Thad's arrangements cannot be denied.[29]

In addition to Thad's new arrangements and the modified instrumentation, the recorded sound of the band was much different than previous albums. Thad and Mel's favorite recording engineer Phil Ramone had begun working more with rock and pop acts and was not available for the session.[30] Engineer Don Hahn is widely believed to have been the engineer at the session; however, in a 1974 interview Thad stated that was not the case. When asked to name his least satisfying album made by his band, Thad replied,

> I'd have to say *Central Park North*, engineering-wise. There was a screw-up in engineers. We had asked for Donny Hahn, but ended up with someone else. To make a long story short, Donny eventually re-mixed the album and saved it. Good thing too, 'cause the guys played like sons o' bitches on that album.[31]

Judging from Thad's comment, the final sound of the album is a credit to the mixing abilities of Don Hahn. While the recording doesn't have the open sonic quality that Ramone produced on the band's early albums, the engineering didn't overshadow Thad's music and band's fantastic interpretation of it.

Mel's drumming on *Central Park North* was at its peak as he swung the band with his ride cymbal beat and propelled the soloists with his interactive drumming. "Big Dipper," "Central Park North," "Quietude," and Thad's arrangement of Jerome Richardson's composition "Groove Merchant" displayed great playing by Mel and proved to be the most popular songs on the album. All three of the charts became staples of the band's repertoire, and to this day, are still performed on Monday nights by the Vanguard Jazz Orchestra, the modern day extension of the Thad Jones/Mel Lewis Orchestra.

After staying in New York for the remainder of June and July, Mel and the band spent much of the remainder of 1969 touring Europe. During the band's first three years the personnel had remained fairly consistent, but the European tour in August brought several new musicians into the group. Mel's friend from the Kenton Orchestra, Al Porcino, had joined the trumpet section and played the second part under lead trumpeter Snooky Young. Saxophonist Joe Farrell had been back with the band on tenor for the *Central Park North* recording, but left soon after, and was replaced by tenor saxophone legend Joe Henderson. Henderson joined the band for the August tour and stayed on the first tenor part for the remainder of 1969.[32]

On August 24, the tour began with a six-night engagement at Ronnie Scott's, London's most famous jazz club. After London, the band performed one night in Birmingham, England, before beginning a two-week stretch that took them all over Europe. Between September 2 and September 14, the band performed in Sweden, Denmark, Germany, France, Amsterdam and Switzerland.[33] Eddie Daniels recalled the tour and Joe Henderson's musical contribution, saying, "The band played at a very high level during that tour and the energy of Joe Henderson's solos really pushed the band to new heights.[34]

Many of the countries' state-sponsored radio and television networks broadcast the band's tour performances. As was often the case, no official studio recordings were made during the tour. Yet years later, record labels released recordings of the live radio broadcasts. *Thad Jones/Mel Lewis Orchestra: Paris 1969—Volume 1* (Royal Jazz) was recorded during the band's Paris concert on September 8. In addition to a very cohesive ensemble, the album featured

154

standout solos by Henderson, Hanna, and Thad. *Paris 1969—Volume 1* is out of print, but worth finding because it features outstanding audio quality with Mel's drums and cymbals very prominent in the mix. Another recording that resulted from the tour is titled *Thad Jones-Mel Lewis Orchestra: Basle 1969* (TCB). It was recorded in Basle, Switzerland, on September 11 and while the audio quality is far from pristine, it features an outstanding performance by Joe Henderson on Thad's blues "The Second Race."

The band's first European tour was much more successful than the previous year's Japan trip, but as Jerry Dodgion stated, "How could it not be?"[35] After spending October and November in the States, the band headed back to Europe in December of 1969 for yet another extended tour. The tour was officially titled "Jazz Wave" and was paid for by United Artists, the parent company of the Solid State record label.[36] In addition to the Thad Jones/Mel Lewis Orchestra, the concerts were headlined by a small group consisting of Freddie Hubbard on trumpet, Stanley Turrentine on saxophone, Ron Carter on bass, Louis Hayes on drums, Kenny Burrell on guitar, Jimmy McGriff on organ, and Jeremy Steig on flute.[37]

The tour's opening performance was on December 6, in Copenhagen, Denmark. Following Denmark, the musicians spent a week playing concerts throughout Germany, Italy, and France. After their engagement in Paris, the tour headed to England to play two very important concerts, one in Manchester and the other at Royal Festival Hall in London. But as Mel later explained, that was when the tour got very interesting:

> Now we were in Paris two nights before and we get on the airplane, we check all our equipment, everything. All our instruments, the book, the works. Everything is checked, the plane takes off, we arrive in Manchester, England and find out that they (the airline) went on strike while our stuff was on the ground. They let us go, but they kept everything. We didn't have anything, not even the bass, we had nothing.[38]

Concert promoters found Mel a drumset, and remarkably the orchestra played their portion of the concert in Manchester. Of course with no music, Thad and the rest of the band had to carefully fake arrangements right on stage, much to Mel's chagrin:

So we get to Manchester, no instruments. They borrow a set of drums for me and we faked a concert up there. Which was no good. Because with all these top-drawer musicians we had they didn't know too much about small group stuff, and Thad starts saying, "Let's play 'Straight No Chaser,'" and that stuff, you know. He tried to actually fake through his arrangements, but nobody remembered those parts, those weird parts, impossible. So it was a little messy.[39]

After creatively making it through the concert in Manchester, the band hoped that their music and instruments would arrive in London before they did. Unfortunately, upon arrival they still had no music or equipment, causing Thad and Mel to debate what to do during the concert that evening at Royal Festival Hall. Mel wanted to tell the audience, some seven thousand people, that their music had been lost due to the airline strike and then perform much like they did the night before, minus the pressure of having to lie to the public.[40] Mel also took into account that earlier in the year the band had played a very successful week at Ronnie Scott's and that the London fans and critics would know that the band was not playing their usual music. On the other hand, Thad was convinced that the band should go on with the concert and that the audience did not need an explanation. In the end, Thad got his way and the band performed without explaining to the audience about their lost music.[41] Mel colorfully described the situation,

Thad starts calling these fake tunes on the stage at Royal Festival Hall. I said to him, "Why don't you tell the audience what happened, so that they'll understand why they're not hearing of your charts." He says, "Fuck 'em." That's his words. I said, "Wrong." He says, "We'll put on a concert for them." Ego, right? All right, so he's entitled. If I'm entitled, he's entitled. It was all right; again it was nothing but solos and everybody playing unison on bebop tunes. It was stupid.[42]

Eddie Daniels also recalled the concert at Royal Festival Hall:

We didn't know any of the band's arrangements by heart, so Thad would count something off and somebody would play a solo right out of the gate. Then he'd sing a lick to the trumpets, and they would grab it. Then he would sing another lick to the saxophones. It was like he was composing live, and we were picking it up out of his mouth. And we're just making up a chart live! And the players were all such great players that it worked. It would have been nice for the audience to hear the arrangements, because of the record being out, but we had no choice … It was scary and exciting, a great and hilarious moment![43]

After the London concerts, the band got their music and instruments back and the tour ended without any further complications. Mel and the band returned to New York City in December just in time for the holidays.

As 1969 ended, so did a very busy decade for Mel. In a ten-year span he had propelled himself to the top of the jazz field, recorded hundreds of albums, toured the world, and most importantly, moved back to the East Coast and started his band with Thad Jones. Mel achieved more between the years 1959 and 1969 than most successful musicians achieve over a lifetime of work. ‖

1 Mel performing with his band at the Village Vanguard in 1971. *Photo by Matthias Kuert © Used by permission of Matthias Kuert.*

2 Recording *Suite for Pops* in 1972. *Used by permission of the University of Missouri-Kansas City Libraries,*

Dr. Kenneth J. LaBudde Department of Special Colle

3 Thad Jones and Mel Lewis publicity sho*t* 1974. *Photo by Chuck Stewart © Used by permiss Chuck Stewart.*

Chapter 16
The Youth Movement

By most accounts, the four-year relationship between Thad, Mel, and Solid State producer Sonny Lester was always a good one. Lester had the reputation of often being overbearing as a producer; yet with Thad and Mel, he seemed to give unprecedented freedom in the studio. Mel recalled Lester's hands-off approach saying, "Manny Albam had more to say at our dates. Sonny sort of stood in the back and kept looking at his watch once in a while."[1] Lester never pressured Thad or Mel to make commercial music, and other than his occasional request for one or two standards per album, he let the men be as creative as they desired.

Sadly, January of 1970 marked the beginning of the end of the Thad Jones/Mel Lewis Orchestra's successful association with Lester. After the merger of United Artist Records and Liberty Records in late 1969, Solid State, the jazz division of United Artist, was merged into Liberty Records' more prestigious jazz label Blue Note.[2] The merger resulted in the cancelation of Thad and Mel's contract with Solid State, but before they left the label they made one more recording that was released on Blue Note titled *Thad Jones/ Mel Lewis: Consummation* (Blue Note).

On January 20, 1970, the Thad Jones/Mel Lewis Orchestra recorded Thad's original compositions "Dedication" and the title track "Consummation." Both arrangements incorporated the additional instrumentation of four French horns and tuba, creating a thick and lush sound. On January 21, the band recorded Thad's arrangements "It Only Happens Every Time" and "Tip Toe."[3]

"Tip Toe" was one of the band's rare arrangements that featured Mel as a soloist. After a technically challenging trombone soli, Mel and the ensemble traded phrases through the thirty-two measure "rhythm changes" song form. Mel expertly used his brushes to solo and set up the band figures as they seamlessly went in and out of double-time. In his instructional book *It's Time for the Big Band Drummer*, Mel provided a written commentary explaining how he approached the trading chorus on "Tip Toe." One description of his thought process was, "I pay close attention to the band figures and play in a call and response style. This first solo should be double-time in response to the band."[4] Mel then described another section of ensemble trading by stating, "I must be very simple here as my fill will lead into seventeen musicians picking a single note out of thin air! The fill must be accurate and definite."[5] "Tip Toe" was custom made for Mel's drumming, and after its initial recording on *Consummation*, he continued to play the arrangement for the rest of his career. He loved the challenge of finding new ways of filling the solo breaks while still playing simply enough to support and lead the ensemble into their written figures.

The band recorded the saxophone section feature "Fingers" on January 28, 1970. "Fingers" was also based on "rhythm changes" and became one of the band's most performed up-tempo pieces, featuring a superlative sax soli and the technical prowess of the entire group. Following the recording on January 28, the band took a lengthy break from the studio. Finally on May 25, they returned to A&R Studios and finished *Consummation* by recording "Ahunk Ahunk," "Us," and Thad's ballad "A Child Is Born."[6] Thad and Mel were always very proud of *Consummation*, and rightfully so, as the album was a successful mixture of ballads, bossa nova, swing, and funk styles.[7] The album marked the band's official departure from Solid State, and to many, the end of the band's first era.

Consummation garnered praise within the music industry and was nominated for a 1971 Grammy in the Best Large Jazz Ensemble category.[8] The Thad Jones/Mel Lewis Orchestra had been nominated for several Grammy Awards throughout the 1960s, but the Duke Ellington Orchestra frequently won in the category of Best Large Jazz Ensemble. Even though Thad and Mel wanted a Grammy, they never felt bad about losing to Ellington because they greatly admired him and the musicians in his band. In February 1971, Thad and Mel spent their own money to travel to Los Angeles and attend the Grammy Awards with hopes of winning their first award and finally receiving larger recognition for their music. When the winner was announced, Thad and Mel received a shock when Miles Davis and his album *Bitches Brew* won the Grammy for Best Large Jazz Ensemble. One can only imagine the thoughts that were racing through Mel's head. *Bitches Brew* represented almost everything he felt was wrong with modern jazz including electronic instruments, the influence of rock music, and the use of tape editing to create the final "performance." Jerry Dodgion remembered Mel's reaction as well as the band's response to losing the Grammy:

> Oh man, that really pissed us off! And Mel was really pissed off because *Bitches Brew* was not a big band; it was thirty-four sessions

of overdubs. No arrangements or anything. But you see Columbia Records was a voting block. The Columbia Records Company had all their employees join NARAS, and when they needed to push someone for a Grammy, they had all their employees vote. So Columbia had their employees who were on NARAS vote for *Bitches Brew*, and we hadn't a chance. That's not really kosher, but it happens.[9]

Adding to the disappointment of the Grammy Award, the remainder of 1971 was a slower year for the band. They remained a strong draw on Monday nights at the Village Vanguard, but with no major tour or recording planned Thad and Mel began to see increased turnover in the band's personnel. When the band assembled for its first rehearsal in 1965, almost every member of the band was an established jazz musician who made his living in the New York City studios. In 1971, the band began a major transition from many of those more established players to younger players who were eager to prove their worth with one of the best big bands in the world. While founding members Jerry Dodgion, Eddie Daniels, Snooky Young, and Richard Davis were still mainstays, by the fall of 1971, younger players such as tenor saxophonist Billy Harper and twenty-year-old trumpet prodigy Jon Faddis were making their mark with the band.[10]

After having led the band for over five years Thad and Mel welcomed these young musicians. Both men were such strong musicians and leaders that even personnel changes did not disrupt their musical focus. Mel continued to be the engine that drove the band on stage, and Thad continued to lead not only with his writing and conducting, but also his playing. Jerry Dodgion recalled the immense inspiration that Thad's playing had on the band:

> Well, over my twelve and a half years we must have played Brookmeyer's arrangement of "Willow Weep for Me" two hundred times. Thad played the melody on it, and he never played the melody the same way twice. I mean never! And his little improvised fill on the ending chord was always, *always*, something different. He was amazing.
>
> He was just such a great improviser and everybody in the band really listened closely when he played. When the band came in and played after his solos, it sounded *really* good. I remember

one night after we played in San Jose, California, Thad came up to me and said, "Gosh, we didn't sound so good tonight." And I said, "I know why!" He said, "*why, why*, I don't understand?" I said, "We didn't sound inspired because you didn't play much tonight. And when you play, we play better." And Thad said, "Oh no, that's totally silly." He didn't see the logic in that at all, but it was true. He played so inventive that even on songs that he must have played hundreds of times, he never repeated himself. Mel's drumming was the same way, it was always creative and always evolving.[11]

By the end of 1971, A&M Records was the new record label of the Thad Jones/Mel Lewis Orchestra. A&M was co-founded by Herb Alpert and Jerry Moss in 1962 and, in only a decade, had become one of the most powerful record labels in the business. In January of 1972, the band began recording their first album for the label titled *Suite for Pops* (A&M). Thad's new arrangements were the result of a commission offered to him the previous year by trumpeter Joe Newman, the president of Jazz Interactions in New York at the time.[12] The arrangements were written as a tribute to Louis Armstrong, who had recently passed away, but unlike many tributes that dealt with songs associated with Armstrong, or transcriptions of his playing, Thad created original music that he said was "reflective of what I remember about Louis."[13] It had been a year and a half since the recording of *Consummation* and Mel and the band were excited to get back into the studio.[14]

On January 25 and 26 they recorded "Meetin' Place" and "The Summary." Both songs featured new members of the band including Faddis, Harper, Cecil Bridgewater on trumpet, and Ed Xiques on alto saxophone. After the departure of alto saxophonist Jerome Richardson, Jerry Dodgion took over the lead alto chair and Xiques took over Dodgion's second alto part. Vocalist Dee Dee Bridgewater, then wife of trumpeter Cecil Bridgewater, had joined the band the previous month and was the first fulltime vocalist whom Thad and Mel hired.[15] Gary McFarland's composition "Toledo by Candlelight" and Jones's "The Great One" were recorded on January 31 and displayed a commanding performance by the rising star vocalist. Dee Dee Bridgewater's ability to blend her voice into the band's sound was also displayed on "The Great One," as she delivered soul and feeling without ever singing a lyric.[16]

With four songs recorded for *Suite for Pops*, the band took an eight-month hiatus from the studio and would not return until later that fall. In the meantime,

Mel spent the spring of 1972 playing a number of commercial sessions for multi-track recording pioneer Don Elliot, playing small group dates with the Thad Jones/Pepper Adams Quintet, and holding down his steady gig at the Vanguard. He and Thad also began preparing for the band's upcoming tour of the Soviet Union in March.

Exactly ten years after he toured the Soviet Union with Benny Goodman, Mel returned to the country on another State Department tour, this time as co-leader of the Thad Jones/Mel Lewis Orchestra. After the band learned of their five-week tour, they added a ten-night engagement at Ronnie Scott's in London to begin the tour. The band departed New York's JFK airport on March 16 and, after arriving in London, enjoyed two days off in the city. Their run at Ronnie Scott's from March 20 to March 30 was an opportunity for the band to amend their "fake arrangements" mishap the last time they were in town.[17] The engagement also gave Mel the chance to play the band's music with substitute bass player George Mraz. Like Richard Davis, great time feel and intonation were a hallmark of Mraz's playing. Additionally, it was Mraz's ability to sight-read the band's difficult music that eventually got him hired on the band fulltime.[18] Richard Davis rejoined the tour for the Soviet Union dates, but it was his final trip with the band. Davis left the group to pursue other musical opportunities and was replaced by Mraz later that summer.

After a day layover in Moscow on April 1, the Soviet Union tour began with a five-night stay in St. Petersburg where the band performed from April 2–6.[19] The performances in St. Petersburg were initially to be held at October Hall, a venue that could hold 3,000 people. However, upon their arrival, the band learned that there was such a high demand for tickets that the concerts had been moved to a converted ice hockey rink that held 6,000 people.[20] This was just the first example of how popular the band was during the tour and how the Soviet people eagerly welcomed American jazz music. Like most State Department tours, the schedule took the band to several cities for about five days each. Those days usually included four performances and one day off, allowing for sight seeing and rest. After St. Petersburg, the band spent April 8–12 in Kiev, April 13–17 in Rostov-on-Don, April 19–22 in Yaroslavl, April 23–28 in Moscow and April 29–May 2 in Tbilisi.[21]

During the tour the band performed arrangements from their Solid State recordings, as well as many of the new compositions from the yet-to-be completed recording *Suite for Pops*. Louis Armstrong was very popular with the audiences, and each night when Thad announced that they were performing a suite dedicated to Armstrong, the crowd erupted with applause. In addition to the Armstrong suite, vocalist Dee Dee Bridgewater's commanding stage presence and beautiful voice made her an instant crowd favorite.[22] During every performance, the musicians witnessed how deeply their music touched the Soviet people. Thad recalled the ovations the band received:

> The response at the end of the concerts was amazing, because instead of staying in their seats, applauding, they immediately rushed to the stage and stood there surrounding the bandstand and giving us an unbelievable ovation.[23]

The band's road manager Cass Lynch remembered sitting in the audience during the performances and witnessing the emotion that the music brought the people. "I noticed that in the audience there were people shedding tears listening to Roland play 'A Child Is Born' and listening to Thad play 'Bringing Together.' They were actually shedding tears. It was really something," recalled Lynch.[24]

Heading back to the Soviet Union after ten years, Mel was anxious to see if its citizens had made progress within the oppressive communist society and if they would embrace the new jazz music:

> I expected to find not too much change and I was very surprised because not only were the audiences even warmer than they had been the first time, but they really did know a lot more about everything, apparently from studying and listening. They still don't have the freedom to do that, and the music is still not accepted by the powers that be, but the people themselves have gone beyond that. Our audiences, our sell-out crowds, were there to hear us and many of them seemed to have a good knowledge of us; they knew who we were, what we were about, and were awfully glad to see us because we finally were bringing something new, modern—what was happening today instead of what they'd been getting.[25]

In addition to Mel, the trip was also special for saxophonist Jerry Dodgion and trombonist Jimmy Knepper, as both men were also on the

Benny Goodman tour ten years prior. The Communist Party's control over civilians was still strong, but for Mel, Dodgion, and Knepper, it was nice to see the citizens with more freedoms.[26] Unlike the very constricting Goodman tour, the government allowed the Thad Jones/Mel Lewis band members to talk and spend time with their Soviet fans. Dodgion recalled that during these conversations he got a good sense of how far the people's freedom had progressed and, equally, how far they still had to go:

> The system the Russians live under is so different from ours that there are things that they find hard to understand. Musicians came to hear our band, and they'd say, "Man, it's terrific, out of sight, this band must be very popular in America." And I'd say, "Yes, we're popular with the jazz community." And they'd think that was terrific, and we'd get to talking, and they'd ask how so-and-so was doing, and I'd say, "Yes, he is in New York." And they'd name all the great jazz musicians, and I'd have to tell them that some of them were not working now, and they don't understand that. They don't understand that in this country, if you don't have a job, you don't get to play.[27]

In addition to having more conversational freedom, band members were also allowed to play jam sessions with Soviet jazz musicians. One jam session in Moscow was so popular that there was not enough time allotted to let every musician get on the stage. Thad remembered the session, saying, "The stamina and vitality of the players was like the old-time sessions we used to have that ran for hours and nobody got tired."[28] The eagerness of the local musicians to learn and play jazz was truly inspiring to the band members.

The tour was a great success and Mel commented that everyone involved seemed to have a nice time musically and personally.[29] The band even had a special guest with them during the first ten days of the tour. Village Vanguard owner Max Gordon met the band in Moscow on their first day and traveled with them throughout the Soviet Union. Gordon grew up in a small Lithuanian town called Vilna. When he learned about the tour, he decided to go, not only to spend time on the road with some of his favorite musicians, but to also take a side trip to Vilna and revisit his Lithuanian roots. Gordon had a great time with the band, and the band loved having him along for the ride.[30]

On September 1, 1972, the band returned to the studio to record two more of Thad's compositions for *Suite for Pops*. As a result of the long layoff between recording sessions, "Only for Now" and "A Great Time Was Had By All" featured vastly different personnel than the songs recorded earlier that January. Jim Bossy, Steve Furtado, and Lew Soloff had joined Jon Faddis in the trumpet section. Cliff Heather was once again playing bass trombone, George Mraz joined on bass, and Frank Foster and Ron Bridgewater were the new tenor saxophonists. After the September 1 session, the band's first album for A&M was complete.[31]

With *Suite for Pops* ready for release, Thad and Mel began taking what they believed was the next step towards the band's success. They had previously discussed taking the group on the road more, and by 1972 both men agreed that it was time to take their music directly to the people. Instead of relying so heavily on their exposure at the Village Vanguard, the band began touring more frequently throughout the United States and Europe. In an August 1972 interview, Mel stated just how deeply he was committed to taking the band on the road:

> We've reached a point where the band is going to start getting out more and I think our name is known a lot better throughout the country and the world now and a lot more people are going to see the band in the years to come. We'll just keep on going. As far as I'm concerned my life is this band.[32]

On November 21, 1972, Thad and Mel were guest artists at North Texas State University in Denton, Texas. In addition to giving clinics, both men were featured performers during a concert with the One O'Clock Lab Band. Even though they had previously given concerts at universities with their big band, the growing popularity of jazz (stage bands) within music departments, such as at North Texas State (now University of North Texas), offered Thad and Mel a new means of earning income as guest artists and clinicians. Because young people no longer danced to big band music, and many jazz clubs were not looking to hire a big band, universities and schools with concert budgets became a major focus of their individual work and of the Thad Jones/Mel Lewis Orchestra.

The Thad Jones/Mel Lewis Orchestra's touring increased greatly in 1973, especially during the spring and summer. The band played several concerts at schools, including performances at Alfred University, Indiana/Purdue University, Queens College, Brooklyn College, and even a concert at a high school in Livonia, Michigan, on April 7.[33] Thad and Mel were actively booking gigs, and would only turn down a job if it was not financially beneficial or if they couldn't book enough work around the date to make it worthwhile. Mel explained the realities of the band's touring schedule:

> Whatever comes along that's right, we take. We've turned down gigs that don't make any sense. We can't go from here to St. Louis to play a job for $2500. That's dumb. But if we can pick up the whole weekend and pick up an amount of money that pays the transportation and pays a decent salary to guys for going, we'll grab it in a minute. It's economics that keeps us mostly at home.[34]

The summer of 1973 brought another European tour. The band performed in Sweden, Finland, Denmark, Belgium, France, Italy, and the Netherlands from August 13 to 27. After playing nine concerts in just over two weeks, they finished the tour with a thirteen-night run at Ronnie Scott's in London and performances in Norwich and Farnworth, England.[35]

During their European tours, the band performed in many of the same locations, including Ronnie Scott's. Each return trip produced a larger fan following and thanks to their persistent traveling the band began to see an increase in their popularity overseas.[36] Mel also experienced an increase in his individual recording opportunities while in Europe. One example of this occurred during the band's week at Ronnie Scott's that September. Mel, along with Thad Jones/Mel Lewis Orchestra rhythm section members Mraz and Hanna, were hired and made a recording with jazz violinist Stephane Grappelli titled *Stephane Grappelli Meets the Rhythm Section* (Black Loin). During their stay in London, the rhythm section also recorded an album led by the band's legendry baritone saxophonist Pepper Adams titled *Ephemera* (Spotlite). The recording took place on September 10 and displayed energetic performances by the group. Even though *Ephemera* has never been reissued on compact disc, it remains a favorite among Pepper Adams enthusiasts.[37]

As the popularity of the band grew, Thad and Mel also began to receive offers for the band to record supporting other artists. The work proved to be a way for the band to make additional income, especially while on tour. This type of work had begun earlier that February while in New York City with a little-known recording titled *Portuguese Soul* (Verve) led by organist Jimmy Smith. While Thad is credited as the arranger, the members of the Thad Jones/Mel Lewis Orchestra backed Smith on the recording but were never officially credited in the album's liner notes.[38] Jerry Dodgion recalled the recording session and resulting album:

> We were hired to do that Jimmy Smith album called *Portuguese Soul* and Thad wrote some beautiful music on that. And when the album came out all you heard was the organ! You couldn't hear a lot of the stuff that Thad wrote because it was covered up. The reason was that Jimmy Smith's wife, Lola I believe was her name, did the mixing and was managing him at the same time. So that was kind of a loss of some beautiful exchanges, which could have been handled better by a professional mixer.[39]

The band's next major recordings came while in Europe in August and September of 1973. Italian vocalist Manuel De Sica hired the band to record an album that featured his vocals and compositions. After De Sica followed the tour from country to country to rehearse his material with the band, they went into a London studio on September 13 and 14 and recorded his extended composition *First Jazz Suite* that was included on *Thad Jones/Mel Lewis and The Jazz Orchestra Meet Manuel De Sica* (Pausa).[40] As the Thad Jones/Mel Lewis Orchestra continued touring, other albums were recorded while on the road that helped cover travel expenses.

The band stayed on the road throughout the remainder of 1973 with performances at the Monterey Jazz Festival in September, a short trip to St. Croix in the Virgin Islands in late November, and an evening at the Jazz Showcase in Chicago on December 16.[41] By December, Thad and Mel felt that they were finally getting their music to a larger live audience; in spite of this, the issue became getting their recorded music into the consumer's hands. Their album *Suite for Pops* had been finished for over a year, but had not yet been released by A&M. With 1970's *Consummation* being the band's last domestic release, it had been over three years since their last album. A&M supposedly did not like the material on *Suite for Pops* and shelved the album indefinitely. When asked about the recording hiatus, Thad responded:

> I don't know exactly how long it's been, but I am sure of one thing: A&M has one of our albums sitting in the vault. They claim it's not commercial. Now there ought to be a law against that. That's placing a restriction against an artist's earning power ... It's a dumb thing to record, then do nothing but sit on it.[42]

Suite for Pops continued to sit at A&M Records and was not released for the entirety of 1974. The frustrating situation led Thad and Mel to look for other record labels as they continued putting pressure on A&M Records to release their finished music.

By the beginning of 1974, the personnel of the Thad Jones/Mel Lewis Orchestra had gone largely unchanged for two years. Longtime members Roland Hanna, Pepper Adams, and Jerry Dodgion were still the stars of the band while Billy Harper and Jon Faddis continued to amaze audiences with their enthusiastic playing. The band spent the majority of 1974 on the road with major tours of the United States, Europe, and Japan.

On February 22, they began three nights of concerts at San Francisco's Basin Street jazz club before flying to Tokyo on February 25. This was the first time that the band had been back to Japan since the disastrous trip in 1968. This time, they stayed in Japan from February 26 through March 14, and while based in Tokyo, they took day trips and performed in cities such as Nagoya.[43] One of the most memorable parts of the tour was a concert in Tokyo's Hibaya Park on March 5. While the band performed Thad's composition "Once Around," an earthquake shook the city, leaving the musicians on stage surprised and confused. Mel recalled the moment:

> We were playing "Once Around," and at the end I had a drum solo. Suddenly everything was shaking, my drums felt like they were going out from under me and I heard this racket—it was the piano sliding away from Roland Hanna. The people were laughing as if it were nothing. By now I saw the bandstand was going in a circular motion, and I stopped. We were right in the middle of an earthquake. It turned out there was a biggie not too

far away and we were getting a good strong piece of the shock ... our first jazz earthquake.[44]

Luckily, no one was hurt and the concert resumed; however, the earthquake gave Mel a great story to tell when he returned to the States.

The band's recorded performances in Tokyo on March 12 and 13 resulted in an album titled *Thad Jones/Mel Lewis and The Jazz Orchestra Live in Tokyo* (Nippon/Columbia). Initially only released in Japan in 1974, the album contained live versions of "Once Around," "Back Bone," "Mean What You Say," and "Little Pixie." Mel's playing on the album was spectacular and revealed him stretching out on many of the arrangements that he had been playing for over seven years.[45]

Mel, Thad, and the band flew back to San Francisco on March 14 after completing their Japan tour. They then played two weeks of gigs as they made their way back to New York City, often traveling hundreds of miles a day by bus to get to the next venue. The trip began with two nights in San Francisco from March 16 to 17, followed by a week in Los Angeles March 18–25 at the new Shelly's Manne-Hole, a night in San Jose on March 26, a night in Denver on March 27, four nights in Chicago from March 28 to 31, before finally arriving back in New York City on April 1.[46]

Later that spring, Thad, who had been searching for a new record label, finally found what he hoped would be the right fit for the band. Philadelphia International Records (PIR) was a fast-growing record label that specialized in R&B and soul music. The label was founded in 1971 by Kenneth Gamble and Leon Huff and became known as the label that pioneered the Philadelphia soul music sound of the 1970s. After PIR's early success they secured an important distribution deal with CBS, the country's largest record label.[47] The opportunity to have distribution through CBS was significant, even if it meant taking a risk as the only jazz artists on the PIR label. Mel recalled the brief negotiations with Gamble and Huff before signing with PIR:

> They get us up there, and now you got Thad and Yvonne Taylor (Thad's girlfriend at the time). They're sitting there all ga-ga by these guys with all their money, and they're talking about doing 10 record sessions. That's a lot of money. And I'm saying, "Hell, we could do this date in 3 sessions, what do we have to do it in 10 for." And Thad's going for all this crap and then they're talking about hits and they're talking about doing "Don't You Worry About a Thing," Stevie Wonder tunes,

and they're talking about doing a couple of their tunes "For the Love of Money" and all that. All of a sudden they talk him into this thing.[48]

While Mel was skeptical of the deal from the beginning, Thad was very optimistic about its possibilities, saying, "Regarding jazz, they've assured us they'll ask nothing of us that will amount to a change."[49]

Soon after signing the deal, the Thad Jones/Mel Lewis Orchestra went into the studio and recorded *Thad Jones and Mel Lewis: Potpourri* (PIR). As was the case for every recording session, Thad wrote incredible new music including "Blues in a Minute," "All My Yesterdays," and "Quiet Lady" which featured him on flugelhorn. Those three compositions, plus Jerry Dodgion's arrangement of Marian McPartland's composition "Ambiance," were the best representation of the band's traditional sound. Several of Thad's other arrangements on the album were well-established R&B songs, such as his arrangement of "For the Love of Money," as well as Stevie Wonder's "Don't You Worry About a Thing" and "Living for the City." Many people assumed that Thad had been pressured into writing the more commercial sounding music by Gamble and Huff, but Jerry Dodgion stated, "People always thought that we did those because Gamble and Huff wanted us to do that, but that was not true. It was Thad's idea to do those songs."[50] Thad's arrangements of the R&B songs gave the recording a more commercial feel than any of the band's previous work. In addition to the arrangements, the sound of Roland Hanna playing the Fender Rhodes electric piano was quite a departure from the band's typical sound. Mel later claimed that the grand piano in the studio was so out of tune that Hanna didn't have any choice but to use the electric piano.[51]

Potpourri was released later that year and eventually sold over 60,000 copies. Even with the impressive sales, Mel found out that Gamble and Huff refused to distribute the album in Canada, possibly costing the band several thousand copies worth of additional sales:[52]

I found this out from the guy that's in charge of distribution at Columbia, he told me, because I got calls from disc jockeys in Canada that would say, "Where's the new record?" I'd say, "I don't know, you should have had it." So I called this guy, Vernon Slaughter, at Columbia and he told me, "Mel, they ordered us not to release it over there." In fact he said the only reason it even got released in Europe at all was because certain distributors over there wanted it, because of those Stevie Wonder tunes and all. So we got screwed out of maybe

40,000 sales, we could have probably had a hit. We could have made the charts and we didn't because of that. These guys, they are deciding what we can do. What do they know about jazz, you know.[53]

The album was eventually nominated for a 1975 Grammy award in the Best Jazz Big Band Performance category. Despite the positive sales and Grammy nomination, Mel considered it his least favorite album the band ever recorded. His initial skepticism of Gamble and Huff were also confirmed when all was said and done:

> Man, this album cost over $70,000 of which it turned out to be padded. They padded it by $15,000 ... In the meantime she (Yvonne) got us into this mess over there, we ended up losing money anyway, because the thing cost so damn much. Thad wrote his butt off though, again. He wrote some great arrangements for that album, though they were poorly recorded if you listen. Those people do not know how to record a big band.[54]

After continued money and distribution disagreements with Gamble and Huff, Thad and Mel soon left the label and never made another album for PIR. After recording *Potpourri*, the band went back on the road, spending June 27 through July 30 touring Europe. During the tour, they made their first trip to Spain and performed for the first time at the Umbria Jazz Festival in Perugia, Italy.[55] The end of the 1974 summer tour finished the band's busiest year of touring to date. Thad and Mel were putting every ounce of energy into their group, and even though the past several years had been tough in terms of studio output, the men were very happy to be on the road with their band. Jerry Dodgion described Thad and Mel's desire to tour:

> There was never any conflict between Thad and Mel as far as touring; they were in agreement all the time. Thad and Mel wanted to have a full time band, and they would have gone out on the road and never come home as far as they were concerned. They loved being on the road with the band.[56] ‖

*See Appendix Transcription and Listening Guide for this chapter

1 Thad Jones/Mel Lewis Jazz Orchestra on tour in 1976. *Used by permission of the University of Missouri-Kansas City Libraries, Dr. Kenneth J. LaBudde Department of Special Collections and the Sokoloff family.*

2 Mel playing his Chinese cymbal in Kans in 1975. *Photo by Matthias Kuert © Used by permission of Matthias Kuert.*

and Mel having a discussion at
ux Jazz Festival.

Matthias Kuert ©
permission of Matthias Kuert.

4 The Thad Jones/Mel Lewis Orchestra in
Waldshut, Germany 1976.

Photo by Matthias Kuert ©
Used by permission of Matthias Kuert.

Chapter 17
Ten Years at the Village
Vanguard / The Road Family

In 1975, Thad and Mel wasted no time getting the band back on the road. On January 19, they began a two-and-a-half-month tour across the United States, one of the longest domestic tours that they ever put together. During the tour the band performed at an astounding number of colleges and universities. The increase of jazz in higher education continued to be seen in the itineraries of the Thad Jones/Mel Lewis Orchestra. In February and March alone, they performed concerts at Arizona State University, Chabot College, Stanford University, University of Texas, University of Wisconsin, Michigan Tech, Florida State University, Dade Community College, Westfield State University, Monroe Community College, Oberlin College, and State Universities of New York in Pottsdam and Oswego.[1] In addition to providing income, the school concerts also provided an opportunity to have their music discovered by the younger "rock" crowd. The average twenty-year-old who did not listen to jazz radio, or read *DownBeat* magazine, could still discover the band through these live performances.

Outside of the Thad Jones/Mel Lewis Orchestra, Mel began to rack up thousands of travel miles as a sideman. After spending May and the beginning of June playing his regular Monday night at the Vanguard (now in its ninth year), and recording a swinging album with trumpeter Buck Clayton titled *A Buck Clayton Jam Session Vol. 2* (Chiaroscuro), he flew to Sweden for a series of concerts and recording with the Swedish Radio Jazz Group. On June 27 and 28, Mel, Thad, and trumpeter Jon Faddis were guest artists with the group and recorded five of Thad's compositions including his newest "Greetings and Salutations."[2] The album also titled *Greeting and Salutations* (Four Leaf), not only showcased Thad's newest arrangements, but also the steadily improved playing of European jazz musicians.

In July, the three men returned to New York City and headed back into the studio with the Thad Jones/Mel Lewis Orchestra. On July 22, 1975, the band recorded "The Farewell," "Forever Lasting," "Love to One Is One to Love," and "Greetings and Salutations" for the A&M label. While the latter three songs were issued at a later date, "The Farewell" officially became the final song added to their album *Suite for Pops*. The recording that began three-and-a-half years earlier, and was supposed to be the follow-up release to 1970's *Consummation*, was finally accepted and released by A&M. After five years, the Thad Jones/Mel Lewis Orchestra finally had an album available for purchase on A&M.[3]

Mel spent much of the remainder of 1975 on the road with the band. On August 15, they began a European tour in Bergen, Norway. They spent the next three weeks performing concerts in Denmark, Finland, Norway, and Germany. After arriving back in New York City in mid-September, they then worked their way to the West Coast during October. The bus trip across the country allowed them to once again perform at schools such as The Ohio State University, North Dakota State University, University of Kansas, and the University of California-Santa Barbara.[4] Upon reaching Los Angeles on October 22, the band flew to Tokyo to begin their third tour of Japan.

For the first time, the band had the opportunity to extensively travel throughout the country. Their previous two trips to Japan were mainly based in Tokyo, but during this tour, the band performed in over ten Japanese cities. After spending October 25–28 in Tokyo, the band performed in Sapporo on October 29, Aomori on October 30, Yamagata on October 31, back to Tokyo from November 1 to 4, Maebashi on November 5, Osaka on November 6, Kurume on November 7, Kagoshima on November 8, Kaga City on November 9, Toyama on November 10, Kyoto on November 11, Nagoya on November 12, and finished the tour with sold-out shows in Tokyo November 13–21.[5]

The band on the Japanese tour featured several new and important additions. Young tenor saxophonist Gregory Herbert was coming off a four-year stint with Woody Herman, and was an outstanding new addition to the band. His modern soloing, ability to blend within the saxophone section, and positive attitude were exactly what Mel and Thad had been looking for in a tenor saxophonist.[6] Earl McIntyre had recently joined the trombone section and was a steady member of the group for many years to come. Also joining the section was a twenty-five-year-old trombonist from New York named John Mosca. Having been awestruck listening to the Thad Jones/Mel Lewis Orchestra as a teenager, Mosca was thrilled to join the band.[7] In October, on short notice, he traveled to Ohio and met Thad and Mel for the first time only moments before taking the stage:

I was the emergency replace for Alex Koffman, who had immigrated to New York from Russia. He had actually met Thad and Mel during their famous tour of Russia in 1972. Anyway, Alex could not get a visa to go to Japan and Al Porcino and Dave Taylor ended up recommending me. The fact that two guys recommended me probably ended up getting me the gig. Thad and Mel were stuck and would not have called a twenty-five year old kid if they could've hired a veteran that they knew. So after being hired, I stayed in New York and ran around with the road manager to get a visa. Meanwhile, the band took the bus out to Columbus, Ohio. After I got my visa, I flew to Ohio, and that's basically when I first met Thad and Mel; right there, twenty minutes before we were supposed to go on stage. It was kind of like shock therapy![8]

Both Herbert and Mosca became standout soloists in the band and also went on to perform and record with Mel's small group in the coming years.

December of 1975 to January of 1976 was a very special milestone for Thad and Mel because it marked the ten-year anniversary of the Thad Jones/Mel Lewis Orchestra. To celebrate the beginning of a new decade, they took the band into A&R Studios and finished recording *New Life* (A&M), their second album on A&M. Both Thad and Mel were extremely proud of the album and considered it one of the band's best.

New Life contained Thad's three arrangements that were recorded earlier on July 22: "Greetings and Salutations," "Forever Lasting," and "Love to One Is One to Love." On December 17, 1975, the band recorded Cecil Bridgewater's composition "Love and Harmony," and Jerry Dodgion's "Thank You." Both compositions were beautiful ballad additions to the album. They finished recording on January 10, 1976, with two of Thad's newest compositions "Little Rascal on a Rock" and "Cherry Juice."[9] With several songs having been recorded in July and the rest recorded in December and January, the album showcased the band with two different lineups. Several of the more notable changes were Al Porcino rejoining the group and replacing Jon Faddis on lead trumpet, Earl McIntyre replacing Dave Taylor on bass trombone, and Walter Norris replacing Roland Hanna on piano. After ten years with the band, Hanna had decided it was time to focus on performing in small groups and as a solo pianist. Hanna's departure left Jerry Dodgion, Pepper Adams, Mel Lewis, and Thad Jones as the last remaining members of the original 1966 band.

February 7, 1976, marked the ten-year anniversary of the band's weekly Monday night gig at the Village Vanguard. To show gratitude for Village Vanguard owner Max Gordon's unwavering support, Lewis and Jones dedicated *New Life* to him. What Gordon and the band had accomplished between 1966 and 1976 was no minor feat. As the album's liner notes state, "The second decade of the Thad Jones/Mel Lewis Orchestra has opened. There have been almost five hundred Monday nights of roughly four hours each for us squirming in the Village Vanguard's drugstore chairs."[10] The band's Monday night performances had become one of the longest running steady gigs in the history of jazz, and as long as Gordon owned the Vanguard, they would continue indefinitely.

During their first decade as leaders, Thad and Mel worked hard to develop not only the band's music, but also its gregarious atmosphere. From its inception the Thad Jones/Mel Lewis Orchestra was more than a band, it was a family. If one has the chance to speak with a musician who played in the band, the words "family" and "marriage" will most likely come up. Thad and Mel were such good friends and worked so closely with one another that the musicians who knew them best often likened their relationship to a marriage. In a 1972 interview, Thad spoke of his relationship with Mel and said, "We've been listening to each other for so many years, we're like two old married people."[11] Like any close relationship, there were times of disagreement, but those times were usually a result of the challenges the men faced while leading eighteen musicians around the world playing original big band music. Mel recalled a conversation that he had with the legendary Count Basie about that very subject:

> You know, Basie, when we saw him recently, said to me (Thad wasn't there), "I hope you argue once in a while, don't you?" I said, "Of course, we do, because if we don't, there's something wrong." "That's good," he said, "Because the only way for it to be a real love affair is to have a fight once in a while."[12]

Thad and Mel were a perfect match on the bandstand and highly respected each other musically. They were also close friends; yet, their distinctly different backgrounds, religions, values, and beliefs also caused the occasional disagreement. They had completely different personalities, and Jerry Dodgion's description of them as the "odd couple" was completely accurate. In 1989, Mel recalled a story that reflected the depth and complexity of his friendship with Thad:

> Thad was my friend, you know. And I felt devoted to him as a musician and the whole thing. We fought, we had our arguments, any partners will. But man, they were nothing like what people thought ... Little things that we had arguments about. I gave him a Jewish star for his fiftieth birthday, a very expensive one. I put it on him. I never saw it on him again. And I thought that was pretty rotten of him. I mentioned it to him after a while, I said, "How come you never wear your star?" He says, "Oh, it bothers me when I sleep." Bullshit, because he always slept on his back. 'Cause I roomed with him and he always slept on his back and snored. So that was a lie. He didn't want to wear the Jewish star. So I have a funny feeling he might have had a slight bit of anti-Semitism and that ... But he could have worn it under his shirt, nobody would have known. The point is I gave it to him as a present, and I had it blessed and everything. It was like, for him. And he was a man that could have used some blessing.[13]

The genuine, if somewhat complex, friendship between the men lifted up the spirit of their entire band. All of the musicians respected each other and were excited to be a part of the group, and the music they made reflected that excitement. The camaraderie that Thad and Mel cultivated in their band was truly something special. Eddie Daniels remembered his time with the band during the 1960s: "Everybody was appreciating each other ... it was almost like a hang. All the guys loved being there with each other and we were all so mutually respectful of one another. It was just a wonderful situation to be in."[14]

As Thad and Mel hired new band members throughout the 1970s, the feeling of group camaraderie never stopped. In many ways, the band members became an even tighter unit during that decade. The band's increased touring resulted in the musicians' spending more time hanging out with each other on the road and more days of consecutive performing, helping to develop their unified sound. Because of the rigorous touring schedule, Thad and Mel often had to hire up-and-coming jazz musicians. The younger players usually did not have steady work or a family keeping them in the city, making them eager for the opportunity to hit the road with the band.[15] Beginning in 1965 with Jimmy Owens and Eddie Daniels, and continuing in the 1970s with players such as Jon Faddis, Gregory Herbert, Larry Schneider, John Mosca, Earl Gardner, Dick Oatts, Harold Danko, and Rich Perry, Thad and Mel always loved hiring and mentoring promising young musicians. When these musicians were hired into the band, they were brought into the family.

Thad and Mel taught musicians in the same manner in which they themselves had learned, on the bandstand playing music for an audience. Pianist Harold Danko joined the band in 1976 and recalled his education on the stage of Village Vanguard stating, "Both Thad and Mel were very much mentors to me. Mel more so in specific things, and Thad as just more of a force. But Mel, if he didn't like something I did, he would tell me."[16] Both men truly cared about the musical growth and development of their band members. Many times when a musician left the band, Mel got hurt feelings and was disappointed because he felt that musician could have learned more if he stayed longer.[17] Trumpeter Marvin Stamm stated, "If you were a member of the Thad Jones/Mel Lewis Jazz Orchestra, you were a family member. If you left the band, Mel felt like he lost a son or a daughter."[18] The Thad Jones/Mel Lewis Orchestra of the 1960s and 1970s was the launching pad for many talented musicians.

While Mel remained extremely active with his band and as a sideman, in 1976 he also accepted a teaching position at the New England Conservatory in Boston where he taught drumset lessons. He remained on faculty in Boston for two years before joining the jazz faculty at William Paterson University in Paterson, New Jersey.

Mel, Doris, and their three daughters had recently moved from their house north of the city in Irvington to an apartment on Manhattan's Upper West Side. The move ended Mel's long commutes and also pleased Doris, who loved the culture and energy of the Upper West Side neighborhood.[19] His new home was 325 West End Avenue, Apartment 2C, which also became the hub for his teaching and mentoring of musicians. Many of today's greatest jazz musicians spent countless hours in that apartment listening to and talking about music with Mel.

The move also resulted in Mel living in the same neighborhood as one of his dearest friends, Buddy Rich. Mel and Buddy had become close friends through the years and by 1976 they were two of the most respected drummers in the world. They loved to hang out together, many times having a bite to eat and talking about the history and future of jazz drumming. Even though they had distinctly different styles of playing, Mel and Buddy had complete respect for each other; simply put, Buddy loved Mel and Mel loved Buddy. Mel recalled their friendship:

> That respect was always there for many years. I used to tell him "Hey, I'll meet you at Gray's," because I used to walk from 75th, and he'd walk from 63rd and we'd meet at a hot dog joint on Broadway and 7th. Then we would just walk around a little bit, for a while. We always had a lot of fun together. Musically, we were opposites but that's what we dug about each other. Buddy couldn't stand Buddy Rich imitators, and I never had that problem as much because not many people understand what I'm doing. Buddy is more understandable, because he really plays the drums. He is probably the greatest drummer who ever lived.[20]

In a 1986 interview with Rick Mattingly, Buddy gave Mel his highest compliments,

> When Mel Lewis was with the Terry Gibbs band, he did some of the best drumming I ever heard with that band. I'm not that free with compliments, but the band was so hot. It was the most perfect way of playing drums with that band. Mel's a marvelous drummer and totally individualistic. He doesn't sound like anybody else. That's the best thing you can say about anybody, and I said it.[21]

Both men sounded great in a small group or when accompanying vocalists, but it was their complete mastery of big band drumming that separated them from nearly every drummer who has ever played. They made a big band shine, Buddy of course through one-of-a-kind chops and energy, and Mel through subtle orchestration that gave the band supreme confidence and clarity. Even though they used drastically different styles of playing, Mel and Buddy shared a supreme touch on the snare drum with both sticks and brushes, tremendous knowledge of the history of jazz drumming, decades of experience playing in big bands, and the ability to memorize every phrase, rhythm, dynamic, and articulation of a big band arrangement. Not only did they memorize a huge amount of written musical information, they also had the ability to acutely listen while performing and make "real-time" musical decisions that made the written music come to life. Mel described Buddy's ability within a big band and how it differed from his own approach, saying,

> He knew every note and figure in an arrangement. See the difference between him and me is night and day. I also know everything that is going on in the band. I'm just as good at that as him, but I only boost certain parts that I know need boosting, and I fill up the space where nothing is going on. Buddy knew the melody, so well he would play the melodies along with the band. That is where I disagreed with him. He forced the music to be played like a drummer, where my bit is I play it like the band is playing. That's where him and I are opposites in big band playing. But behind it, we have the same talent for hearing. This is what he liked about me and what I liked about him. In other words, what we liked about each other was the things neither one of us could do, the respect for each other's signature.[22]

Because of his unsurpassed expertise in a big band, Mel, as well as Buddy, was often pigeonholed as only a great big band drummer. By 1976 Mel had recorded hundreds of small group albums over the course of two decades; unfortunately many jazz fans still failed to realize how well he also played in a small group. However on June 8 and 9, Mel once again had the opportunity to lead his own small group recording session.[23] It had been nineteen years since he recorded *The Mel Lewis Sextet* for Mode Records (1957), and Mel was long overdue for a small group release under his own name. Recorded at Generation Sound Studio in Manhattan, *Mel Lewis and Friends* (A&M) featured Ron Carter on bass, Hank Jones on piano, Freddie Hubbard on trumpet, Cecil Bridgewater on trumpet, Michael Brecker on tenor saxophone, and Gregory Herbert on alto and tenor saxophone. Much like his big band, the lineup of musicians was a mix of up-and-coming stars (Brecker and Herbert) and mature veterans (Hank Jones, Ron Carter, and Freddie Hubbard).

The recording had the feel of an old-fashioned "blowing session," and displayed inspired playing by the all-star cast. Thad Jones's composition "Ain't Nothin' Nu" gave the album an energetic start and showed the energy that Mel created in a small group without ever overplaying. "Moose the Mooche" featured a half-time funk groove by Mel that, to this day, sounds modern and hip. Hank Jones's piano playing on the song mixed beautifully with Mel's beat and created a funky rhythmic backdrop for the melody played by Michael Brecker and Freddie Hubbard. Other highlights of the album included the trio interaction of Jones, Carter, and Mel on Sarah Cassey's composition "Windflower," and the driving swing feel of "Sho' Nuff Did."[24] In Bill Kirchner's review of the album he stated, "There's a lot to recommend about this fine album: some excellent playing, simple but highly effective arrangements by Thad Jones, and thoughtfully chosen tunes."[25] The album also received favorable reviews from Mel's fans, who had waited nearly two decades for a new small group album under his name.

After a shorter European tour in the spring and recording *Rhoda Scott in New York with the Thad Jones/Mel Lewis Orchestra* (Barclay) in early June, the Thad Jones/Mel Lewis Orchestra returned to Europe from June 18 through September 20, 1976.[26] The three-month tour of Europe included concerts in Germany, Poland, The Netherlands, France, Spain, Norway, Sweden, Belgium, Denmark, Italy, and performances at the International NOS Jazz Festival, North Sea Jazz Festival, and Antibes Jazz Festival. The most important performance of the tour proved to be their September 9 concert at the Domicile in Munich, Germany. The concert was recorded and released as *Thad Jones and Mel Lewis: Live in Munich* (A&M/Horizon), featuring the compositions "Mach II," "A That's Freedom," "Mornin' Reverend," "Come Sunday," and "Central Park North." The recording eventually won the Grammy in 1978 for Best Large Jazz Ensemble Recording, finally becoming the first Grammy award for the band. Ironically, A&M recorded and released *Live in Munich* after letting Thad and Mel know that the band had been dropped from the A&M/Horizon label. Mel recalled a frustrating conversation with A&M founder and president Jerry Moss during the band's time in Munich:

> Jerry Moss didn't want any of it. Herb Alpert had to fight for that label. Herb wanted the jazz label, Moss didn't want it at all. In fact, he outwardly told Thad and I that in Munich, while we were recording the Munich album. After we had already been dropped

from the label, he says, "You can blame me for the whole thing, and if you want to hit me you can hit me, but I just don't have any feeling for any of this. And I don't think it's worth any of our investment. But I have to admit, that being here to watch you guys live, I wish we could make it work." That's what he said. I said, "I'd love to hit you, but it wouldn't look good in the trade papers." He's standing there telling us how great it is live.[27]

Live in Munich was the last album that the Thad Jones/Mel Lewis Orchestra recorded for an American record label. For the next several years the band toured extensively, but never recorded another studio album or signed a deal with a new label. Thad and Mel refused to compromise or commercialize their music and were forced to push forward without the support, distribution, or funds of a major label.

After the European tour, the Thad Jones/Mel Lewis Orchestra remained in the United States from November of 1976 to July of 1977. These nine months off the road gave Mel the chance to continue teaching at the New England Conservatory, play gigs as a sideman, travel to Sweden with Thad to make an album with Swedish vocalist Aura Rully (*Thad Jones and Aura Rully*), and record with legendary trumpeter Chet Baker.

After substance abuse problems and health related issues sidelined the career of Chet Baker a decade earlier, he had made a comeback in New York City during the mid 1970s.[28] On February 20, 1977, Mel joined Baker, bassist Ron Carter, tenor saxophonist Gregory Herbert, and pianist Harold Danko to record Baker's album *Once Upon a Summertime* (Artists House). The album exhibited Baker lyrically navigating some of the most harmonically challenging material he ever recorded, including "The Song Is You," "ESP," and Danko's original composition "Tidal Breeze."[29]

Pianist Harold Danko had joined the Thad Jones/Mel Lewis Orchestra several months prior to recording *Once Upon a Summertime*, and was delighted to be in the studio with Baker. Coincidentally, Danko had previously played in Baker's working band; however, he was never offered the opportunity to record. To help sell records, Baker's management urged him to record with well-established jazz musicians, leaving out his younger working band. The odd twist to the story is that when Baker asked Mel whom he wanted to play piano on the session, Mel suggested Danko. Even though he performed with

Baker for years, Danko most likely would never have recorded with Baker if he hadn't joined Mel's band.[30] Danko recalled the ironic circumstances that led to his inclusion on the recording:

> It was Mel that got Gregory, and probably myself, on Chet's album *Once Upon A Summertime*. It became a pretty good record for Chet and I got my tune "Tidal Breeze" on there, which really helped me. So it was one of those instances where Mel might not get any credit, but if you get the real story, he had a lot to do with me being on that record. He had everything to do with it actually.[31]

The story of Mel getting Harold Danko on *Once Upon a Summertime* is just one example of the type of friend Mel was to the musicians in his band. When Mel could have recommended any piano player in the world, he recommended his own.

After remaining in New York City for much of the spring, in July the Thad Jones/Mel Lewis Orchestra embarked on another busy summer of touring. After performing a concert at New York's Carnegie Hall on July 1, the band toured Europe for the remainder of July and August. It was the first tour for two new members of the saxophone section, Rich Perry and Dick Oatts. The young saxophonists, both playing tenor at the time, quickly became prominent soloists in the band and were an important part of the saxophone section for years to come. Perry recalled joining the band during the 1977 European summer tour, and how it quickly shaped his concept of playing in a saxophone section:

> When I came on the band, I was sitting between Jerry Dodgion and Pepper Adams. That was school. That's where I really learned how to play in a section. I joined the band and two weeks later we were in Europe on an eight-week tour. I played every night sitting between Pepper and Jerry![32]

Bassist Rufus Reid had recently moved to New York City from Chicago and replaced Bob Bowman on bass. Reid recalled his first time playing with the Thad Jones/Mel Lewis Orchestra:

> Of course there were no rehearsals, it was just right out of the

box. The very first tune that I played was "Tip-Toe", which was the tune that Thad and Mel used to *really* see if a bass player could hang in that band. It had lots of really nice bass lines that were in unison with the trombones, so that was my audition. I survived and played well enough because Mel invited me to stay with the band.[33]

Reid also frequently performed with Danko and Mel throughout New York City in various small groups and as a piano trio, when not on the road with the big band.[34]

From July 8 through August 24, the band performed throughout Europe with extended stays in Nice, France; Copenhagen, Denmark; and Helsinki, Finland. In Nice, Thad and Mel spent time hanging out with their mentor and friend Count Basie, who was also performing at the Nice Jazz Festival. Basie told Thad and Mel how proud he was of them and that the success of their band was keeping the big band tradition alive. Right there in his hotel room, Basie made Thad and Mel promise that neither of them would ever walk away from the band. It turned into a prophetic promise that would soon come back to haunt Mel.

While in Helsinki, the band recorded an album with Swedish singer Monica Zetterlund. *It Only Happens Every Time* (EMI) was recorded on August 20 and 21 and featured Zetterlund singing nine arrangements by Thad, including vocal versions of "Groove Merchant" and the album's title track "It Only Happens Every Time."[35] Even though the album was never officially released in the United States, it was an important milestone as Dick Oatts, Rufus Reid, and Rich Perry's first recording with the band. It also turned out to be the last recording that Pepper Adams made with the band. After over eleven years in the group, he left at the end of the European tour to focus on his career as a leader.[36] The summer tour of 1977 was another positive step for the band as they saw their popularity and paychecks in Europe continue to rise.[37]

By most accounts, the long European tours were enjoyed by the band members. For the younger members, it was a chance to play great music with veteran musicians, and see the world. For the older musicians who had "been there" and "done that," the high level of the music each night made the extended time away from home worthwhile.[38] While it wasn't always fun, comfortable, or lavish, the tour bus was where the musicians really got to know each other, for better or for worse. Harold Danko recalled the contrasting personalities of

Thad and Mel while on the road:

Being on the road with the band was great! The funny thing was that we could always complain about things to Mel, but we'd never complain to Thad because he was kind of in his own world, not in a bad way though. Mel was like the mom and Thad was like the dad. You could always hang out with Mel and voice your dislikes. His thing was always, "Well in 1948, it was *this* much worse." He'd always tell you a story about how everything used to be worse; there was nothing you could say that Mel couldn't find a way to top you.

The other thing we used to laugh about on the road was that Mel was always the hero in any story he told. Mel was *always* the hero! One time on the band bus, Gregory Herbert grabbed Mel, because Gregory was really close to both Thad and Mel and he was a very important character in that band. Anyway, he got Mel in a headlock and started dragging him through the bus. And we're all laughing, even Mel is laughing. Gregory is messing up Mel's hair and asking him why he is always the hero in his stories. This may not be exact, but Mel's stories would always be something like—him describing Billy Higgins wanting to sit in, and how he would always let Higgins sit on the West Coast. And Higgins eventually became this big guy with Ornette. So the implication from Mel was that he facilitated the free jazz movement!

You know, Mel was just so into stories. We used to joke about not sitting on the inside of Mel in those old diner booths, because he would start telling stories and just talk until he was done. So if you had to go to the bathroom or get out, you better sit on the outside! He just loved to tell stories, and even though we joked with him, we always loved to listen.[39]

On the road and on the bandstand, Mel was the glue that held the Thad Jones/Mel Lewis Orchestra together. That is said in no way to diminish the role of Thad, but as Mel would prove during the following year, his dedication to the future and success of the band was unparalleled.

In September of 1977, Thad and Mel recorded their first quartet album as co-leaders, *Thad Jones and Mel Lewis: The Thad Jones/Mel Lewis Quartet*

(Artists House). They had worked and recorded previously in a quintet with Pepper Adams, but had begun their own quartet in 1972.[40] When playing gigs around New York City, Thad and Mel's quartet usually consisted of the rhythm section of their big band. In this case, new members of the band, bassist Rufus Reid and pianist Harold Danko, made up the other half of the quartet. The album was recorded live on September 24, 1977, during the quartet's weeklong engagement at the Airliner Lounge in Miami, Florida.[41] Rufus Reid recalled the recording, saying, "Every time we played as a quartet it was a joyous occasion and that recording is a true reflection of our joy."[42] The recording displayed the group's ability to interact while playing American songbook standards such as "But Not for Me," "This Can't Be Love," and "Love for Sale." The group's ability to listen to each other created jazz music that was elastic, yet never directionless. In the album's liner notes, Mel made mention of their ability to listen to each other by saying, "We had an exciting time making this record and we hope you will listen as closely to us as we listened to each other."[43]

While the group interaction on the album is outstanding, the solos of Thad and Mel are also highlights. Even though Thad wasn't taking the number of solos he once did in the big band and wasn't recording many small group albums, his cornet solos were still a display of flawless rhythmic feel and harmonic mastery. What also made the solos so memorable was Mel's ability to listen closely to Thad's phrasing and react instantaneously with seemingly the perfect musical response.

Mel's solos, especially his solo on "This Can't Be Love," are examples of his constantly evolving drumming style. By 1977 much of the vocabulary he played was a result of improvisation in its purest form. Within the structure of the music, Mel played almost free and constantly searched for new phrases, sounds, and textures that emulated the sounds of an instrumental soloist. He was proud of his drumming and solos on the recording, stating, "This is my idea of what jazz is all about. Spontaneous, co-operative, changing, surprising, and a whole lot of fun."[44]

1978 was a year full of major events for Mel, some which forever changed his career. The first was the Thad Jones/Mel Lewis Orchestra's spring tour of the United States. In previous years, the band had toured domestically, but never to the extent of this eight-week bus trip across the country. The tour was saxophonist Jerry Dodgion's last with the group. After twelve years in the band, the only members to stay longer than him were Thad and Mel.[45] Dodgion remembered the extent of his last tour with the band:

> As far as domestic tours, we only did one extended bus tour. It was a ten thousand mile tour, which was a long time to be on a bus! We left on the bus from New York and traveled to New Orleans, through Texas, Arizona, Southern California and to the San Diego area. Then we traveled up to L.A. and played one or two nights at Donte's, which was a well-known jazz club in L.A. at the time. Then we headed up to San Francisco where we played the Great American Music Hall, and then up to Portland and Seattle. From Seattle we started back east and went through Idaho and Montana, making our way to Denver, Cleveland, and Chicago, of course. That was our ten thousand mile bus tour in the spring of '78.[46]

The eight-week tour included shows in jazz clubs, hotels, high schools, and universities. If the band could pick up a concert and make decent money, they played it. After the lengthy tour, there was major turnover in band personnel before the next tour of Europe that September. Dodgion, who was the most famous sideman to leave, explained that it wasn't the bus tour across the United States that caused his departure, but simply the reality that extended tours resulted in having to turn down other performing opportunities and paychecks.[47]

The next major event for Mel was the return of composer and valve trombonist Bob Brookmeyer to the New York City jazz scene. Brookmeyer had spent the previous decade in Los Angeles working commercial studio jobs, recording the occasional jazz album, and fighting an alcohol addiction. By the spring of 1978, he had overcome his battle with substance abuse and moved back to the East Coast to begin the "second half" of his legendary jazz career.

Recorded on May 23, 24, and 25, the aptly titled *Bob Brookmeyer: Back Again* (Sonet), marked the first recording for Brookmeyer as a sole leader since his album *Bob Brookmeyer and Friends* (Columbia) recorded fourteen years earlier in 1965. Brookmeyer hired many of his longtime friends to record *Back Again*, including Mel on drums, George Mraz on bass, Thad

Jones on cornet and flugelhorn, and Jimmy Rowles on piano. In addition to several standards, the album featured two new Brookmeyer compositions, "In a Rotten Mood," and "Carib."[48] The swinging sound of *Back Again* marked the return of the Bob Brookmeyer/Mel Lewis collaboration that would become increasingly important to both men's careers. ‖

*See Appendix Transcription and Listening Guide for this chapter: "This Can't Be Love"

1 Thad and Mel in Montreux during one of their final European tours together. *Photo by Matthias Used by permission of Matthias Kuert.*

Chapter 18
Thad Leaves for Denmark

In the fall of 1978, only weeks after their bus tour of the United States, the Thad Jones/Mel Lewis Orchestra set out on a three-month tour of Europe. The tour and the weeks that followed were a defining moment in Mel's career. As previously stated, there had been many personnel changes in the band following their spring tour across the United States. Many of the changes had taken place in the saxophone section. Bob Rockwell joined Rich Perry on tenor saxophone, Steve Coleman had recently moved to New York City and joined on second alto, while Charles Davis took over baritone saxophone duties. The most important change in the saxophone section was Dick Oatts taking over Jerry Dodgion's vacated lead alto chair. Oatts recalled his hesitation to become the lead alto player:

> Thad asked me to play lead, and I told him I didn't really want to. He then proceeded to tell me that I didn't have any choice. It was kind of a drag for me because I really enjoyed playing second alto under Dodgion. In a way, I was also trying to focus more on the jazz end of things and didn't want the responsibility of playing the lead part.[1]

After his initial hesitation, Oatts became a superb lead alto, in addition to one of the band's greatest soloists, and continued playing the chair with Mel for the next twelve years. Mel thought so highly of Oatts that he once stated, "Along came Dick Oatts, who is the best alto player we've ever had in the band ... I'm going to hang on to him for as long as I can. Dick Oatts is a monster player."[2] Oatts joined lead trombonist John Mosca and lead trumpeter Earl Gardner to form the core of the 1978 band. Importantly, all three men continued to serve as musical leaders of their sections for the next decade. Other major changes to the band personnel included Jim McNeely, who replaced Harold Danko on piano, and Douglas Purviance, who joined on bass trombone.[3]

As always, the music on the 1978 fall tour was performed at an extremely high level. The average age of the musicians in the band was now under thirty, and while some critics claimed that the youthful bands of the 70s didn't have the precision of the veteran 1966 lineup, the band on this European tour played with as much precision, fire, and spirit as any previous aggregation. Several live recordings from the tour were later released, including *The Thad Jones/Mel Lewis Orchestra: Body and Soul* (West Wind) and *The Thad Jones/ Mel Lewis Orchestra: The Complete Poland Concerts 1976 and 1978* (Gambit).[4] The latter featured a performance in Warsaw, Poland, in October of 1978. John Mosca recalled that the recording was not planned ahead of time and took place in far from ideal conditions:

> That album was funny because Thad and Mel actually gave them permission to record. They let them record because at that time, the Iron Curtain was still up and it was very grim back there. Everything was grey cinder block, but the people were very nice to us and we had a good time. So Thad and Mel said, "Oh hell, let them record it, they don't have anything here." The recording was not done in great conditions. One of the gigs was outside and we couldn't hear anything, it was freezing cold, you know all of this kind of stuff. It was far from optimal for the band to do that recording.[5]

The tour was long, often with grueling bus travel, and was not without several negative incidents. The first occurred in November while the band was in Yugoslavia and, in an instant, changed Thad Jones's career. While sitting in a car, Thad was abruptly punched in the mouth through the glass car window by an unknown assailant. As Thad would later state, "A guy I'd never seen before hit me in the chops through a car window. I got glass in it, and it got infected."[6] The injury was so severe that he eventually needed surgery. The injury had a devastating effect on Thad as it forced him to take time away from playing, ultimately coming back to play the valve trombone (with its larger mouthpiece) for a time, and made it difficult for him to ever perform regularly on cornet. The accident may have been the tipping point for Thad, who unbeknownst to anyone had already decided to leave Mel and the band at the end of the year.[7]

The remainder of the tour was stressful as Thad dealt with his injured mouth, and Mel dealt with Thad. It was reported that the men had a heated argument while in Germany, ending with Thad telling Mel that he was quitting the band. Mel didn't take the claim seriously because Thad had said that to him before in frustration, but the two of them had always worked things out.[8] The band members' comparison to Thad and Mel as a married couple was not meant to be "cute"; it was very real. As Mel recalled:

> Thad quit the band many times. He'd get this thing going in his head about something he'd be mad about and never say anything, and then all of a sudden he'd build up this thing. I'd see it coming and think, "Well we're going to have a big fight."[9]

From Thad's perspective, the end of the 1978 fall tour had to be extremely frustrating. Secretly, he had already accepted a position to move to Denmark and lead the Danish Radio Orchestra; he was ready for a life change.[10] To add to the stress of keeping his departure a secret he had to deal with his injured and infected mouth, wondering if he would ever be able to perform on his cornet again. The tour officially ended in late December and the band returned to New York City to recuperate after an eventful tour and a long year on the road.

In January, Mel abruptly realized that Thad's threat was serious and he had indeed quit the band. "We found out Thad was really gone on the first Monday in January 1979, when he didn't show up at the Vanguard," remembered Mel.[11] In what must have felt like a surreal moment, Mel counted off the band at the Village Vanguard without the presence of Thad. While Mel, the band members, and the audience, did not know exactly why Thad was not at the club, the group performed through the evening as usual. In the days that followed, Mel finally learned of Thad's plan to relocate to Denmark immediately and lead the Danish Radio Orchestra. The band's booking manager, Willard Alexander, worked as a mediator between both sides, trying to find solutions to Thad's desire to leave the country immediately and Mel's contractual commitments to the band's upcoming five-week tour of the Midwest. Mel recalled that several possible solutions were presented to Thad:

> What Willard had asked him to do, is to do this tour. And then, just before the tour ends, or even during the tour, or before it even starts, we'll have a press conference and announce that this is going to be the last tour of the Thad Jones/Mel Lewis Orchestra, but that the orchestra is going to continue.[12]

After a week of uncertainty, Mel received a call from Thad that quickly brought the Thad Jones/Mel Lewis Orchestra to its official end. Mel remembered the conversation, and the last time that he saw Thad before he left for Denmark:

> On the following Monday he called me at ten a.m. and he said, "I'm leaving today for Europe." I said, "Man, I can't really understand why you didn't talk to me. Look why don't you come over." He said, "I need some scores you got." I said, "Fine, but I'm keeping the parts, because you can have them recopied over there. Come over today, man, let's have lunch, let's talk."
>
> At twelve o'clock I was downstairs in the basement, getting scores out of a case and I hear his voice. He walked in with his coat on and I said, "Were you upstairs? You should've waited for me; I'm coming right up and we'll have some lunch." He said, "I'm double parked, Mel, and I've got to go."
>
> So we went upstairs and we stood at the door and we looked at each other and we shook hands—we used to always hug each other and all that crap, but we didn't do it this time—we shook hands, we looked at each other, and he said, "I'll be back in March with the band." And I said, "I think this is *it*, isn't it?" He didn't have any intention of coming back anytime.[13]

Thad Jones was really gone, and his departure was a shock to Mel and everyone associated with the band. Thad and Mel seemed to be the closest of friends, and Mel never imagined Thad would abruptly leave everything that they had worked so hard to achieve. Thad had seemingly become disillusioned by the American music scene and left without thinking of anyone but himself. Months after leaving New York he made his feelings known: "You have to concern yourself with quality. America makes a mockery of higher aesthetic yearning, like music that makes them turn inward ... and maybe think."[14] Naturally Mel was upset that Thad walked out on their band and often stated his hurt during interviews:

> In this case, man, he [Thad] did all the screwing to me all through the years. He screwed me many times. He did a lot of things that were dishonest. I never did anything to him, ever. I mean I can honestly

say that with a clear conscience. All those times he quit and left me out there and walked away. And he also made money, you know, I never made any money in this band. He used to complain about not making any money, but who wrote the music, who made all the royalties? I never got a cent. Every record we sold he got something, I got nothing ... And I got stuck with all the debts when he walked away. But he always had money, he was always buying new cars, things like that. You know I never knew what he was talking about. And he had a steady job at CBS there, for years.[15]

Mel felt betrayed, yet tried to remain positive about the situation. When Mel made statements in interviews that came across as jaded they were often simply the truth, and Mel was never one to shy away from stating the truth. In a 1982 interview with Les Tomkins he voiced his sincere feelings and acknowledged that even Thad's family had been left in the dark:[16]

> Thad decided to change his life-style, and he moved to Europe. A lot of people thought that he and I had argued, but we had no arguments between ourselves. He just wanted to do this, and rather than allow me, his family or anybody else to try and talk him out of it, he just made up his mind and just did it ... thirteen years of your life, and reaching a peak of goodness. I mean, we were doing very well; we were finally on our way—and he walked away from it. But I guess he had to do it; so I'm glad for him. I don't know what he's actually had going on in his life, but I wish him nothing but the best. I don't think everything worked out the way he planned, so far; it will, though, because he's a great talent.[16]

After Thad left that January, Mel was faced with many decisions regarding the future of the band. But before the initial shock of Thad's departure had a chance to sink in, or decisions could be made, the band had to hit the road for a tour of the Midwest. In a move that Mel and manager Willard Alexander hoped would smooth over negative reactions to the absence of Thad, clarinetist Buddy DeFranco joined the tour as a guest artist. "At each town, we had to go to the promoter and tell the truth, that Thad wasn't with us. We had no recourse, we were breaching contracts daily," recalled Mel.[17]

Considering everything that Mel and the band had dealt with, the tour ended as a public relations nightmare, but as always, a musical success. After the tour, Mel was forced to decide whether to continue running the band or call it quits and focus his career in a new direction. In the weeks that followed, Dick Oatts spent countless hours at Mel's apartment talking with him about the future of the band. Oatts recalled Mel's mindset at the time:

> After the Buddy DeFranco tour during the spring of 1979, I think Mel still felt that Thad might come back. He hoped Thad's departure was just a passing fancy. But to tell you the truth, Thad's mind was pretty made up. I don't think Mel really knew how serious Thad was about leaving. It really felt like a divorce, and as Brookmeyer said, "Thad left and Mel inherited the kids," which was us, the band. Thad left him, and chose something different, and Mel would never have done that.
>
> Thad was a very diverse jazz artist and his playing and composing were extremely sought after for that obvious reason. He was always highly in demand and would often be writing or performing in different arenas than Mel. Thad's direction in playing and composing had been the direction of the band since 1966. When he left, Mel needed a new direction to recover and move on. I told him that he had a young band that was up for anything and wanted to keep playing great music. Mosca, McNeely, and myself had Mel's back, especially during his first years as a leader. We all missed Thad, but the musical direction would never be the same without him. It had to change and develop new concepts. Once Mel understood that, it became his band.[18]

In the end, Mel was not willing to let go of everything that the band had achieved and he remained committed to seeing it continue. As easy as it would have been for Mel to walk away from the band, he never did. It helped his decision knowing that since Thad's departure, the band personnel had gone virtually unchanged. Just when the band might have fallen apart, Mel reinvented it and made it his own:

> My mind is made up, Thad and I made a promise to Count Basie that we'd never quit. Basie said, "You can't do it, you know if

you guys quit, if your band ever breaks up, that'll be the end of the big band era. If you fail, if you throw in the towel, nobody will start a band." And now that Thad is gone, if *I* quit now and said that I can't make it, everybody else would be a fool to even start. And I'm not quitting. Hell, I'm having a better time now than I ever was.[19]

Mel forged ahead with the support of his family, band members, and also a vote of confidence from Vanguard owner Max Gordon. Gordon told Mel that as long as he had the band, he would always retain the normal Monday night gig at the Vanguard.[20] After entertaining the idea of hiring a new co-leader (Brookmeyer was offered the spot, but turned it down because he was performing in Stan Getz's small group at the time), Mel decided to run the band himself. Mel Lewis and The Jazz Orchestra became the group's new name, but even something as simple as the name change took time for people to get used to. "I think the moment of truth came when I was finally able to convince Max [Gordon] that the band's name on the Monday-night sign outside the Vanguard had to be changed. That's when we all knew it was for real," recalled Mel.[21]

At the time, Mel still did not fully understand the reasons why Thad walked out on the band, his American career, and even his family. Surprisingly though, in an interview Mel recalled an incident in Denmark during the band's 1978 European tour that should have been a sign that Thad was planning something:

> There was a scene that went on in Denmark where these Danish radio musicians were talking to him and they wouldn't talk to me. And I went to sit down with them and he said, "I'm having a private conversation here, would you mind leaving?" When he came on like that to me I thought, "What kind of shit is this?" And I said, "What do you mean? I know these people." He said, "But I'm talking business." And I thought to myself, "Oh," then I thought there's something fishy going on. And sure enough someone snuck out a copy of the contract he signed a year previously. He knew a year before he did this that he was going to leave.[22]

Harold Danko had left the band only months before Thad. During 1978 he sensed that something was changing within Thad:

Mel and Thad were really close, and that's the sad part of it; they were just so close. When Thad decided to leave and Mel was left with the "kids," all of the loyalty that was in that band was because they realized that he was really trying to keep the band together. I wouldn't even call it a divorce. It was a walk out, total abandonment … I was fairly close to Thad, about as close as you could get as a musician that wasn't in his generation. In 1978, we often drove to gigs together and I just sensed that there was something changing in him. As it turned out, maybe Thad was already negotiating a contract in Europe or something. But I just kind of felt like it was time for me to move on to other things.[23]

When asked about his new Danish big band, Thad admitted that leaving the Thad Jones/Mel Lewis Orchestra and relocating to Denmark was a very calculated move:

It represents a change … one I've had in the back of my mind for a long time … I've received from the music society in Denmark open, warm acceptance. The audiences are phenomenal, loving, and honest. Here I've found acceptance of music as an *art* form, not a commercial form like in the States. There (in America) there's nothing you can do. Even your best isn't appreciated … What's really important? More than anything I just want happiness.[24]

As the months passed, Mel learned that in addition to taking the job with the Danish Radio Orchestra, Thad was also in a romantic relationship with a young Danish woman who had just given birth to their first child.[25] Even with Thad's negative statements about the American music scene, his new family was most likely the principal factor in his relocation to Denmark. Thad wanted a completely new life and, instead of communicating with his wife, family, or friends, left his former existence behind with no explanation. As Mel put it, "The point is, he was walking out on his family here, without telling them either. You know he didn't do a very good job of this at all, I mean a very honest job, let's put it that way."[26]

Chapter 19
Mel Lewis and
The Jazz Orchestra

Only three months after Thad departed for Europe, Mel Lewis and The Jazz Orchestra recorded their debut album. *Naturally* (Telarc) was recorded on March 20 and 21 in Englewood, New Jersey, and was a much-needed step in the continuation of the band. Mel believed that the purpose of releasing an album was "To promote the band. To let people know we exist, to get people coming. To me a record is a promotional thing, but in our case I consider it a piece of history because we are playing music."[1] *Naturally* was important because it signaled that Mel Lewis and The Jazz Orchestra were continuing the musical journey that began in 1965. Even as the band pushed forward, the presence of Thad was still strongly felt as the entire album featured his compositions and arrangements (several that had never been recorded), including "Two as One," "Que Pasa Bossa," "My Centennial," and "61st and Richard." In a 1983 interview, Mel stated that he had sent Thad a copy of *Naturally* and that Thad replied with a positive review.[2] The album was also significant because it introduced fans of the Thad Jones/Mel Lewis Orchestra to the playing of more recent band members such as Dick Oatts, John Mosca, Rich Perry, Earl Gardner, and Jim McNeely. These musicians were the foundation of Mel's band, and stayed loyal to him and the group for the next decade.

After the drama of Thad's departure and the recording of *Naturally*, Mel still had big decisions to make about the group's future. Thad's writing and arranging had been a huge part of the band's sound and identity. The only other aspect that was as imperative to the band's sound was Mel's drumming. Mel knew that if the group was going to create a new identity it would have to play new arrangements that were at the same level as Thad's. Dick Oatts recalled urging Mel to think about the band's future and suggested that Bob Brookmeyer compose for the group:

> Mel knew I was a faithful member of the band, and he knew I'd come over to his apartment and talk to him about a lot of stuff. In 1979, Mel and I got together a lot and talked about

the direction of the band. The first few months after Thad left I said, "Mel you have so many friends and you know so many great writers." We had just spent a day listening to Brookmeyer's earlier compositions, so I said, "Mel, why don't you just call Brookmeyer and ask him to do a record with us?" So Mel went to the bathroom and came back fifteen minutes later and said, "Oatts, I got an idea. What if I call Brookmeyer and ask him to do a record with us?" I said, "Great idea Mel." You see, at that time, Mel was still thinking so hard about keeping the band together that he wasn't even thinking about it going forward. Truth be told, he was too busy bitching about what Thad did to realize that he was going to be fine. But that was Mel![3]

Even though Brookmeyer had earlier turned down his offer of co-leadership, Mel contacted him about composing for the band. In the spring of 1979, Brookmeyer was looking for new opportunities to compose for a big band and Mel's group was an ideal situation. The first arrangement that Brookmeyer brought to the band was his version of Hoagy Carmichael's composition "Skylark."[4] Brookmeyer's beautiful arrangement was a stylistic fit for the band, but most importantly, he enjoyed composing it for the group. Mel quickly asked Brookmeyer to be musical director, and he gladly accepted the offer. Mel recalled the agreement that he and Brookmeyer settled on:

> I told him, "Look, you're not going to be my partner, it's my band and you have your own group." So we worked it out where I would play with his band, and he would work with me and he could *write*. The main thing is for him to write. And, occasionally, if a tour or something came up where I really needed him or he wanted to go, we'd ask for a little more money and he'd go.[5]

Soon after Brookmeyer submitted his arrangement of "Skylark," he started composing original works for the band. His new music was experimental, and as Mel explained, audiences at the Village Vanguard didn't immediately accept it:

> When Bobby started writing for the band and we were trying to present the music at the Vanguard, oh people turned left on

us. That's when business all of a sudden got bad and we had to change it fast. So I had to tell Bob, "Bob, we're going to have to swing. We're just gonna have to." What resulted was the album you like, the Gryphon (*Live at the Village Vanguard*), that was the beginning of getting back into swing ... we were trying so hard, maybe overly trying, to acquire our Mel Lewis identity instead of our Thad Jones identity.[6]

Dick Oatts had a slightly different opinion as to why the band's Monday night audiences had diminished:

> After Thad left, the attendance at the Vanguard was terrible. It really dropped off. But the lack of a crowd wasn't because of Brookmeyer, it wasn't the music as much as it was the simple fact that Thad wasn't there. People wanted to see Thad and they wanted to feel that vibe that he always brought to the club. The first year and a half after I joined the band, when Thad was still there, every week it was just packed down there. There were still lines way down the block for the first and second set. But during Mel's reign, a lot of people thought that the band had broken up because Thad was not there. When Mel took over it felt like we were starting a new band. Thankfully we had Max Gordon on our side.[7]

While Brookmeyer composed new music, Mel spent the summer of 1979 promoting his band and solidifying its personnel. Now that he had adjusted to Thad's departure, he viewed it as an opportunity to make the band even stronger, and to achieve that he looked to his section leaders. Mel never considered his leadership position as one of total control; as a result, he trusted his most loyal musicians with the task of developing the band personnel.[8] "I decided that I should let each section leader run his musicians because I didn't play their instruments," said Mel.[9] He recalled gathering the lead players at his apartment and explaining their role:

> I brought the lead men up here, to this apartment, the three of them, and I sat them down: Dick Oatts, Earl Gardner and John Mosca and I said, "Guys we're on our own. I'm gonna need your

help ... I want you guys to slowly, but surely, put together your dream section. The kind of section you would want to play with the rest of your life, if possible." And you know something, they just looked at me, they couldn't believe I was telling them this. I said, "I mean take your time, try different guys. If anybody that's there now has to be fired, I will let them go. But not until we find somebody to replace them or we give them a proper chance, you know. If you think anybody here has the potential we'll keep them."[10]

Mel's musical trust in Oatts, Mosca, and Gardner, showed confidence in them and also in his belief that the band could be even better than when Thad was there. Similar to how Mel was influenced by working for and observing Stan Kenton, he became a defining musical mentor for the young musicians who played in his band throughout 1980s. Dick Oatts summed up Mel's dedication to the band and the musicians in it:

That cat never gave up on us, and never gave up on the potential of that band. He could have made so much more money doing other things, but he was dedicated to making music with us. If I could come even halfway close to dedicating my life to music the way Mel Lewis did; that's the shit![11]

As Mel embraced his new role as the sole leader, he also began booking more gigs as leader of his own small group. He had led his own small group in 1957, but during the 1960s and 1970s, studio work, gigs as a sideman, and the Thad Jones/Mel Lewis Orchestra left little time for a small group of his own. By 1979, Mel had the time and international reputation to once again frequently work and record as a small group leader.

In September 1979, Mel traveled to Austria and led a small group consisting of Bill Hardman on trumpet, Kai Winding on trombone, Joe Gallardo on piano, and Wilber Little on bass. The group's performance on September 9 was recorded and released as *The New Mel Lewis Quintet Live* (Sandra).[12] The simple four-track recording captured a truly superb live performance by the group. Mel played aggressively throughout and took very modern solos on "Once I Loved" and "Pell Mel." Mel was very much himself during the date, yet one can clearly hear the influence of other modern jazz drummers, such as Tony Williams and Elvin Jones, in his playing. The album ends with a blues titled "Ending Shuffle," during which Mel played a shuffle that was so full of energy that the joyful vibe audibly moved from the bandstand into the audience.

With their 1979 recording *Naturally*, Mel Lewis and The Jazz Orchestra had demonstrated that with or without Thad Jones, they were one of the best big bands in the world. However, the inclusion of Thad's compositions and arrangements did not give the album the feel of a "new beginning." Their next recording in February of 1980 clearly signaled the new era of the band. *Mel Lewis/Bob Brookmeyer: Live at the Village Vanguard* (Gryphon) was the debut of Brookmeyer as musical director of the band, and his rebirth as a big band composer.[13] It was an important album, as he felt his new compositions helped establish his writing credentials with a new generation:

> I think the best example was Mel Lewis' band. They were all new to me. And I came down, and I was the old geezer who'd written some of the fifteen-year old arrangements that they were playing. They could look at me and say, "Well, he did that," but that was no wedge for me in the door. I had to spend time the first year and a half in New York getting to know them and saying, "Well, now look, here's what I do, what do you think of that?" So it was really reestablishing credentials, because not many people of the younger generation would say, "Gee, that's really great you played with Gerry Mulligan or Stan Getz." They couldn't care less, you know. If I'd played with maybe Herbie Hancock or Chick Corea or John Coltrane—those were the people who were important to them. So it was a different set of heroes and a different set of judgmental values.[14]

The blues and Basie traditions had often inspired Thad Jones's compositions, and while Brookmeyer's new works were certainly not without the blues or swing, they were very experimental and modern sounding. Simply put, Brookmeyer treated the big band like a classical chamber ensemble. Each composition was focused on constant harmonic and melodic developments, textures, colors, and moods, rather than preexisting song forms or well-known chord progressions. His refined compositional style highlighted the ensemble;

any solo that took place was to sound as if it seamlessly blended in and out of the composition. Brookmeyer explained that he changed the function of the soloist, stating, "Solos became the background to the background."[15] The contemporary music was immediately accepted by Mel and performed with intensity and enthusiasm on *Live at the Village Vanguard*. In addition to his new works, Brookmeyer was also featured playing valve trombone on "El CO" and "The Fan Club," alongside special guest Clark Terry. The joy and applause from the Village Vanguard audience was proof that the band and Brookmeyer's new music were appreciated.

During the summer of 1980, the band traveled to Europe for their first overseas tour as Mel Lewis and The Jazz Orchestra. Brookmeyer fronted the band, and thanks to Mel's drumming, the band's inspired playing, and the new arrangements by Brookmeyer and tenor saxophonist Bob Mintzer, the band was well-received by audiences and critics. Mintzer had played tenor saxophone in the band throughout the spring. He was also one of several band members who had recently written arrangements for the group. After a suggestion from the band's road manager Sherman Darby, Mintzer wrote arrangements of several Herbie Hancock compositions.[16] Even though Mintzer did not play tenor with the band during the European summer tour, his arrangements of "One Finger Snap," "Eye of the Hurricane," "Wiggle Waggle," "Speak Like a Child," and "Dolphin Dance" were frequently performed. The band's performance at the Montreux Jazz Festival on July 16 was recorded and featured Mintzer's arrangements. The recording was titled *Mel Lewis and The Jazz Orchestra: Live in Montreux* (MPS) and was the third release by Mel Lewis and The Jazz Orchestra.

Filling Mintzer's vacated tenor chair was Joe Lovano, a young saxophonist from Cleveland, Ohio. Lovano had played in Woody Herman's band from 1976 through 1979, before relocating to New York City. It was through his employment with Herman that Lovano first met Mel.[17] "The first time I really met Mel was in Berlin, at the Berlin Jazz Festival. I was playing with Woody Herman at the time, it might have been 1977, and we played opposite Thad and Mel that night," recalled Lovano.[18] After settling in New York City, Lovano subbed in Mel's band at various times throughout 1979, before getting the call to join the band for the 1980 summer tour. After the tour, Lovano stayed and played first tenor for the next ten years.

Mel's hard work with Mel Lewis and The Jazz Orchestra resulted in an increase in small group work with the members of the band. On March 31,

1981, Mel returned to Rudy Van Gelder's studio in New Jersey and recorded *Mellifluous* (Gatemouth), a new small group album under his name. The entire group consisted of members of the big band including Dick Oatts on alto saxophone, John Mosca on trombone, Jim McNeely on piano, and Marc Johnson on bass. Mosca explained that in the months leading up to the recording, Mel had played several gigs with that same small group lineup:

> Basically that group started because Thad and Mel had some gigs, and then Thad left to live in Copenhagen. So Dick and I approached him and said, "Mel if it's cool we would love to play those gigs with you." So we went out and did a gig and had a good time, and this kept going for a little while. We were considerably less drawing power than having Thad Jones out there, with good reason, but we had fun.[19]

The session originated because producer David Feinman wanted to record another album with pianist Jim McNeely; the two had previously collaborated on McNeely's 1979 album *The Plot Thickens*. As it turned out, *Mellifluous* was really McNeely's album; he composed and arranged all of the music and scheduled the recording date. It was also because of McNeely's involvement that Feinman helped pay for the recording.[20] However, in the end, Mel's name was used as the leader, and it became known as his session. *Mellifluous* featured great playing throughout, and McNeely's writing for the date was outstanding.

Throughout the spring and summer of 1981, Mel worked as a leader and sideman in New York City. Mel Lewis and The Jazz Orchestra began to get more publicity due to the innovative composing of Brookmeyer and the inspired playing of the young musicians in the band. It had been two years since Thad's departure, and while the band continued forming a new identity, their Monday night engagements at the Village Vanguard were slowly gaining a larger crowd.[21] The reality of the situation was that even though the music was at the same, or even higher, level than it was in the 1960s, a band full of young talent could not draw as well as a band of established musicians led by someone the stature of Thad Jones. While the general public and certain jazz critics were slow to acknowledge Mel Lewis and The Jazz Orchestra, jazz musicians and fans "in the know" still went down to the Village Vanguard to check out the band. On any given Monday night, patrons could brush shoulders with any number of legendary musicians in attendance. Mel recalled that in the summer of 1981, even Miles Davis came down on Monday nights to listen to the band:

> One night I was on break in the kitchen of the Vanguard, and the guys come in and say, "Miles Davis is here." He was getting ready for his debut and he was sitting at a table talking to Max. All the guys were buzzing, they had never even *seen* him this close. I came out and Miles said, "Hey Mel." And we hugged each other, gave kisses on the cheek French style and all that, and I stood back and said, "Man, am I glad to see you." He said, "You too, I hear you've got a good band here." I said, "I sure do – look at 'em." They were all standing around staring, and I became even bigger in their eyes because they saw me talking to Miles.[22]

After his initial visit, Miles came back to hear the band several times that summer. On one of his later visits, Mel finally said, "C'mon man, you've been here a lot, why don't you come up and play with us?"[23] Miles got up from his table and used the band members' trumpets to play several choruses on a blues, much to the delight of everyone in the audience and on stage. The visits from Miles were not only exciting for the band, but brought new publicity and exposure to Monday nights at the Vanguard. Several weeks after Miles sat in with the band, Leonard Feather interviewed him in a nationally syndicated publication and asked how Mel Lewis and The Jazz Orchestra sounded, Miles responded, "Out of sight! The brass section is better than ever."[24]

Another exciting moment for Mel during the summer of 1981 was the opportunity to perform a concert in his hometown of Buffalo. On the evening of June 28, Mel Lewis and The Jazz Orchestra played a concert at Kleinhans Music Hall. They shared the bill with singer Mel Torme, but the main attraction of the night was the return of the hometown hero, Mel Lewis.[25] The performance was the first time that Mel performed in his hometown with his band; even when it was the Thad Jones/Mel Lewis Orchestra they had never played Buffalo. Before the beginning of the concert, a proclamation was read on stage, officially naming June 28 "Mel Lewis Day in Buffalo." Mel was also presented with a key to the city before leading his band through the concert. For Mel, the respect that he was shown during his trip back to Buffalo was extremely rewarding.

Throughout the fall and winter of 1981, Mel Lewis and The Jazz Orchestra performed several new Brookmeyer arrangements in preparation for their upcoming recording. Max Gordon gave the band a weeklong engagement at the Village Vanguard January 7–11, 1982. It was during that week that they recorded the live album *Mel Lewis and The Jazz Orchestra: Make Me Smile and Other New Works by Bob Brookmeyer* (Finesse). Mel explained the band's recording process at the Vanguard:

> Our newest album, *Make Me Smile* on Finesse Records, was recorded live in a club with a two-track machine, with two microphones hanging from the center of the club. The engineer, Jay Yampolsky, is a young man who's been working at the club for years; basically, he was the handyman around the club— dishwasher, waiter, whatever you want to call him—and also an engineer. He found out just what to do, and he's turning out some beautiful tapes; we decided that's the way to do it. He knows the band inside-out, and this new album proves that you don't need all that other stuff. All you need is two microphones that are open, and leave it all on the band. All the dynamics, everything there belongs to us; so if there are any mistakes, it's *ours*, and everything good is *ours*.[26]

Make Me Smile was another major step towards the band's new identity. Brookmeyer's original compositions "Make Me Smile," "The Nasty Dance," "McNeely's Piece," "Nevermore," and "Goodbye World" were extremely forward thinking big band compositions. Many of them were regularly performed by the band in concert, usually programmed between two of Thad's arrangements.[27] "My Funny Valentine" is the only standard on the album, but Brookmeyer's complete reworking turned the classic composition into an almost completely different song. Every aspect of Brookmeyer's writing on the album was cutting edge and thoughtful; Mel couldn't have been happier with the end results:

> As far as I'm concerned, the new one, *Make Me Smile* is a masterpiece—it's a trend-setting album. Everybody might not like it, but if they listen to it closely, they'll have to admit; it's

new. It's had nothing but good reviews so far. And the record's selling pretty well ... I'm proud of the album; the performance is unique—it shows what the band is.[28]

The album's artistic achievement was due to the band's ability to bring Brookmeyer's inventive compositions to life. Oatts, Mosca, and Gardner were still the section leaders in the band, and several new musicians were making strong contributions as well. Joe Lovano continued to bring fire and creativity to the first tenor chair and was joined in the section by young alto saxophonist Kenny Garrett and baritone saxophonist Gary Smulyan. Important new additions to the brass section included Tom Harrell on trumpet and Ed Neumeister on trombone. *Make Me Smile* featured a band that was stacked with talented players who put their heart and soul into every performance, just like their leader. After recording four albums in four years, Mel Lewis and The Jazz Orchestra had firmly established themselves as a forward thinking ensemble that performed original cutting-edge music. ‖

Chapter 20
The Musical Mentor

1 Mel performing with bassist Dennis Irwin. *Photo by Joan Powers © Used by permission of Joan Powers.*

2 Mel in front of his second home, the Village Vanguard. *Photo by Rick Mattingly © Used by permission of Rick Mattingly.*

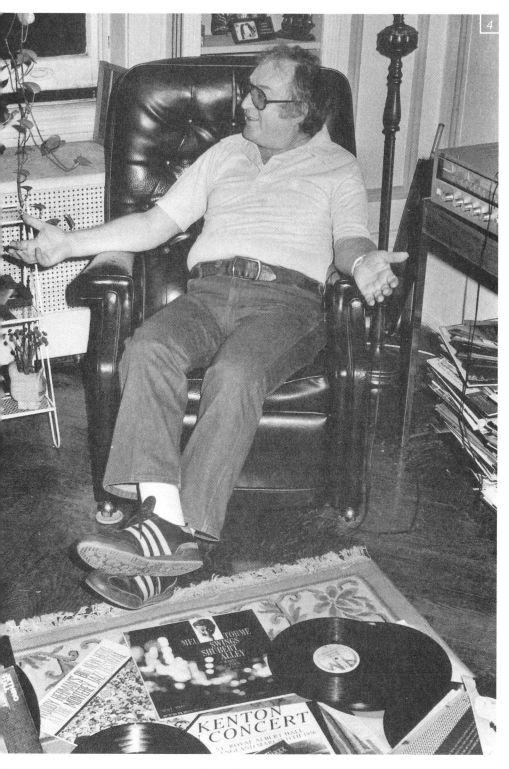

Lewis and The Jazz Orchestra at the Village Vanguard in the 1980s. *Used by permission of the Uni-* *Missouri-Kansas City Libraries, Dr. Kenneth J. LaBudde Department of Special Collections and the Sokoloff family.*

at home in his lounge chair discussing his past recording projects. *Used by permission of Sokoloff family.*

5 Mel, Doris, granddaugher Samantha, Donna, Mel's brother Lewis, Anita, and Lori.
Used by permission of Sokoloff family.

Chapter 20
The Musical Mentor

In January of 1982, Mel recorded a small group album under the leadership of Brookmeyer titled *Bob Brookmeyer: Through a Looking Glass* (Finesse). The recording consisted of a small group of players from the big band; in addition to Mel and Brookmeyer, it included Tom Harrell on trumpet, Dick Oatts on soprano saxophone, Jim McNeely on piano, and Marc Johnson on bass. The recording showcased many of Brookmeyer's newest compositions including "The Magic Shop," "Daisy," and "April March."[1]

On February 21, 1982, Mel Lewis and The Jazz Orchestra performed a concert in Washington D.C. at the Smithsonian Institute's Baird Auditorium. Several years earlier Mel had played a concert at the Smithsonian with his small group, and that performance was so popular that it resulted in an invitation for the big band.[2] The big band performance was video recorded and released as *Mel Lewis and The Jazz Orchestra* (Shanachie).[3] Bob Mintzer's arrangements of "One Finger Snap" and "Dolphin Dance" were featured along with Brookmeyer's composition "Make Me Smile." The program featured inspired playing by the band, but the highlight was the exciting musical interaction between Mel and Lovano on "Eye of the Hurricane." Mel masterfully supported and energized the big band through a challenging shout section, then continued to intensify the music by playing modern phrases behind Lovano's rousing solo. "Eye of the Hurricane" presented Mel completely in his element, at home in his band and fueling its musical fire.

The remainder of 1982 found the band on the road for several weeks at a time playing festivals, clubs, and universities. They were also a part of several higher profile opportunities, such as taping a television show for ABC Arts in New York City about the making of a song. The show filmed Brookmeyer and the band during rehearsal and performance, demonstrating how a big band composition was built, rehearsed, and performed. Another high profile opportunity for the band was their inclusion in the Stan Kenton tribute concert at Avery Fisher Hall as part of the New York City Kool Jazz Festival.[4] They were the house big band for the evening with guest section leaders Maynard Ferguson, Eddie Bert, and Ernie Royal. The all-star led group performed many of Kenton's famous charts with notable alumni such as Shelly Manne, Bud

Shank, Kai Winding, and Anita O'Day.[5] For Mel, it was a surreal experience having his band play the tribute concert to his old boss, a man whom he had learned from and respected very much.[6]

In addition to his opportunities as leader, Mel also played several interesting engagements as a sideman during 1982. When asked to join a tour with Benny Goodman, Mel accepted the invitation. Twenty years after his tour of Russia with Goodman, Mel realized that not much had changed in their relationship. Goodman was still eccentric and difficult to work with, but Mel respected his musicianship and knew how to deal with his personality quirks:

> No, nothing about him [Goodman] has changed—except that he's older and I'm older. So I do understand him a lot better. He's still a great musician—which is the reason I would work for him. I respect him for that; I always have and I always will. You have to put up with some of those eccentricities of his—but I've learned how to handle them better, being a lot older and smarter myself.[7]

Mel was also happy to accept the tour because it was a rare chance for him and Doris to travel together. Surprisingly, it was the first time that Doris traveled with him to Europe:

> It was my thirtieth year of marriage, and my wife had never been over here [Europe], I'd promised her that this year she was going to finally come on a tour that would be a little more sensible, where she could see something and do something ... Benny offered me his tour and it was a very nice one, as far as having an opportunity to enjoy ourselves besides playing, I accepted it. And I'm glad I did, because I was able to make some connections, do some business on the side for myself, and make sure that we're ok for next year.[8]

Doris had joined Mel on the road during his tenure with Beneke in the early 1950s when the couple was engaged, and she also traveled with the Mel Lewis/ Thad Jones Orchestra to Japan in 1968. However as Mel's European trips became more frequent throughout the 1970s and 1980s, she stayed in New York with their three daughters Anita, Lori, and Donna. As Doris put it, "I did some traveling with Mel, but of course I had my obligations at home. Somebody had to mind the store!"[9]

During the spring of 1982, Mel flew to Cologne, Germany, and joined Bill Holman as a guest artist with the newly reorganized WDR Big Band. Prior to 1982, the WDR Big Band was a German government-sponsored radio band that mainly functioned as a dance band. The government's reorganization of the project in the early '80s resulted in the WDR Big Band becoming a contemporary jazz ensemble that focused on performing and recording new music.[10] Mel, Holman, and trombonist Jiggs Whigham were invited to Cologne during the last week in May to record the band's first album, *Jiggs Whigham/Bill Holman with the WDR Big Band: The Third Stone* (Koala).[11] Holman wrote the arrangements and conducted the group, while Mel and Whigham were featured soloists and also played within the ensemble. *The Third Stone* was an important recording as it marked the beginning of the WDR Big Band as an artistic endeavor and the beginning of seven years of Mel's working with the band.

The WDR Big Band became one of Mel's main sources of income for the remainder of his career. When the band hired writers such as Holman and Brookmeyer, they also hired Mel to play drums. After his initial trip in 1982, he usually traveled to Cologne four times a year, twice with Brookmeyer and twice with Holman, to perform.[12] As a result of his guest artist work with this and other European groups, the majority of Mel's income came from playing overseas:

> I make a living in Europe, traveling. I make my living as a guest artist with bands, other bands. I make my living from other bands, not my own. I never made a penny from my own band, that's a fact. What I make from my own band is my reputation, which gets me the other work.[13]

In addition to his own employment, Mel started the tradition of the WDR Big Band hiring American jazz drummers as regular guest artists. Drummers such as John Riley, Dennis Mackrel, Jeff Hamilton, Danny Gottlieb, Peter Erskine, and Adam Nussbaum all traveled to Germany to perform with the band during the 1980s. Riley recalled,

> Mel was basically making a good percentage of his living with that band in the 1980s. But for tax reasons, he could only work in Germany a certain number of weeks per year. So the rest of the year they had other guest drummers do projects they thought they would be suitable for.[14]

Mel had the final say about who got hired to play drums for the WDR Band. If he liked the way a drummer played, he would give their name to WDR management and the drummer would join the guest artist rotation.[15]

The WDR Band is another example of how Mel helped to promote younger jazz musicians. Much like the love he showed for the members of his band, Mel also extended his friendship, advice, and equipment to the young jazz drummers whom he thought showed promise. Drummer Adam Nussbaum recalled his relationship with Mel:

> I really got to know Mel when I was playing with John Scofield and Michael Moore at a club "Palsson's" on West 72nd street in New York City; that was not too far from where Mel lived. He showed up to the gig and saw me playing with these cats. He kind of knew about me because I was playing with some of the guys in his band like Dennis Irwin, Dick Oatts, Joe Lovano, Jim McNeely, we were all buddies. At the time I had a set of walnut finish Gretsch drums, was using old K's, and had calfskin heads on my snare and bass drum. I guess he may have seen me as a younger version of himself; I also had red hair and was Jewish. After we said hello to each other, I said, "Hey Mel why don't you come up and play a little bit." So Mel sat in and played a couple tunes with Scofield.
>
> After the gig was done Mel said to me, "What are you doing tomorrow? I want you to come to my house tomorrow around noon, you free?" So I went over the next day, I ring the bell, and Mel said, "Wait for me in the lobby." So I waited for him in the lobby, and then we went down to the basement, to his storage place. When we got down there he took out a snare drum and floor tom. He said, "Here man, I want you to have these." I said, "*What*?" He goes, "Yeah man, these match your Gretsch drums perfectly, they stole the rest from me and I am using Slingerland now, so you should have them." Just real matter of fact, it was just so sweet of him!
>
> Mel didn't have a son, so I think he saw a bunch of us guys in New York—of the younger generation (Kenny Washington, Danny Gottlieb, and others) whom he felt had some talent—kind of like his family. He was very supportive and encouraging to us, like a

father. I would have to say that he is one of my musical fathers. We'd
go out to eat, we'd go to his apartment and he would sit in his big
chair and play recordings that he played on. I'd bring up things that
I played on. We'd listen and we'd talk. We spent time just hanging
out, not necessarily talking about drums per say, just talking about
music and life. He watched out for the guys that he cared about. If
Mel cared about you and liked you, he really took to you.[16]

Mel was supportive and often brutally honest with the drummers he
befriended. As far as specific drumming advice, he rarely told them what they
might have wanted to hear; rather he told them what they needed to hear
to improve as musicians.[17] Pianist and Director of Jazz Studies at Purchase
College Pete Malinverni, recalled Mel's humorous and blunt teaching style:

> I took my friend Tom Melito, who is a wonderful drummer,
> to the "Don't Be Shy" recording session. He was talking to Mel
> during one of our breaks and Mel said, "Hey you want a lesson?"
> And of course Tom said, "Absolutely!" So Mel said, "Ok, sit down
> and play me a roll." Tom proceeded to play this absolutely clean
> and perfect drum roll on the snare drum. All Mel said was, "*That's
> your problem.*" It was hilarious, perfectly Mel![18]

Even though Mel spent several years teaching at New England
Conservatory, William Paterson University, and New York University, he
was never one to give a typical drum lesson. When approached about giving
lessons he often replied, "I teach every Monday night at the Vanguard."[19]

As Mel continued to perform in Europe during the 1980s, he hired his favorite
young drummers to play with his band at the Vanguard when he was out of town.
Danny Gottlieb, Joey Baron, Kenny Washington, Dennis Mackrel, Peter Erskine,
and John Riley all subbed for Mel. To add to their excitement of playing that music,
on that night, the drummers always played Mel's personal set of drums and cymbals
he kept at the club. Joey Baron remembered his time subbing for Mel and what he
took away from the experience:

> What a supreme drum instruction. I mean I was sitting on
> Mel's instrument, with the same band, playing the same music,

wondering why it sucked? I found myself on stage trying to figure out why it didn't feel half as good as it did when I was in the audience listening to Mel play. That experience really taught me the importance of having a developed musical voice. Mel had one and it complimented the band's music perfectly. Thad Jones, Bill Holman, and Bob Brookmeyer all wrote charts with Mel's drumming in mind and that is a very powerful thing.[20]

John Riley also recalled subbing with the band and the influence Mel's equipment had on his playing:

> It was a perfectly natural situation, and much easier to fit into the band, to play his instrument than it would have been on my drums or on a rental kit. I think it certainly made the band feel more comfortable to have a sound that they were used to, even if the feeling and vocabulary were a little different. It certainly made me play a little more like Mel, without a doubt.[21]

Peter Erskine echoed Riley's statement saying, "I didn't intend to try to sound like Mel, but as soon as I sat down behind his drums and cymbals, a certain 'Melness' started coming out of me."[22]

The impact that Mel had on jazz drumming is far greater than just his own performances and recordings; it also includes his influence and friendship with the drummers he helped along the way. Just as Gene Krupa watched over him as a young drummer in Buffalo, Mel spent the 1980s watching over his drummers in New York City, making sure that jazz drumming continued on the proper path for years to come.

The year 1983 was the first in a decade that Mel did not record an album as a leader or co-leader; yet, he continued taking his band on tour. In the band's new booking agent Abby Hoffer, Mel finally found a booking agent who, he felt, worked hard for the band. "Abby is the only one that has ever really gotten us anywhere. You know, there have been other agencies, promises, promises, promises, and Abby has a hard time booking us, but he still tries all the time and he's the one that comes through," stated Mel.[23] In March of 1983, thanks to Hoffer, the band traveled to Israel for the first time for a two-week tour. They arrived in Israel on March 7 and were in Tel Aviv for a week. During their stay, the band performed four concerts and had the opportunity to see the city and surrounding area. After Tel Aviv, the band traveled the country and performed in Haifa and Jerusalem. The band's performances in Jerusalem on March 20 were video recorded and released as *Mel Lewis and His Big Band* (View Video).[24] The performance featured arrangements by both Thad Jones and Bob Brookmeyer and stand out solos by new members of the band: Phil Markowitz on piano, Billy Drewes on alto saxophone, and Dennis Irwin on bass.

In bassist Dennis Irwin, Mel had found a kindred musical spirit. Like Mel, Irwin was known as a "musician's musician" in part because he listened so closely to the musical ideas being played by other members of the group, and in turn used their ideas to inform his own musical choices. This resulted in Irwin being a bass player who supported a group and also inspired it by seamlessly introducing his own voice into the musical mix. In short, he played in a way that made all the musicians on the bandstand feel comfortable and sound good. The musical connection between Irwin and Mel was incredibly special. Their performances together were a model of the profound musical feel a drummer and bass player could generate when being unselfish and giving to the music.

As the Mel Lewis Jazz Orchestra remained in New York City for much of 1983 and 1984, Mel split his time between Europe and the United States working as a guest artist. His career continually revealed his musical versatility and desire to play whenever possible. This was especially true in the vibrant jazz scene of New York City, where one night he could make a decent paycheck playing in the Great Jazz Trio with Hank Jones and Ron Carter at Fat Tuesday's and the next night make little to no money playing original compositions in a small group with members of his own band.[25] For Mel true happiness was found at the drums and he played them nearly every chance he got.

On July 19 and 20, 1984, Mel recorded his first album with tenor saxophonist Loren Schoenberg. *Loren Schoenberg Jazz Orchestra: That's The Way It Goes* (Musicmasters) showcased arrangements of classic jazz standards, and in addition to Mel, included jazz legends Eddie Bert on trombone, Ken Peplowski on clarinet and tenor saxophone, and Dick Katz on piano.

Schoenberg and Mel had performed together for the first time years earlier at a tribute concert to Lester Young and Charlie Parker at Carnegie Recital Hall. In his early twenties at the time, Schoenberg organized the entire concert (including writing the arrangements, hiring the band, and paying for the event), and was thrilled to have Mel on drums.[26] In the early 1980s, when he was looking for a drummer in his newly formed big band, Schoenberg once again contacted Mel:

> I had a good band, the musicians in it were really great, and I figured the worst Mel could do was say no. After Mel accepted and started playing in my band, I could get anybody I wanted because they knew Mel was on drums. I was twenty-two at the time, and fact that he was willing to play in my band says so much about him. He was a world famous bandleader, one of the world's greatest drummers, and he was willing to put up with all my crap and immaturity at twenty-two. What an incredible gift that was of him! On occasion he would cut me down to size, but always he acted like he was a member of *my* band.[27]

Schoenberg and Mel became close friends throughout the 1980s and recorded together several times with Schoenberg's Jazz Orchestra (*Time Waits for No One, Solid Ground, Just A-settin' and A-rockin', That's The Way It Goes*) and as members of the American Jazz Orchestra (*Central City Sketches, Ellington Masterpieces*), many on the Musicmasters label.

Mel's ability to record on the Musicmasters label became a very important part of his career. In addition to the five Musicmasters recordings previously listed, he also recorded three big band albums and one small group album as a leader on the label during 1988 and 1989.[28] Unlike many of the larger labels that Mel had recorded for, Musicmasters was specifically formed to record prominent American classical and jazz musicians. The label's president Jeff Nissim was more interested in giving artists a chance to document their work than he was in trying to make huge sums of money selling popular music. Mel held Musicmasters in high regard: "I think the label we're on now, Musicmasters, can turn out to be one of the best deals I ever had. Only because Jeff Nissim has such a high regard for music and the fact that the company is a classical label."[29] Thanks to Mel's relationship with Musicmasters, he was able to record his groups, on his terms, for the remainder of his career.

In addition to their recordings, Mel and Schoenberg also collaborated on radio station WKCR New York and presented a multi-part series on the history of jazz drumming. The radio shows consisted of Mel speaking about famous drummers throughout jazz history, and featured the on-air playing of musical examples from each drummer discussed. The shows originally aired in 1982 and were so popular that people urged Mel and Schoenberg to repeat the series.[30] In 1987, five years after the original shows, the men once again presented the history of jazz drumming. This time it was a thirty-two-part series that included several recordings that were not played during the first series. Musicians all over the New York area were ready for Mel's history lesson and tape-recorded the live radio shows. The cassette tapes from those shows have famously been circulated through the jazz community for over twenty-five years. They allow generations of musicians to learn the history of jazz drumming through Mel's insight and first hand knowledge. Recently Loren Schoenberg and John Riley donated the taped interviews to the Percussive Arts Society, and as a free service the PAS has posted the audio from each of Mel's famous history lessons on its website. ‖

1 "Uncle Mel" celebrating his birthday at the Village Vanguard with owner Max Gordon. *Photo of the Sokoloff family.*

2 Mel performing in Switzerland in 1986. *Photo by Matthias Kuert ©*
Used by permission of Matthias Kuert.

3

Lewis and The Jazz Orchestra live at the Village Vanguard. *Used by permission of the University of Kansas City Libraries, Dr. Kenneth J. LaBudde Department of Special Collections.*

Chapter 21
Twenty Years at the Vanguard / A New Fight

After a two-year absence, Mel Lewis and The Jazz Orchestra recorded a new album in May of 1985. Unfortunately, Atlantic Records would not release the album until later the next year, making fans wait four years for the band's follow-up release to *Make Me Smile*. When the album was finally released in 1986, it was titled *Mel Lewis and The Jazz Orchestra: 20 Years at the Village Vanguard* (Atlantic) and coincided with the band's twenty-year anniversary of playing Monday nights at the Vanguard.[1]

By 1985, the band was performing music by a wider variety of arrangers. Brookmeyer still wrote for the group but was no longer the musical director, giving extra incentive for band members such as Jim McNeely, Kenny Werner, and Ted Nash to write new compositions. Nash recalled,

> My first composing and arranging for a big band was for Mel's band. Mel said, "Hey if anybody wants to write music bring it in and we'll play it." We rarely rehearsed so most of the time when people brought in new charts we read them during the second set at the Vanguard. It was a very cool situation.[2]

Kenny Werner composed frequently for the band and explained that Mel allowed him and others to take musical chances:

> Mel was always cool with people bringing in new music for the band. Funny story; I recall going to a composition seminar that Brookmeyer gave and where he talked about composing music based on cells of ideas and themes. As a result, I composed a chart based on cells and titled it "Bob Brookmeyer." Well I sort of created a monster because that chart ended up being over one thousand measures long! I didn't know just how long it was until we played it for the first time with the band. And Mel was cool but said, "Nice chart, it's ridiculous, cut it down!" So I did, but

Mel never told you what *your* music was supposed to sound like. We all felt very free to bring new compositions into the band because we knew that the band would play the shit out of them and Mel would support our creative vision. It was an honor to get to add a couple of my pieces to that incredible book of music.[3]

In addition to the new music, Mel started to program more of Thad Jones' classic compositions into the band's weekly performances. *20 Years at the Village Vanguard* is also a good reflection of how the band performed music from a variety of arrangers such as Richard De Rosa, Bill Finegan, Jerry Dodgion, and Jim McNeely in addition to the classics written by Bob Brookmeyer and Thad Jones.[4] Outside of the players in his band, Mel often asked composers and arrangers throughout the jazz community to write for the group. This included the well-known composers mentioned above such as Bill Finegan and Bill Holman, up and coming composers such as Richard De Rosa and Michael Abene, and even composers who usually wrote for military bands such as Mike Crotty with the U.S. Air Force Airmen of Note. Ted Nash relayed a story that demonstrated just how receptive Mel was to new compositions for the group:

> Cecil Taylor used to be one of our biggest fans. He used to hang out in the kitchen of the Vanguard and hear us play at least a couple times a month. Cecil loved the band and at one point told Mel that he wanted to write some new music for us and Mel said, "Great, let's do it!" Mel loved seeing other people get excited about the band and he was way more open-minded than most people give him credit for. So Mel set up a rehearsal and Cecil showed up without any music, he literally had nothing. We were all sitting there and Cecil said, "Alright lets get started, trombones play this." And he started playing random notes on the piano, meanwhile the trombones were trying to write them down on old pieces of music paper and guys were running out to the store to get Cecil a pencil because he didn't bring that either. It was a complete disaster! We spent three hours with Cecil and we had about twenty bars of music. Eventually Mel got really mad and got in a big fight with

Cecil about wasting our time and ended the rehearsal. We never saw Cecil down in the Vanguard again! But that gives you a sense of just how much Mel wanted new creative music for the band.[5]

Mel was always searching for new music, and as Dick Oatts explained, new music was important because it allowed the band to record frequently and helped to further develop its identity. "A lot of these good arrangers started coming through because Mel *needed* to record. He *needed* new music and he *needed* to record the band," recalled Oatts.[6] Mel also had the luxury of having veteran section leaders who knew his musical preferences regardless of style, tempo, or arranger. "No matter who wrote for the band, we knew what Mel wanted as far as the interpretation of the charts. That was very comforting to him. It allowed us to play a lot of different music from a lot of different writers," said Oatts.[7]

The 1985 band was one of the strongest that Mel ever led, and the personnel remained largely unchanged for the next five years. Pianist and composer Kenny Werner replaced Phil Markowitz and joined Mel and Dennis Irwin in the rhythm section. The trombone section of John Mosca, Ed Neumeister, Douglas Purviance, and Earl McIntyre also included Stephanie Fauber on French horn. Joe Mosello, Jim Powell, and Glenn Drewes joined Earl Gardner in the trumpet section. The saxophone section consisted of Dick Oatts on lead alto saxophone, Ted Nash on alto saxophone, Joe Lovano on tenor saxophone, Ralph Lalama on tenor saxophone, and Gary Smulyan on baritone saxophone. (Depending on schedules, Rich Perry and Billy Drewes both subbed in the section throughout the decade).[8] Mel often referred to that particular saxophone section as the greatest he ever played with. Ted Nash was the youngest member of the section and recalled the tremendous inspiration he received from the musicians he was surrounded by:

That saxophone section with Gary, Ralph, Dick, and Joe was truly amazing! I play both alto and tenor so sitting between Dick Oatts and Joe Lovano was just incredible. Dick's passionate bright sound and Lovano's creativity both really influenced me a lot. There were times when I felt a little overwhelmed with how strong and developed everyone in that section was; everyone was swinging so hard and playing very creatively. Many times the environment was like a competitive inspiration where I wanted to jump up and try to play on that level of the people I was surrounded by, the people I greatly respect. I wanted to stand up and make a meaningful statement too.[9]

Nash's comment mirrors Rich Perry's statement about joining the band nearly ten years prior and performing along side Jerry Dodgion and Pepper Adams. Mel's band continued to be an onstage apprentice system where musicians developed their skills by performing with and deeply listening to their mentors. Many of the musicians who were lucky enough to learn in such an environment refer to it as "real school."

Mel was ecstatic about all the members of his band, and like a proud parent, sang their praises every chance he got. "They stuck with me, and through them we built a whole new band that today is better than any band we ever had, including the original band ... this band plays together as a unit much better than that first band did," said Mel.[10] As the drummer and leader, Mel had the unique ability to lead, not by waving his arms in front of the group or by forceful intimidation, but by playing his drums in an unselfish and musical manner. His drumming acted as a huge cushion of support, allowing the band members to relax and play their best. As Jeff Levenson once stated, "Mel powers his band with an unobtrusive hand, controlling the degree of swing with a knowing sense of space, time, and embellishment."[11] Joe Lovano recalled Mel's musical leadership and how it inspired the band members, saying, "I was really proud to be a part of Mel Lewis and The Jazz Orchestra. He treated everyone in the band like it was *their* band. He accompanied you like it was *your* band. And that in turn made all of us play for him."[12]

With all of the positive momentum that Mel had achieved in the past several years, 1985 marked the beginning of a very difficult period in his life. It was during a tour that summer that Mel first came to grips with the possibility that he might be ill. Dick Oatts recalled the tour and how he witnessed the first signs of Mel's skin cancer:

> We were on tour in '85; it was the summer tour and I sat across from Mel on the bus. Within the two and a half weeks of that tour I saw the scab, which I think was his left forearm, go from a dime size to a quarter size. By the end of the tour it was the size of a fifty-cent

piece and I said, "Mel, really, that doesn't look good you need to have it checked out." He said, "Oh, yeah sure, I will when I get back home." But you know, I think he let it go too long. When he went in they did tests and told him he had Melanoma. Mel had light skin, and probably didn't realize skin cancer was a possibility. He could have gotten it when he was a kid and it laid dormant until then.[13]

At the time, information regarding Melanoma was not as prevalent as today and many people weren't aware of what caused it or how deadly it could be. Mel explained the situation saying, "It's a condition from being a redhead and from being burned up when I was a little boy on the beaches. That's the only thing they can attribute it to. This kind of thing has nothing to do with smoke or anything. Melanoma is a cancer all by itself, and it's the worst of all skin cancers."[14] Soon after his initial diagnosis, the growth was removed from his arm and he began treatments to fight the disease. Even during regular treatments and checkups, Mel continued drumming and traveling as much as he always had. The arrival of his Melanoma did not mark the decline of his drumming or the slowing of his career. Mel was as determined as ever to keep growing as a musician, lead the band that he had spent twenty years building, and beat cancer. "The doctor is totally optimistic about me beating the cancer. They're not even worried about it, and neither am I. I told them I was going to beat it as soon as I found out I had it," declared Mel.[15]

After touring most of the summer, Mel recorded two excellent small group albums in the fall of 1985. First, in August he recorded with pianist Kenny Barron, tenor saxophonist Harold Land, bassist Ray Brown, and trumpeter Jon Faddis, on Faddis's album *Legacy* (Concord). As Dizzy Gillespie stated in the album's liner notes, "And then, 'the Old Father,' Mel Lewis ... I have never heard him better. He is there on time when he is supposed to be. He's beautiful!"[16] *Legacy* gave Mel the chance to once again record with Ray Brown. Both men were two of the most recorded jazz musicians of all-time, yet hadn't recorded together since Brown's 1956 release *Ray Brown: Bass Hit* (Verve). [17]

On November 21, Mel recorded Joe Lovano's debut album as a leader *Tones, Shapes and Colors* (Soul Note) at the Jazz Centre of New York. In addition to Mel, the live recording featured Kenny Werner and Dennis Irwin, Lovano's working quartet at the time. Becoming known through his frequent tours to Europe as a sideman, Lovano was approached with the opportunity to record as a leader by the European Soul Note label. Lovano explained the origins of *Tones, Shapes and Colors*:

> The way the album happened for me was a very natural progression. After recording several albums with Paul (Motion) for ECM, we began to record for the Black Saint-Soul Note label. I developed a relationship with Giovanni Bonandrini, the president of Soul Note Records, and he approached me about doing an album as leader. I wanted my first recording as leader to be a live concert. I thought it was really important for people to hear me play in a live performance, a complete performance situation. I chose the quartet with Mel, Dennis, and Kenny, because we had been playing together and developing a repertoire. It felt so beautiful to explore music with that particular quartet, at that particular time.[18]

Kenny Werner recalled the intensity of that quartet and the inspired gigs they played in Boston leading up to the recording:

> The week before we recorded *Tones, Shapes and Colors* we played at the 1369 club in Boston. I don't know if it was because of the small stage or what, but those gigs in Boston were *killing.* And I know people really dig the record that came out, but Joe and I always joke that people should have heard us in Boston. It was super happening and very organic.[19]

Tones, Shapes and Colors is one of Mel's greatest small group recordings. His cymbal colors and textures created a continually shifting sonic backdrop, and in typical Mel fashion, when it was time to swing his cymbal beat wrapped a comforting blanket of sound around the whole band. His bass drum and toms were used as both melodic voices and low register textures. Most importantly, his drumming demonstrated that orchestration and patience were as powerful musical tools as chops and speed. For an example of this, listen to how he accompanied Joe Lovano's solo on the song "Chess Mates." After building the solo for over two minutes Mel pushed the intensity to new heights by moving from his main ride cymbal to his Chinese cymbal. At the point where other drummers might have added volume or overplayed, Mel elevated the music by changing his cymbal sound and intensifying the texture.

In the fall of 1985 Mel Lewis and The Jazz Orchestra once again toured Europe. The tour included a stop in Stockholm to perform at the Stockholm Jazz Festival. The performance was significant because the band shared the concert bill with the Count Basie Orchestra led by Thad Jones. Count Basie had passed in April of 1984, and in February of 1985, Thad had taken over the Basie band as leader.[20] Thad had finished his commitments in Denmark and relocated back to the United States with his Danish wife, Lis, and their six-year-old son, Thad Jr. While at the Stockholm Jazz Festival, Thad sat in with Mel's band, giving them a brief chance to reconnect musically.[21] Dick Oatts recalled the Thad Jones/Mel Lewis reunion in Stockholm:

> You know, when all was said and done, Mel loved Thad. Eventually Mel realized that his band was a result of the choices Thad had made. And by 1985, Mel was feeling a lot better about his own career.
>
> We spent twenty-two hours on a bus to play at the Stockholm Jazz Festival, after our gig in Lugano, Switzerland. We performed as soon as we arrived. Mel's band played first and the Basie band, fronted by Thad, played second. Mel called a great set of music. To his credit, it was a celebration of Thad Jones and Bob Brookmeyer, his favorite composers. We had a fantastic set and so did the Basie band. It was an amazing night of two different approaches in music and performance. Mel was extremely happy about his ability to keep his (and Thad's) direction going on his own.[22]

The Stockholm Jazz Festival was not the first time that Thad and Mel had reunited since their "separation" in 1979. Their first reunion occurred years prior when Thad brought his Danish band Eclipse to New York City for a series of concerts. Exactly what the men said to each other during their conversation is unknown, and at that very personal and private moment, their words were no one else's business. What is important, and what has often been untold in publications, is that the two men spoke to each other again and achieved some type of reconciliation in their friendship. Dennis Mackrel recalled the night Thad and Mel reconnected at the Village Vanguard:

People often rewrite history and I don't want to do that. I want to respect their privacy. But, I can tell you they both were very respectful to each other, they hugged each other, and I remember seeing them talk. They seemed to talk all night, and it was a good thing, it *definitely* was a good thing. I wasn't privy to the conversation, but I remember that there was a nice feeling being there at that moment. It was a very dignified meeting.[23]

Thad and Mel's conversation that night at the Vanguard, and their performance later at the Stockholm Jazz Festival, went a long way to healing some of Mel's personal wounds.[24] Mel later recalled a conversation he had with Thad in 1985, and how they discussed plans for the future:

> We had a nice conversation; we were talking about some future things together, hopefully with the Basie Band and our band, my band. That we would try to connect and do some things like Basie and Ellington used to do, and we thought that he could do some writing and all.[25]

They remained in touch, but unfortunately a musical collaboration never took place. As Mel continued his career and fight with cancer, unknown to most, including Mel, Thad was silently fighting his own.

After the extreme highs and lows of 1985, the beginning of 1986 was an exciting time for Mel as February marked the twenty-year anniversary of the Thad Jones/Mel Lewis Orchestra at the Village Vanguard. He and Max Gordon had no visions of ending what had become the longest steady gig in the history of jazz. On February 10, the band celebrated its twentieth anniversary and played to a standing-room-only crowd at the Village Vanguard.[26] Then February 17–24, the band continued the celebration with nightly performances that featured alumni of the band. Musicians who performed throughout the week included: Harold Danko and Jim NcNeely on piano, Bob Brookmeyer on trombone, Rufus Reid on bass, Jon Faddis and Lew Soloff on trumpet, and Pepper Adams and Jerry Dodgion on saxophone.[27]

Thad Jones was also scheduled to make a surprise guest appearance during the week. Mel had even planned to record the final evening of performances featuring Thad, in hopes of releasing an album titled *Thad Jones with Mel Lewis and The Jazz Orchestra.*[28] Unfortunately, Mel's communication with Thad abruptly stopped only days before the engagement. After leaving several phone messages, Mel finally spoke to Thad's wife Lis and learned that Thad was feeling very ill and would not be able to make the performance on February 24.[29] Thad's cancelation was disappointing, and at the time, his lack of communication made it look like he had skipped out on Mel once again. Several days later, it was learned that Thad's absence was a result of being hospitalized in Denmark with severe stomach ulcers.[30] Thad was becoming very sick, yet no one knew the severity at the time. Sadly, his health rapidly deteriorated throughout the spring of 1986.

Jazz historian and journalist Ira Gitler attended the last night of the anniversary celebration on February 24 and gave the performance a rave review in *JazzTimes*. Speaking to Gitler that night, Mel stated, "I've never been as happy as I've been this week with the band. I don't think a band could be any better as far as playing together is concerned. We care about each other on and off the stand."[31] The week was a fitting celebration for the band that helped define the club, and for the club that helped define the band.

Mel recorded several albums throughout the spring of 1986, including *Hank Crawford/Jimmy McGriff: Soul Survivors* (Milestone), *Jimmy Knepper: Dream Dancing* (Criss Cross), *Renee Manning: Uhm…Uhm…Uhmmm!* (Ken), *Bob Stewart: In a Sentimental Mood* (Stash), and *Al Porcino Big Band: In Oblivion* (Jazz Mark).[32] For the rest of the summer he worked Monday nights at the Vanguard, traveled to Finland to be a guest artist, and took freelance work in New York City.[33]

During the summer of 1986, while battling his own disease, Mel abruptly learned of the severity of Thad Jones's illness. After multiple health issues earlier that spring, including the stomach ulcers that kept him from the band's twentieth anniversary celebration, Thad had been diagnosed with cancer in May. When discovered, his cancer was already in the severe stages, and after a short four-month battle, Thad Jones passed away on August 21, 1986.[34] His death was so unexpected that it sent shock waves through the jazz community. Mel recalled how abruptly he learned that Thad was ill:

> I didn't know how sick he was until six days before he passed. I was over in Helsinki for a festival and I called him, and that's when he told me for the first time. I mean I had heard rumors, but that was the first time I found out what he really had. Less than a week

later he was gone. He left the band back at the end of 1978; he left the band to live over in Denmark. But we kept in touch, and we didn't part enemies like so many people thought.[35]

When Thad died, Mel lost a dear friend and someone he considered family. Together they created some of the greatest big band music the world has ever known. Along the way, they positively affected the lives of so many young jazz musicians. When asked how he remembered his longtime partner, Mel responded, "He was a big, happy guy, who loved to party and to teach younger musicians."[36]

After the shock of Thad's death, Mel spent the remainder of 1986 traveling the world as a guest artist. He played and recorded with pianist and arranger Joe Haider in Switzerland, took part in the 1986 Floating Jazz Festival in late October, and returned to Cologne several times to work with the WDR Big Band.[37] The next year, 1987, was also a busy year of travel for Mel, spending time in Germany, Holland, and Austria. Much like his contemporaries Bob Brookmeyer and Bill Holman, because of the European interest and love of jazz music, coupled with many European governments' funding of the arts, Mel could make a comfortable living by teaching and playing in Europe. When not in Europe, he was in New York City playing Monday night at the Village Vanguard, as well as regularly with Loren Schoenberg's Jazz Orchestra and the American Jazz Orchestra.

In April, Mel and Dennis Irwin recorded a trio album led by pianist Pete Malinverni. Recorded by Rudy Van Gelder at his studio in Englewood Cliffs, New Jersey, the pristinely recorded session captured Mel's remarkable brushwork. The audio quality on *Pete Malinverni: Don't Be Shy* (Sea Breeze) is so clear that listening to it makes one feel as though Mel is sitting right beside you playing brushes. His brush playing on George Gershwin's classic composition "Who Cares" is a prime example of his ability to subdivide a time feel in a multitude of ways, while always maintaining legato-sounding strokes and quietly blending the sound of his hi-hat into the sound of his snare drum. *Don't Be Shy* is one of Mel's lesser-known small group recordings, but one that should be sought out and listened to as it features some of Mel's finest brushwork, as well as great playing from Dennis Irwin and Pete Malinverni. As he approached his fifty-ninth birthday Mel was musically in his prime; even with continued cancer treatments, he showed few signs of slowing down.

One of the most painful and emotionally trying times in Mel's life came at the end of 1987. On November 23, he tragically lost his daughter Anita who had just turned thirty-four that October. Mel loved his daughters more than anything in the world, and Anita's heartbreaking suicide felt nearly too much to bear. The tragedy left Mel utterly distressed and saddened; yet he found solace in Doris and daughters Lori and Donna who still lived in the area. Mel also found relief from his heartache behind the drums, where the never-ending worries of the world always seemed so far away. ‖

1 Mel and Doris at their daughter Lori's wedding.

Photo courtesy of the Sokoloff family.

el Lewis *Photo by Joan Powers © Used by permission of Joan*
rs.

Chapter 22
Hello and Goodbye

In February of 1988, Mel Lewis and The Jazz Orchestra played their annual weeklong engagement at the Village Vanguard, this time celebrating their twenty-second birthday. The band used the week at the Vanguard, February 11–15, to record three new albums for the Musicmasters label. Throughout the five nights, the band recorded nine new arrangements for *Mel Lewis and The Jazz Orchestra: Soft Lights and Hot Music* (Musicmasters). The recording featured the writing and arranging of Mike Abene, Ted Nash, Kenny Werner, Jim McNeely, Bill Finegan, and Mike Crotty. *Soft Lights and Hot Music* showcased the band's ability to make challenging music sound effortless and swinging, such as McNeely's composition "Off the Cuff," and Werner's "Compensation." The album also displayed the band's ability to play incredibly cohesive ensemble passages, thanks to the leadership once again of Mosca, Oatts, and Gardner. When the ensemble dissolved into a solo section, Mel, Dennis Irwin, and Kenny Werner gave the soloists the freedom to create and develop their solo with few musical limits. Ralph Lalama, Glenn Drewes, Ted Nash, Dick Oatts, Joe Lovano, Kenny Werner, Jim Powell, John Mosca, and Ed Neumeister were all featured soloists on the album.

The second and third albums the band recorded that week were titled *Mel Lewis Jazz Orchestra: The Definitive Thad Jones Vol. 1* and *Mel Lewis Jazz Orchestra: The Definitive Thad Jones Vol. 2* (Musicmasters). Both recordings featured several of Thad Jones's most famous arrangements from the Thad Jones/Lewis Orchestra era including "Low Down," "Quietude," "Three in One," "Walkin' About," "The Little Pixie," "Second Race," "Tip Toe," "Don't Get Sassy," "Rhoda Map," and "Cherry Juice." *The Definitive Thad Jones Vol. 1* and *Vol. 2* became an interesting bookend in Mel's career. The recordings served as a tribute to Thad and also became the last recorded performance of Mel playing the music that defined much of his career. Interestingly, Dick Oatts explained that the recordings were never planned:

> *The Definitive Thad Jones* recordings were afterthoughts. They were the charts we played in between what we recorded for *Soft Lights and Hot Music*. We were playing Thad's charts as filler material. When Musicmasters was down at the Vanguard that week, they recorded

everything we played. So Mel said, "Let's put out two more records because we have the music in the can. We'll call it *The Definitive Thad Jones* because they are all Thad's charts." However, it wasn't like we sat down and thought about those albums from start to finish.

Mel just needed product out there. Releasing those albums was the best way for him to promote Mel Lewis and The Jazz Orchestra. And to be honest, I was against the *Definitive Thad Jones* recordings because I thought maybe some of the takes weren't good enough. But Mel said, "Oh, Oatts you are too picky." And he was right.[1]

Thanks to the inspired playing by Mel and the band, the music on *The Definitive Thad Jones* has never sounded anything close to an afterthought. As Loren Schoenberg stated in the album's liner notes, "Mel was his own sternest critic, and most protective of the band's reputation. He felt that these new interpretations were valid both on their own, and in comparison to the originals."[2] Even though Mel continually persuaded the band members to compose for the group, he always kept Thad's arrangements in heavy rotation. As Mel put it,

> I knew that I could never stop playing Thad's arrangements because we were going to get requests anyway and because if we stopped playing Thad that would be the end of Thad. Period. Because he had nobody in Europe who could play his music, even with him conducting. Because, now this sounds like braggadocio, but Thad Jones' music, without me, means nothing. I'm the only one who can make this music happen. We've proved it. [3]

Soft Lights and Hot Music and *The Definitive Thad Jones* continued Mel's tradition of recording the band during live performances. As the music world adopted new technology, computers, and high-tech recording studios, Mel continued to record live at the Village Vanguard with two microphones:

> I insist on setup, it has to be exactly the way the band sets up normally at the Vanguard. So that we're comfortable. If the engineer doesn't like it, then he's not going to be the engineer. I also insist on and prefer two-track recording. I don't like them to have control over our dynamics. Which takes me back to the old days when I was

recording 78's. Because I think a musician is entitled to be himself
on a record.[4]

After the recording of *Naturally* in 1979, which was the first ever digital
recording of a big band, Mel rarely took the band back into a recording studio.[5]
Thanks to his unenthusiastic attitude for recording big bands in studios, the six
live albums that the band released during the 1980s give the feeling of sitting and
listening to the band live at the Village Vanguard on a Monday night.

During 1988, Mel traveled to Europe several times with his band and also
returned frequently as a guest artist. While in New York City, he continued
recording as a sideman, making albums with pianist Harold Danko, Loren
Schoenberg and his Jazz Orchestra, Garry Dial and Dick Oatts, Buck Clayton,
and the American Jazz Orchestra.

Mel also continued his lengthy battle with Melanoma. That spring, he
underwent surgery to remove his underarm lymph nodes, because they too had
been taken over with cancer. After the procedure he healed quickly and began
chemotherapy treatments. Despite the growing challenges of his health, Mel
rarely spoke about his condition. It was not that he was afraid to talk about it;
sometimes he would, but he always preferred to converse about sports, politics,
or the future plans of his band. Dick Oatts explained Mel's positive attitude saying,
"Mel always wanted to give guys hope, so he never basked in the misery of his
cancer. He was always open to talk about it, but in a very positive way. He'd say,
'Oh, they're going to get this stuff, don't worry about it.'"[6] Always looking to the
future, Mel made plans to record a new small group album in the spring of 1989.

One month shy of his sixtieth birthday, Mel led a sextet of some of his
favorite musicians into RCA Recording Studios and recorded a new small group
album as leader. *Mel Lewis Sextet: The Lost Art* (Musicmasters) was recorded on
April 11 and 12, 1989, and is one of most adventurous small group albums Mel
ever recorded. Joining him were Kenny Werner on piano, Dennis Irwin on bass,
Gary Smulyan on baritone saxophone, Dick Oatts on tenor, alto, and soprano
saxophones, John Mosca on trombone, and Jim Powell on flugelhorn.[7]

The recording included original compositions from Smulyan ("One for
Max") and Oatts ("Face Value" and "Native American"). However, the largest
compositional contribution was that of Werner, who composed "Voyager,"
"Bulgaria," "Allanjuneally," "Trio for B.B.," and "Oold Ranger." The contemporary
music on the album allowed Mel to push his own musical boundaries and play in a

very modern drumming style. For some listeners, Mel's drumming on the album was a vast departure from his "normal" style. However, for those who had closely followed his playing throughout the decade, his drumming on the recording was simply the continued evolution of his style. On *The Lost Art*, Mel expanded on the sounds and textures that he played during Brookmeyer's compositions on *Make Me Smile* and Joe Lovano's *Tones, Shapes and Colors*.[8] Mel explained his drumming on *The Lost Art* by stating,

> What am I supposed to do? Stay in mold? No way. Yeah, it's a modern album of music that goes in a variety of directions. But time is there in one form or another; it remains the determining factor in everything I play.
>
> Because I really know "inside" music, conventional modern jazz, I have the basis to move "outside." Only musicians who have this foundation, like Coltrane, who work out all the possibilities of the "inside," can really do the thing on the "outside."
>
> What I do on this album is something that was bound to happen. I just had to get into the right environment. I had been playing only with beboppers. I didn't get with musicians who stepped out on a limb and tried things. Now I do—with Kenny Werner, Dick Oatts, Jim McNeely, Bob Brookmeyer, and others.[9]

Even as late as the April recording of *The Lost Art*, the musicians who worked with Mel did not sense that he was in pain or physically struggling from cancer. The album not only proved his continued drive to make music, but was also evidence that he had lost no musical ability and was still one of the world's greatest drummers. John Mosca recalled *The Lost Art* session, as well as Mel's playing and health at the time:

> At the time, and at the age I was then, it was very easy to be in denial about the whole situation (Lewis's cancer) because Mel was largely denying it himself. Through force of will, and the fact that he loved to play, he was a strong guy who was very determined to beat the cancer. You know, at the time there was nothing like the awareness there is now of how lethal skin cancer could be. It was very hard to believe how sick he really was because he was still playing his ass off. There

was no diminution of his skills, until maybe the last couple of jobs …
Even less than one year before his death he was really playing great. I
mean you can really hear it on that record; he seemed to be quite well
in most respects.[10]

Dick Oatts also remembered the intensity of Mel's drumming during the
recording. However, for Oatts, a conversation during the session prompted his
first realization of just how sick Mel really was:

When we recorded *The Lost Art* Mel played his ass off. I remember
him being skinnier at the time, maybe from his treatments, but it
was business as usual. I had written this tune, it was the last one on
the date and it was really fast ("Face Value"). It was really up there in
tempo and I felt badly about what I played, meanwhile Smulyan and
Mosca were just tearing it up. So I said, "Mel can we just do one more
take?" And Mel said, "Oatts, I am just too wasted. I'm just too tired."
And Mel would *never* say that if he had any energy at all. And when
he said that I said ok, because you had to respect that. Mel never, *ever*,
complained about energy or things like that. That was the beginning
of me realizing that this great drummer was really suffering.[11]

Mel began and ended *The Lost Art* with two unaccompanied drum solos
titled "Hello" and "Goodbye." Sadly, the recording was the last of Mel's career as a
leader and became one of his final musical goodbyes.

For much of the summer of 1989, Mel traveled and performed internationally.
His first notable gig took place in Paris that June, when he performed on an all-star
tribute concert to Charlie Parker. The big band assembled for the event included
jazz legends Jimmy Heath, James Moody, Benny Carter, Clark Terry, Phil Woods,
and was led by pianist Jay McShann. A thirty-minute video documentary was
made of the rehearsal and concert, as well as an audio recording released as a two-
compact-disc set titled *The Jay McShann Kansas City Band: Paris All-Star Blues*
(Heritage Jazz).

In July, Mel toured with his friend and colleague Loren Schoenberg. The
two men performed with the American Jazz Orchestra on a tour of Japan and
Southeast Asia that featured the group performing classic arrangements of the
Duke Ellington Orchestra. For Mel, one of the highlights of the tour was an

impromptu jam session during the band's stay in Hong Kong. Members of the American Jazz Orchestra as well as members of saxophonist Michael Brecker's group turned up at the Jazz Club and surprised management by asking to use the stage, jamming until the early hours of the morning. Mel took to the stage with Schoenberg, bassist Marc Johnson, and Brecker's pianist Joey Calderazzo. Adam Nussbuam, who was on tour with Brecker, also sat in on drums and spent the rest of the evening hanging out with Mel.

During Mel's final tour that summer, Doris traveled with him to Germany as he once again performed with the WDR Band. Sadly, during the tour Mel's deteriorating health finally caught up with his ability to play. In an article published by *JazzTimes*, Mel colorfully described his health issues during his trip to Germany. As usual, Mel was positive about his struggle with cancer and excited to talk about the future of his band. Ira Gitler's article displayed Mel's undying spirit and motivation; it was simply titled *"Mel Lewis: Road Warrior"*:

...If you are not aware of it, Lewis has been battling cancer and when I say "battling" I mean this "road warrior" (and he was on the scene before that other Mel—Gibson) has his sticks, brushes and mallets at the ready. Sometimes he tries to do too much.

His recent trip to Germany is a case in point. "They bring me over there approximately 12 months a year," Mel told me on a mid-December Sunday afternoon in his living room. "I work there with Bob Brookmeyer, Bill Holman, with Jiggs Whigham; and as a leader, myself."

This time the Cologne Radio Band, of which the aforementioned Eardley is a member, was scheduled to go to the east to play in Leipzig. "I took my wife Doris, and we had no idea "the wall" was going to come down," he explains. "It was a thrill to be there when it happened."

Lewis began in Cologne by playing with "the large orchestra, strings and the whole thing. I just did a regular program with Jerry Van Rooyen conducting. No problem. And we had Saturday and Sunday off. My project for Leipzig started on Monday and was supposed to be a definitive Thad Jones thing. We rehearsed Monday from 10 to 4, Tuesday, 10 to 4, bla, bla, bla—'til Friday. I'm taking my medicine every day, and the weather was lovely in Cologne. I'm playing *Groove Merchant* after rehearsing *Cherry Juice* many times. *Groove Merchant* is a shuffle —all of a sudden I'm on the floor. I lost complete control of my left arm. And I'm on the floor because I'm trying to get the stick. And I'm still playing with my right hand up on top. I finished the piece of music. That's me. That's the way I am. But that was it. No feeling in the arm. They took me to one of the best hospitals and figured out I taking too strong a dose of my medicine."

Mel relaxed on Saturday and Sunday and was told he shouldn't go to Leipzig. "But that's what I was hired for," he protested.

Dennis Mackrel, the former Count Basie drummer who was in Vienna playing a Bix Beiderbecke program with Loren Schoenberg, agreed to come in and stand by. "We flew to Leipzig," Mel narrates. "The air was bad, it looked like Pittsburgh in the old days. All of this was for radio. I got through the first night. The second night, which was not recorded, I lost control of my nerves in my left arm. Dennis did the whole show. On the third day's broadcast we both played."

Back in Cologne, Lewis was told he was going home. "No I can do Stuttgart," he protested. It took a phone call from his old buddy Brookmeyer who called and "gave me hell." The next day Bob called again and convinced him to return to New York. Back in Manhattan Mel went right to the hospital. "That first week I lost my memory," he says. "I was in 'No-No Land.' So everybody was right. I couldn't have played."

But when he was let out the following Monday the first question he asked as "When can I go back to work?" He was told, "Go back but don't overdo it. And if you can't don't."

The Mel Lewis Jazz Orchestra has used John Riley and Danny Gottlieb as subs. Mel calls then "excellent drummers" but his number one deputy is Mackrel, as he was on the Monday after this interview, December 18, at the Vanguard. Dennis and Mel split the night.

"Dennis has been *listening* to this band and he knows what's going on," Lewis informs. "He loves me. He's willing to make the sacrifices. He can't be Mel Lewis, just like I can't be Tiny Kahn and I don't want to be. But most of his Mondays are free and he's just going to be there. It means I can go there and not worry. If I play one tune, three tunes, half the night, the first set, he's there. I can go home and get into bed or go out front, relax and just listen. As soon as I can avoid this, I will. I want to really get well, and I want to be able to play. Especially since we've got a new album to make."

When it comes to the band's recording activities, Lewis is very upbeat, not surprising with the results of the last two Musicmasters' CDs—*Soft Lights and Sweet Music* and a collection of Thad Jones charts—both done live at the Vanguard. The next one will be a studio date, featuring the writing of former band pianist Jim McNeely and present keyboarder Kenny Werner.

"They're writing beyond Thad Jones, beyond Bob Brookmeyer, but *from* that." Mel emphasizes. "This is from playing with the band. This is what they learned with me but, harmonically, what they learned from those guys (Jones and Brookmeyer) just playing piano, sitting in front of the band. "Who did Thad learn from?" he continues. "Ellington. Sitting in Basie's band he wasn't thrilled. He didn't play enough or write enough. Brookmeyer didn't write enough and didn't play enough in that period either."

The Thad Jones-Mel Lewis Orchestra gave both these men an important outlet. One of Mel's regrets is that he never got Al Cohn to write for his band. "The last years, his eyes were gone and he just wanted to play," Lewis reflects. Then he returns to the present. "Now Ted Nash is writing. Earl McIntyre. Practically everybody's studying with Brookmeyer and Manny Albam at the EMI classes, one day every week. Ed Neumeister just brought in a new chart and (alumnus) Jerry Dodgion always comes up with something.

"We want to take longer with this new album because it's going to be more difficult and because it's going to be a departure. We're going to shock a lot of people. But it's not crazy. It's not Globe Unity. But it's going to take this band somewhere no other band in this United States ever went. I think McNeely is the man of the future. He really is."

Lewis is justifiably proud of his sections and soloists, as well as his writers. "This band has a unique way of playing ensemble—totally different from those (Jones-Lewis) days," he feels. "I think if Thad were around he'd be very proud of it. I'm sure he would."

I agree that Thad would be proud. We certainly are.[12]

What the article did not mention was that after meeting with his doctor back in New York, Mel learned that the Melanoma had spread to his lungs. "It must have got in there in August, we discovered it in September," he recalled.[13] His health issues in Germany were not solely a result of his medication; they were a result of his body being taken over with disease. After years of fighting his initial Melanoma, Mel was now more than ever in the fight for his life. The severity of the cancer on his lungs led to intense chemotherapy treatments that quickly took a toll on his body, resulting in weight and hair loss. The treatments often drained his energy, yet never diminished his optimism:

> I've been taking chemotherapy ever since, and this Interferon. I've taken all the miracle drugs, and it's holding it in check. We're watching, and we're just hoping and waiting for shrinkage, which will happen one day. As long as it's not getting bigger it means we've got it under control. But until it shrinks, I'm not cured ... I'm lucky it didn't get into my liver or somewhere where it could have done some real damage. My lungs are in such good shape I can breathe deeply. I'm more careful about what I eat now. I get more rest that I used to. You know, I really take advantage of resting so that I've got plenty of energy. I had to get a blood transfusion yesterday, for the second time now, because the chemo eats up all my red blood corpuscles. Chemo cures one thing and kills another, so you've got to fight all these different things. But I've learned to appreciate life more now. Now I realize how close I've been to losing it.
>
> I'm straight ahead now where I used to take the saying before, "Don't worry about something, screw it." Now I feel I've got to get it done, and less procrastination. Now I feel like I haven't got that much time, so there's not that much time for compromise. Oh, I mean I'll always be a compromiser, but still I figure, you know to be fair, but not when it comes to music. As you will see with the future albums I'm going to make. I don't give a damn about standards and airplay and all that crap. From now on I'm going back. I'm gonna be what I always was, like we were when we first started, you know, the best music possible, artistic and for the sake of the music.[14]

In August, Mel recorded what would be his last small group album. *The Spirit* was led by pianist Pete Malinverni and took place once again at Rudy Van Gelder's studio in Edgewood Cliffs, New Jersey. Malinverni recalled the circumstances surrounding the recording and how Mel's astounding strength throughout the process resulted in the album being titled *The Spirit*:

> I had the opportunity, on Joe Lovano's recommendation, to sub in Mel's band at the Vanguard many times. I always marveled at how, no matter how many instruments were playing at no matter what dynamic level, the band always sounded like a small group, with all the attendant agility and subtlety. I'd already made my first trio recording, "Don't Be Shy," with Mel and Dennis Irwin and we continued to work together until 1989, when I played a quartet gig with Mel, Ralph Lalama and bassist Pat O'Leary that, unbeknownst to me, Pat recorded on his Sony Walkman. We listened to it afterward and I thought, "wow, this group really sounds great." Since I had a bunch of music together that was fit for that quartet, I decided it was time to make my second album as leader. Everyone was into the session so I called Rudy Van Gelder to see if he could record it. Mel was doing both radiation and chemotherapy at the time and we had to schedule the recording on a date when Mel would be strong enough to do it. Rudy told me he would be out of town on the date we had settled on and that he couldn't do the session. I said, "Alright, Rudy, thanks anyway," and hung up the phone. Only about a half hour later Rudy called me back and said, "I'm going to cancel my vacation and do this for you—I understand what you're trying to do and it's important." People don't give Rudy Van Gelder enough credit for the generous person he is. He really loves the music, appreciates relationships, and will do what he can for you.
>
> On the day of the recording, when I picked Mel up at his place on the Upper West Side he told me that the chemo drugs had been making him sick that morning. I had a banana in the car and gave it to him; thankfully he was able to keep it down and settle his stomach as we drove to Jersey. In between takes, Mel would go into Rudy's booth and lay down on his couch to rest. All of this was going on with Mel, but when you listen to the record, he is the youngest guy

on the date! We were recording tunes, some of them with odd forms, that we'd rehearsed only once at his apartment—but Mel played that music like he had written it. It was amazing! I named the album, which turned out to be his final recording, "The Spirit," because I saw, through Mel Lewis, that the spirit is truly stronger than the flesh.

That fall, while maintaining his band and continuing extensive medical treatments, Mel played two of the most exciting performances of his career. On September 17, 1989, he had the privilege of performing at the White House for President George H. W. Bush. Mel joined fellow jazz legends Benny Carter, Milt Hinton, and Dick Hyman as they performed and were honored as part of the "In Performance at the White House" series.[15] During the White House visit Mel and Doris were invited into the president's private living quarters. Doris recalled the experience and her husband's conversation with President Bush:

> We were sitting in the President's private living space, and he came over and talked with us. Mel immediately said, "I can't believe I am sitting here with the President of The United States." And you know the President responded, "I can't believe I am sitting here with the world's greatest drummer." Mel saw his opening and replied, "You know mister President, I have a seventeen-piece band and I'd sure like to bring it to the White House." Can you imagine! We are sitting there with the President of The United States, who had the burdens of the world on his shoulders, and Mel is trying to book a gig! The President was very gracious and said, "You'll just have to speak with my private secretary about that."[16]

For Mel, the opportunity to spend time with and perform for the president was a thrilling experience. Additionally, the White House's recognition of him as a "jazz legend" was an overdue and well-deserved honor.

Mel's second memorable performance that fall took place at Cooper Union Hall in Manhattan on October 26. The evening was a musical retrospective of Mel's career and he was the featured performer with the American Jazz Orchestra. Loren Schoenberg was responsible for organizing the concert and spent countless hours tracking down musical arrangements from Mel's past.[17] Thanks to Schoenberg's efforts, the historic event showcased Mel masterfully leading the band through charts that he hadn't played in decades. The concert included arrangements by Al Cohn, Bill Holman, Bob Brookmeyer, and others. At the conclusion of the performance, the crowd and musicians on stage erupted in a standing ovation for Mel. It was a fitting and emotional tribute to Mel Lewis, a man who was still giving all he had to the music he loved.

Throughout November and December of 1989, Mel performed as much as possible with the Loren Schoenberg Jazz Orchestra, the American Jazz Orchestra, and his own big band. Even as his health deteriorated, he was at the Village Vanguard every Monday night. Only weeks before he passed Mel told journalist Rick Mattingly, "I'll be at the Vanguard Monday night, I'm not sure if I'll feel like playing, so there will be a sub on hand. But I'll be there."[18]

Mel played the drums right up until the very end of his life. He never stopped believing that he would beat cancer and he never quit planning his next great recording. When asked how he viewed himself, he responded, "I think Mel Lewis is a person who has made up his mind that there is going to be great music in this world for as long as there is life, and in his time, he is going to do everything that he can to perpetuate it, even at the cost of the good life."[19] Much like the sixty years that proceeded, Mel's final weeks were devoted to his family and music. On January 13, 1990, Mel Lewis and The Jazz Orchestra performed in New Orleans for a standing-room-only crowd at the International Association of Jazz Educators convention.[20] Mel's doctor had advised him against the performance, but Mel responded by simply saying, "I have to show those people what a *real* band sounds like."[21] By that time, the cancer had spread to Mel's brain and taken quite a toll on his body and physical appearance. He had to be assisted onto the stage, making it apparent to those in attendance that the performance was likely to be his last. The sobering reality of the moment was not lost on the band members, many of whom were openly crying throughout the performance. After leading his band through an emotional rendition of Thad Jones's ballad "To You," Mel Lewis left the bandstand for the last time.

On February 2, 1990, Mel Lewis passed away at the age of sixty.[22] Sadly, he was one week shy of celebrating his twenty-fourth anniversary at the Village Vanguard. With his untimely passing, jazz music lost one of its greatest musicians and biggest advocates. Mel was born a jazz drummer and died a jazz drummer; few have ever contributed as much to the art form as he did. ‖

See Appendix Transcriptions and Listening Guides for this chapter: "Three and One" and "Tip-Toe"

1 The View From the Back of the Band.

Used by permission of the University of Missouri-Kansas City Libraries,
Dr. Kenneth J. LaBudde Department of Special Collections.

Chapter 23
Memories of Mel

Mel Lewis devoted his life to developing a unique style of drumming in hopes of making a lasting contribution to jazz music. In a 1967 *DownBeat* interview he stated,

> I hope that I've really fallen into something new and valid in terms of big band drumming. I hope that I'm doing something that will make a real contribution. That's what a musician really strives for—not to be taken for granted as just a good player, but having made a real contribution to the music.[1]

Mel succeeded. His contributions to jazz drumming and music are unsurpassed.

While Mel's musical contributions will forever be preserved with the music he recorded, his spirit is carried on within the musicians he mentored and performed with. At the time of Mel's death, all of the members of his big band had been with him for at least five years, and several for over a decade. Many of these musicians continue to perform every Monday night at the Village Vanguard in the Vanguard Jazz Orchestra. The group is the modern extension of the Thad Jones/Mel Lewis Jazz Orchestra and Mel Lewis and The Jazz Orchestra. Dick Oatts explained that the Vanguard Jazz Orchestra is the continuation of what Mel spent his life creating:

> From the beginning it was always Thad Jones/Mel Lewis *and* The Jazz Orchestra. It was the Jazz Orchestra with two stars out front, Thad Jones and Mel Lewis. Then it became Mel Lewis *and* The Jazz Orchestra. Even after Mel died, we were still The Jazz Orchestra, just not with Thad Jones or Mel Lewis. Now we are the Vanguard Jazz Orchestra. And even though we play at the Village Vanguard, we don't call ourselves the Village Vanguard Orchestra. We call ourselves the Vanguard Jazz Orchestra because the word vanguard means going forward, and that's what we decided to do. That's what Mel would have wanted us to do.[2]

The Vanguard Jazz Orchestra honors Mel's legacy by remaining one of the most influential big bands in jazz. Each Monday they still perform the classic music of Thad Jones and Bob Brookmeyer, but by also presenting creative new music by composers such as Jim McNeely, they truly keep Mel's spirit alive and moving forward. ▮

Many of the people who were interviewed for this project wanted their stories and memories of Mel preserved and shared. The following quotations from those interviews serve as a tribute to Mel Lewis and provide unique insight into his personality and drumming.

It is difficult to find the proper words to say. I think of Melvin every day, I miss our life together. Sadly, I cannot reach out to touch him, but his presence is always with me.
—*Doris Sokoloff*

People reading this book and listening to great Jazz music, knew my father as world famous jazz drummer, Mel Lewis. I knew him as "Daddy." Growing up with a famous father certainly had its special moments, but for me, he was just my Dad. He scolded me, he was proud of me, he was my teacher and my hero.

I remember he traveled a lot when we were young. Sometimes gone for a month or more at a time, but he always would write and, when he was finally home, he would bring us special gifts from all over the world. I remember he was always home for Thanksgiving and at Christmas time. We lived far from family, which meant it was usually just the five of us; it was nice to be together. It took many years to get him to agree to decorate for Christmas, because we are Jewish. Out of respect, he never allowed it while my grandparents were still living, but I will never forget the year he finally let us buy a real Christmas tree. He was powerless in a house of all women! I recall him sitting in his recliner, admiring the small nod to Christmas. It became a tradition.

I remember when he took me on my first roller coaster ride at Playland Amusement Park, and he and my sister Anita would ride the racehorses. I remember Saturday mornings when he would take me to my piano lessons and the half hour lesson always turned into an hour because of Dad's lengthy conversations (Dad loved to talk as you all well know), followed by a stop at the Deli for lunch; he would talk and I would listen. I remember he and Mom took me to my first Mets game, his favorite team. He would also come to my high school's football games and watch me cheerlead.

I remember family vacations always were planned around his gigs, mostly jazz festivals. I remember him coming to Wildwood, New Jersey, with us just for a regular vacation with Mom and me. I remember bringing friends to fun gigs like Festival on the River and Glen Island Casino. I remember trips to the Vanguard and getting to hang out with all the musicians in the band; they always made me feel special.

I remember when we moved to NYC and taking walks to the park with him. I remember after I moved out, I spoke to him every day. I remember him walking me down the aisle on my wedding day and at the reception he got up to play the drums with the band he hired because, after all, he's Mel Lewis and everyone wanted to hear him play. I remember when I was getting close to the birth of our daughter Samantha, his first grandchild, he had to fly to Europe and he said to me, "Now don't give birth until I get back." I went into labor the day after he left. I cried when I spoke to him, apologizing because Samantha just couldn't wait. He laughed and was so happy and couldn't wait to get home to see her. He was so proud she was named after his father, Sam. I remember him being the funniest Grandpa, he loved and spoiled her and he called her "Sam."

I remember what Dad told us when he was diagnosed the first time with melanoma, and then it subsequently spread, that he would never give up and he would beat the disease. I believed that unquestionably. In 1989, he decided he was having a 60th birthday party because he said he didn't know if he would make his 61st birthday. So he celebrated with the friends and family he loved dearly. Later that year, my sister remarried, and my son Alex was born. Moments he cherished, and thankfully for us, he could be a part of. He fought hard every day and continued to work and travel; he was remarkable.

I remember vividly the last time he played the Village Vanguard. It was my 30th birthday, December 18, 1989, and he played three tunes. It was hard for him to step down and pass the drumsticks to his back up drummer. It was emotional for him, our family, and every person in the club. There wasn't a dry eye in the house. He had such strength and grace that night.

I remember up until the day he passed, he kept telling me, "I'm not going anywhere." I believed him. I miss him every day. He was my Daddy first and he was also Mel Lewis, one of the best jazz drummers in the world, and I want to thank all of you who still support his legacy. I want to personally thank Chris Smith for writing this wonderful tribute to him.

He loved his music, he loved us all.

—*Donna Jeanne Sokoloff Bauman*

Over these many years, I have made peace with the varying emotions that come about when you are the child of a famous person. They are never quite yours alone, and your little life never seems big enough in the shadows of such a large one. Of course you don't realize any of this as a young child caught up in all the side-stream excitement and notoriety you experience when everyone you meet "loves your dad."

So this for me, this is my opportunity to say what I loved about Melvin Sokoloff just being my dad. I loved my father deeply; he was quite a complicated person in a very simple way. I loved that he was an eternal optimist (those who knew him well, know exactly what I mean). I loved that he never compromised on his integrity when choosing his jobs; walking away from jobs when he was asked to do so. I loved that when he was asked by Ray Anthony to change his name, he chose his brother's name, Lewis. I love that all the years he traveled, he always wrote to my mother, my sisters, and me from wherever he was. I loved the nights he came home from long tours, and we would run to the garage so happy that he was back after what seemed an eternity. I loved that he wasn't disappointed in me when I couldn't learn an instrument. I loved that he took us to Playland Amusement Park every year, and the fireworks at Matheson Park. I loved that we would watch the Mets and Giants together on those rare weekends he was home. I don't even remember if I even liked baseball and football, but I do remember that it was uninterrupted "me" time. I loved that, even when I was a teen, he still talked on the phone more than me. I loved that he taught me to drive, and hugged me when I cried as the first car I bought on my own drove away with its new owner. I loved that when I married my first husband, he said "you know you don't have to go thru with this, we can just have a great party," and he loved that he didn't have to say that when I married Ken. I loved that when he called me he always said "hi kiddo," and I loved that he was always so proud of my accomplishments, as humble as they may seem in the shadow of his. I loved and was endlessly amazed that when we walked down the streets of New York City, where millions of strangers are passing us by, we always met more than one person he knew. I loved that on Passover he made the best fried matzah. I loved that he was so unpretentious that on one of his album covers he is actually wearing his pajamas. Finally, I love that when he was dying, he apologized to my mother for leaving her alone.

The essence of my father is engraved on his head stone. He was totally devoted to his music, but also deeply loved his family. I feel gypped that he is not here, that he hasn't met my children: Melanie his name sake, Matthew who, like me, would challenge him always needing the last word, and Jennifer who looks just like him. He would have loved watching them all grow and, undoubtedly, his influence would have been enriching. I miss him terribly.

We are so grateful to Chris for writing this book to keep his unique contribution to jazz history alive and to allow his family to offer a personal perspective on the little life inside the big.

—Lori Sokoloff Lowell

How did Mel Lewis affect your life and career?

I was twenty-six or twenty-seven when I first came to New York and Mel really became almost a father figure, in how much he helped me to adjust to the city, and with advice. And later on after our friendship grew to real friends, he would share things with me about his family, and so forth, like real friends do. This man that I looked up to so much, had become my real friend, and that was so meaningful to me. Our friendship made a great contribution to my coming to New York and my first years there. I can never express in words how much I appreciate everything Mel did for me.

—Marvin Stamm

Man those records Mel made with Terry Gibbs really lit me up, and they are still my favorite. His playing inspired me to write down ten questions that I had about drumming on a piece of paper. One Sunday afternoon I called Mel up out of the blue. He really didn't know me at all at the time, but I desperately wanted to ask him these questions, so I called. Well to my surprise he was at home with his family; they lived up in Irvington, New York at the time. I said, "I am sorry to bother you." And the first thing Mel said, "It is ok, I understand." So I asked him my ten questions and he was really great about it. One of the questions I asked was about tuning and Mel told me, "on the tom-toms you should tune the bottom head to about medium, where it's not loose or tight. Then on the top head, you should tune it to medium-low. Tune your snare drum just a little bit higher than your highest tom-tom. With your bass drum just keep both heads as loose as possible." Mel was a natural drummer so his explanations were really pretty simple. I also asked him about kicking a big band, more specifically if I should always kick the band with my snare drum and never my tom-tom. Mel said, "Well most of the time I use my snare drum, but sometimes I use my tom-tom depending on what the music calls for." I don't know what happened to that list and I can't remember everything I asked him, but I tell you he couldn't have been nicer to me. He took plenty of time with me that day and always did from that point forward. He was so generous and I could never fully thank him for everything he gave me musically. His drumming changed my life.

—John Von Ohlen

Mel Lewis was one of those gentlemen who would tell you exactly what was on his mind. A lot of other people might think about telling you things, but they wouldn't because they didn't want to hurt your feelings. Mel didn't care about that, he wanted to tell you the truth and that was a quality I really liked about him. He was a real sweetheart of a man who loved to play music. His band loved him, and I remember fondly how they used to call him "Uncle Mel."

He would have given anybody that he cared about the shirt off his back if they needed it. I have a set of drums at my house, in my little studio here, that Mel gave me. I was looking to buy a used set and went to him thinking he would know someone who was selling a kit, but he said, "Man I have four sets in my basement, and you can have one on permanent loan." Mel was very generous like that.

—Rufus Reid

He was a true improviser and he absolutely *loved* to play! He played in Boston with me a number of times and the bread was sad, but he didn't care and never even asked about the money. Mel just loved to play and explore music with all kinds of cats, especially the young musicians. That's why he always had such a fresh band, and a band of cats that stayed with him. We were loyal to the band because it was so much fun. You couldn't wait till Monday night, that's how I always felt!

—Joe Lovano

Once Mel became your friend and musical supporter he stayed incredibly loyal and wanted to see your continued musical success. When I decided to leave Mel's band in 1984, I called him up on the phone. I told him that my touring obligations with Stan Getz were becoming more frequent and I felt it was time for him to get a new piano player in the band, one that could make more of the weekly gigs. Well, Mel's first response was silence. It was probably only ten seconds, but it felt like a half hour because Mel speechless was something I had never experienced before! Then he said, "Frankly I am surprised you stayed as long as you did." I took that as a compliment. Then the third thing Mel said really represented him, he said, "Well as far as I am concerned you're not leaving the band, you're just not going to play piano anymore." I was in Mel's circle and even though he would widen the circle with a new piano player, he wanted to keep me involved. His attitude allowed me to stay involved and I really started composing for the band from that point on.

I still think of Mel as "Uncle Mel," his relationship with you was that deep. Of course he had his idiosyncrasies and would often say things that might have been better kept to himself, but Mel was genuine. He had a big heart and a *hell* of a ride beat, I'll say that!

—*Jim McNeely*

The first time I went over to Mel's apartment he started playing me records. We just hung out, listened to music, and he told me stories about my dad from when they worked together with Tex Beneke and in Los Angeles. It was a great introduction to Mel and how he was as a human being. He really loved to sit and talk with people. He was so passionate about his experiences and the music that he had been involved with, that he made me realize it's ok to love what you do and share it with other people.

—*Ted Nash*

I had been writing tunes for years, but being in Mel's band really started my career as a large ensemble writer. I have a very distinct memory of being at IAJE and sitting and talking with Brookmeyer and Mel. Brookmeyer made this outlandish statement, a challenge really, he said, "Jim will be the next Bob Brookmeyer composer for the band and you'll be the next Thad Jones composer for the band." And I said, "*What*? How could you possibly know that is going to happen?" I think he thought Jim's writing had a similar sensibility as his, and I think he felt like some of the grease of Thad's writing might have been more up my alley. When I wrote my first chart for the band "Compensation" I was not trying to sound like Thad, I was trying to channel Thad's spirit through my own voice.

—*Kenny Werner*

What I remember most about Mel was that he always seemed to be looking into the next direction, the next step in life. I don't ever remember having conversations with him that were based on his past. He always wanted to talk about what was currently happening, whether it was the Knicks, or Israel, or new music. It was always about what is happening *right now*, not what we were or what we had been doing. He was always interested in the right now, who was in the band *right now*, and what we're going to do *right now*. His attitude really inspired me in a lot of ways.

—*Dennis Mackrel*

I moved to New York after living in Los Angeles for seven years. I remember going out after I arrived in town and meeting up with Billy Hart, whom I had befriended several years before. Billy is another incredible drummer and a very supportive guy. He took me over to Sweet Basil to meet Mel because even though I had seen Mel play several times I was never formally introduced. As I recall Mel wasn't playing that night, he was just hanging out and listening to music. So Billy walked me over and said, "Mel this is Joey Baron he's new in town, have you heard him? He's a really great player." Billy really gave me a big compliment. And Mel said, "Ok if you're *that* good do you want to play with my band?" And I thought he was putting me on so I just went along with it. I said, "Sure what time do you start?" Mel told me what time to be at the Vanguard and at that very moment I realized that he was being serious! I thought to myself, "Shit he's calling my bluff!" That was the beginning of my relationship with Mel, subbing for him, and my career in New York. Many other drummers throughout the years had subbed, but after that I became one of his first calls. It was timing really because during that period Mel was dealing with carpal tunnel issues and he couldn't play all night. He gave me some tapes to check out and I would go over to his apartment and we would sit and listen to the music together. He would sit in his chair, twiddle his thumbs and talk for hours. I always tried to get him going because I wanted to learn from him and hear about his experiences.

—*Joey Baron*

Mel was a very kind man and if he was your friend he would do anything for you. One day I got a call from him and he said "Ralph, man you've lost a lot of weight lately. I have three brand new three-piece suits that I can't wear, you want them?" And I said, "Yeah!" I was still a young guy at the time and I didn't have the money to go out and buy suits. So I went to his pad and picked up the suits and they fit me perfectly. I wore those suits on gigs for years! Something that simple and thoughtful is a perfect example of how generous Mel was.

—*Ralph Lalama*

There is an album called *Mel Lewis and Friends*. Well, Mel invited me to come to that recording session and I was pretty much there during that entire process. I think the reason that he wanted me to be at that date was to observe Hank Jones. Mel had expressed to me that Hank's comping and time were the best, you know, Mel thought Hank was *it*! So I went and was really able to observe Hank in the studio, which was a little different than seeing him live. I saw how everything he did was perfect, and I think that was one of those times where Mel brought me along so that I could learn. He was helping me grow as a musician.

—Harold Danko

Lee Konitz introduced me to Mel during our gig one night. After Lee introduced us, he just walked away, leaving me alone with Mel. So Mel kicked a chair over in front of him and said, "Yeah man, have a seat." The chair set right in front of him and so we're just sitting there face to face. Mel said, "Yeah you play good. You have good time, you have good sound on the instrument, *but you play too goddamn loud!*" And he just went off on me, man! He said, "You'll knock all the windows out of this joint. It doesn't make any sense to play drums that loud. And that ride cymbal you're using is not a good ride cymbal." Then he said, "You young drummers never use your bass drum, now if it was a funk record and you didn't hear any bass drum you'd think something was wrong, wouldn't you?" So because he said the thing about my ride cymbal I said to him, "Mel you must have lots of cymbals why don't you lay one on me?" So, he's still staring me in the face as he writes down his number and he said, "Call me, we have a lot of work to do."

Four or five days later I called him and he told me to come up to his apartment. It was right after the dinner hour, and I come in and he sits me down and said, "If you want to be a success in New York City in this music, you have to be adaptable." And from about 7:30 p.m. to around 3:15 in the morning, he played records for me. That night I learned a valuable lesson about how to play with different people in different situations. Mel totally changed my whole way of thinking about the drums. One thing that he said that I will never forget was, "If you can't hear everybody in the band clearly, you are playing too loud and it's your fault. If you can hear everybody, then everyone sitting in the audience can clearly hear everybody on the bandstand." And I'll also never forget him saying, "That will work whether you are playing Carnegie Hall or a Dixie roadside diner." I *never* will forget that!

—Kenny Washington

What made Mel Lewis such a special drummer?

Mel really knew how to hear what was right for the music. Like most good musicians, he had the ability to adapt to a situation and play what was appropriate in a very natural way. He really knew how to orchestrate. What I also loved so much about Mel was his ability to "shade" the time of the music. He knew when to get up on it, and he knew when to get back on it, depending on what was happening with the band. He knew how to "dig in the stirrups," or "pull back the reins," you know. He had an amazing ability to know how and when to do that. A real gift!
—*Adam Nussbaum*

Mel was capable of contributing many things to an album, and he did it in ways that only he could do. His musical approach to drumming never forced people to play a certain way. He allowed people to play the way they play, and then he made his musical contribution while that was happening.
—*Jerry Dodgion*

He really embodied the idea of being a team player, rather than drawing attention to himself. He tried to keep the small group feeling in the big band, and I think that he proved that great music could be made without making bold technical statements. I also think that he showed that it's really possible to play a wide range of music *well* over the course of a career. Even though he may have been "pigeon holed" as a certain type of player, he found a way to bring life to all kinds of musical situations.
—*John Riley*

Mel's wasn't an incredibly technical drummer, he kind of rumbled back there, but he could just explode with energy when the music called for it. He was the only drummer that I have ever played with that told me he had a specific cymbal for my sound. That really blew me away! He said, "Yeah I have a cymbal for George, I had a cymbal for Richard, and I have a cymbal for you."

Mel and I once recorded these play-along albums for Ramon Ricker. After recording the whole day it was suggested that since everyone had settled in we go back and rerecord the very first song. The recording engineer said, "Should I playback the tempo of the first take?" And Mel said, "No I got it." So we recorded the song again and when we finished we listened back. The new version ended up

being one second different than the original take! The song was six or seven minutes in length and the two recordings were done at least six hours apart. Everybody that was in the control booth kind of fell silent and looked at each other and said, "Wow that's incredible!" Mel had a very unique internal clock; that was one of his gifts.
—*Rufus Reid*

Mel played to make everybody else in the band sound as good as possible. He did this by thinking of their phrasing and thinking like a horn player. He was totally unselfish; he always played what the band needed.
—*Jeff Hamilton*

Mel didn't sound like anybody else; he was a true original. I loved the way he sounded and I loved playing with him. He had a very wonderful and personal way of playing that sure made the band feel good.
—*Bill Crow*

Mel created space for the music to breathe and grow. He had the unique ability to create that space, yet still play enough to support the band through some very difficult music. Mel was the best; he was truly amazing.
—*John Mosca*

Mel played very musical. All the drummers that have played with my band, after Mel left and the records came out, they sort of played the same licks that Mel played because it was almost like someone had written them out, they fit the music perfect! He was so musical.
—*Terry Gibbs*

First, Mel's time feel was so swinging and down the middle. Secondly, the sound of his drums made his playing unique. He tuned his drums on the loose side and that gave him a very wide-open sound. Mel's sound really spread through the band like a warm blanket. Finally, and most importantly, Mel never got in the way of a chart. He had a way of playing fills that were ridiculously simple, but musically perfect. The example I always go back to is his fills during the shout chorus of Bill Holman's "Stomping at the Savoy" chart. During the shout chorus Mel played quarter notes on beats one and two as his fills and it was simply perfect. Other drummers would have played a lot more in those gaps, but it wasn't needed. Similar to how Basie could play one note and it would be a perfect musical fill, Mel had the same gift. By playing one simple quarter note on his tom Mel gave the music exactly what it needed and nothing more.

—Jim McNeely

When we played "Little Pixie," number seven in the book, all the sax players stood up and took a solo. Lovano played the first solo and Mel played perfectly for the style that Joe played in. When Ted Nash stood up, Mel played perfectly for the way that Ted played. Same thing happened when Oatts, Smulyan, or I played! Mel got deep inside our personal styles, it didn't matter if you played in front of the beat, behind the beat, right down the middle, straight ahead or avant-garde, Mel was always right there with you. He had great compassion for the music and everyone on the stage. He played to make *you* sound good.

—Ralph Lalama

I love Mel's brush playing! I remember one of the last times I was at his house, this was after he had already gotten sick and lost his hair, I got him to pull out a snare drum. I said, "Mel I know you got a snare drum lying around here, would you please just play the snare drum for me?" And he did. Man I was in heaven! He showed me this little pattern he played at medium tempos and I really ran with it. I still work on it *all* the time. Mel also inspired me to further develop the approach of supporting an ensemble from underneath and getting the ensemble to be buoyant.

Mel was a model of someone who could swing his ass off and at the same time sound very modern and blend into any musical situation. The way Mel was as a leader, along with his deep sense of swing defied the small-minded stereotypes of race, religion, age, gender, and identity. He was a model of excellence.

—Joey Baron

I was recently listening to the album *Thad Jones and Mel Lewis: Live at the Village Vanguard*. I have listened to the Thad Jones/Mel Lewis albums for years, but each time I go back and listen again, Mel's drumming never ceases to amaze me. He always seemed to hear the perfect thing to play, and he always played it on the perfect part of the kit. Mel played with perfect articulation and perfect dynamic support. It is almost unbelievable that a drummer could be that subtle and musical. It's no wonder he was Buddy Rich's favorite big band drummer.

Mel also had such a beautiful touch on the instrument. He could get so many sounds out of his cymbals. For example, he integrated shoulder crashes into the "Rub-a-Dub" sticking when he played the sticking between the snare and his cymbal. He also would utilize his bass drum with some of those cymbal shoulder crashes. The unique aspect of this was that he would do it in such a way that the dynamic integrity of the phrase was not compromised. It all came out consistently, and that was due to his amazing touch.

—*Ed Soph*

Mel didn't really have a leader mentality or great business acumen, but what he did instead was swing his ass off like nobody else. For us, just being in a band with him was enough to keep the band together and strong.

—*Ted Nash*

Well, it boils down to the fact that Mel played music on the drums. He absorbed what everyone in the band was doing and found things to play that complimented it. His time was so relaxed that sometimes he got in trouble for it. I remember one time, while we were playing with Terry Gibbs, hearing Al Porcino pounding his heel on the floor and saying, "Let's go Mel!" Because Mel was so easy that sometimes he would drag a little bit. But, to me it was a perfect solution to big band drumming.

—*Bill Holman*

As a soloist, there was always a beautiful communication and dialog with Mel. There was a lot of interplay within the phrases because Mel would breathe with you. The way he would also breathe and phrase with the band was just incredible. To play an ensemble passage with Mel was a life changing experience. He really taught me about the levels of sound within a big band. The way he played the bass drum with the trombones, the snare drum with the trumpets, and the way he used cymbals with the saxophone section. He was in all of these beautiful areas at the same time, and punctuated all the parts within his own sound. He didn't just play your part with you; he would set you up and then come off of it. As a result, it never felt like a big band, it felt like a trio. His sound and concept were all about the feeling of the music. That was Mel's approach, and it was amazing!

—Joe Lovano

Through the years I played various gigs with Mel, everything from big band, to piano trio at Jazz clubs, to wedding gigs. He was always so relaxed when he played it looked like he was up there reading the paper! Mel's *absolute* first priority, no matter what, was the *feel* of the music. He knew that if it didn't feel good, neither the band nor the audience would like it. It didn't matter what you wanted to do harmonically, melodically, formally or any of that—if the music didn't start from a place of good feel, forget it! Trust your body, trust your instincts and let the music flow—it will be ok.

Of the many things I learned from Mel, one really stands out in my mind. He told me a story about how Art Tatum played opposite him once on a gig. He explained that the venue's dressing room was directly under the stage, and Mel was down there on a break listening to Tatum playing above. He could hear Tatum's piano of course, but more interestingly, he could hear Tatum's foot tap the floor. Mel said, "of course, Tatum tapped his foot on beats one and three because that's where the swing is," something I later heard from many, including Barry Harris and Vernel Fournier. The concept stuck with me and I tell that story to my students at SUNY Purchase College all the time. A lot of players think only about beats two and four, but those beats are actually just the reaction to beats one and three.

—Pete Malinverni

Mel's touch and brush work were two of the things that really set his drumming apart. I also think he was unique in his use of the bass drum. The way he supported the brass section with his bass drum was really an art. He also had such a special groove and his time was so centered. Everything he played was like a Zen groove. He never tried to *do* anything to the music; he became the music. He sat there and looked like a Buddha sitting on the drum bench with his arms just moving freely. He was a truly organic musician. His drumming was similar to looking at a tree and watching the leaves blow in the wind at different speeds and directions, all while its trunk is always centered. Even with lots of complex motions going on it is still very organic. That was Mel; *plus* he swung harder than anybody else!

—*Kenny Werner*

1 The Vanguard Jazz Orchestra.

Used by permission of Douglas Purviance and the Vanguard Jazz Orchestra.

AFTERWORD
Mel Lewis's Example

Mel Lewis was a very strong, passionate, and opinionated man but he selflessly chose making other musicians comfortable his prime mission. At this Mel had great success.

I have been listening to Mel's playing since I first became aware of him and the Thad Jones/Mel Lewis Jazz Orchestra in 1971. Like many young players, I was drawn to the more flamboyant players of the day and didn't understand what was special about Mel because I didn't hear anything flamboyant in Mel's playing. Now, having known him, discussed music with him, seen him live many times and listened to numerous recorded performances of that band's classic repertoire (along with playing that music with the band myself for over 20 years) my appreciation of Mel's special feeling and ever evolving approach to the music is deeper than ever.

What Mel told Burt Korall in *Drummin' Men: Bebop Years* sums up Mel's attitude: "I found that to really make money, you had to give up music. So I gave up money." Mel was the ultimate team player but he wasn't a follower. Mel had great instincts and musical taste and with these attributes he would propel even the corniest musical situation into something worth listening to.

People refer to great players as "a musician's musician" and to great drummers as "a drummer's drummer." Throughout his long career Mel Lewis showed that it's possible to be a musician's musician and a drummer's drummer. It is to be hoped that Chris Smith's great tribute will inspire more young drummers to follow Mel's example by putting the music first.

—*John Riley*

TRANSCRIPTIONS
AND LISTENING GUIDES

Notation Key:

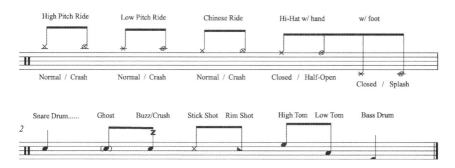

R = Right Hand
L = Left Hand
R/L = Unison or Right on Left Stick Shot

I've included suggested stickings that work well for me and are similar to what Mel *might* have used; they are intended only as a guide to help you explore his playing. Finally, don't get stuck in the page! These transcriptions should inspire a deeper *listening* to Mel's drumming.

Transcription 1—"Stompin' at the Savoy"

Stan Kenton: *Contemporary Concepts*
Capitol Records CDP 7243 5 42310 2 5 (CD 2002)
Recorded on July 22, 1955, in Chicago, IL

"'Stompin' at the Savoy,' yeah that was the tune that really made me with Stan. My reputation was built off of that one arrangement."
    —Mel Lewis, radio interview 1978

At the time of this recording, Mel's ride cymbal beat was still developing. You can hear him focus on beats one and three so much that they sounded accented. His reasons for this were to counterbalance the sound of the hi-hat on two and four and clearly define beat one for the large ensemble. Over the next two years Mel refined his ride cymbal beat by playing beats one and three slightly softer, creating a driving quarter-note feel.

Whether done consciously or not, Mel played his snare drum on the "and" of beats two and four throughout this arrangement. This repetition created continuity in his comping and sounded like a written part of the original arrangement.

Pay close attention to the way in which Mel propelled the band during the shout sections (E, K). His fills were simple, perfectly in time, and seamlessly prepared the other musicians to play their parts. The legato eighth-note phrases Mel played to set up many of the brass figures extended the legato eighth-note lines of the saxophone section.

Mel created rhythmic dialog during the shout chorus without interrupting the flow of the music. He played simple accents on beat two and the "and" of one, that are prime examples of this dialog (mm. 52, 54, 62, 64, 70, 72). While Mel often played ensemble figures in unison with the band, he was more concerned with improvising counterpoint and rhythmic dialog to them. His approach to big band drumming supported the group and created a new layer of rhythm that was musical and perfectly placed.

"My whole approach to playing is reaction. I don't listen to myself play. I'm too busy listening to everything going on around me. All my body is doing is reacting to that. I augment, compliment, round out. I can make anybody sound good. I have my own style, but I play uniquely with everyone that I play with ... Sometimes I'm forcing things, making things happen another way, but I'm still reacting to everything I hear. The composition I'm creating as I play in a big band is also because of what I'm hearing ... Everything depends on your ears. If I'm busy listening to me, then I'm not hearing the rest of the band. When the band is playing as an ensemble, I'm part of that ensemble."
—Mel Lewis, clinic in Hilversum, Netherlands 1985

Stompin' at the Savoy

Stan Kenton Orchestra
July 22, 1955

Mel Lewis Drums
@ Beginning of chart

Low Pitch Cymbal on Left
High Pitch Cymbal on Right

"Stompin' at the Savoy"

"Stompin' at the Savoy"

"Stompin' at the Savoy"

"Stompin' at the Savoy"

Transcription 2 — "You Took Advantage of Me"

The Mel Lewis Sextet
V.S.O.P #18 (CD 1996)
June 1957; Los Angeles

"The bass drum is not just a tom-tom holder! This was the first and most important drum in a band; it is the timekeeper. The whole idea of the bass drum is that it is the pulse, the heartbeat of the entire rhythm section. Besides, when you don't play your bass drum you are completely taking out the dancing part of your body! There's no way the music will feel like it's dancing if that bass drum foundation isn't there ... The only time that I don't play my bass drum is when the music says don't play it."
—Mel Lewis, clinic in Hilversum, Netherlands, 1985

Although difficult to hear, Mel softly played quarter notes on his bass drum. This "four on the floor" bass drum pattern was originally used to enhance the sound of the acoustic bass and create a pulse for dancers. Even after the advent of amplifiers and the decline of dancing, Mel continued to play his bass drum while keeping time. He was adamant that lightly playing the bass drum was an essential component of a drummer's swing feel.

Whether using a 14X20 inch bass drum or one that was slightly larger or smaller, Mel always tuned the bass drum about as loose and as low at it could handle and still produce a good tone. This low pitch sat underneath the upright bass frequency and never competed with the range of any instruments in the group. As Mel said, "The bass drum sound should be as deep [low pitched] as possible without any rattling and the drum should have some ring, not a completely dead sound."

Mel's quiet snare drum rhythms blended with his "four on the floor" bass drum, hi-hat, and ride cymbal to create a unified feel and sound. The snare drum was a component of the overall groove and *not* a separate interactive voice.

Author Rick Mattingly wrote, "For Mel, 'chops' had to do with control of the instrument, a sense of color, and above all, the ability to swing." Mel's light touch, consistent sound, and swing feel throughout this excerpt are evidence of his "chops."

The rhythms Mel played with his left hand never affected the accent, speed, or feel of his right hand. His repetitive ride cymbal beat was consistent and very swinging.

"Technique must be functional: the means by which a drummer communicates his 'feeling' and ideas. Speed by itself isn't worth a cent. It is the control of hands and feet,

281

whether playing fast or slow, and sensitivity of touch, that are all-important."
—Mel Lewis, *International Musician,* 1961

You Took Advantage of Me
Mel Lewis Sextet
June 1957

Mel Lewis Drums
@ 0:53 - Marty Paich piano solo

Transcription 3—"Baubles, Bangles, and Beads"

Pepper Adams Quintet
V.S.O.P. #5 (CD 1987)
July 10, 1957; Los Angeles

"I do everything easy. All these things are happening but it looks as though I'm doing nothing. That's the way I want it. I have limited technique. I work all this stuff out of this little amount of technique. I can't play fast single strokes. I'm basically a double-stroker, and lots of press rolls. I make sounds. Whatever I hear, I do. I don't even know how, I just do it. I know what I do isn't easy."
—Mel Lewis, *Modern Drummer*, April 1978

Much of Mel's solo vocabulary consisted of double-strokes (RR, LL), paradiddles (RLRR, LRLL), and buzz rolls. In this excerpt he utilized all three, voicing them around the drumset in a multitude of ways:
Measure 11: Mel played a paradiddle between his snare drum and hi-tom.
Measure 12: Mel played double-strokes to get to his left-side ride cymbal.
Measures 12–15, 35–36, 61–63: Mel played buzz rolls for texture and suspense.
Measures 29–34, 51–52, 64–68: Mel played double-strokes and paradiddles.
Mel's melodic use of cymbals is one of the most distinctive traits of his drumming. He used cymbals as melodic voices within fills *and* timekeeping, playing on the top of a cymbal was as valid as playing the snare drum or tom. Utilizing lateral motions with his wrists, he moved efficiently mixing drum and cymbal sounds in unique ways. Examples of Mel applying this concept include:
Measures 29–31: Mel played on top of his ride cymbal within the solo phrase.
Measures 49–50: Mel played on top of his ride, crashed, and splashed his hi-hats.
Measures 65–67: Mel used his open hi-hat as a prominent sound within his fill.
By 1957 Mel had developed a smoother-sounding ride cymbal beat by giving equal emphasis to beats one, two, three, and four. In true bebop fashion, his cymbal beat created a driving 4/4 pulse that drove the group's rhythmic feel.

"If you like my playing that much, absorb and be influenced, but take it and change it around a little bit. Turn it into your own thing. Use it, use me, use others. Use it in some kind of way, but not deliberately. When you get deliberate, when you actually try to copy note for note, lick for lick, you're not doing anything to help yourself ... Be

influenced by the fact that I have a good sound, but you don't have to get my sound. You can't get my sound. My touch has to do with my sound, and nobody has my touch except me. I don't have anybody else's touch either. Find your sound."
    —Mel Lewis, *Modern Drummer*, April 1978

Baubles, Bangles and Beads

Pepper Adams Quintet
July 10, 1957

Mel Lewis Drums
@ 6:58 - Pepper Adams trading

Low Pitch Cymbal on Left
High Pitch Cymbal on Right

"Baubles, Bangles and Beads"

Transcription 4 — "Bernie's Tune"

Art Pepper + Eleven: *Modern Jazz Classics*
Contemporary/Original Jazz Classics OJCCD 341 2 (CD 1991)
May 12, 1959; Los Angeles

Mel believed that his drumming should sound as deliberate and thoughtful as the composer's written notes. On "Bernie's Tune" he played several musical concepts that greatly added to the written arrangement.

During the introduction (mm. 2, 4) Mel used his cymbals to match the pitches of the ensemble hits. When the ensemble played higher notes, he joined them and played with his higher pitched cymbal.

During the melody statement (mm. 11–22) Mel alternated playing two measures on his slightly open hi-hat and two measures on his left ride cymbal. His texture change mirrored the musical changes that took place in the band: one being the melody changing from a syncopated pattern to sustained notes, and another being the upright bass alternating between rhythmic hits and a walking bass line.

During the first sixteen measures of the alto solo (m. 43) the ensemble played active backgrounds, resulting in sparse accompaniment from Mel. When the backgrounds stopped for the bridge (mm. 59–66) Mel increased his rhythmic activity to maintain the music's energy. His rhythmic density changed depending on what was happening in the ensemble. As a general rule, when the ensemble played dense rhythmic activity Mel played simpler. When the ensemble played simpler, Mel played more.

"I think drummers should create their own fills based on what they are hearing, instead of the old standard fill before a dotted quarter ... Drummers can create their own fills based on the music itself, based on what will follow or what proceeded."
—Mel Lewis, *Modern Drummer*, February 1985

During the final two measures of the introduction (mm. 9–10), Mel cleverly played the melody of "Bernie's Tune" to set up Art Pepper's melodic entrance. This is an example of Mel using rhythmic foreshadowing, the performance of a rhythmic figure to set up or cue a subsequent performance of that same figure.

Mel commonly played eighth-note fills that have became known as "Rub-a-Dub." He produced the "Rub-a-Dub" by incorporating three sticking patterns (RRL, RRLR, and RLLR) into his timekeeping. By playing these patterns between his snare drum and cymbals, Mel created smooth eighth-note phrases that connected ensemble figures and provided polyrhythmic accompaniment behind soloists. Examples of Mel using the "Rub-a-Dub" in "Bernie's Tune" include measures 33-34, 65–66, 92–94, and 96.

In the late 1950s, Mel began to significantly vary the pattern of his ride cymbal beat (measures 60–61 and 69–70). Many times his non-repetitive cymbal beat was a result of using "Rub-a-Dub" and playing in a more interactive fashion with the soloist. Mel continued to evolve his non-repetitive cymbal beat during the 1960s and, alongside Roy Haynes, was a pioneer of the post-bebop "broken-time feel."

Bernie's Tune

Art Pepper Plus Eleven: Modern Jazz Classics
May 12, 1959

"Bernie's Tune"

"Bernie's Tune"

"Bernie's Tune"

Transcription 5—"Nose Cone"

Terry Gibbs Dream Band: *Volume 4—Main Stem*
Contemporary CCD 7656 25 (CD 2002)
January 20-22, 1961; Los Angeles (Summit Club)

"This is the greatest swing band I ever played in. It saved my life, musically, and the same goes for the rest of the guys. Before we went into the Seville, who was hiring big bands to work in L.A. clubs? Since then, several big bands have worked clubs in L.A., but we were the only band that did any business in a club. We started the big band era in Los Angeles."
—Mel Lewis, "Vamp Till Ready," *DownBeat*, 1962

Notice how Mel played his slightly open hi-hat during the boisterous four-measure introduction. The sound of the two cymbals cut through the volume of the band and added to the thick texture of the introduction.

"Young drummers should learn that the hi-hat is another ride cymbal to be played properly; open/closed, all open, half open, half closed. There are a lot of effects. To me, the hi-hat is another ride cymbal."
—Mel Lewis, *Modern Drummer* 1985

Mel's playing on the introduction is an example of how he used the "Rub-a-Dub" to connect ensemble figures. His open hi-hat complimented the brass's loud sustained notes, while his "Rub-a-Dub" sticking on the snare drum reinforced the saxophone's eighth-note lines underneath.

Mel also used the "Rub-a-Dub" in measures 44–45, 85, 101, and 116.

Mel played articulations and accents that matched the band's interpretation, resulting in a very precise-sounding ensemble. When the band played a short accent, Mel played a short accent. When the band played a sustained sound, Mel also played a sustained sound. This concept was not unique to Mel, but so deeply ingrained in his musical subconscious that he utilized it constantly.

"When playing figures with the ensemble, duplicate its effects: loud or soft, long or short. For short sound, strike the center of the snare drum; snap the hi-hats shut tightly; press the stick into the head of a tom; make a cross-stick shot. For a long sound, strike a cymbal; hit the bass drum; instantly snapping the beater back; snap the hi-hats in an open position and let them ring. Strike a tom and let the note sustain. Strike the off-center area of the snare drum (a semi-long sound). Never, unless it is called for, play a figure with just one sound (every note sounding alike). Each note has a different texture and requires varying treatment ... Always sing the figure, either aloud or to yourself. This applies when studying the figure (before playing it) and at the moment of execution. And sing with the feeling and articulation of the horn. Then duplicate this feeling on the drum set. In this way you will get a better blend between the drums and the horns."

—Mel Lewis, *International Musician*, 1961

Mel was just as conscious of pitch as he was accent and articulation. During the melody (mm. 7, 9, 23, 25) Mel matched the sound of the low brass and bass hits by playing his bass drum. Also, at the end of the arrangement (mm. 146–157) he used his floor tom to support the low trombone and baritone rhythms, while he played his cymbals to accentuate the sustained saxophone notes. Mel masterfully matched the sounds of his drums and cymbals to the orchestration of the band.

"The drummers should be sitting up there knowing the music inside and out. There is no reason to be sitting at a concert reading anything. The reading should have been done at the first rehearsal, maybe the second or third rehearsal, maybe even the fourth rehearsal. After that they shouldn't even be looking at the music. They should know the part, and they should be listening and finding the inside of everything."

—Mel Lewis, *Modern Drummer*, 1985

When rehearsing an arrangement for the first time, Mel was not concerned with reading figures or creating rhythmic dialog. He played simple time and listened so that he could internalize the arrangement as quickly as possible. He listened past the most obvious band figures to hear what the saxophone section or bass trombonist played, the "inner parts" of the arrangement. Mel's playing supported the parts of an arrangement that most drummers never heard. Examples of Mel supporting these "inner parts" include:

At letters G, H, and I (mm. 54–77) Mel played responses to the saxophone figures. Instead of playing in unison with the saxophones, he created dialog that supported their part.

During the solo interlude Mel beautifully reinforced the saxophones by playing a fill that matched their rhythm and pitch. (m. 81)

At letters K and M (mm. 86 and 102) the brass took over the figure that the saxophones had played at letter G. Meanwhile the saxophones played a written response nearly identical to what Mel had played minutes prior! What Mel played at letter G foreshadowed what the saxophones eventually played at letter K.

At letter K, Mel continued to support the "inner part" by playing his snare drum with the saxophone rhythms.

"In many cases, the point where drummers would put a fill, there is something musical going on underneath, which is a written fill for another section. So the drum fill should, perhaps, reinforce what's already written."
—Mel Lewis, *Modern Drummer*, 1985

Nose Cone

Terry Gibbs Dream Band Volume 4: Main Stem
Recorded January 1961

Mel Lewis Drums
@ Introduction

Low Pitch Cymbal on Right
High Pitch Cymbal on Left

"Nose Cone"

"Nose Cone"

"Nose Cone"

"Nose Cone"

"Nose Cone"

"Nose Cone"

"Nose Cone"

Transcription 6 — "Three and One"

Presenting Thad Jones/Mel Lewis and The Jazz Orchestra
Reissued as *The Complete Solid State Recordings of The Thad Jones/Mel Lewis Orchestra.* Mosaic MD5-151 (CD 1994)
May 6, 1966; New York City

"With the saxophones, you want a roaring sound to envelop, because reeds don't have the power that the brass has. That's why I believe that during a sax soli—where you have all five saxophone players standing up playing together—nothing sounds better behind them than a Chinese ride cymbal, because there's a blend."
—Mel Lewis, *Modern Drummer*, 1985

Presenting Thad Jones/Mel Lewis and The Jazz Orchestra showcased the continued maturation of Mel's drumming. After ten years of developing his style in the bands of Stan Kenton, Bill Holman, Terry Gibbs, and Gerry Mulligan, Mel found the ideal platform for his drumming in the music of Thad Jones.

Mel's brushwork was the foundation for the melody. While keeping the sound of his brushes steady he reinforced ensemble accents with his snare drum or hi-hat, playing the hi-hat with his right hand (slightly open) or left foot (quickly splashing cymbals open).

When the saxophone or brass sections played loud responses to the melody, Mel broke his brush pattern and played eighth-note phrases that matched the band's subdivision and dynamics. Examples can be seen/heard in measures 5, 12, 17, 20–21, and 28–31.

Mel employed typical "Rub-a-Dub" fills in measures 29-31.

To accompany the sax soli Mel played on his Chinese cymbal, located just above his floor tom. After having two measures (mm. 31–32) to switch from brushes to sticks, Mel joined the saxophones on the "and" of four with a soft touch that allowed his entrance to be *felt* more than *heard*. The complex tone of his Chinese cymbal perfectly blended into the sound of the saxophone section.

Mel interjected rhythmic dialog during the sax soli, many times by simply playing a single snare drum or cymbal accent. He was able to add dialog to the saxophone phrases because he had internalized their parts and could vocalize everything they played. Several examples of Mel's dialog can be seen/heard in measures 33, 36, 37, 41, 43, and 58.

"I get a lot of credit for lightening the band up. If you play just about the way you would play loudly in a small group, and the band is aware of what you are doing, they'll come down in their

volume and the whole thing will swing more ... This small group approach keeps it flowing along, and it's so much easier to work with dynamics that way. The real word is not drive or kick; it's intensity, and intensity can be real soft. The whole thing is motion."
—Mel Lewis, *Modern Drummer* 1985

During the shout chorus Mel played several clear downbeats that simultaneously set up a band figure and maintained a flowing time feel. By accenting beat one, he gave the band the information they needed to play their note on the "and" of one in perfect time. While other drummers might have focused on playing the hit in unison with the band, Mel ultimately created a smoother time-feel by setting up a big beat one, then immediately going back to playing time. Additional examples appear in measures 102, 104, 115, and 118.

When the ensemble played sparse rhythmically, Mel usually played more. This concept was apparent in the shout chorus during measures 118 and 119. When the ensemble played quarter notes, Mel played a dense shuffle pattern on his snare drum and maintained quarter notes on his ride cymbal. By playing the eighth-note subdivision with his shuffle he subtly energized the music and subdivided the band's quarter notes.

There are two examples of Mel using rhythmic foreshadowing in the "Three and One" shout chorus. The first occurred in measures 119 and 120, where Mel set up the ensemble by playing "offbeat" hits on the "and" of four and one. He played the syncopated rhythm so that when the band came in with their "offbeat" hits, they fit perfectly into what he had already established. The second example occurred in measures 127 and 128, where Mel played a one-measure fill that was then repeated back by the ensemble the very next measure. Listening to these examples gives valuable insight into the way Mel supported a band. In a very friendly manner, his drumming allowed the band to realize the music's full potential.

Throughout the shout chorus Mel used all four of his cymbals (left ride, right ride, Chinese ride, and hi-hats) for color, accents, and time. "There is nothing worse than the monotony of one cymbal going on behind everything," Mel once said.

"When the band is playing along and they keep hearing the same cymbal sound, it just disappears in their minds. But when you make a change to another ride cymbal, it wakes them up again. Even in my dark sounds there is still a higher sound, a medium sound, and a lower sound. I'll use the high sound behind the piano. I'll also use the lowest sound behind the piano. But I won't use the middle sound behind the piano because it's too much in the piano's range ...When I'm playing behind, say, a trumpet solo followed by a tenor solo, and I know the tenor player is a

hard-blower, I'll use the Chinese cymbal behind the tenor. Now, if it's just going to be a trumpet solo, or if the tenor player has a lighter sound, I'll use my normal 20" ride cymbal. But I'll always save my Chinese for the hardest blowing soloist. I don't work it out; it's just automatic—which cymbal suits which soloist."

—Mel Lewis, *Modern Drummer* 1985

Three And One
Presenting Thad Jones/Mel Lewis and The Jazz Orchestra
May 6, 1966

Mel Lewis Drums
@ Beginning

High Pitch Cymbal on Right
Low Pitch Cymbal on Left
Chinese Cymbal on Far Right

"Three and One 1966"

303

2

"Three and One 1966"

"Three and One 1966"

"Three and One 1966"

"Three and One 1966"

"Three and One 1966"

Transcription 7 — "Tip-Toe"

Thad Jones/Mel Lewis: *Consummation*
Blue Note CDP 7243 5 38226 2 0 (CD 2002)
Also reissued as *The Complete Solid State Recordings of the Thad Jones/
Mel Lewis Orchestra.* Mosaic MD5-151 (CD 1994)
January 28, 1970; New York City

"As a drummer, you have to build the band's confidence in you, so that you can try anything and it won't bother them. Don't get them in a habit of waiting for a specific thing that you're going to do so that they don't have to count. Be unpredictable, but make them have a lot of confidence in you, so that they won't worry about it, because they know that no matter what you play, it will be right."
—Mel Lewis, *Modern Drummer*, 1985

During the solo trading Mel flawlessly set up the band's written responses. He often played triplet fills to lead the band into a swing response and double-time eighth-note fills to lead the band into a straight response.

The legato sound of Mel's brushes was a result of the smooth lateral motions of his hands. This motion allowed his brushes to stay in contact with the drumhead nearly constantly. By using the same lateral motion, he produced accents by simply pushing the brush across the drumhead at a faster rate. To achieve a legato sound when playing with sticks, Mel used a similar lateral motion and approached his drums and cymbals more from the side than the top.

Mel's solo vocabulary with brushes was very similar to the vocabulary he used when playing with sticks. During his solo breaks on "Tip-Toe" Mel frequently used double strokes and paradiddles for sixteenth-note phrases and "Rub-a-Dub" sticking or single strokes for eighth-note phrases.

When playing with brushes Mel frequently played his slightly open hi-hat for a sustained crash sound. Using his hi-hat pedal, he controlled the length of sustain and matched the ensemble's note lengths.

Mel used brushes during the shout chorus and rarely played fills. By leading the dynamic changes, playing steady time, and interjecting simple dialog Mel allowed the sound of the ensemble to be the highlight. To hear a drummer play so tastefully and simply during a shout chorus is refreshing.

"Drummers are going to have to start becoming more musicians, rather than fillers. Just because there are a few beats, or a beat, or an eighth of a beat, they don't have to play a fill there. Space is beautiful too—silence, or just a time figure."
—Mel Lewis, *Modern Drummer,* 1985

Tip -Toe

Thad Jones/Mel Lewis Orchestra: Consummation
January 21, 1970

Mel Lewis Drums
@ 2:25 - Solo Trading

"Tip Toe 1970"

"Tip Toe 1970"

"Tip Toe 1970"

Transcription 8 — "This Can't Be Love"

Thad Jones And Mel Lewis: *The Thad Jones/Mel Lewis Quartet*
A&M CD 0830 (CD 1989)
September 24, 1977; Miami, Florida (Airliner Lounge)

"I began the changeover process in 1977 on an album with Thad, bassist Rufus Reid, and pianist Harold Danko. I loosened up my playing and became freer. But, make no mistake, the traditional part of me is still very much alive. Listen to what I do. It's uninhibited and controlled, and all of my experience is used."
—Mel Lewis, *The Lost Art* liner notes, 1989

On this recording, Mel improvised using a different approach than he had in the 1950s and early 1960s. His new concept did not rely on repetitive sticking patterns or cliché drumming vocabulary. Instead, Mel thought like an instrumentalist and played long phrases that often focused on texture and shape. The beginnings of his approach can be heard in his open drum solos on the Thad Jones / Mel Lewis Orchestra's recordings of "Once Around" and "Fingers."

If you try to count measures through Mel's solo you are likely to conclude that he did not keep the form of the song. However, when you stop counting and start listening to his phrases, you will hear that he kept the form through all three choruses. Mel was very clear about marking the beginning of most song sections (AABA), but in between those markers he played very unconventional and loose-sounding phrases.

"I think like a horn player. I like to cross bar lines, to think meters without thinking anything other than 4/4. I sort of think like Thad. He'll start phrases in the middle of nowhere, continue them on through, and end up where you're supposed to. You really have to have a very good awareness of where you are."
—Mel Lewis, *Modern Drummer*, April 1978, p. 32.

The second A section of the third chorus (mm. 105–112) was one of Mel's most experimental phrases. His use of quarter-note triplets was an effective way to give the illusion of playing at a slower tempo. He also played quarter note triplets during the bridge of his second chorus (mm. 80–86), where he stuck with them long enough to have the listener internalize the slower feel. When Mel went back to playing phrases at the original tempo it felt like a substantial musical shift had occurred.

Mel orchestrated at the drumset. Listen to this solo and imagine him as a one-man jazz orchestra: his snare drum and high tom are saxophones, his cymbals are trumpets, and his floor tom and bass drum are trombones. There is phrasing, accent, call and response, repetition, dynamics, unison and soli sections, tension and release, and a natural sounding beginning and end.

During the third chorus Mel frequently played flams and unison hits on his toms and snare drum (mm. 97, 102, 113, and 121). He also used these sounds to achieve "fat" sounding eighth notes or quarter notes when setting up ensemble figures. Listen to him apply these sounds in "Bernie's Tune" (mm. 50, 76–77) and "Three and One" (mm. 102, 113).

Mel's hands were always in motion, especially his right hand, which continually moved around the kit playing a variety of sounds. During his first solo chorus (mm. 49–59) every time he played a cymbal with his right hand it resulted in a different sound. Even though Mel only used three ride cymbals, it sounded like hundreds surrounded him. He achieved this variety by playing on different spots of the cymbals, playing on the bells, employing rolls, using dead strokes, crashing with the tip, butt-end, or shoulder of the stick, and by having complete dynamic control of each cymbal.

"Playing from hand to hand and constantly moving the cymbal pattern, gets the feeling of straight ahead motion without getting into a rigid situation. The only thing that really has to keep going and stay rigid is the hi-hat. But you never think about your hi-hat, it just goes. But you keep moving your hands with different patterns while listening to the soloist and reacting to what they play."
—Mel Lewis, clinic in Hilversum, Netherlands, 1985

By 1977 Mel had also further developed his concept of the "broken time feel." He rarely used a repetitive ride cymbal beat when keeping time; instead he played eighth-note ideas between hands to produce pulse. This resulted in active snare drum comping, an irregular ride cymbal beat, and a smooth "open" feel. The majority of Mel's "broken time feel" came from his hands, while his feet maintained their traditional roles. Listen to the forward momentum that Mel's "broken time feel" created behind Thad's solo.

Mel regularly used the aforementioned "Rub-a-Dub" to achieve his "broken time feel." Several examples of his "Rub-a-Dub" between ride cymbal and snare drum are heard/seen in measures 5, 9, 15, 21, and 27.

"Today it's very simple to record yourself anytime. So instead of sitting home and listening all day to your favorite drummer, spend more time listening to cassettes of yourself. In the beginning, you'll hear things that you don't like. Great. Eliminate those things or make them better. You will hear

things you do like. Keep those and improve upon them. After a while, by listening to yourself and believing in yourself, you will start to influence yourself...You will hear your sound or you will hear yourself changing, and before you know it, you will have developed a style of your own. The whole idea is to find yourself, get your own sound, your own feeling, your own ideas, and your own clichés."

- Mel Lewis, *Modern Drummer* 1985

This Can't Be Love
Thad Jones / Mel Lewis Quartet
September 24, 1977

Mel Lewis Drums
@ 1:23 - Thad Solos One Chorus

High Pitch Cymbal on Left
Low Pitch Cymbal on Right
Chinese Cymbal on Far Right

"This Can't be Love"

315

"This Can't be Love"

"This Can't be Love"

"This Can't be Love"

Transcriptions 9 and 10—"Three and One" and "Tip-Toe"

The Mel Lewis Jazz Orchestra: *The Definitive Thad Jones Vol.1*
Nimbus Records NI 2706 (CD 2009)
February 11-15, 1988; New York City (Village Vanguard)

Throughout Mel's career the sounds he preferred out of his drumset and cymbals remained largely unchanged. Dark-sounding cymbals, calfskin heads, and loose low tuning of his drums were three of the characteristics that defined "his sound." This listening guide features quotes from Mel speaking about of his drums and cymbals.

Mel on his cymbals:
I've been playing original K. Zildjian cymbals practically all my life. The early hand-me-downs from my father were all K.'s, because that's what he used. Then I bought my first A., which I still have to this day. That's the famous one with the pieces cut out. Buddy Rich says it's probably the greatest ride of all time. I feel the same way about it. Everybody seems to know that cymbal ... When I joined the Kenton band, I needed to use A.'s because they are louder and I needed the volume. So I stayed with the A.'s there for a while. One of my ride cymbals was that famous one, with two rivets in it, which is my trademark. To this day, I've been using two rivets in my ride cymbal. Of course, as soon as I left the Kenton band I switched to K.'s completely. That was the end of '56. With my small-group playing, actually, I was using K.'s all along, but I became a permanent K. player from '56 on ... The more high-pitched cymbals you have, the more trouble you're going to give a band. Also for riding in a big band, I think that the pingier a cymbal is and the less overtone and spread it has, the emptier everything will be. It's important that you have a good, full, fat-sounding cymbal.
—Mel Lewis, *Modern Drummer*, 1985

One thing about cymbals is that once your ears get tuned into the sound you like, you'll always be looking for cymbals with that sound. That is what you'll always buy, that's what you'll always get. Once you find something you like, that's your sound. Your touch, on your cymbals, equals your sound.
—Mel Lewis, clinic in Hilversum, Netherlands, 1985

See, I still believe in the old lightweight concept. When you put a cymbal on a heavy stand, that muffles the cymbal—it really kills the sound. The old flush-base-type stands

are still the best. Now, no company wants to hear that, because they're trying to sell this other junk. But who are they selling them to?
—Mel Lewis, *Crescendo International*, 1983

Mel on his bass drum:
With the bass drum, I only use a piece of paper napkin with a couple pieces of tape to the right side of my foot pedal, and that drum has nothing inside at all. I just control it with my foot with the largest possible beater I can get. I have a lot of those old Ghost beaters. They're nice and big and round, and I get a big, fat sound.
—Mel Lewis, *Modern Drummer*, 1985

I used a 26" bass drum with Boyd Raeburn and Alvino Rey. From '49 on I went to the 22", which I used through 1957. It had calf heads on both sides. In the Kenton band, I used a timpani head on the batter side, and as little muffling as possible ... I've gone back to using calfskin timpani head on the batter side and calf on the front. If you really want to get that sound, you have to use calf, especially on the bass drum ... When I got off the road and started lugging my drums around, and as cars were getting smaller, I thought I'd go to the 20". Well it worked, and to this day I use a 20" bass drum in big bands. A 20" with proper tuning has all you need for big band.
—Mel Lewis, *Modern Drummer* 1985

Mel on his snare drum:
I use a 6 ½" snare drum. With a metal snare drum there is a metallic sound, and you have enough metal in the band as it is. All the horns are made out of metal. You need some wood in there, so you have your acoustic bass and wooden drums. A wooden snare drum sounds much better. It's a deeper, gutsier sound. I really prefer a 6 ½" snare drum in a big band. That's what we played in the old days, and I missed it for a long time while I went to the 5 ½". I had it tuned down. Now I can actually play a medium-tight snare drum, and with that extra inch there, I get that depth that I used to get, without having to have the drum slack.
—Mel Lewis, *Modern Drummer* 1985

Mel on the tuning of his drums
Drums that are too tight get a shallow and choked sound. I personally prefer fairly loose tuning. It enables me to get the loud sounds with a minimum of effort.
—Mel Lewis, *Modern Drumming* by Charles Perry, 1961

The tuning of my drums isn't exact. As long as the sound is right, I don't care. I start out trying to be exact but it never ends up that way. I don't always have time to finish tuning, so sometimes everything is sitting there a little crooked. Nothing is perfect, but I get a sound. I strive for a full sound. I try to make my drums sound like a fat sounding trumpet.
—Mel Lewis, *Modern Drummer,* 1978

As you listen to the 1988 *Definitive Thad Jones* versions of "Three and One" and "Tip-Toe" notice the differences and similarities in Mel's sound between the newer versions and the originals recorded twenty years prior. Some noticeable changes to Mel's approach include:

- The use of sticks instead of brushes.
- The constant changing of his ride cymbal pattern behind the ensemble and soloists.
- Increased comping with his snare drum, due to his increased use of "Rub-a-Dub."
- More active playing throughout both shout sections, especially "Tip-Toe."

Three And One

Mel Lewis and The Jazz Orchestra: The Definitive Thad Jones

February 1988

l Lewis Drums
Beginning

High Pitch Cymbal on Left
Low Pitch Cymbal on Right
Chinese Cymbal on Far Right

"Three And One 1988"

322

"Three And One 1988"

"Three And One 1988"

"Three And One 1988"

"Three And One 1988"

"Three And One 1988"

Tip -Toe

Mel Lewis and The Jazz Orchestra: The Definitive Thad Jones
February 1988

Mel Lewis Drums
@ 4:46 - Solo Trading

High Pitch Cymbal on Left
Low Pitch Cymbal on Right
Chinese Cymbal on Far Right

"Tip Toe 1988"

"Tip Toe1988"

"Tip Toe1988"

Mel Lewis Equipment Timeline
Compiled by Paul Wells and Chris Smith

1935–1947
Leedy, 3 Ply shells with reinforcement hoops, Blue Duco Painted Finish, Calfskin Heads, with a tacked single-tension tom-tom: 14 X 26 Bass Drum, 7X11 Tom Tom 14X14 Floor Tom, 7X14 Snare Drum with Dual Tension and dual-tension snare drum.
(This was his father's hand-me-down and officially Mel's first set of drums.)

1944
At 15 years old, Mel picked out and bought a 20-inch A Zildjian cymbal. That cymbal later had two sections cut out of it to stop the spreading of cracks around the edges. Mel used that iconic cymbal on hundreds of recording sessions in the 1950s and early 1960s. Buddy Rich claimed it was one of the greatest cymbals ever made.

1944–1949
Gretsch, 3 ply shells, Gold Sparkle Finish, Round Badge, "Rocket" Lugs, Calfskin Heads: 14X26 BD, 9X13 TT, 16X16 FT, 6.5X14 SD Calfskin Heads
(Personally bought by Mel)

Because Ray Anthony did not like the gold color of Mel's personal drums, Mel often used the Anthony band's Gretsch kit: Gretsch, 3 ply shells, White Marine Pearl Finish, Round Badge, "Rocket" lugs, Calfskin Heads: 14 X 26 BD, 9 X 13 TT, 16 X 16 FT, 5 X 14 SD
(Ray Anthony Equipment)

1949–1954
Gretsch, 3 ply shells, Midnight Blue Finish, Round Badge, Broadkaster Lugs: 14X22 BD, 9X13 TT (with large lugs), 16X16 FT, 5.5X14 SD
(Personally bought by Mel)

1954–1961
Gretsch "Birdland" Model, 3 ply shells, Cadillac Green Finish w/Gold Plated Hardware, Round Badge, Calfskin Heads: 14 X22 BD (with a calfskin

timpani batter head), 9X13 TT (with large lugs), 16 X 16 FT, 5.5 X 14 SD (Mel received this Cadillac Green kit as his first free endorsement kit from Gretsch.)

1957–61
Gretsch, 3 ply shells, Starlight Sparkle Finish, Round Badge, Calfskin Heads: 14X20 BD, 8X12 TT, 14X14 FT, 5.5X14 SD

During these years, Mel switched between these two sets (12/14/20 and 13/16/22.) He didn't seem to prefer the larger set for big bands, or the smaller set for small groups; both were used interchangeably.

1961
Mel began using the distinctive sound of a Chinese cymbal.

1961–1970
During this period, Mel switched between three set-ups:

Gretsch, 6 ply shells, Burgundy Sparkle Finish, Round Badge, Calfskin Heads: 14X20 BD, 9x13 TT, 16x16 FT, 5.5X14 SD

Gretsch, 6 ply shells, Burgundy Sparkle Finish, Round Badge, Calfskin Heads: 14 X 18 BD, 8 X1 2 TT, 14x14 FT, 5.5x14 SD (Used for small group gigs and recordings.)

Gretsch, 6 ply shells, Burgundy Sparkle Finish, Round Badge, Calfskin Heads: 14 X 20 BD, 8 X 12 TT, 14 X 14 FT, 5.5 X 14 SD (It is believed that Mel used this set-up on the first studio record by the Thad Jones/ Mel Lewis Jazz Orchestra. He may have later left this kit at the Village Vanguard for use on Monday nights.)

Mel also used a vintage 5 X 14 Ludwig Black Beauty snare drum (circa late 1920s) on recording sessions. Though he never liked metal snare drums, his Black Beauty was the one exception.

The Gretch Drum Company released a Mel Lewis Model stick in the mid

1960s. The stick was a version of their 7D model and had a wood tip; Mel used it exclusively for 15 years.

1970–1974

Gretsch, 6 ply shells, Walnut Lacquer Finish, Stop Sign Badge, Calfskin Heads: 14X20 BD, 9X13 TT, 16X16 FT, 5.5X14 SD (After 1974, Mel left this kit at the Village Vanguard for use on Monday nights.)

Gretsch, 6 ply shells, Walnut Lacquer Finish, Stop Sign Badge, Calfskin Heads: 14X18 BD, 8 X 12 TT, 14 X 14 FT, 5.5 X 14 SD (Used for small group gigs and recordings.)

ASBA Nesting Kit, Black Finish: 10X18 BD, 4X14 SD
This French-made ASBA kit featured a cut bass drum shell, so that the snare drum could be transported inside of it. Mel received this kit as a gift from Daniel Humair, who also gave ASBA nesting kits to drummers Jake Hanna and Stan Levey. Mel often used this small kit when playing around New York City.

1974–1979

Gretsch, 6 ply shells, Natural Maple Lacquer, Stop Sign Badge: 14X20 BD, 8 X 12 TT, 9 X 13 TT, 16 X 16 FT, 5.5 X 14 SD
Calfskin heads on snare drum and bass drum, plastic on the toms.

Gretsch, 6 ply shells, Natural Maple Lacquer Finish, Stop Sign Badge, Calfskin Heads: 14X18 BD, 8x12 TT, 14x14 FT, 5.5X14 SD (Used for small group gigs and recordings.)

1979–1984

Slingerland, 6 ply shells, Natural Maple Lacquer, Calfskin Heads: 14X20 BD, 8X12 TT, 9X13 TT, 16X16 FT, 5.5X14 SD (Mel had two identical kits like this: one for traveling and one to keep at the Vanguard for Monday nights.)

Slingerland, 6 ply shells, Natural Maple Lacquer, Calfskin Heads: 14x18 BD, 8x12 TT, 9x13 TT, 14x14 FT, 5.5x14 SD (Used for small group gigs and recordings.)

Slingerland also made a Mel Lewis model stick after he became an endorser in 1979. Similar to the Gretch stick, it was a version of a 7D wood tip stick.

1984–1990
Pearl, 8 ply Keller Maple Shells, Natural Maple Lacquer, Calfskin Heads: 16X20 BD, 8X12 TT, 9X13 TT, 16X16 FT, 6.5X14 SD (This kit Mel kept at the Vanguard for Monday nights.)

Pearl, 8 ply Keller Maple Shells, Natural Maple Laquer, Calfskin Heads: 14x18 BD, 8x12 TT, 9x13 TT, 14x14 FT, 5x14 SD (Used for tours, local gigs, and recordings)

These Pearl kits were custom made for Mel by Al Duffy. Duffy previously worked at Frank Ippolito's Pro Percussion, a drum shop in New York City. He later joined Pearl Drums as a consultant.

In 1984 Mel began playing and endorsing Istanbul cymbals. "I'm very happy to find out now that this new Istanbul Cymbal Company are the makers of the old cymbal. I found them up at Barry Greenspon's Drummers World. I tried some of them and thought my God, they're back. These are the cymbals," stated Mel.[1] In 1995 the Istanbul cymbal company launched a line of cymbals based on the profile and sound of Mel's called the Mel Lewis Signature Series.

In the mid 1980s Mel began using wood tip Mel Lewis model sticks made by Cappella. Currently Bop Works still makes a Mel Lewis model stick that is based on the design of Mel's Cappella sticks. ∥

Notes
1. Mattingly, "Mel Lewis," 44.

SELECTED
DISCOGRAPHY

"Jealousy" —**Private Acetate Recording**
Recording was played on air during Lewis's interview
WKCR *Profiles* with Loren Schoenberg
1946

"One for Mel" —**Private Acetate Recording**
Recording was played on air during Lewis's interview
WKCR *Profiles* with Loren Schoenberg
1948

Ray Anthony: *Ray Anthony Capitol Collectors Series*
Capitol Records CDP 7 94079 2 (CD 1991)
July 25, 1953; New York City

Stan Kenton Orchestra: *Stan Kenton Festival*
Status CD 101 (CD 2000)
September 21, 1954; Portland, OR (Civic Auditorium)

Frank Rosolino: *Stan Kenton Presents Frank Rosolino*
Mosaic Box Set MD4 185 (CD 1999)
November 6, 1954; Los Angeles

Bob Brookmeyer: *The Modernity of Bob Brookmeyer*
Reissued as: *The Modernity of Bob Brookmeyer: The 1954 Quartets*
Fresh Sound Records FSRCD 499 (CD 2008)
December 26, 1954: Los Angeles

Pete Jolly Quintet: *The Five*
Reissued as *Pete Jolly: Quartet, Quintet and Sextet*
Fresh Sound Records FSRCD 2241 (CD 2007)
March 10–11, 1955; Los Angeles

Herb Geller Quartet: *The Gellers*
Reissued as *The Gellers: Complete Recordings 1954–1955*
Fresh Sound Records FSRCD 412 (CD 2006)
April 20-21, 1955: Los Angeles

Bud Shank-Bill Perkins
Pacific Jazz/Capitol Records CDP 7243 4 93159 2 1 (CD 1998)
May 2, 1955; Los Angeles

Stan Kenton: *Live at Palo Alto*
Status DSTS 1036 (CD 1990)
May 13, 1955; Palo Alto, California (Surf Club/Stanford University)

Stan Kenton: *Contemporary Concepts*
Capitol Records CDP 7243 5 42310 2 5 (CD 2002)
July 20, 22, 1955; Chicago

Mel Torme with the Marty Paich Dek-tette
Reissued as *The 1956 Torme/Paich Legendary Sessions*
Fresh Sound Records FSRCD 2230 (CD 2006)
January 16-18, 1956; Los Angeles

Stan Kenton and His Orchestra: *Kenton in Hi-Fi*
Capitol Records CDP 7 98451 2 (CD 1992)
February 11-12, 1956; Los Angeles

Stan Kenton and His Orchestra: *Cuban Fire!*
Capitol Records CDP 7 96260 2 (CD 1991)
May 22-24, 1956; New York City

Bill Usselton Sextet: *Modern Jazz Gallery*
Reissued as *Billy Usselton Sextet: Complete Recordings*
Fresh Sound Records FSRCD 2220 (CD 2006)
October 17, 1956; Los Angeles

336

Marty Paich: *Modern Jazz Gallery*
Reissued as *Paich-ence: Complete Recordings as a Leader 1955–1965*
Fresh Sound Records FSRCD 2217 (CD 2006)
October 23, 1956; Los Angeles

Bill Perkins: *Just Friends*
Lone Hill Jazz LHJ 10237 (CD 2006)
October 29, 1956: Los Angeles

Stan Kenton and His Orchestra: *Kenton '56 In Concert*
Artistry ARCD 002 (CD)
November 5, 1956; San Francisco (Live at Macumba Club)

Got'cha: Music of the Mel Lewis Septet
Fresh Sound Records FSRCD 73 (CD 1991)
November 19-20, 1956; San Francisco

Ray Brown: *Bass Hit!*
Reissued as *Ray Brown: The Man—Complete Recordings 1946–1959*
Fresh Sound Records FSRCD 560-2 (CD 2009)
November 23, 1956; Los Angeles

Lennie Niehaus Octet
Reissued as *Lennie Niehaus: Complete Fifties
Recordings Vol.3 —Sextet, Quintet, Octet*
Lone Hill Jazz LHJ 10240 (CD 2006)
December 10, 1956; Los Angeles

Maynard Ferguson and His Orchestra: *Live at Peacock Lane January 6, 1957*
Reissued as *Maynard Ferguson and His Dream Band
Orchestra: Live at Peacock Lane 1956-1957.*
Fresh Sound Records FSRCD 346-2 (CD 2007)
January 4-6, 1957; Los Angeles

Dave Pell's Jazz Octet: *A Pell of a Time*
RCA Victor ND 74408 (CD 1989)
January 21, 23, 1957; Los Angeles

John Graas/Paul Chambers: *East/West Controversy*
Reissued as *Westlake Bounce: The Music of John Graas*
Fresh Sound Records FSRCD 508 (CD 2004)
January 22, 1957; Los Angeles

Quincy Jones: *Go West, Man!*
Reissued as *Quincy Jones: This Is How I Feel About Jazz*
Lone Hill Jazz LHJ 10273 (CD 2006)
February 25, 1957; Los Angeles

Bill Holman: *The Fabulous Bill Holman*
Reissued as *The Original Bill Holman Big Band: Complete Recordings*
Lone Hill Jazz LHJ 10298 (CD 2007)
April 25, 29, 1957; Los Angeles

Med Flory and His Orchestra: *Jazz Wave*
Reissued as *Med Flory and His Orchestras 1954–1959: Go West Young Med!*
Fresh Sound Records FSRCD 506 - (CD 2004)
May 13 and June 3, 1957; Los Angeles

The Mel Lewis Sextet
V.S.O.P #18 (CD 1996)
June 1957; Los Angeles

Marty Paich: *Marty Paich 3*
V.S.O.P #64 (CD 1997)
June 1957; Los Angeles

Marty Paich: *A Jazz Band Ball*
V.S.O.P #64 (CD 1996)
July 1957; Los Angeles

Pepper Adams Quintet
V.S.O.P. #5 (CD 1987)
July 10, 1957; Los Angeles

Pepper Adams: *Critics' Choice*
Mighty Quinn Productions MQP 1103 (CD 2005)
August 23, 1957; Los Angeles

The Music of Bob Cooper: *Coop*
Original Jazz Classics OJC 161 (CD 1991)
August 26–27, 1957; Los Angeles

Terry Gibbs: *A Jazz Band Ball (Second Set)*
V.S.O.P #40 (CD 1998)
September 1957; Los Angeles

Don Fagerquist Octet: *Eight by Eight*
V.S.O.P #4 (CD 1987)
September 14, 1957; Los Angeles

Jeri Southern: *Southern Breeze*
Fresh Sound Records FSRCD 104 (CD 2007)
January 23–25, 1958; Los Angeles

Shorty Rogers and His Giants: *Gigi in Jazz*
RCA Victor SP 74321125882 (CD 2004)
January 27, 30, 1958; Los Angeles

Shorty Rogers and His Giants: *Boots Brown and His Blockbusters*
RCA Victor 20-7269 (LP 1958)
February 2, 1958; Los Angeles

Bill Holman: *Big Band in a Jazz Orbit*
Reissued as *The Original Bill Holman Big Band: Complete Recordings*
Lone Hill Jazz LHJ 10298 (CD 2007)
February 11-14, 1958; Los Angeles

Anita O'Day: *Anita O'Day Sings the Winners*
Verve 837939-2 (CD 1990)
April 2-3, 1958; Los Angeles

The Axidentals: *Hello, We're the Axidentals*
Jasmine 512 (CD 2009)
May, 1958; Los Angeles

Bill Holman/Mel Lewis Quintet: *Jive for Five*
V.S.O.P. #19 (CD 1997)
May 29 and June 6, 1958; Los Angeles

Jimmy Rowles Quintet: *Let's Get Acquainted
with Jazz (For People Who Hate Jazz)*
V.S.O.P. #11 (CD 2009)
June 20, 1958; Los Angeles

June Christy: *June's Got Rhythm*
Capitol Jazz 4 775490 2 (CD 2005)
June 27 and July 3, 1958; Los Angeles

The Hi-Lo's with the Marty Paich Dek-Tette: *And All That Jazz*
Collectables COL-CD 6026 (CD 1995)
June 30, July 2 and August 4-5, 1958; Los Angeles

Sammy Davis Jr. and Carmen McRae: *Porgy and Bess*
Reissued as *Boy Meets Girl: Sammy Davis Jr. and Carmen McRae on Decca*
Verve 314 589546 2 (CD 2005)
October 9 and 28, 1958; Los Angeles

Bobby Troup: *Stars of Jazz*
RCA Victor/BMG 35027 (CD 1999)
October 24 and November 10, 1958; Los Angeles

Terry Gibbs Dream Band: *Volume 3—Flying Home*
Contemporary CCD 7654 25 (CD 1991)
March 17–19 and November, 1959; Los Angeles (Seville, Sundown Club)

Terry Gibbs Dream Band: *Volume 6—One More Time*
Contemporary CCD 7658 25 (CD 2002)
March and November, 1959; Los Angeles (Seville, Sundown Club)

Jimmy Witherspoon: *At the Monterey Jazz Festival*
Reissued as *Jimmy Witherspoon: The Concerts*
Fantasy Jazz FCD 24701 2 (CD 2002)
October 2, 1959; Monterey, CA

Woody Herman's Big New Herd: *At the Monterey Jazz Festival*
Koch Jazz KOC-CD 8508 (CD 1999)
October 3, 1959; Monterey, CA

Terry Gibbs Dream Band: *Volume 2—The Sundown Sessions*
Contemporary CCD 7652 25 (CD 1999)
November 1959; Los Angeles (Sundown Club)

Gerry Mulligan Meets Ben Webster
Verve 841661 2 (CD 2000)
November 3 and December 2, 1959; Los Angeles

Witherspoon, Mulligan, Webster at the Renaissance
Reissued as *Jimmy Witherspoon: The Concerts*
Fantasy Jazz FCD 24701 2 (CD 2002)
December 2, 1959; Monterey, CA

Sonny Stitt: *Blows the Blues*
Fresh Sound Records FSRCD 591 (CD 2010)
December 21–22, 1959; Los Angeles

Mel Torme Swings Shubert Alley
Verve/Polygram 821 581 2 (CD 1990)
January 4 and February 4, 11, 1960; Los Angeles

Benny Carter Quartet: *Sax a la Carter*
Capitol Jazz 5 93513 2 (CD 2004)
February 5, 1960; Los Angeles

"Alley Oop" —Hollywood Argyles
Marginal 120 (CD 1994)
Spring 1960; Los Angeles

Terry Gibbs and His Big Band: *Swing Is Here!*
Reissued as *Terry Gibbs and His Dream Band: Swing
Is Here! / Launching a New Sound in Music*
Fresh Sound Records FSRCD 583 (CD 2010)
February 23–24, 1960; Los Angeles

Bob Brookmeyer Quartet: *Blues, Hot and Cold*
Reissued as *Bob Brookmeyer Quartet: The Blues, Hot and Cold + 7X Wilder*
Lone Hill Jazz LHJ 10378 (CD 2009)
June 16, 1960; Los Angeles

Bill Holman's Great Big Band
Reissued as *The Original Bill Holman Big Band: Complete Recordings*
Lone Hill Jazz LHJ 10298 - (CD 2007)
June 29–30 and July 1, 1960; Los Angeles

Gerry Mulligan: *The Concert Jazz Band*
Reissued as *Gerry Mulligan: The Concert Jazz Band (The First Album)*
Poll Winners Records PWR 124537 (CD 2011)
July 25, 27, 1960; New York City

Al Cohn: *Son of Drum Suite*
RCA Victor LPM 2312 (LP 1960)
August 24, 26, 1960; New York City

Terry Gibbs: *More Vibes on Velvet*
EmArcy MG36148 (LP 1958)
November 1958; Los Angeles

Ella Fitzgerald: *Ella Swings Lightly*
Essential Jazz Classics EJC 55470 (CD 2010)
November 22–23, 1958; Los Angeles

Mark Murphy: *This Could Be the Start of Something*
Reissued as *Mark Murphy: Orchestra Conducted and Arranged by Bill Holman*
Fresh Sound Records FSRCD 608 (CD 2010)
December 1958 and August 26, 28, 1959; Los Angeles

Shorty Rogers: *Chances Are It Swings*
Reissued as *Shorty Rogers: Four Classic Albums (The Big
Shorty Rogers Express / Shorty Rogers and His Giants /
Wherever the Five Winds Blow / Chances Are It Swings)*
Avid Records UK AMSC 1041 (CD 2011)
December 9, 12, 20, 1958; Los Angeles

Terry Gibbs and His Orchestra: *Launching a New Sound in Music*
Reissued as *Terry Gibbs and His Dream Band: Swing
Is Here! / Launching a New Sound in Music*
Fresh Sound Records FSRCD 583 (CD 2010)
February 17–18, 1959; Los Angeles

Art Pepper + Eleven: *Modern Jazz Classics*
Contemporary/Original Jazz Classics OJCCD 341 2 (CD 1991)
March 14, 28 and May 12, 1959; Los Angeles

Terry Gibbs Dream Band: *Volume 1*
Contemporary CCD 7647 25 (CD 1991)
March 17-19, 1959; Los Angeles (Seville Club)

Gerry Mulligan and the Concert Jazz Band featuring Zoot
Sims—1960 Zurich: *Swiss Radio Days Jazz Series 12*
TCB Montreux Jazz Label 02122 (CD 1999)
November 17, 1960; Basel, Switzerland

Gerry Mulligan Concert Jazz Band: *Live at the Olympia Paris 1960*
Gambit 69249 (CD 2006)
November 19, 1960; Paris, France

Gerry Mulligan and the Concert Jazz Band: *At the Village Vanguard*
Verve 589488 2 (CD 2002)
December 11, 1960; New York City

The Exciting Terry Gibbs Big Band
Reissued as *Terry Gibbs Dream Band: Volume 4—Main Stem*
Contemporary CCD 7656 25 (CD 2002)
January 20-22, 1961; Los Angeles (Summit Club)

Mavis Rivers: *Mavis*
Reprise R2002 (LP 1961)
January 25, 26, 30, 1961; Los Angeles

Johnny Hodges: *The Complete 1960 Jazz Cellar Sessions*
Solar Records 4569895 (CD 2011)
January 31, 1961; Los Angeles

Sammy Davis Jr.: *The Wham of Sam*
Rhino/Warner Bros. 603497058266 (CD 2007)
February 7, 1961; Los Angeles

Shorty Rogers and His Orchestra featuring
The Giants: *An Invisible Orchard*
RCA Victor 74321495602 (CD 2004)
February 28 and April 18, 26, 1961; Los Angeles

Jimmy Hamilton: *It's About Time!*
Reissued as *Jimmy Hamilton: Can't Help Swingin'*
Prestige/Original Jazz Classics 25218521420 (CD 1999)
March 21, 1961; Englewood Cliffs, NJ

Judy Holliday: *Holliday with Mulligan*
DRG CDSL 5191 (CD 1990)
April 10–12, 14, 17, 1961; New York City

Explosion: Terry Gibbs and His Exciting Big Band
Reissued as Terry Gibbs Dream Band: *Volume 5—The Big Cat*
Contemporary CCD 7657 25 (CD 2002)
June 1961; Los Angeles (Summit Club)

Ray Charles and Betty Carter
Reissued as *Ray Charles: Ray Charles and Betty Carter / Dedicated to You*
Rhino 75259 (CD 1998)
June 13–14, 1961; Los Angeles

Bob Brookmeyer: *7 X Wilder*
Reissued as *Bob Brookmeyer Quartet: The Blues Hot and Cold + 7X Wilder*
Lone Hill Jazz LHJ 10378 (CD 2009)
June 29, 1961; New York City

Gerry Mulligan Concert Jazz Band: *Gerry*
Mulligan Presents a Concert in Jazz
Reissued as *The Complete Verve Gerry Mulligan Concert Band Sessions*
Mosaic Box Set MD4-221 (CD 1997)
July 10–11, 1961; New York City

Gerald Wilson Orchestra: *You Better Believe It*
Reissued as *The Complete Pacific Jazz Recordings*
of Gerald Wilson and His Orchestra
Mosaic Box Set MD5-198 (CD 2000)
September 9, 30, 1961; Los Angeles

Anita O'Day: *All the Sad Young Men*
Reissued as *Anita O'Day: Trav'lin' Light / All the Sad Young Men*
Fresh Sound Records FSRCD 673 (CD 2011)
October 16, 1961; New York City

Bob Brookmeyer: *Gloomy Sunday and Other Bright Moments*
Verve 314 527 658 2 (CD 1995)
November 6-8, 1961; New York City

Gary McFarland: *How to Succeed in Business Without Really Trying*
Verve 314 527 658 2 (CD 1995)
November 8, 15, 1961; New York City

Dizzy Gillespie Quintet: *Legends Live*
Jazz Haus 101711 (CD 2012)
November 27, 29, 1961; Stuttgart and Frankfurt, Germany

Eric Dolphy Quartet: *Softly, as in a Morning Sunrise*
Reissued as *Eric Dolphy with McCoy Tyner, Reggie Workman and
Mel Lewis: Softly, as in a Morning Sunrise (Munich 1961)*
Random Chance 13 (CD 2003)
December 2, 1961; Munich, Germany

Peggy Lee: *Sugar 'n' Spice*
Capitol Jazz 5 25249 2 (CD 2011)
March 28 and April 2, 4, 1962; Los Angeles

Benny Carter with Ben Webster and Barney Bigard: *BBB and Co.*
Original Jazz Classics OJC CD 758 2 (CD 1994)
April 10, 1962; Los Angeles

Gerald Wilson Big Band: *Moment of Truth*
Reissued as *The Complete Pacific Jazz Recordings
of Gerald Wilson and His Orchestra*
Mosaic Box Set MD5-198 (CD 2000)
August 27 and September, 1962; Los Angeles

The Barbra Streisand Album
Columbia CK 57374 (CD 1993)
January 23–25, 1963; New York City

James Moody: *Great Day*
Reissued as *James Moody / Thad Jones: The Legendary 1963–64 Sessions*
Lone Hill Jazz LHJ 10313 (CD 2007)
June 17–18, 1963; New York City

The Second Barbra Streisand Album
Columbia CK 57378 (CD 1993)
June 1963; New York City

Jimmy Smith and Kenny Burrell: *Blue Bash!*
Verve 557453 2 (CD 1999)
July 16, 26, 29, 1963; New York City

Clark Terry and His Friends: *What Makes Sammy Swing*
Reissued as *Clark Terry Septet: What Makes Sammy Swing*
Lone Hill Jazz LHJ 10333 (CD 2008)
August 1963; New York City

Gary McFarland Sextet: *Point of Departure*
Verve A 46 (LP 1963)
September 4–6, 1963; New York City

Stan Getz: *Reflections*
Verve 513631 2 (CD 2003)
October 21–22, 1963; New York City

Brother Jack McDuff Big Band: *Prelude*
Prestige PRCD 24283 2 (CD 2003)
December 24, 1963; New York City

Barbra Streisand: *The Third Album*
Columbia CK 57379 (CD 1993)
December and January, 1963; New York City

Morgana King: *With a Taste of Honey*
Mainstream CD 707 (CD 1991)
1964; New York City
Sylvia Syms: *The Fabulous Sylvia Syms*
20ᵗʰ Century Fox TFM 3123 (LP 1964)
1964; New York City

Barbra Streisand: *People*
Columbia CK 86103 (CD 2002)
July and August 1964; New York City

Joe Williams: *The Song Is You*
Reissued as *Joe Williams: Me and the Blues / The Song is You*
Collectables Jazz Classics COL 2703 (CD 2006)
November 11–12, 1964; New York City (Webster Hall)

Jimmy Ricks: *Vibrations (Arranged and Conducted by Don Sebesky)*
Mainstream 56060 (LP 1965)
1965; New York City

Barbra Streisand: *My Name is Barbra*
Columbia CK 9136 (CD 1994)
1965; New York City

Barbra Streisand: *My Name is Barbra, Two...*
Columbia CK 9209 (CD 1994)
1965; New York City

Jimmy Witherspoon: *Blues for Easy Livers*
Prestige/Original Blues Classics OBC CD 585 2 (CD 1996)
1965; New York City

Zoot Sims: *Live at the Half Note Again!*
Lone Hill Jazz LHJ 10207 (CD 2006)
1965; New York City (Half Note)

Carmen McRae: *Haven't We Met?*
Reissued as *Carmen McRae: The 1964 Orchestra Recordings*
Lone Hill Jazz LHJ 10256 (CD 2006)
February 2–3, 1965; New York City

Music from the Sound Track of "Mickey One" played
by Stan Getz / Composed by Eddie Sauter
MGM 4312 (LP 1965)
April, May and June 1965; New York City

Shirley Scott: *Latin Shadows*
Impulse AS 93 (LP 1965)
July 21–22, 1965; New York City
Oscar Peterson Trio: *With Respect to Nat*
Verve 314 557486 2 (CD 1998)
November 13, 1965; New York City

Tijuana Jazz with Gary McFarland and Co./ Clark Terry
Impulse AS 9104 (LP 1965)
December 3, 6, 7, 1965; New York City

Barbra Streisand: *Color Me Barbra*
Columbia CK 9278 (CD 1994)
1966; New York City

Thad Jones/Mel Lewis Big Band: *Opening Night February 7, 1966*
Alan Grant Presents 74321519312 (CD 2002)
February 7, 1966; New York City (Village Vanguard)
Thad Jones/Pepper Adams Quintet: *Mean What You Say*
Milestone/Original Jazz Classics OJCCD 464 2 (CD 1990)
April 26 and May 4, 9, 1966; New York City

Manny Albam: *Brass on Fire*
Solid State SM 17000 (LP 1966)
April 26–28, 1966; New York City

Presenting Thad Jones/Mel Lewis and The Jazz Orchestra
Reissued as *The Complete Solid State Recordings of
the Thad Jones / Mel Lewis Orchestra*
Mosaic MD5-151 (CD 1994)
May 4–6, 1966; New York City

Eddie Daniels: *First Prize!*
Prestige/ Original Jazz Classics OJCCD 771 2 (CD 1993)
September 8, 1966; New York City

Presenting Joe Williams and Thad Jones/Mel Lewis Jazz Orchestra
Blue Note CDP 7243 8 30454 2 6 - (CD 1994)
September 30, 1966; New York City

James Moody: *Moody and the Brass Figures*
Milestone/Original Jazz Classics OJCCD 1099 2 (CD 2004)
October and November, 1966; New York City

Thad Jones and Mel Lewis: Live at the Village Vanguard
Blue Note CDP 7243 5 60438 2 4 (CD 2004)
Also reissued as *The Complete Solid State Recordings of The Thad
Jones / Mel Lewis Orchestra* Mosaic MD5-151 (CD 1994)
April 28, 1967; New York City

Jimmy McGriff: *A Bag Full of Blues*
Solid State SM 17017 (LP 1967)
June 1967; New York City

Dizzy Gillespie: *Solid State Jazz for a Sunday Afternoon Vol. 1 and Vol. 2*
Reissued as *Dizzy Gillespie: Live at the Village Vanguard*
Blue Note CDP 0777 7 80507 2 8 (CD 1992)
October 1, 1967; New York City (Village Vanguard)

Jazz Casual: *Thad Jones-Mel Lewis Orchestra /*
Woody Herman and His Swinging Herd
Koch Jazz KOCCD 8563 (CD 2001)
April 22, 1968; San Francisco (Live on *Jazz Casual*)

The Great Joe Williams: *Something Old, New and Blue*
Reissued as *Joe Williams with the Thad Jones/Mel
Lewis Orchestra: One More for My Baby*
LaserLight 17 135 (CD 2008)
April 22–27, 1968; Los Angeles

The Big Band Sound of Thad Jones/Mel Lewis featuring Miss Ruth Brown
Reissued as *Ruth Brown with the Thad Jones / Mel
Lewis Orchestra: Fine Brown Flame*
Capitol Jazz CDP 7 81200 2 (CD 1994)
July 18, 1968; New York City

Jimmy McGriff: *The Worm*
Blue Note CDP 7243 5 38699 2 2 (CD 2002)
August 1968; New York City

Stanley Turrentine: *Always Something There*
Reissued as *Easy!—Stanley Turrentine Plays the Pop Hits*
Blue Note CDP 7243 4 93991 2 9 (CD 1998)
October 1, 14, 1968; Englewood Cliffs, NJ

Thad Jones/Mel Lewis Jazz Orchestra: *Monday Night*
Reissued as *The Complete Solid State Recordings of
the Thad Jones / Mel Lewis Orchestra*
Mosaic MD5-151 (CD 1994)
October 17, 1968; New York City (Village Vanguard)

Thad Jones/Mel Lewis Jazz Orchestra: *Central Park North*
Blue Note CDP 7243 5 76852 2 (CD 2004)
Also reissued as *The Complete Solid State Recordings of the Thad
Jones / Mel Lewis Orchestra* Mosaic MD5-151 (CD 1994)
June 17–18, 1969; New York City

Thad Jones/Mel Lewis Orchestra: *Paris 1969—Volume 1*
Royal Jazz RJD 511 (CD)
September 8, 1969; Paris, France (Maison De L'Ortf)
Thad Jones-Mel Lewis Orchestra: *Basle 1969*
TCB Montreaux Jazz Label 02042 (CD 2011)
September 11, 1969; Basel, Switzerland (Stadt Theatre)

Thad Jones/Mel Lewis: *Consummation*
Blue Note CDP 7243 5 38226 2 0 (CD 2002)
Also reissued as *The Complete Solid State Recordings of the Thad Jones / Mel Lewis Orchestra* Mosaic MD5-151 (CD 1994)
January 20, 21, 28 and May 25, 1970; New York City

Thad Jones and Mel Lewis: *Suite for Pops*
Horizon SP 701 - (LP 1972)
January 25, 26, 31 and September 1, 1972: New York City
July 22, 1975; New York City

Jimmy Smith: *Portuguese Soul*
Verve V6-8832 (LP 1973)
February 8–9, 1973; New York City

Stephane Grapelli Meets The Rhythm Section
Reissued as *Stephane Grapelli: Parisian Thoroughfare*
Black Lion BLCD 760132 (CD 1999)
September 5, 7, 1973; London, England

Pepper Adams Quartet: *Ephemera*
Spotlite PA 6 (LP 1973)
September 10, 1973; London, England

Thad Jones/Mel Lewis and The Jazz Orchestra Meet Manuel De Sica: *First Jazz Suite*
PAUSA PR 7012 (LP 1973)
September 13–14, 1973; London, England

Thad Jones/Mel Lewis and The Jazz Orchestra: *Live in Tokyo*
Nippon/Columbia COCB 53510 (CD 2005)
March 12–13, 1974; Tokyo, Japan (Yubin Chockin Hall, Toshi Center Hall)

Thad Jones and Mel Lewis: *Potpourri*
Philadelphia International Records KZ 33152 (LP 1974)
June 1974; Philadelphia

A Buck Clayton Jam Session Vol.2
Reissued as *A Buck Clayton Jam Session: 1975*
Chiaroscuro CR 143 (CD 1995)
June 5–6, 1975; New York City

Greeting and Salutations: Thad Jones / Swedish Radio
Jazz Group featuring Mel Lewis and Jon Faddis
Four Leaf Clover FLCCD 125 (CD)
June 27–28, 1975; Stockholm, Sweden

Thad Jones/Mel Lewis: *New Life*
A&M CD 0810 (CD 1989)
December 16–17, 1975; New York City
January 8, 10, 1976; New York City

Rhoda Scott in New York with the Thad Jones/Mel Lewis Orchestra
Universal/EmArcy 981120 6 (CD 2003)
June 2–3, 1976; New York City

Mel Lewis and Friends
A&M CD 0823 (CD 1990)
June 8–9, 1976; New York City

Thad Jones/Mel Lewis Orchestra: *Live at Jazz Jantar*
Reissued as *Thad Jones/Mel Lewis Orchestra: The*
Complete Poland Concerts 1976 and 1978
Gambit Records 69320 (CD 2009)
August 6, 1976; Sopot, Poland (Jazz Jantar)

Thad Jones and Mel Lewis: *Live in Munich*
Horizon/A&M SP 724 (LP 1976)
September 9, 1976; Munich, Germany (Domicile Club)

Thad Jones and Aura Rully
Four Leaf Clover FLC 5020 (LP 1977)
January 28-29, 1977; Stockholm, Sweden

Chet Baker: *Once Upon a Summertime*
Galaxy/Original Jazz Classics OJCCD 405 2 (CD 1984)
February 20, 1977; New York City

**Monica Zetterlund and the Thad Jones/Mel Lewis
Orchestra:** *It Only Happens Every Time*
EMI Sweden 7CO62 35454 (LP 1977)
August 20, 21, 23, 1977; Helsinki, Finland

Thad Jones and Mel Lewis: *The Thad Jones/Mel Lewis Quartet*
A&M CD 0830 (CD 1989)
September 24, 1977; Miami, Florida (Airliner Lounge)

Bob Brookmeyer: *Back Again*
Gazell Records GJCD 1015 (CD 1995)
May 23–25, 1978; New York City

The Thad Jones/Mel Lewis Orchestra: *Body and Soul*
West Wind 2407 (CD 2002)
October 2, 1978; Berlin, Germany (Filmtheater Kosmos)

Thad Jones/Mel Lewis Orchestra: *One More Time*
Reissued as *Thad Jones/Mel Lewis Orchestra: The
Complete Poland Concerts 1976 and 1978*
Gambit Records 69320 (CD 2009)
October 26, 1978; Warsaw, Poland (Jazz Jamboree)

Mel Lewis and The Jazz Orchestra: *Naturally*
Telarc CD 83301 (CD 1988)
March 20–21, 1979; Englewood, New Jersey

The New Mel Lewis Quintet: *Live*
Inak 8611 (CD 1992)
September 9, 1979; Saalfelden, Austria (Festival Im Stall)

Bob Brookmeyer / Mel Lewis and The Jazz
Orchestra: Live at the Village Vanguard
DCC Jazz DJZ 616 (CD 1991)
February 1980; New York City (Village Vanguard)

Mel Lewis And The Jazz Orchestra: *Live at Montreux*
PAUSA PR 7115 (LP 1981)
July 16, 1980; Montreux, Switzerland (Montreux Jazz Festival)

Mel Lewis: *Mellifluous*
Landmark LCD 1543 2 (CD 1995)
March 31, 1981; Englewood Cliffs, NJ

Bob Brookmeyer: *Through a Looking Glass*
Finesse FW 37488 (LP 1982)
January 1982; New York City

Mel Lewis and The Jazz Orchestra: *Make Me Smile*
and Other New Works by Bob Brookmeyer
Reissued as *Mel Lewis and The Jazz Orchestra:*
Featuring the Music of Bob Brookmeyer
Red Baron JK 53752 (CD 1993)
January 7–11, 1982; New York City (Village Vanguard)

WDR Big Band featuring Jiggs Whigham, Bill
Holman, Mel Lewis: *The Third Stone*
Koala Music CD P4 (CD 1989)
May 24–28, 1982; Cologne, Germany

Loren Schoenberg, His Orchestra and His
Quartet: *That's the Way It Goes*
Aviva 6005 (LP 1984)
July 19–20, 1984; New York City

The Mel Lewis Orchestra: *20 Years at the Village Vanguard*
Atlantic 81655 2 (CD 1991)
March 20–22, 1985; New York City

Jon Faddis: *Legacy*
Concord Jazz CCD 4291 (CD 1990)
August 1985: New York City

Joe Lovano Quartet: *Tones, Shapes and Colors*
Soul Note 121132 2 (CD 1993)
November 21, 1985; New York City (Jazz Center)
The American Jazz Orchestra with Benny Carter: *Central City Sketches*
Musicmasters CIJD 60126X (CD 1992)
1986; New York City

Hank Crawford / Jimmy McGriff: *Soul Survivors*
Milestone MCD 9142 2 (CD 1990)
January 29–30, 1986; Englewood Cliffs, NJ

Jimmy Knepper Quintet: *Dream Dancing*
Criss Cross 1024 (CD 1994)
April 3, 1986; Englewood Cliffs, NJ

Al Porcino Big Band: *In Oblivion*
Jazz Mark CD 106 (CD 2000)
April 6, 1986; New York City

Renee Manning: *Uhm…Uhm…Uhmmm!*
Ken 022 (CD 1987)
May 4, 1986; New York City

Loren Schoenberg and His Jazz Orchestra: *Time Waits for No One*
Musicmasters CIJD 60137K (CD 1992)
1987; New York City

Pete Malinverni: *Don't Be Shy*
Sound Hills 80000APV8V JP (CD 2003)
April 1987; Englewood Cliffs, NJ

The Mel Lewis Jazz Orchestra: *The Definitive Thad Jones Vol. 1*
Reissued as *The Mel Lewis Jazz Orchestra: The Definitive*
Thad Jones—Live from the Village Vanguard
Nimbus Records NI 2706 (CD 2009)
February 11–15, 1988; New York City (Village Vanguard)

Mel Lewis Jazz Orchestra: *The Definitive Thad Jones Vol. 2*
Reissued as *The Mel Lewis Jazz Orchestra: The Definitive*
Thad Jones—Live from the Village Vanguard
Nimbus Records NI 2706 (CD 2009)
February 11–15, 1988; New York City (Village Vanguard)

Mel Lewis Jazz Orchestra: *Soft Lights and Hot Music*
Musicmasters CIJD 60172F (CD 1992)
February 11–15, 1988; New York City (Village Vanguard)

The American Jazz Orchestra Conducted by
John Lewis: *Ellington Masterpieces*
East-West 91423 (CD 2010)
November 21–23, 1988; New York City

Mel Lewis Sextet: *The Lost Art*
Musicmasters CIJD 50232C (CD 1992)
April 11–12, 1989; New York City

The Jay McShann Kansas City Band: *Paris All-Star Blues*
Heritage Jazz 522804 H (CD 1991)
June 13, 1989; Paris, France (Live at La Villette)

357

Pete Malinverni: *The Spirit*
Saranac SR1001 (CD 1995)
August 17, 1989; Englewood Cliffs, NJ

Loren Schoenberg and His Jazz Orchestra: *Just A-settin' and A-rockin'*
Musicmasters CIJD 50392C (CD 1992)
September 6–7, 1989; New York City

Notes

Preface

1. Tom Lord Online Jazz Discography, s.v. "Mel Lewis," http://www.lordisco.com (accessed December 28, 2011).

2. Burt Korall, *Drummin' Men: The Heartbeat of Jazz—The Bebop Years* (New York City: Oxford University Press, 2002), 248.

Chapter 1

1. Bob Rusch and Beth Jenne, "Mel Lewis: Interview Part Three," *Cadence*, March 1990, 22.

2. Mel Lewis, "The View from the Back of the Band" (ca. 1988), unpublished memoirs, Mel Lewis Collection, Miller Nichols Library, Kansas City.

3. Mel Lewis, interviewed by Ben Sidran on *Talking Jazz: An Oral History*, October 16, 1987, CD, Unlimited Media Ltd. (2006), transcription by author.

4. Mel Lewis, interviewed by Loren Schoenberg, December 1982, WKCR *Profiles*, transcription by author.

5. Diane Spear, "Mel Lewis," *The West Side Spirit*, n.d.

6. Rusch and Jenne, "Mel Lewis: Interview Part Three," 10.

7. Rusch and Jenne, "Mel Lewis: Interview Part Three," 9.

8. Ibid., 10.

9. Mel Lewis, interview with Jim Marcus, November 29, 1985.

10. Lewis, interviewed by Loren Schoenberg, WKCR *Profiles*.

11. Ibid.

12. Spear, "Mel Lewis."

13. Lewis, interviewed by Loren Schoenberg, WKCR *Profiles*.

14. Ibid.

15. Ibid.

16. Lewis, interviewed by Loren Schoenberg, WKCR *Profiles*.

17. Arnold Jay Smith, "Staunch But Swinging," *DownBeat*, June 1, 1978, 16.

18. Lewis, interviewed by Loren Schoenberg.

19. Ibid.

20. Ibid.

21. Ibid.

22. Ibid.

23. Bob Rusch and Beth Jenne, "Mel Lewis: Interview Part One," *Cadence*, January 1990, 7.

24. Arnold Jay Smith, "Mel Lewis: Staunch But Swinging," *DownBeat,* June 1, 1978, 16.

25. Rusch and Jenne, "Mel Lewis: Interview Part Three," 19.

26. Lewis, interview with Jim Marcus.

27. Ibid.

28. Lewis, interviewed by Loren Schoenberg, WKCR *Profiles*.

29. Ibid.

30. Lewis, interviewed by Loren Schoenberg, WKCR *Profiles*.

Chapter 2

1. Bob Rusch and Beth Jenne, "Mel Lewis: Interview Part One," *Cadence,* January 1990, 8.

2. John Tynan, "Time Is the Quality Mel Lewis Has," *DownBeat,* December 12, 1957, 22.

3. Gene Cipriano, interview by author, May 16, 2013.

4. Lewis, interviewed by Loren Schoenberg.

5. Lewis, interviewed by Loren Schoenberg, WKCR *Profiles.*

6. Ibid.

7. Ibid.

8. Scott Kevin Fish, "Mel Lewis: Straight Ahead," *Modern Drummer*, April 1978, 14

9. Frank King, "Meet Mel Lewis," *Crescendo*, October 1969, 39.

10. Mel Lewis, interviewed by Will Moyle, n.d., AM 1370 *Essence of Jazz,* transcription by author.

11. Lewis, interviewed by Loren Schoenberg, WKCR *Profiles.*

12. Ibid.

13. Rusch and Jenne, "Mel Lewis: Interview Part Three," 10.

14. Ibid.

15. Lewis, interviewed by Loren Schoenberg, WKCR *Profiles.*

16. Ibid.

17. Ibid.

18. Ibid.

19. Ibid.

20. Ibid.

21. Ibid.

22. Ibid.

23. Ibid.

24. Rusch and Jenne, "Mel Lewis: Interview Part Three," 11.

25. Lewis Sokoloff, interview by author, February 18, 2014.

26. Rusch and Jenne, "Mel Lewis: Interview Part Three," 11.

27. Ibid.

28. Doris Sokoloff, interview by author, April 2, 2012.

29. Rusch and Jenne, "Mel Lewis: Interview Part One," 7.

30. Lewis, interviewed by Loren Schoenberg, WKCR *Profiles.*

31. Tom Lord Online Jazz Discography, s.v. "Mel Lewis."

32. N.a., "Music—As Written," *The Billboard*, April 22, 1950, 26.

33. Lewis, interviewed by Loren Schoenberg, WKCR *Profiles.*

34. Ibid.

35. Ibid.

36. Ibid.

37. Ibid.

38. Ibid.

39. Ibid.

40. Gene Cipriano, interview.

41. Tynan, "Time Is the Quality Mel Lewis Has," 22.
42. Tom Lord Online Jazz Discography, s.v. "Mel Lewis."
43. Lewis, interviewed by Loren Schoenberg, WKCR *Profiles*.
44. Ibid.
45. Bob Rusch and Beth Jenne, "Mel Lewis: Interview Part Two," *Cadence*, February 1990, 9.
46. Ibid.
47. Doris Sokoloff, interview by author, April 2, 2012.

Chapter 3

1. Mel Lewis, interviewed by Will Moyle, n.d., AM 1370 *Essence of Jazz*, transcription by author.
2. Tynan, "Time Is the Quality Mel Lewis Has," 22.
3. *The New Grove Dictionary of Jazz,* 2nd ed. (New York City: Macmillan Publishers, 2002), s.v. "Bob Brookmeyer."
4. N.a., "Beneke-Haynes-Miller Team Hits Bumpy Road," *The Billboard*, December 16, 1950, 14.
5. Lewis, interviewed by Loren Schoenberg, WKCR *Profiles*.
6. Ibid.
7. Ibid.
8. Ibid.
9. Ibid.
10. Ibid.
11. Sokoloff, interview.
12. Lewis, interviewed by Loren Schoenberg, WKCR *Profiles*.
13. Ibid.
14. Ibid.
15. Ibid.
16. Ibid.
17. Ibid.
18. Rusch and Jenne, "Mel Lewis: Interview Part Two," 12.
19. Robin Callot and Jerry Burling, notes to *Ray Anthony Collectors Series*, CD (1991), Capitol Records CDP 7 94079 2, 10.
20. N.a., "Kudos Pile on Anthony for Dragnet," *The Billboard*, September 26, 1953, 24.
21. Callot and Burling, notes to *Ray Anthony Collectors Series*, 7.
22. Lewis, interviewed by Loren Schoenberg, WKCR *Profiles*.

Chapter 4

1. Lewis, interviewed by Will Moyle, AM 1370 *Essence of Jazz*.
2. Jack Brand and Bill Korst, *Shelly Manne: Sounds of the Different Drummer* (Rockford, IL: Percussion Express, 1997), 70.
3. Ibid., 53.
4. Mel Lewis, interviewed by Loren Schoenberg, 1987, WKCR *History of Jazz Drums* (Shelly Manne), transcription by author.

5. Korall, *Drummin' Men: The Heartbeat of Jazz—The Bebop Years*, 239.

6. Lewis, interviewed by Loren Schoenberg, WKCR *History of Jazz Drums* (Shelly Manne).

7. Bill Holman, interview by author, July 21, 2011.

8. Holman, interview.

9. Michael Sparke, *Stan Kenton: This Is an Orchestra!* (Denton: University of North Texas Press, 2010), 123.

10. Marc Myers, "Bill Holman: I Told You So," http://www.jazzwax.com/2010/05/bill-holman-i-told-you-so.html (accessed December 29, 2011).

11. Tynan, "Time Is the Quality Mel Lewis Has," 56.

12. Jordi Pujol, notes to *The Modernity of Bob Brookmeyer*, CD (2008), Fresh Sound Records FSR-CD 499.

13. Ibid.

14. Lewis, interviewed by Will Moyle, AM 1370 *Essence of Jazz*.

15. Tom Lord Online Jazz Discography, s.v. "Mel Lewis."

16. Rusch and Jenne, "Mel Lewis: Interview Part Three," 12.

17. *The New Grove Dictionary of Jazz*, 2nd ed., s.v. "Al Porcino."

18. Sparke, *Stan Kenton: This Is an Orchestra!*, 126.

19. Ibid., 126.

20. Ibid.

Chapter 5

1. Nat Hentoff, "Are You Sure This Is Kenton? Asks Listener," *DownBeat*, July 27, 1955, 17.

2. Burt Korall, "Mel Lewis," *International Musician*, n.d., 28.

3. John Von Ohlen, interview by author, March 14, 2013.

4. Lewis, interviewed by Will Moyle, AM 1370 *Essence of Jazz*.

5. Michael Sparke, notes to *Stan Kenton: Contemporary Concepts*, CD (2002), Capitol Records 42310.

6. Sparke, *Stan Kenton: This Is an Orchestra!*, 130.

7. Sparke, notes to *Stan Kenton: Contemporary Concepts*.

8. Lewis, interviewed by Will Moyle, AM 1370 *Essence of Jazz*.

9. Ibid.

10. Tom Lord Online Jazz Discography, s.v. "Thad Jones."

11. Francis Davis, notes to *Thad Jones Legacy: Vanguard Jazz Orchestra*, CD (1999), New World Records 80581.

12. Sparke, *Stan Kenton: This Is an Orchestra!*, 131.

13. Holman, interview.

14. Sparke, *Stan Kenton: This Is an Orchestra!*, 133.

15. Ibid.

16. Ibid., 134.

17. Tony Brown, "Kenton's Impact," *Melody Maker*, April 7, 1956, 3.

18. Ibid.

19. Leslie Mallory, "Kenton Band Is Far Ahead," n.p., April 8, 1956, n.p.

20. Sparke, *Stan Kenton: This Is an Orchestra!*, 138.
21. Ibid.
22. Mel Lewis, *Queen Elizabeth* boarding pass, May 10, 1956.
23. Sparke, *Stan Kenton: This Is an Orchestra!*, 138.
24. Gioia, *The History of Jazz*, 217.
25. Bill Coss, notes to *Stan Kenton: Cuban Fire*, LP (1965), Capitol Records SM-11794.
26. Sparke, *Stan Kenton: This Is an Orchestra!*, 142.
27. Tom Lord Online Jazz Discography, s.v. "Mel Lewis."
28. Ibid.
29. Ibid.
30. Rusch and Jenne, "Mel Lewis: Interview Part Two," 14.
31. Ibid.
32. Ibid.
33. N.a., notes to *Got'cha: Music of the Mel Lewis Septet*, CD (1989), Fresh Sound Records FSR-CD 73.
34. Rusch and Jenne, "Mel Lewis: Interview Part Two," 14.
35. Sparke, *Stan Kenton: This Is an Orchestra!*, 142.
36. Sokoloff, interview.
37. Tynan, "Time Is the Quality Mel Lewis Has," 22.
38. Rusch and Jenne, "Mel Lewis: Interview Part Two," 10.

Chapter 6

1. Tom Lord Online Jazz Discography, s.v. "Mel Lewis."
2. Russ Wilson, "Ferguson Gassed by Career as Leader," *The Oakland Tribune,* 6 January 1957, n.p.
3. Holman, interview.
4. Ibid.
5. Ibid.
6. Stewart Clay, notes to *The Original Bill Holman Big Band: Complete Recordings*, CD (2007), Lone Hill Jazz LHJ 10298.
7. Holman, interview.
8. Jeff Hamilton, interview by author, September 20, 2011.
9. Holman, interview.
10. Tom Lord Online Jazz Discography, s.v. "Mel Lewis."
11. Rusch and Jenne, "Mel Lewis: Interview Part Two," 15.
12. Tynan, "Time Is the Quality Mel Lewis Has," 55.
13. Joe Quinn, notes to *Pepper Adams Quintet*, CD (1987), V.S.O.P. #5.
14. Ted Panken, notes to *Pepper Adams: Critics' Choice*, CD (2005), Mighty Quinn Productions MQP 1103.
15. Ibid.
16. Ibid.
17. Tynan, "Time Is the Quality Mel Lewis Has," 22.

18. Holman, interview.

19. Tynan, "Time Is the Quality Mel Lewis Has," 56.

20. Lewis, interviewed by Will Moyle, AM 1370 *Essence of Jazz.*

21. Holman, interview.

22. Helen LaFaro-Fernandez, *Jade Visions: The Life and Music of Scott LaFaro* (Denton: University of North Texas Press, 2009), 83.

23. Holman, interview.

24. Ibid.

25. John Tynan, "Heard in Person: Mel Lewis-Bill Holman Quintet," *DownBeat*, July 24, 1958, n.p.

26. Ibid.

27. Holman, interview.

28. Paul Conley, "Monterey Jazz Festival Celebrates 50th Year," http://www.npr.org/templates/story/story.php?storyId=14566084 (accessed February 11, 2012).

29. N.a., official program, Monterey Jazz Festival, 1958.

30. Ibid.

31. Tynan, "Time Is the Quality Mel Lewis Has," 55.

32. Tom Lord Online Jazz Discography, s.v. "Mel Lewis."

33. Hamilton, interview.

34. *The New Grove Dictionary of Jazz,* 2nd ed., s.v. "Shorty Rogers."

35. Tom Lord Online Jazz Discography, s.v. "Mel Lewis."

Chapter 7

1. Terry Gibbs, interview by author, July 25, 2011.

2. Tom Lord Online Jazz Discography, s.v. "Mel Lewis."

3. Gibbs, interview.

4. Ibid.

5. Ibid.

6. John Tynan, "Vamp Till Ready—Terry Gibbs' Big Band," *DownBeat*, November 8, 1962, 18.

7. Gibbs, interview.

8. Tynan, "Vamp Till Ready—Terry Gibbs' Big Band," 18.

9. Ibid.

10. Ibid.

11. Gibbs, interview.

12. Ibid.

13. Tynan, "Vamp Till Ready—Terry Gibbs' Big Band," 19.

14. Gibbs, interview.

15. Holman, interview.

16. N.a., notes to *Terry Gibbs and His Orchestra: Launching a New Sound in Music*, LP (1959), Mercury SR-60112.

17. Ibid.

18. Gibbs, interview.

19. Tynan, "Vamp Till Ready—Terry Gibbs' Big Band," 19.

20. Terry Gibbs, *Good Vibes: A Life in Jazz* (Lanham, MD: The Scarecrow Press Inc, 2003), 193.

21. Pat Tobin, "Recording Wally Heider: Memories of W-W-Wally," http://wallyheider.com/wordpress/2006/10/memories-of-w-w-wally/#more-42 (accessed February 5, 2012).

22. Ibid.

23. *The New Grove Dictionary of Jazz,* 2nd ed., s.v. "Wally Heider."

24. Gibbs, *Good Vibes: A Life in Jazz*, 208.

25. Ibid.

26. Gibbs, interview.

27. N.a., notes to *Terry Gibbs Dream Band: Volume 1*, CD (1986), Contemporary Records CCD-7647-2.

28. Rusch and Jenne, "Mel Lewis: Interview Part One," 6.

Chapter 8

1. Ibid.

2. Sokoloff, interview.

3. Tom Lord Online Jazz Discography, s.v. "Mel Lewis."

4. Ibid.

5. Ralph J. Gleason, notes to *Woody Herman's Big New Herd at the Monterey Jazz Festival*, CD (1999), Koch Jazz KOC-CD8508.

6. Hamilton, interview.

7. *The New Grove Dictionary of Jazz,* 2nd ed., s.v. "Jimmy Witherspoon."

8. Frank Buchmann-Moller, *Someone to Watch Over Me: The Life and Music of Ben Webster* (Ann Arbor: The University of Michigan Press, 2009), 180.

9. Jack Gordon, *Fifties Jazz Talk: An Oral Retrospective* (Lanham, MD: Scarecrow Press, 2004), 151.

10. John Tynan, notes to *Jimmy Witherspoon: The Concerts*, CD (2009), Fantasy Records FCD-24701-2.

11. Rusch and Jenne, "Mel Lewis: Interview Part Two," 9.

12. Fred Bronson, *The Billboard Book of Number One Hits: 5th Edition* (New York City: Watson-Guptill Publications, 2003), 70.

13. Rusch and Jenne, "Mel Lewis: Interview Part Two," 9.

14. Bronson, *The Billboard Book of Number One Hits: 5th Edition*, 70.

15. Joseph Carucci, "The Contributions of Gerry Mulligan's Concert Jazz Band to the Jazz Tradition " (DMA diss., University of Kentucky, 2009), 28.

16. Ibid.

17. Gordon, *Fifties Jazz Talk: An Oral Retrospective*, 151.

18. Alan Raph, interview by author, December 14, 2011.

19. Tom Lord Online Jazz Discography, s.v. "Mel Lewis."

20. Korall, *Drummin' Men: The Heartbeat of Jazz—The Bebop Years*, 243.

21. Ibid.

22. Lewis, interviewed by Will Moyle, AM 1370 *Essence of Jazz.*
23. John Tynan, "The Peripatetic Mel Lewis," *DownBeat*, n.m. 1962, 40.
24. Rusch and Jenne, "Mel Lewis: Interview Part Two," 10.
25. Tom Lord Online Jazz Discography, s.v. "Mel Lewis."
26. Ibid.
27. Raph, interview.
28. Korall, *Drummin' Men: The Heartbeat of Jazz—The Bebop Years*, 243.
29. Ibid.
30. Carucci, "The Contributions of Gerry Mulligan's Concert Jazz Band to the Jazz Tradition," 32.
31. Tom Lord Online Jazz Discography, s.v. "Mel Lewis."
32. Bill Crow, interview by author, December 20, 2011.
33. Ibid.
34. Ibid.
35. Ibid.
36. Nat Hentoff, notes to *Gerry Mulligan and the Concert Jazz Band at the Village Vanguard*, LP (1961), Verve Records V-8396.
37. Crow, interview.
38. Ibid.

Chapter 9

1. Carucci, "The Contributions of Gerry Mulligan's Concert Jazz Band to the Jazz Tradition," 34.
2. Ibid., 32.
3. Ibid., 34.
4. Ibid., 32.
5. Tom Lord Online Jazz Discography, s.v. "Mel Lewis."
6. Tynan, "The Peripatetic Mel Lewis," 40.
7. Tom Lord Online Jazz Discography, s.v. "Mel Lewis."
8. Ibid.
9. Rusch and Jenne, "Mel Lewis: Interview Part Three," 18.
10. Ibid.
11. Max Jones, "Dizzy Knows His Drums—I Adapt to Him," *Melody Maker*, February 24, 1962, 4.
12. Tynan, "The Peripatetic Mel Lewis," 40.
13. Jones, "Dizzy Knows His Drums—I Adapt to Him," 4.
14. N.a., official program, *Jazz at the Philharmonic*: British Tour, 1961.
15. Tynan, "The Peripatetic Mel Lewis," 40.
16. Mel Lewis, interviewed by Loren Schoenberg, 1987, WKCR *History of Jazz Drums* (Elvin Jones), transcription by author.
17. Don DeMichael, "John Coltrane and Eric Dolphy Answer the Jazz Critics," *DownBeat*, April 12, 1962, 20.
18. *The New Grove Dictionary of Jazz,* 2nd ed., s.v. "Eric Dolphy."
19. Rusch and Jenne, "Mel Lewis: Interview Part Three," 13.
20. Jones, "Dizzy Knows His Drums—I Adapt to Him," 4.

21. Rusch and Jenne, "Mel Lewis: Interview Part Three," 13.
22. Tynan, "The Peripatetic Mel Lewis," 40.
23. Sokoloff, interview.

Chapter 10

1. Paul J. Byrne, *The Cuban Missile Crisis: To the Brink of War* (Minneapolis: Compass Point Books, 2006), 86.
2. Crow, interview.
3. Bill Crow, "To Russia Without Love: The Benny Goodman Tour of the USSR—Part One," *Gene Lees Jazzletter*, August 1986, 1.
4. Ibid., 2.
5. Ibid., 4.
6. Ibid., 6.
7. Ibid., 8.
8. Mel Lewis, Goodman U.S.S.R tour itinerary, June 1962.
9. Rusch and Jenne, "Mel Lewis: Interview Part Three," 13.
10. Crow, interview.
11. Rusch and Jenne, "Mel Lewis: Interview Part Three," 13.
12. Ibid.
13. Ibid.
14. Ibid.
15. Crow, interview.
16. Mel Lewis, personal letter to Doris Sokoloff, June 20, 1962.
17. Tom Lord Online Jazz Discography, s.v. "Mel Lewis."
18. *The New Grove Dictionary of Jazz,* 2nd ed., s.v. "Gerald Wilson."
19. Gerald Wilson Big Band, DVD, *Frankly Jazz: Featuring the Gerald Wilson Big Band* (Los Angeles, CA: not commercially released, 1962).
20. Ralph J. Gleason, "A Salute to the Trojan Jazzmen," *San Francisco Chronicle*, September 27, 1962, 45.
21. Donald L. Maggin, *Dizzy: The Life and Times of John Birks Gillespie* (New York City: Harper Collins Publishers, 2005), 310.
22. David L. Abell, program notes, UCLA Concert Series: Dizzy Gillespie, November 1962, 22–23.
23. Mel Lewis, personal letter to Doris Sokoloff, June 20, 1962.
24. Gibbs, interview.
25. Carucci, "The Contributions of Gerry Mulligan's Concert Jazz Band to the Jazz Tradition," 33.
26. Hamilton, interview.
27. Holman, interview.
28. Ibid.
29. Rusch and Jenne, "Mel Lewis: Interview Part Three," 17.
30. Lewis, interviewed by Ben Sidran, *Talking Jazz: An Oral History.*
31. Sokoloff, interview.
32. Lewis, interviewed by Will Moyle, AM 1370 *Essence of Jazz.*

33. Lewis, interviewed by Ben Sidran, *Talking Jazz: An Oral History*.

Chapter 11

1. Lewis, interviewed by Ben Sidran, *Talking Jazz: An Oral History*.
2. Ibid.
3. Ibid.
4. Ibid.
5. Jeroen de Valk, *Ben Webster: His Life and Music* (Berkeley: Berkeley Hill Books, 2001), 124.
6. Ibid., 123.
7. John Riley, interview by author, January 24, 2012.
8. Valk, *Ben Webster: His Life and Music*, 124.
9. Benny Golson, notes to *James Moody: Great Day*, CD (2007), Lone Hill Jazz LHJ10313.
10. Lewis, interviewed by Will Moyle, AM 1370 *Essence of Jazz*.
11. Tom Lord Online Jazz Discography, s.v. "Mel Lewis."
12. Dan Morgenstern, "Mel Lewis: The Big Band Man," 20.
13. Sokoloff, interview.
14. Marvin Stamm, interview by author, January 18, 2012.
15. Lewis, interviewed by Ben Sidran, *Talking Jazz: An Oral History*.
16. Morgenstern, "Mel Lewis: The Big Band Man," 20.
17. Ibid.
18. Tim Brooks and Earle Marsh, *The Complete Directory to Prime Time Network and Cable TV Shows: 1946–Present* (New York City: Ballantine Books, 2007), 702.
19. Ibid.
20. Kirchner, notes to *The Complete Solid State Recordings of the Thad Jones/Mel Lewis Orchestra*, 3.
21. Frank King, "Meet Mel Lewis," *Crescendo*, October 1969, 40.
22. Lewis, interviewed by Will Moyle, AM 1370 *Essence of Jazz*.
23. Jerry Dodgion, interview by author, March 1, 2012.
24. Rusch and Jenne, "Mel Lewis: Interview Part Two," 11.
25. Duke Ellington, *Music Is My Mistress* (New York City: Da Capo Press, 1973), 330.
26. Ibid., 331.
27. Tom Lord Online Jazz Discography, s.v. "Mel Lewis."
28. Rusch and Jenne, "Mel Lewis: Interview Part Three," 20.
29. Ibid.
30. *The New Grove Dictionary of Jazz*, 2nd ed., s.v. "Friedrich Gulda."
31. Mel Lewis, Euro-Jazz Orchestra concert programs, 1964–1966.

Chapter 12

1. Mike Bourne, "Soulmates: Thad Jones-Mel Lewis," *DownBeat*, April 16, 1970, 14.
2. Crow, interview.
3. Les Tomkins, "The Thad Jones Story: Music Should Not Be Confined to One Narrow Road," *Crescendo*, June 1972, 14.

4. Lewis, interviewed by Will Moyle, AM 1370 *Essence of Jazz.*
5. Lewis, interviewed by Ben Sidran, *Talking Jazz: An Oral History.*
6. Lewis, interviewed by Will Moyle, AM 1370 *Essence of Jazz.*
7. Tom Lord Online Jazz Discography, s.v. "Mel Lewis."
8. Sokoloff, interview.
9. Morgenstern, "Mel Lewis: The Big Band Man," 20.
10. Ibid.
11. Stamm, interview.
12. *The New Grove Dictionary of Jazz,* 2nd ed., s.v. "Manny Albam."
13. Rusch and Jenne, "Mel Lewis: Interview Part Three," 16.
14. Dodgion, interview.
15. Lewis, interviewed by Ben Sidran, *Talking Jazz: An Oral History.*
16. Rusch and Jenne, "Mel Lewis: Interview Part Three," 16.
17. Bill Kirchner, notes to *The Complete Solid State Recordings of the Thad Jones/Mel Lewis Orchestra,* CD (1994), Mosaic Records MD5-151, 2.

Chapter 13

1. Bourne, "Soulmates: Thad Jones-Mel Lewis," 14.
2. Kirchner, notes to The Complete Solid State Recordings of the Thad Jones/Mel Lewis Orchestra, 2.
3. Les Tomkins, "Thad Jones and Mel Lewis: We're Just Two Lucky Guys," Crescendo, n.m., 1969, 20.
4. Rusch and Jenne, "Mel Lewis: Interview Part Three," 17.
5. Eddie Daniels, interview by author, February 17, 2012.
6. Dodgion, interview.
7. Dick Oatts, interview by author, April 7, 2012.
8. Dodgion, interview.
9. Ibid.
10. Tomkins, "The Thad Jones Story," 14-15.
11. Dodgion, interview.
12. Les Tomkins, "Thad Jones and Mel Lewis: We're Just Two Lucky Guys," 21.
13. Dodgion, interview.
14. Ibid.
15. Tomkins, "Thad Jones and Mel Lewis: We're Just Two Lucky Guys," 21.
16. Ibid.
17. Kirchner, notes to The Complete Solid State Recordings of the Thad Jones/Mel Lewis Orchestra, 2.
18. Ibid.
19. Ibid., 3.
20. Dodgion interview.
21. Jean Elliot, "An Injection of Musical Hormones," Melody Maker, August 30, 1969, 6.
22. Kirchner, notes to The Complete Solid State Recordings of the Thad Jones/Mel Lewis Orchestra, 3.

23. N.a., "Lewis Bows the Jazz Band at Vanguard," The Billboard, February 19, 1966, n.p.
24. Dodgion, interview.
25. Dan Morgenstern, "The Big Bands: In New York...Signs of Life," DownBeat, April 21, 1966, 20.
26. Dodgion, interview.
27. John S. Wilson, "2 New Big Bands Here Appeal to More than Old Memories," New York Times, February 12, 1966, 17.
28. Dodgion, interview.
29. Gary Carner, Pepper Adams' Joy Road: An Annotated Discography (Lanham, MD: Scarecrow Press, 2012), 150.
30. Dodgion, interview.
31. John Mosca, interview by author, August 25, 2011.
32. Dodgion, interview.
33. Mel Lewis, personal datebook, March 1966.
34. Lewis, personal datebook, April 1966.
35. Claude Hall, "Jazz Alive, Well and Thriving as Beat in Commercials Field," The Billboard, March 15, 1969, 34.
36. Ibid.
37. N.a., "Commercial Co. to Debut LP," The Billboard, June 20, 1970, 10.
38. Stamm, interview

Chapter 14

1. Rusch and Jenne, "Mel Lewis: Interview Part Three," 15.
2. Ibid.
3. Ibid., 16.
4. Ibid.
5. Daniels, interview.
6. Ibid.
7. Kirchner, notes to The Complete Solid State Recordings of the Thad Jones/Mel Lewis Orchestra, 15.
8. Ibid., 6.
9. Ibid.
10. Dodgion, interview.
11. Daniels, interview.
12. Kirchner, notes to The Complete Solid State Recordings of the Thad Jones/Mel Lewis Orchestra, 3.
13. Dodgion, interview.
14. Lewis, personal datebook, August 1966.
15. Rusch and Jenne, "Mel Lewis: Interview Part Two," 12.
16. Tom Lord Online Jazz Discography, s.v. "Mel Lewis."
17. Orrin Keepnews, notes to James Moody: Moody and the Brass Figures, CD (2004), Milestone/Original Jazz Classics OJCCD-1099-2.
18. Hamilton, interview.

19. King, "Meet Mel Lewis," *Crescendo,* October 1969, 40.
20. Ibid.
21. Morgenstern, "Mel Lewis: The Big Band Man," 53.
22. Lewis, interviewed by Ben Sidran on *Talking Jazz: An Oral History.*
23. Stamm, interview.
24. Lewis, personal datebook, 1967.
25. Lewis, personal incorporation contract, February 1, 1967.
26. Lewis, personal datebooks, January–April 1967.
27. Morgenstern, "Mel Lewis: The Big Band Man," 20.
28. Harvey Siders, "In-Siders' Groove: Thad and Mel," *Different Drummer,* June 1974, 29.
29. Ira Gitler, "Thad's Thing, *DownBeat,* February 22, 1968, 18.
30. Dodgion, interview.
31. Tomkins, "The Thad Jones Story," 15.
32. Dodgion, interview.
33. Tomkins, "Thad Jones and Mel Lewis: We're Just Two Lucky Guys," 21.
34. Dodgion, interview.
35. Daniels, interview.
36. Stamm, interview.
37. Ibid.
38. Dodgion, interview.
39. Lewis, personal datebooks, May–November 1967.

Chapter 15

1. Ibid.
2. Thad Jones and Mel Lewis Band, DVD, *Ralph Gleason's Jazz Casual* (San Francisco, CA: Idem Home Video, 2001).
3. Gary Carner, "Pepper Adams Chronology: Thaddeus 1965–1977," http://pepperadams.com/Chronology/Thaddeus.html (accessed March 28, 2012).
4. Rusch and Jenne, "Mel Lewis: Interview Part Three," 16.
5. Lewis, personal datebook, July 1968.
6. Dodgion, interview.
7. Ibid.
8. Ibid.
9. Ibid.
10. Ibid.
11. Ibid.
12. Ibid.
13. Ibid.
14. Ibid.
15. Daniels, interview.
16. Ibid.
17. Dodgion, interview.

18. Rusch and Jenne, "Mel Lewis: Interview Part One," 16.
19. Ibid.
20. Rusch and Jenne, "Mel Lewis: Interview Part Two," 12.
21. Kirchner, notes to *The Complete Solid State Recordings of the Thad Jones/Mel Lewis Orchestra*, 9.
22. Mosca, interview.
23. Ira Gitler, "New York's Big Band Community: A Discussion with Clark Terry, Thad Jones, Mel Lewis, Duke Pearson, Ira Gitler," *DownBeat*, April 17, 1969, 19.
24. Ira Gitler, "Thad's Thing," 19.
25. Ira Gitler, "New York's Big Band Community," 19.
26. Ibid.
27. Lewis, interviewed by Will Moyle, AM 1370 *Essence of Jazz*.
28. Scott Kevin Fish, "Mel Lewis: Straight Ahead," *Modern Drummer*, April 1978, 15.
29. Kirchner, notes to *The Complete Solid State Recordings of the Thad Jones/Mel Lewis Orchestra*, 10.
30. Dodgion, interview.
31. Siders, "In-Siders' Groove: Thad and Mel," 29.
32. Daniels, interview.
33. Lewis, personal datebook, August–September 1969.
34. Daniels, interview.
35. Dodgion, interview.
36. Rusch and Jenne, "Mel Lewis: Interview Part Two," 16.
37. Carner, "Pepper Adams Chronology" (accessed March 29, 2012).
38. Rusch and Jenne, "Mel Lewis: Interview Part Two," 16.
39. Ibid.
40. Ibid.
41. Ibid.
42. Ibid.
43. Daniels, interview.

Chapter 16

1. Rusch and Jenne, "Mel Lewis: Interview Part Two," 17.
2. *The New Grove Dictionary of Jazz,* 2nd ed., s.v. "Blue Note."
3. Tom Lord Online Jazz Discography, s.v. "Mel Lewis."
4. Mel Lewis and Clem DeRosa, *It's Time for the Big Band Drummer* (Delevan, NY: Kendor Music Publisher, 1978), 32.
5. Ibid., 33.
6. Kirchner, notes to *The Complete Solid State Recordings of the Thad Jones/Mel Lewis Orchestra*, 11.
7. Siders, "In-Siders' Groove: Thad and Mel," 29.
8. Dodgion, interview.
9. Ibid.

10. Tomkins, "The Thad Jones Story," 15.

11. Dodgion, interview.

12. Christian Renninger, "Horizon-Part II: Mel Lewis/Thad Jones," *Radio Free Jazz*, n.m., 1975, 10.

13. Ibid.

14. Dodgion, interview.

15. John S. Wilson, "Jazz Band Steps Into Its 6th Year," *New York Times*, n.m., 1972, n.p.

16. Renninger, "Horizon-Part II: Mel Lewis/Thad Jones," 10.

17. Lewis, personal datebook, March 1972.

18. Jim Schaffer, "Thad Jones/Mel Lewis—4/4 Swing," *DownBeat*, July 19, 1973, 39.

19. Dan Morgenstern, "With Thad and Mel in Russia," *DownBeat*, August 17, 1972, 19.

20. Max Gordon, *Live at the Village Vanguard* (New York City: Da Capo Press, 1980), 131.

21. Lewis, personal datebook, April 1972.

22. Morgenstern, "With Thad and Mel in Russia," 20.

23. Ibid., 40.

24. Ibid.

25. Ibid.,19.

26. Dodgion, interview.

27. Morgenstern, "With Thad and Mel in Russia," 20.

28. Ibid., 19.

29. Ibid., 40.

30. Ibid.

31. Tom Lord Online Jazz Discography, s.v. "Mel Lewis."

32. Morgenstern, "With Thad and Mel in Russia," 41.

33. Lewis, personal datebooks, March–May 1973.

34. Bourne, "Soulmates: Thad Jones-Mel Lewis," 15.

35. Lewis, personal datebooks, August 1973.

36. Dodgion, interview.

37. Tom Lord Online Jazz Discography, s.v. "Mel Lewis."

38. Dodgion, interview.

39. Ibid.

40. Ibid.

41. Lewis, personal datebooks, October–December 1973.

42. Siders, "In-Siders' Groove: Thad and Mel," 27.

43. Carner, "Pepper Adams Chronology" (accessed April 7, 2012).

44. Leonard Feather, "Thad Jones-Mel Lewis: Blindfold Test Part I," *DownBeat*, June 6, 1974, 31.

45. Tom Lord Online Jazz Discography, s.v. "Mel Lewis."

46. Lewis, personal datebook, March 1974.

47. *The Encyclopedia of Popular Music*, 3rd ed. (New York City: MUZE Inc., 1998), s.v. "Philadelphia International Records."

48. Rusch and Jenne, "Mel Lewis: Interview Part Two," 9.

49. Siders, "In-Siders' Groove: Thad and Mel," 27.

50. Dodgion, interview.

51. Rusch and Jenne, "Mel Lewis: Interview Part Two," 9.

52. Ibid.

53. Ibid.

54. Ibid.

55. Lewis, personal datebook, July 1975.

56. Dodgion, interview.

Chapter 17

1. Lewis, personal datebooks, February–March 1973.

2. Tom Lord Online Jazz Discography, s.v. "Mel Lewis."

3. Dodgion, interview.

4. Carner, "Pepper Adams Chronology" (accessed April 10, 2012).

5. Ibid.

6. Rusch and Jenne, "Mel Lewis: Interview Part Two," 11.

7. Mosca, interview.

8. Ibid.

9. Tom Lord Online Jazz Discography, s.v. "Mel Lewis."

10. Arnold Jay Smith, notes to *New Life,* LP (1976), A&M Horizon SP707.

11. Tomkins, "The Thad Jones Story," 16.

12. Pawel Brodowski, "Thad Jones and Mel Lewis on Jazz in the Big Apple," *Jazz Forum,* no. 44, 1976, 59.

13. Rusch and Jenne, "Mel Lewis: Interview Part One," 13.

14. Daniels, interview.

15. Danko, interview.

16. Ibid.

17. Stamm, interview.

18. Ibid.

19. Sokoloff, interview.

20. Lewis, interviewed by Loren Schoenberg, 1987, WKCR *History of Jazz Drums.*

21. Rick Mattingly, *The Drummer's Time* (Cedar Grove, NJ: Modern Drummer Publications, 1998), 53.

22. Lewis, interviewed by Loren Schoenberg, 1987, WKCR *History of Jazz Drums.*

23. John Snyder, notes to *Mel Lewis and Friends,* CD (1988), A&M Records 0823.

24. Ibid.

25. Bill Kirchner, "Record Reviews: Mel Lewis and Friends," *Radio Free Jazz,* May 1977, n.p.

26. Dodgion, interview.

27. Rusch and Jenne, "Mel Lewis: Interview Part Two," 17.

28. Danko, interview.

29. Ibid.

30. Ibid.

31. Ibid.

32. Bret Primack, "Mel Lewis Orchestra: Thad Jones Roams But Nobody Moans," *DownBeat,* June 7, 1979, 15.

33. Rufus Reid, interview by author, February 20, 2013.

34. Danko, interview.
35. Tom Lord Online Jazz Discography, s.v. "Mel Lewis."
36. Carner, "Pepper Adams Chronology," (accessed April 11, 2012).
37. Ed Newton, "Thad and Mel Go *Pffft*," *Jazz Magazine*, Summer 1979, 41.
38. Dodgion, interview.
39. Danko, interview.
40. Carner, "Pepper Adams Chronology" (accessed April 13, 2012).
41. Danko, interview.
42. Reid, interview.
43. Ibid.
44. Mel Lewis, notes to *The Thad Jones/Mel Lewis Quartet*, CD (1989), A&M Records 0830.
45. Dodgion, interview.
46. Ibid.
47. Ibid.
48. Tom Lord Online Jazz Discography, s.v. "Mel Lewis."

Chapter 18

1. Oatts, interview.
2. Lewis, interviewed by Will Moyle, AM 1370 *Essence of Jazz*.
3. Tom Lord Online Jazz Discography, s.v. "Mel Lewis."
4. Ibid.
5. Mosca, interview.
6. Newton, "Thad and Mel Go *Pffft*," 42.
7. Chip Deffaa, "Thad Jones: New Directions for the Basie Band," *DownBeat*, August 1985, 17-18.
8. Lee Jeske, "Mel Lewis: Not Throwing in the Towel," *JAZZ Magazine*, January/February 1983, 4.
9. Rusch and Jenne, "Mel Lewis: Interview Part One," 12.
10. Ibid.
11. Ibid.
12. Ibid., 5.
13. Ibid.
14. David Froman, "Thad Jones Today," *Jazz Journal International*, 1979, 11.
15. Rusch and Jenne, "Mel Lewis: Interview Part One," 12.
16. Les Tomkins, "Mel Lewis Today: Making the Jazz Orchestra Even Better," *Crescendo*, October 1982, 6.
17. Newton, "Thad and Mel Go *Pffft*," 40.
18. Oatts, interview.
19. Jeske, "Mel Lewis: Not Throwing in the Towel," 7.
20. Ibid., 5.
21. Dan Morgenstern, notes to *Mel Lewis and the Jazz Orchestra: Naturally*, CD (1979), Telarc Records CD-83301.
22. Rusch and Jenne, "Mel Lewis: Interview Part One," 12.
23. Danko, interview.

24. David Froman, "Thad Jones Today," 11.

25. Lewis, interviewed by Will Moyle, AM 1370 *Essence of Jazz*.

26. Rusch and Jenne, "Mel Lewis: Interview Part One," 12.

Chapter 19

1. Rusch and Jenne, "Mel Lewis: Interview Part Two," 17.

2. Les Tomkins, "Mel Lewis: Tailoring the Ensemble to the Individual," *Crescendo*, March 1983, 26.

3. Oatts, interview.

4. Jeske, "Mel Lewis: Not Throwing in the Towel," 6.

5. Ibid.

6. Rusch and Jenne, "Mel Lewis: Interview Part Two," 15.

7. Oatts, interview.

8. Lewis, interviewed by Will Moyle, AM 1370 *Essence of Jazz*.

9. Stanley Crouch, "1000 Nights at the Village Vanguard," *Village Voice*, March 4, 1986, 79.

10. Rusch and Jenne, "Mel Lewis: Interview Part One," 14.

11. Oatts, interview.

12. Tom Lord Online Jazz Discography, s.v. "Mel Lewis."

13. Bob Brookmeyer, notes to *Mel Lewis/Bob Brookmeyer: Live at the Village Vanguard*, CD (1991), DCC Jazz DJZ-616.

14. Wayne Enstice and Paul Rubin, *Jazz Spoken Here: Conversations with 22 Musicians* (New York City: Da Capo Press, 1994), 60.

15. Ben Ratliff, "Bob Brookmeyer: Raging and Composing Against the Jazz Machine," *The New York Times*, May 12, 2006.

16. Rusch and Jenne, "Mel Lewis: Interview Part One," 13.

17. Joe Lovano, interview by author, February 25, 2012.

18. Ibid.

19. Mosca, interview.

20. McNeely, interview.

21. Oatts, interview.

22. Jeske, "Mel Lewis: Not Throwing in the Towel," 7.

23. Ibid.

24. Leonard Feather, "Miles Davis' Comeback a Jazz Event," *The Buffalo News*, n.d. 4.

25. John Hunt, "Jazz: Mel Lewis Jazz Orchestra," *Buffalo Around Town*, July 16, 1981, n.p.

26. Les Tomkins, "Get Out There on that Road: Mel Lewis Advises Young Musicians," *Crescendo*, November 1982, 24.

27. Rusch and Jenne, "Mel Lewis: Interview Part Two," 15.

28. Tomkins, "Mel Lewis: Tailoring the Ensemble to the Individual," 26.
Tom Lord Online Jazz Discography, s.v. "Mel Lewis."

Chapter 20

1. Tom Lord Online Jazz Discography, s.v. "Mel Lewis."

2. Tomkins, "Mel Lewis: Tailoring the Ensemble to the Individual," 31.

3. Mel Lewis and The Jazz Orchestra, DVD, *Jazz Masters Series: Mel Lewis and The Jazz Orchestra* (Washington D.C.: Shanachie, 2005).

4. Mosca interview.

5. Richard M. Sudhalter, "Kenton Tribute: Just Like Old Times," article in unidentified newspaper.

6. Lewis, interviewed by Will Moyle, AM 1370 *Essence of Jazz.*

7. Tomkins, "Mel Lewis Today: Making the Jazz Orchestra Even Better," 6.

8. Ibid.

9. Sokoloff, interview.

10. Gabriela A. Richmond, "The WDR Big Band: A Brief History" (master's thesis, University of Nebraska-Lincoln, 2011), 48.

11. Ibid.

12. Mattingly, "Mel Lewis," 44.

13. Rusch and Jenne, "Mel Lewis: Interview Part One," 16.

14. Riley, interview.

15. Ibid.

16. Adam Nussbaum, interview by author, March 23, 2012.

17. Ibid.

18. Pete Malinverni, interview by author, November, 8, 2013.

19. Rick Mattingly, "In Memoriam—Mel Lewis: 1929–1990," *Modern Drummer*, June 1990, 70.

20. Joey Baron, interview.

21. Riley, interview.

22. Mattingly, "In Memoriam—Mel Lewis: 1929–1990," 70.

23. Rusch and Jenne, "Mel Lewis: Interview Part One," 15.

24. Mel Lewis and The Jazz Orchestra, DVD, *Mel Lewis and His Big Band* (Israel: View Video, 2007).

25. Lovano, interview.

26. Loren Schoenberg, interview by author, May 16, 2011.

27. Schoenberg, interview.

28. Tom Lord Online Jazz Discography, s.v. "Mel Lewis."

29. Rusch and Jenne, "Mel Lewis: Interview Part Two," 17.

30. Schoenberg, interview.

Chapter 21

1. Tom Lord Online Jazz Discography, s.v. "Mel Lewis."

2. Nash, interview.

3. Werner, interview.

4. N.a., notes to *The Mel Lewis Jazz Orchestra: 20 Years at the Village Vanguard*, CD (1990), Atlantic 81566-2.

5. Nash, interview.

6. Oatts, interview.

7. Ibid.

8. Ibid.
9. Ted Nash, interview.
10. Rusch and Jenne, "Mel Lewis: Interview Part One," 13.
11. Jeff Levenson, "The Vanguards Own Fanta(sticks): Mel Lewis," *Hot House*, September 1989, 15.
12. Lovano, interview.
13. Oatts, interview.
14. Rusch and Jenne, "Mel Lewis: Interview Part One," 6.
15. Rusch and Jenne, "Mel Lewis: Interview Part Two," 13.
16. Dizzy Gillespie, notes to *Jon Faddis: Legacy*, CD (1985), Concord Jazz CCD-4291.
17. Tom Lord Online Jazz Discography, s.v. "Mel Lewis."
18. Lovano, interview.
19. Werner, interview.
20. Deffaa, "Thad Jones: New Directions for the Basie Band," 17.
21. Ibid.
22. Oatts, interview.
23. Dennis Mackrel, interview by author, February 22, 2012.
24. Sokoloff, interview.
25. Rusch and Jenne, "Mel Lewis: Interview Part One," 12.
26. Ira Gitler, "1001 Nights at the Vanguard," *JazzTimes*, April 1986, 9.
27. Ibid., 12.
28. Sokoloff, interview.
29. Gitler, "1001 Nights at the Vanguard," *JazzTimes*, 9.
30. Ibid.
31. Ibid.
32. Tom Lord Online Jazz Discography, s.v. "Mel Lewis."
33. Lewis, personal datebooks, June–August 1986.
34. Dennis Hevesi, "Thad Jones Dies in Denmark; Trumpeter and Band Leader," *New York Times*, August 21, 1986, 23.
35. Mel Lewis, interviewed by Jack Ellsworth, 1987, 1580 WLIM Long Island, transcription by author.
36. Hevesi, "Thad Jones Dies in Denmark; Trumpeter and Band Leader," 23.
37. Lewis, personal datebooks, September–December 1986.

Chapter 22

1. Oatts, interview.
2. Loren Schoenberg, notes to *The Mel Lewis Jazz Orchestra: The Definitive Thad Jones Vol. 2*, CD (2004), Jazz Heritage Society 5179024.
3. Rusch and Jenne, "Mel Lewis: Interview Part One," 14.
4. Rusch and Jenne, "Mel Lewis: Interview Part Two," 17.
5. Morgenstern, notes to *Mel Lewis and The Jazz Orchestra: Naturally*.
6. Oatts, interview.
7. Tom Lord Online Jazz Discography, s.v. "Mel Lewis."

8. Burt Korall, notes to *Mel Lewis Sextet: The Lost Art*, CD (1989), Musicmasters CIJD 60222.
9. Ibid.
10. Mosca, interview.
11. Oatts, interview.
12. Ira Gitler, "Mel Lewis: Road Warrior," *JazzTimes*, February 1990, 15.
13. Rusch and Jenne, "Mel Lewis: Interview Part One," 5.
14. Ibid.
15. Sokoloff, interview.
16. Ibid.
17. Peter Watrous, "Jazz Review: A Salute to Mel Lewis," *New York Times*, October 28, 1989.
18. Mattingly, "In Memoriam—Mel Lewis: 1929–1990," 70.
19. Rusch and Jenne, "Mel Lewis: Interview Part One," 5.
20. Bob Young, "Mel Lewis: Breathing Swing to Life's End (1929–1990)," *JAZZIZ*, April/May 1990, 28.
21. Mattingly, "In Memoriam—Mel Lewis: 1929–1990," 71.
22. Young, "Mel Lewis: Breathing Swing to Life's End (1929–1990)," 28.

Chapter 23

1. Morgenstern, "Mel Lewis: The Big Band Man," 53.
2. Oatts, interview.

BIBLIOGRAPHY

Books / Dissertations / Theses

Brand, Jack and Bill Korst. *Shelly Manne: Sounds of the Different Drummer.* Rockford, IL: Percussion Express, 1997.

Bronson, Fred. *The Billboard Book of Number One Hits: 5th Edition.* New York City: Watson-Guptill Publications, 2003.

Brooks, Tim and Earle Marsh. *The Complete Directory to Prime Time Network and Cable TV Shows: 1946–Present.* New York City: Ballantine Books, 2007.

Buchmann-Moller, Frank. *Someone to Watch Over Me: The Life and Music of Ben Webster.* Ann Arbor: The University of Michigan Press, 2009.

Byrne, Paul J. *The Cuban Missile Crisis: To the Brink of War.* Minneapolis: Compass Point Books, 2006.

Carner, Gary. *Pepper Adams' Joy Road: An Annotated Discography.* Lanham, MD: Scarecrow Press, 2012.

Carucci, Joseph. *"The Contributions of Gerry Mulligan's Concert Jazz Band to the Jazz Tradition."* DMA diss., University of Kentucky, 2009.

Ellington, Duke. *Music Is My Mistress.* New York City: Da Capo Press, 1973.

Enstice, Wayne and Paul Rubin. *Jazz Spoken Here: Conversations with 22 Musicians.* New York City: Da Capo Press, 1994.

Gibbs, Terry. *Good Vibes: A Life in Jazz.* Lanham, MD: The Scarecrow Press Inc, 2003.

Gioia, Ted. *The History of Jazz.* Oxford: Oxford University Press, 1997.

Gordon, Jack. *Fifties Jazz Talk: An Oral Retrospective.* Lanham, MD: Scarecrow Press, 2004.

Gordon, Max. *Live at the Village Vanguard.* New York City: Da Capo Press, 1980.

Korall, Burt. *Drummin' Men: The Heartbeat of Jazz— The Bebop Years.* New York City: Oxford University Press, 2002.

LaFaro-Fernandez, Helen. *Jade Visions: The Life and Music of Scott LaFaro.* Denton: University of North Texas Press, 2009.

Lewis, Mel, and Clem DeRosa. *It's Time for the Big Band Drummer.* Delevan, NY: Kendor Music Publisher, 1978.

Maggin, Donald L. *Dizzy: The Life and Times of John Birks Gillespie.* New York City: Harper Collins Publishers, 2005.

Mattingly, Rick. *The Drummer's Time.* Cedar Grove, NJ: Modern Drummer Publications, 1998.

Richmond, Gabriela A. "The WDR Big Band: A Brief History." Master's thesis, University of Nebraska-Lincoln, 2011.

Sparke, Michael. *Stan Kenton: This Is an Orchestra!* Denton: University of North Texas Press, 2010.

The Encyclopedia of Popular Music. 3rd ed. New York City: MUZE Inc., 1998.

The New Grove Dictionary of Jazz. 2nd ed. New York City: Macmillan Publishers, 2002.

Valk, Jeroen de. *Ben Webster: His Life and Music.* Berkeley, CA: Berkeley Hill Books, 2001.

Magazines / Newspapers

Bourne, Mike. "Soulmates: Thad Jones-Mel Lewis." *DownBeat,* April 16, 1970.

Brodowski, Pawel. "Thad Jones and Mel Lewis on Jazz in the Big Apple." *Jazz Forum,* no. 44, 1976.

Brown, Tony. "Kenton's Impact." *Melody Maker,* April 7, 1956.

Crouch, Stanley. "1000 Nights at the Village Vanguard." *Village Voice,* March 4, 1986.

Crow, Bill. "To Russia Without Love: The Benny Goodman Tour of the USSR—Part One." *Gene Lees Jazzletter,* August 1986.

Deffaa, Chip. "Thad Jones: New Directions for the Basie Band." *DownBeat,* August 1985.

DeMichael, Don. "John Coltrane and Eric Dolphy Answer the Jazz Critics." *DownBeat,* April 12, 1962.

Elliot, Jean. "An Injection of Musical Hormones." *Melody Maker,* August 30, 1969.

Feather, Leonard. "Miles Davis' Comback A Jazz Event." *The Buffalo News,* n.d.

———. "Thad Jones-Mel Lewis: Blindfold Test Part I." *DownBeat,* June 6, 1974.

Fish, Scott Kevin. "Mel Lewis: Straight Ahead." *Modern Drummer,* April 1978.

Froman, David. "Thad Jones Today." *Jazz Journal International,* 1979.

Gitler, Ira. "New York's Big Band Community: A Discussion with Clark Terry, Thad Jones, Mel Lewis, Duke Pearson, Ira Gitler." *DownBeat,* April 17, 1969.

———. "Mel Lewis: Road Warrior." *JazzTimes,* February 1990.

———. "Thad's Thing." *DownBeat*, February 22, 1968.

———. "1001 Nights at the Vanguard." *JazzTimes*, April 1986.

Gleason, Ralph J. "A Salute to the Trojan Jazzmen." *San Francisco Chronicle*, September 27, 1962.

———. "Krupa Role Tough for Mel Lewis." *San Francisco Chronicle*, n.d., n.p.

Hall, Claude. "Jazz Alive, Well and Thriving as Beat in Commercials Field." *The Billboard*, March 15, 1969.

Hentoff, Nat. "Are You Sure This Is Kenton? Asks Listener." *DownBeat*, July 27, 1955.

Hevesi, Dennis. "Thad Jones Dies in Denmark; Trumpeter and Band Leader." *New York Times*, August 21, 1986.

Hunt, John. "Jazz: Mel Lewis Jazz Orchestra." *Buffalo Around Town*, July 16, 1981.

Jeske, Lee. "Mel Lewis: Not Throwing in the Towel." *JAZZ Magazine*, January/February 1983.

Jones, Max. "Dizzy Knows His Drums—I Adapt to Him." *Melody Maker*, February 24, 1962.

King, Frank. "Meet Mel Lewis." *Crescendo*, October 1969.

Kirchner, Bill. "Record Reviews: Mel Lewis and Friends." *Radio Free Jazz*, May 1977.

Korall, Burt. "Mel Lewis." *International Musician*, n.d.

Levenson, Jeff. "The Vanguards Own Fanta(sticks): Mel Lewis." *Hot House*, September 1989.

Mallory, Leslie. "Kenton Band Is Far Ahead." n.p., April 8, 1956.

Mattingly, Rick. "In Memoriam—Mel Lewis: 1929–1990." *Modern Drummer*, June 1990.

———. "Mel Lewis." *Modern Drummer*, February 1985.

Morgenstern, Dan. "Mel Lewis: The Big Band Man." *DownBeat*, March 23, 1967.

———. "The Big Bands: In New York … Signs of Life." *DownBeat*, April 21, 1966.

———. "With Thad and Mel in Russia." *DownBeat*, August 1972.

N.a. "Beneke-Haynes-Miller Team Hits Bumpy Road." *The Billboard*, December 16, 1950.

———. "Commercial Co. To Debut LP." *The Billboard*, June 20, 1970.

———. "Kudos Pile on Anthony for Dragnet." *The Billboard*, September 26, 1953.

———. "Lewis Bows The Jazz Band At Vanguard." *The Billboard*, February 19, 1966.

———. "Music—As Written." *The Billboard*, April 22, 1950.

Newton, Ed. "Thad and Mel Go *Pffft*." *Jazz Magazine*, Summer 1979.

Perry, Charlie. "Modern Drumming: Interview with Mel Lewis." *International Musician*, 1961.

Primack, Bret. "Mel Lewis Orchestra: Thad Jones Roams But Nobody Moans." *DownBeat*, June 7, 1979.

Ratliff, Ben. "Bob Brookmeyer: Raging and Composing Against the Jazz Machine." *The New York Times*, May 12, 2006.

Renninger, Christian. "Horizon-Part II: Mel Lewis/Thad Jones." *Radio Free Jazz*, n.m., 1975.

Rusch, Bob, and Beth Jenne. "Mel Lewis: Interview Part Three." *Cadence*, March 1990.

———. "Mel Lewis: Interview Part Two." *Cadence*, February 1990.

———. "Mel Lewis: Interview Part One." *Cadence*, January 1990. www.cadencebuilding.com

Schaffer, Jim. "Thad Jones/Mel Lewis—4/4 Swing." *DownBeat*, July 19, 1973.

Siders, Harvey. "In-Siders' Groove: Thad and Mel." *Different Drummer*, June 1974.

Smith, Arnold Jay. "Mel Lewis: Staunch But Swinging." *DownBeat*, June 1, 1978.

Spear, Diane. "Mel Lewis." *The West Side Spirit*, n.d.

Sudhalter, Richard M. "Kenton Tribute: Just Like Old Times." n.p., n.d.

Tomkins, Les. "Get Out There on That Road: Mel Lewis Advises Young Musicians." *Crescendo*, November 1982.

———. "Mel Lewis: Tailoring the Ensemble to the Individual." *Crescendo*, March 1983.

———. "Mel Lewis Today: Making the Jazz Orchestra Even Better." *Crescendo*, October 1982.

———. "Thad Jones and Mel Lewis: We're Just Two Lucky Guys." *Crescendo*, n.m. 1969.

———. "The Thad Jones Story: Music Should Not Be Confined to One Narrow Road." *Crescendo*, June 1972.

Tynan, John. "Heard in Person: Mel Lewis-Bill Holman Quintet." *DownBeat*, July 24, 1958.

———. "The Peripatetic Mel Lewis." *DownBeat*, n.m. 1962.

———. "Time Is the Quality Mel Lewis Has." *DownBeat*, December 12, 1957.

———. "Vamp Till Ready—Terry Gibbs' Big Band." *DownBeat*, November 8, 1962.

Watrous, Peter. "Jazz Review: A Salute to Mel Lewis." *New York Times*, October 28, 1989.

Wilson, John S. "Jazz Band Steps into Its 6th Year." *New York Times*, n.m. 1972.
———. "2 New Big Bands Here Appeal to More than Old Memories." *New York Times*, February 12, 1966.
Wilson, Russ. "Ferguson Gassed by Career as Leader." *Oakland Tribune*, January 6, 1957.
Young, Bob. "Mel Lewis: Breathing Swing to Life's End (1929–1990)." *JAZZIZ*, April/May 1990.

Online Databases / Websites

Carner, Gary. "Pepper Adams Chronology: Thaddeus 1965–1977." http://pepperadams.com/Chronology/Thaddeus.html (accessed March–April, 2012).
Conley, Paul. "Monterey Jazz Festival Celebrates 50th Year." http://www.npr.org/templates/story/story.php?storyId=14566084 (accessed February 11, 2012).
Delmonico, Edward. "Brit Jazz: Stan Kenton Tour 1956." http://britjazz.blogspot.com/2010/07/stan-kenton-kenton-in-europe-1956-flac.html (accessed January–February, 2012).
Myers, Marc. "Bill Holman: I Told You So." http://www.jazzwax.com/2010/05/bill-holman-i-told-you-so.html (accessed December 29, 2011).
Tobin, Pat. "Recording Wally Heider: Memories of W-W-Wally." http://wallyheider.com/wordpress/2006/10/memories-of-w-w-wally/#more-42 (accessed February 5, 2012).
Lord, Tom. "Tom Lord Online Jazz Discography." http://www.lordisco.com (accessed December 2011-June 2012).

Album Liner Notes

Beach, Ed. Notes to *Thad Jones and Mel Lewis: Live at the Village Vanguard*. CD, Blue Note 7243 5 60438 2 4. 2005.

Brookmeyer, Bob. Notes to *Mel Lewis/Bob Brookmeyer: Live at the Village Vanguard*. CD, DCC Jazz DJZ-616. 1991.

Callot, Robin and Jerry Burling. Notes to *Ray Anthony Collectors Series*. CD, Capitol Records CDP 7 94079 2. 1991.

Clay, Stewart. Notes to *The Original Bill Holman Big Band: Complete Recordings*. CD, Lone Hill Jazz LHJ 10298. 2007.

Coss, Bill. Notes to *Stan Kenton: Cuban Fire*. LP, Capitol Records SM-11794. 1956.

Davis, Francis. Notes to *Thad Jones Legacy: Vanguard Jazz Orchestra*. CD, New World Records 80581. 1999.

Gillespie, Dizzy. Notes to *Jon Faddis: Legacy*. CD, Concord Jazz CCD-4291. 1985.

Gleason, Ralph J. Notes to *Woody Herman's Big New Herd at the Monterey Jazz Festival*. CD, Koch Jazz KOC-CD8508. 1999.

Golson, Benny. Notes to *James Moody: Great Day*. CD, Lone Hill Jazz LHJ10313. 2007.

Hentoff, Nat. Notes to *Gerry Mulligan and the Concert Jazz Band at the Village Vanguard*. LP, Verve Records V-8396. 1961.

Keepnews, Orrin. Notes to *James Moody: Moody and the Brass Figures*. CD, Milestone/Original Jazz Classics OJCCD-1099-2. 2004.

Kirchner, Bill. Notes to *The Complete Solid State Recordings of the Thad Jones/Mel Lewis Orchestra*. CD, Mosaic Records MD5-151. 1994.

Korall, Burt. Notes to *Mel Lewis Sextet: The Lost Art*. CD, Musicmasters CIJD 60222. 1989.

Lewis, Mel. Notes to *The Thad Jones/Mel Lewis Quartet*. CD, A&M Records CD 0830. 1989.

Morgenstern, Dan. Notes to *Mel Lewis and The Jazz Orchestra: Naturally*. CD, Telarc Records CD-83301. 1979.

N.a. Notes to *Music of the Mel Lewis Septet: Got'cha*. CD, Fresh Sound Records FSR-CD 73. 1989.

———. Notes to *Terry Gibbs and His Orchestra: Launching a New Sound in Music*. LP, Mercury SR-60112. 1959.

———. Notes to *The Mel Lewis Jazz Orchestra: 20 Years at the Village Vanguard*. CD, Atlantic 81566-2. 1990.

———. Notes to *Terry Gibbs Dream Band: Volume 1*. CD, Contemporary Records CCD-7647-2. 1986.

Panken, Ted. Notes to *Pepper Adams: Critics' Choice*. CD, Mighty Quinn Productions MQP 1103. 2005.

385

Pujol, Jordi. Notes to *Bob Brookmeyer: The Modernity of Bob Brookmeyer*. CD, Fresh Sound Records FSR-CD 499. 2008.

Schoenberg, Loren. Notes to *The Mel Lewis Jazz Orchestra: The Definitive Thad Jones Vol. 2*. CD, Jazz Heritage Society 5179024. 2004.

Smith, Arnold Jay. Notes to *Thad Jones/Mel Lewis: New Life*. LP, A&M Horizon SP707. 1976.

Snyder, John. Notes to *Mel Lewis and Friends*. CD, A&M Records CD 0823. 1988.

Sparke, Michael. Notes to *Stan Kenton: Contemporary Concepts*. CD, Capitol Records 42310. 2002.

Tynan, John. Notes to *Jimmy Witherspoon: The Concerts*. CD, Fantasy Records FCD-24701-2. 2009.

Quinn, Joe. Notes to *Pepper Adams Quintet*. CD, V.S.O.P. #5. 1987.

Interviews and Unpublished

Abell, David L. Program notes to UCLA Concert Series: Dizzy Gillespie. November 1962.

Baron, Joey. Interview by author. May 4, 2013.

Cipriano, Gene. Interview by author. May 16, 2013.

Crow, Bill. Interview by author. December 20, 2011.

Daniels, Eddie. Interview by author. February 17, 2012.

Danko, Harold. Interview by author. January 15, 2012.

Dodgion, Jerry. Interview by author. March 1, 2012.

Gibbs, Terry. Interview by author. July 25, 2011.

Hamilton, Jeff. Interview by author. September 20, 2011.

Holman, Bill. Interview by author. July 21, 2011.

Lalama, Ralph. Interview by author. April 19, 2013.

Lewis, Mel. Goodman tour itinerary. June 1962.

———. Interviewed by Jack Ellsworth. 1987, AM 1580 WLIM Long Island. Transcription by author.

———. Interviewed by Jim Marcus. November 29, 1985.

———. Interviewed by Will Moyle. n.d., AM 1370 *Essence of Jazz*. Transcription by author.

———. Interviewed by Loren Schoenberg. 1987, WKCR *History of Jazz Drums*. Transcription by author.

———. Interviewed by Loren Schoenberg. December 1982, WKCR *Profiles.* Transcription by author.

———. Interviewed by Ben Sidran on *Talking Jazz: An Oral History.* October 16, 1987, CD, Unlimited Media Ltd. 2006. Transcription by author.

———. Personal datebooks. 1966-1989.

———. Personal letter to Doris Sokoloff, June 20, 1962.

———. *Queen Elizabeth* boarding pass. May 10, 1956.

———. "The View from the Back of the Band." 1988, unpublished memoirs. Mel Lewis Collection, Miller Nichols Library, Kansas City.

Lovano, Joe. Interview by author. February 25, 2012.

Mackrel, Dennis. Interview by author. February 22, 2012.

Malinverni, Pete. Interview by author. November 8, 2013.

Mattingly, Rick. Interview by author. April 15, 2013.

McNeely, Jim. Interviewed by Aurthor. April 20, 2013.

Mosca, John. Interview by author. August 25, 2011, May 2012, and May 17, 2013.

N.a. Official program. Euro-Jazz Orchestra concert programs, 1964-1966.

———. Official program. Jazz at the Philharmonic: British Tour, 1961.

———. Official program. Monterey Jazz Festival, 1958.

Nash, Dick. Interview by author. May 5, 2013.

Nash, Ted. Interview by author. April 23, 2013.

Nussbaum, Adam. Interview by author. March 23, 2012.

Oatts, Dick. Interview by author. April 7, 2012.

Raph, Alan. Interview by author. December 14, 2011.

Reid, Rufus. Interview by author. February 20, 2013.

Riley, John. Interview by author. January 24, 2012, May 19, 2012, and May 2013.

Schoenberg, Loren. Interview by author. May 16, 2011.

Sokoloff Bauman, Donna. Interview by author. March 17, 2012.

Sokoloff, Doris. Interview by author. April 2, 2012.

Sokoloff, Lewis. Interview by author. February 18, 2014.

Sokoloff Lowell, Lori. Interview by author. April 2, 2012.

Soph, Ed. Interview by author. June 22, 2012.

Stamm, Marvin. Interview by author. January 18, 2012.

Von Ohlen, John. Interview by author. April 6, 2013.

Washington, Kenny. Interview by author. May 7, 2012.

Werner, Kenny. Interview by author. May 2, 2013.

Video Recordings

Gerald Wilson Big Band. *Frankly Jazz: Featuring the Gerald Wilson Big Band.* DVD. Los Angeles, CA: not commercially released, 1962.

Mel Lewis and The Jazz Orchestra. *Mel Lewis and His Big Band.* DVD. Israel: View Video, 2007.

Mel Lewis and The Jazz Orchestra. *Jazz Masters Series: Mel Lewis and The Jazz Orchestra.* DVD. Washington D.C.: Shanachie, 2005.

Mel Lewis Workshop. N.p. Hilversum, Netherlands 1985.

Thad Jones and Mel Lewis Band. *Ralph Gleason's Jazz Casual.* DVD. San Francisco, CA: Idem Home Video, 2001.

Index

G

H